£2.99

C000174204

The Public Schools Battalion in the Great War

THE PUBLIC SCHOOLS BATTALION IN THE GREAT WAR

A History of the 16th (Public Schools) Battalion
of the Middlesex Regiment
(Duke of Cambridge's Own).
August 1914 to July 1916.

Steve Hurst

Pen & Sword
MILITARY

First published in Great Britain in 2007 by
Pen & Sword Military
an imprint of
Pen & Sword Books Ltd
47 Church Street
Barnsley
South Yorkshire
S70 2AS

ISBN 978-1-84415-510-1

A CIP catalogue record for this book is
available from the British Library.

Typeset in Palatino 9pt

Printed and bound in the United Kingdom by CPI

Pen & Sword Books Ltd incorporates the imprints of Pen & Sword Aviation, Pen & Sword
Maritime, Pen & Sword Military, Wharncliffe Local History, Pen and Sword Select, Pen and
Sword Military Classics and Leo Cooper.
For a complete list of Pen & Sword titles, please contact
Pen & Sword Books Limited
47 Church Street, Barnsley, South Yorkshire, S70 2AS, England
E-mail: enquiries@pen-and-sword.co.uk
Website: www.pen-and-sword.co.uk

CONTENTS

MAPS

No map exists giving all the details of the attack on the first of July 1916. Maps were given very high security gradings. Where there was any possibility that a map might fall into the hands of the enemy that map showed nothing that might be of value to the opposing intelligence officers.

There are accurate trench maps in collections, both pubic and private, that are corrected on dates before and after the battle. These do not name individual trenches, nor do they show trench positions on the British side of the line. The only map that does was corrected after the capture of the Ancre Heights and the ruins of Beaumont Hamel in November 1916.

To attempt to give an accurate picture of the landscape and the trenches on 1.7.1916 one has to accept a compromise. This may not be accurate in every detail but it is as faithful to an ideal picture as anyone can make it. The intelligence officers, the topographical draftsmen, and the tactical sketchers, at GS Intelligence branch at GHQ, who knew every inch of the original trench maps, are now dead, nor did I meet anyone who had worked on these maps during the research period more than twenty years ago. What I can claim is that my sketches and crude sketch maps were approved, or corrected, by men who were there. They were not cartographers, it is true, but these were the trenches in which they lived.

LIST OF MAPS

PART ONE

Chapter 1

UNFINISHED BUSINESS

ALL DAY AND ALL NIGHT the special trains steamed down the valley. The main line of the Caledonian Railway followed the valley. A wooded ridge muffled the sound of the locomotives, but in the stillness of the night Noel could hear them. The room that Noel shared with two other boys was a small one, under the roof, and the Lodge was built on high ground almost a mile from the railway, but at night he could hear the trains passing. It was Noel's morning duty to cycle to the small rural station to collect the telegrams for the guests. He stood watching the trains pass. They carried the Scottish Naval and Army reservists south to Aldershot and Portsmouth, Chatham, Portland and Salisbury Plain. Some of the servicemen waved to the lad with his bike leaning against the fence. Noel waved back. Then he pushed his cycle up the hill, the leather bag with the telegrams slung over his shoulder. The reservists seemed like beings from another world. Noel's world was the house in London and the Lodge in Scotland and his diligent acquisition of the knowledge that would ensure his elevation in his trade in kitchen and hall. The notion of joining either the Army or the Royal Navy did not enter his head.

Noel Peters began his training as a junior footman and cook in 1913, when he was

Mobilisation of the Royal Naval Reserve. Sailors say goodbye to their families and sweethearts.

fourteen. By the following summer he had completed his first year with his employer, Mr Ebden. In mid-July the staff of the London house moved to Scotland to prepare the Lodge for the start of the grouse shooting season. The deputy butler, cook, maids and part of the kitchen staff travelled north on the Caledonian Railway, just as they had done every year. That summer seemed different. Cook told him that some of the guests had cancelled their holiday in the Highlands in July. Noel noticed that the party that arrived at the beginning of August seemed unusually subdued, the gentlemen preoccupied with the news from central Europe. Some of Mr Ebden's guests held high positions in the Civil Service while a smaller number were senior officers in the Army and Royal Navy.

After he had collected the telegrams Noel laid them out on the table in the library and then notified each of the guests. That day he found one of the telegrams thrown into the waste paper basket. He glanced at it before putting it back. The strips of typed paper gummed to the Telegraph form summoned one of the guests, a senior civil servant, to his post at the Admiralty in Queen Anne's Gate. The newspapers remarked that the Grand Fleet had remained at sea since the July manoeuvres. What they did not relate was that the fleet was already at it's war station. On the 2nd of August all Naval personnel were recalled from leave and the reserves mobilised. On the morning of the 4th the War Office ordered full mobilisation of the regular army reserve. There was no grouse shooting that season. In the gun room the engraved Purdy and Manlicher twelve bores were lightly oiled and placed in their felt lined mahogany cases. Valets packed their masters' plus-fours, thick woollen stockings, walking boots and Norfolk jackets for the journey south. The Highland shooting lodge emptied of guests. Noel and the other servants cleaned, packed and spread dustsheets over the furniture.

That summer the Lewisham Boy Scouts assembled near Goring. The weather was perfect for camping, warm and dry with a light breeze. The 5th of August was a Sunday. The early morning sun warmed the line of pale green canvas tents pitched on a flat meadow, flanked by woodland of dark leafed oak and ash trees. The smoke of the cooking fire rose against the bright blue sky. Alf Damon was one of thirty scouts who paraded before breakfast that morning. Owl, Peewit and Wren troops paraded in lines. Alf, like many of the boys, was barefoot, the dew-wet grass cool underfoot and the sun warming the back of his khaki shirt.

One of the Scout-masters cycled into the village to fetch the Sunday papers. Alf Damon saw him return, cycling fast, shouting and waving the newspaper. The masters talked together then the senior master announced to the boys that he had some important news. The previous night, at 11 pm, Great Britain and her Empire had declared war on Germany.

Flying the red, white and blue horizontal stripes of Holland the four masted barque sailed into Puento Arenas harbour. The port lies at the southern tip of Chile's long coastline. A small steam tugboat guided the barque to a pier and the mixed Dutch and English crew made fast the mooring ropes. From childhood Lionel Renton had nursed

Shepherd's Bush at the turn of the century.

a dream to sail round Cape Horn. At the age of seventeen he ran away from his boarding school and signed on as an apprentice seaman on the Dutch ship. When the barque sailed into Puento Arenas there were two steamers docked in the harbour, one British and one German. The Germans were the first to hear news of war and they taunted the British sailors in one of the waterfront bars. A fight started and some of the English crew of the barque joined in. Lionel Renton was on duty watch so he missed the excitement. The angry crews returned to their ships to arm themselves with any crude weapon they could find. Blood would have been spilled had not a force of well-armed Chilean *Carabinieri* arrived. Both sides were confined to their ships. Lionel was impatient to reach England to enlist before the war ended. He hoped that their next port would be Rotterdam. But when the barque sailed a few days later, to his disappointment, the captain turned to starboard instead of port and the neutral Dutch ship headed northwards along the coast of Chile.

Edmund Tennant was acting in Jamaica when the war started. The Glossop-Harris Travelling Theatre Company toured the East Indies and Panama; Edmund was a junior member of the cast. He argued with the company manager that England's declaration of war against Germany forced him to break his contract and took the first steamer back to Europe. He wrote to his younger brother Philip that he was going to join up and urged him to join too. Philip Tennant was a junior clerk in the London and South Western Bank. His job was routine and irksome and Philip wanted an excuse to escape the boredom of life in the City.

Piccadilly Circus five years before the Great War.

More mature than any one of these, his future companions, Arthur Graham-West set off on a walking tour of the lakes with a small group of university friends, young men and young women. Only when the party reached Keswick did they hear of the outbreak of war. Graham-West still had a year to go before he could complete his study for an MA in philosophy at Oxford. The walkers discussed the situation in Europe. They agreed that the war could not last more than a few months. The economic effects of such an industrial and geographical upheaval would bring the leaders of Europe to their senses. The European powers could not prolong the war. Neither Britain, the richest power with the largest navy, nor Germany, the most advanced in science and technology, nor France, commanding the largest European army, could afford it. Returning to the peace of Oxford, emptied by its long vacation, the dull grey stones seeming to doze in the sunshine, Graham-West opened his diary to record his walking holiday. War was a diversion from the purpose of real life. It was a distraction, a moment of hysteria, before Europe returned to serious matters.

One who took the war seriously was, at that moment, the chairman of a committee of patriotic, wealthy and influential North London businessmen. The individual members had their differences, but on one thing they were agreed: it was their patriotic duty to form a volunteer battalion of infantry and their battalion should be the finest in London, or even in England. The committee approached the county regiment for affiliation. This military unit, the battalion that was to bring the six volunteers together, did not exist at the outbreak of war. It took an eccentric business-man, entrepreneur, former mayor of Harrow, and, one must add, a bit of a charlatan, to have the imagination to propose that Harrow should raise, uniform and equip the battalion. When the committee met, in a private room above an inn at Harrow-on-the-Hill, Major Mackay was applauded when he proposed his imaginative plan. The battalion should be an elite, accepting only the finest and fittest of volunteers. Recruiting should be exclusive; open only to former Public Schoolboys and University men. This new military unit should be called 'The Public Schools Battalion'. His rousing speech inspired more applause and Mackay, with touching modesty, proposed that he lead it, with the rank of Colonel. This, like the first motion, was carried unanimously.

During that same week when the patriotic elders of Harrow held their meeting, the newly appointed Secretary for War, Lord Kitchener, appealed for young men to come forward to defend their country. He was supported by the Bishop of London and many other leaders, civil and religious. Kitchener appealed for 100,000 volunteers. The volunteers would train, serve and fight together, workmates, brothers, pals. The newly formed units would be called the New Army Battalions, to distinguish them from the Regular and Territorial battalions. This was how the Pals battalions were conceived. The Pals recruited in the manufacturing cities of the Midlands and North of England. They were joined by commercial battalions, tramway, railway, post office and public works battalions and, not least, the sporting battalions. Second only in numbers to the Pals came the football battalions raised all over the country.

By negotiation with the county authorities and the War Office, Major Mackay's battalion was adopted into the Middlesex Regiment and so earned its full title: 'The 16th (Public Schools Battalion) The Middlesex Regiment. The Duke of Cambridge's Own.' Recruiting began 4th September with advertisements in the London morning and evening papers.

THE PUBLIC SCHOOLS BATTALION
THE MIDDLESEX REGIMENT

THE ABOVE HAS BEEN AUTHORISED BY THE ARMY COUNCIL AND IS
COMPRISED SOLELY OF PUBLIC SCHOOL MEN WHO WILL SERVE TOGETHER.
THOSE DESIROUS OF JOINING SHOULD APPLY IMMEDIATELY TO:
24 ST JAMES STREET. SW.
WHICH IS THE ONLY AUTHORISED OFFICE FOR THE BATTALION

13

Chapter 2

LONDON: THE HUB OF EMPIRE

T HE CHAIRMAN OF THE COMMITTEE may have been Mayor of Harrow, or may not, and the title of Colonel was one that he bestowed on himself. He has been described variously as Major, Captain and Lieutenant Mackay, late of the Westminster Dragoon Yeomanry. At this late date it is impossible to disentangle fact from fantasy. Whatever his past, Mackay was a man of vision and great energy and he must be acknowledged as the founder of a Battalion that caught the public imagination and is a subject of argument to this day. Mackay was as creative as he was controversial. To him must go the credit for the instantly manufactured traditions and customs of the Battalion; the wolfhound mascot, the pipes and drums, the new kilts, plaids and bonnets of the bandsmen and the bright forage caps that could be worn by the rank and file.

The patriotic committee of citizens of the county of Middlesex were part of a massive popular movement that created the 'Pals battalions'. The Public Schools Battalion retained its title right up to its disbandment, when the British army reduced brigades from four to three battalions late in 1917. One can be misled by the title and underestimate the importance of the Middlesex Regiment and that special regional pride. Some survivors spoke of 'the PSB', or '16thPSB', with affection but did not stress the regimental title. No doubt this was because they were posted to other regiments when commissioned or after a long period in hospital. Others, like Noel Peters, stayed with the Middlesex through the duration of the war, serving with other battalions. The original Public Schools Battalion was both class-based and cosmopolitan. This changed rapidly during the first months in England, and the changes accelerated once the battalion went into the line in Flanders. By the spring of 1916 very little remained of the original composition, and yet a certain elan, the fighting spirit of an elite, remained special to 16PSB.

Middlesex, one hardly needs to emphasise, was, and is, one of the counties that make up Greater London. During Kitchener's recruiting drive of autumn 1914 the county regiments divided the great city by crude rule of thumb. The Middlesex recruited north of the Thames; the Queen's East Surreys south and west, while the Royal Fusiliers and the Essex regiment took the city and east end of London. If one takes the British Army, at any period of rapid expansion, whether by the recruiting of volunteers or by conscription, one encounters a fierce regional pride. Recruits go from barrack hut to hut seeking out neighbours and fellow townsmen, and nowhere is this stronger than amongst young men from the great cities, Glasgow, Birmingham, Manchester or Liverpool. With her population of over seven million. London, in 1914, was the largest city in the world. The economic and political facts, that we read today, were unknown to the mass of the population. Had some visionary stood upon a soap box at Hyde Park Corner and declared that the Empire was in decline, and that both Germany and America had outstripped Britain in the production of steel and those chemicals vital to industry, trade and the manufacture of weapons and ammunition, the Londoner would have either laughed at him or punched him on the nose. To have dared to mention such unwelcome statistics to the patriotic group that assembled to join 16PSB would have been judged close to treason. Britain had the largest navy on the high seas and Britannia ruled the waves. The Indian army, policing the Empire, was the largest land fighting force in the world. And at the hub of this vast and unvanquishable empire stood London, banking, trading and administrative capital of the world.

The worn and battle stained banners of the Middlesex Regiment hang in St Paul's Cathedral in the heart of the City of London. To be a member of that regiment gave the volunteer a special place in the world. It may have been this Londoners' swagger that so irritated Robert Graves, and perhaps he mistook it for Public School snobbery. (Graves was himself a Londoner by birth, but, once commissioned in a Welsh regiment, he adopted the pose of a wild Celt.) The two factors that emerged clearly, in conversations with survivors, were, firstly, relations between the Middlesex Regiment and the grammar schools and day-public schools of north London, particularly Highgate and Mill Hill schools. The second important factor was the sporting clubs of the region, of which the most prominent examples were Wasps RFC and Tottenham AFC. Nor should one forget that the great stadium itself, the home of British football, was built in Wembley.[1]

At the outbreak of war the Middlesex Regiment (The Duke of Cambridge's Own) consisted of ten battalions. Four were regular, two regular reserve, and there were four battalions of Territorials. Once the war of mobility was over and trench war commenced, the Middlesex Regiment sent twenty-six battalions into the line while the total of those serving at home and abroad numbered forty-six. By November 1918 London had lost 125,000 men, killed in action.[2]

1. Football Bns. Following the recruitment of 16PSB, wealthy and patriotic citizens raised two sporting battalions, the 17th (1st Football) and the 23rd (2nd Football). Both football battalions were raised by W. Joynson Hicks, MP, the 1st in December 1914 and the 2nd in June 1915.)

2. Peter Ackroyd. *London: The Biography.* P722. Pub. Vintage books 2001.

Chapter 3

WATERLOO: THE SPECIAL TRAIN

It's Tommy this and Tommy that and Tommy step outside,
But it's a special train for Atkins when the troopers on the tide.
The troopers on the tide, my boys,
The troopers on the tide.
And it's a special train for Atkins when the troopers on the tide.

Rudyard Kipling

CHARLES LAWSON, ONE OF THE ORIGINAL VOLUNTEERS who joined the train at Waterloo on that September morning remarked that it was 'like a delightful picnic.' His memory of that carefree morning was shared by many others who, like him, falsified their ages to enlist. Others left routine jobs in the City of London, or families that had become burdensome, and joined in a spirit of adventure. It was all a great lark, an escape from one's normal responsibilities. The rivalry between England and Germany went back over thirty years. It would be decided by a short war of movement, and every man and boy was anxious to get out to France before it ended. Filling the ranks, at this stage in the war, was not a problem for the Public Schools Battalion.

Colonel Mackay aimed at a battalion strength of over a thousand all ranks. These included: 29 Officers; 50 NCOs; 16 Drummers and Buglers (sic: later titled Pipers) and 1005 Rank and file. Whether the Battalion ever reached this number is not recorded because War office regulations quickly superseded Mackay's eccentric plans. Numbers ebbed and flowed as recruits came and trained soldiers left to train to be officers. At one point while in England, Battalion numbers rose to 50 officers with 631 other ranks. In France, before the Somme battle, officer numbers dropped to 24 and other ranks rose to 750. This was high for an infantry battalion in 1916.

The recruiting office for the Public Schools Battalion was in St James, close to the

The Central Recruiting Office, London. Some of Kitchener's First Hundred Thousand assembling to volunteer.

Wilkinson's Swords shop. Tony Chubb had good reason to remember the place because a thief stole his precious bicycle while he was signing on and he had to walk home to Swiss Cottage. Tony was one of many boys who enlisted under age. One forgetful child gave his real birth date. Captain Ryan, who was in charge of recruiting, told him to come back when he was older. He returned next day aged by three years. Lieutenant Jackson had difficulty controlling his laughter at the lad's impudence as he recorded his name in the nominal role. One of that first wave of volunteers was Alf Damon. 'I always had itchy feet so, when I saw the advertisement in the Evening Standard, I welcomed the chance to join up.' He too was below the age of enlistment and declared a false date of birth.

Those that were accepted by the new battalion received a telegram on the 12th of September: 'Parade Waterloo Station on Tuesday morning. Bring enough kit for ten days and one blanket. (Signed) OC. Public Schools Battalion.'

The volunteers gathered at Waterloo Station on Tuesday the 15th of September. Each volunteer received a copy of Battalion Standing Orders, part one and part two. They boarded a special train for Kempton Park. One or two friends joined up together but the majority went to the station alone. The train left Waterloo at 11.30am, under the command of Captain Ryan. The party reached Kempton Park in time for lunch on the racecourse. Both Alf Damon and Charles Lawson described a glorious sunny morning. Alf remembered the variety of casual clothing worn by the volunteers made more colourful, here and there, by bits of uniform. Men wore belts, riding breeches and tall boots. Some even wore spurs, though the more military looking were outnumbered by men in tweed suits or Norfolk jackets. Hats covered every style and variety, ranging from Bowlers and Homburgs to the slouch hats of the Canadians and 'The League of Frontiersmen'. The majority wore sensible tweed caps to go with their jackets and stout walking boots.

Alf described the group as middle of the middle-class, touched neither by want nor great responsibilities. Dressed as though for a weekend's hiking no one stood out as particularly affluent nor particularly poverty stricken. There is no record of the 'Son of a Duke' reported in the *Evening Standard*, nor of the 'Belted Earl', though no doubt there was a fair sample of 'Fellows down on their luck' reported by the paper. The latter group viewed the war as a temporary diversion which would give them bed and board until something better turned up. The volunteers were a friendly, easy-going crowd and by the time the train reached the Surrey countryside, and the men marched to the race course, most felt at ease and at home in their strange surroundings. Alf Damon described that journey 'As though setting off in high spirits for a beano at some quiet spot on the pier.'

Charles Lawson was impressed by the age range, from the very young, like himself, who had taken liberties with their birth certificates, to the more elderly and experienced who advised the youngsters on what they should, or should not, carry in their ruck-sacks. He wrote: 'In retrospect, it seems to me that many of the more mature and prosperous recruits took less kindly to the rigours of camping, which included sleeping on the ground or in horse-boxes, than did the less-experienced and weedy. These boys, in many cases, took to the life and blossomed like roses.'

Charles Lawson also commented on the variety of military experience. 'It was noticeable that the schools that encouraged OTC training had supplied their Old Boys with experience that made drilling on the barrack square almost unnecessary. Indeed they did almost as much as the small number of Regular Army NCOs to indoctrinate the uninitiated.'

Amongst the 'elderly', as Charles Lawson described the experienced recruits, was Arthur Channing Purnell, who was thirty-three years old and an official in the National Provincial bank. He was an athlete, footballer and oarsman who held the record for winning the double-sculling skiff championship on the Thames for three years running and the Thames skiff marathon. He had also served in the ranks of the Honourable Artillery Company for four years and was as fit, or fitter, than most of the younger recruits.

Alf Damon ended his letter (one of many) with some thoughts on those unusual, and strangely innocent, first few weeks of the war.

'For some of us this introduction was little more than a coming together in comradeship before starting away again. For others, a few months before they took their leave to serve elsewhere. But for many of us, this began a long period in camps and huts before the final selection of those who should go to France and those who should remain with the Service Battalion.'

Some gained commissions, others transferred to other units. Some were too old or unfit for service. Some moved to the 24th (Service) Battalion. Some fell sick and were invalided out of the army. Apart from the first list of all the volunteers who assembled at Kempton Park, Colonel Mackay's record keeping was not very exact. When the War Office took control and appointed a regular officer to command, Colonel J. Hamilton Hall, records conformed to regular army standards. Later, Colonel Hall, in his methodical staff officer's way, kept lists of those volunteers sent forward to officers' training schools. Colonel Hall's list did not include the early days when his predecessor, the flamboyant Colonel Mackay, commanded the Battalion. Less easy to understand is Hall's omission of the first winter in France when a smaller, but significant number applied for commissions.

SOURCES
For the description of the train and assembly at Kempton Park I used extracts from a letter sent to me by Charles Lawson, and a long series of letters from Alf Damon, writing from Hobart, Tasmania. Alf wrote in bursts of enthusiasm and it was often hard to tell which year of the war he was describing. He would jump from one incident to another without warning in a form of stream-of-consciousness writing. With practice I became skilled at interpreting and decoding these changes in narrative. But, apart from this eccentricity, Alf's memory was clear and accurate. The general description of the first few weeks in the life of 16PSB are based on H.W. Wallace Grain's privately printed pamphlet, The 16th (Public Schools) Service Battalion Middlesex Regiment and The Great War 1914-1918. The rest of the chapter uses letters from several of the original volunteers who left the Battalion to be commissioned in other regiments.

Chapter 4

THE ORIGINALS

*Here we are Public Schoolboys, and above everything Englishmen, and we want to fight.
Whether in trench or bayonet charge we will show the Teuton that one Englishman is worth
twenty Germans.*

Report in *The Evening Standard.* 8th October 1914

THE BATTALION CAMPED ON FLAT MEADOWS beside the race track. The
civilian world had not caught up with the reality of war and the racing
programme continued well into October. Alf described an incongruous
combination of festival on one side of the fence and drill and weapon training on the
other. One Saturday most of Alf's company backed a favourite and watched it come
home. The bookie ran for it chased by fit and very angry soldiers. Fear for his life lent
him extra adrenalin and the bookie escaped. The company titled themselves 'The
Welshed Rabbits'.

More volunteers arrived at Kempton and the instructors, a mixture of old reservists
of the regular army and former officers of the Territorials, strove to turn the new recruits
into soldiers. Once the racing season ended the Battalion headquarters, offices,
armoury and stores made temporary homes in the racecourse buildings and stable

*'The Originals'. The Public Schools Battalion (16th Middlesex) assemble at Kempton Park. A C Purnell
to the left facing the camera.*

PUBLIC SCHOOL BATTALION.

The Duke of Cambridge's Own (Middlesex Regiment).

BATTALION ORDERS, PART I.

London, 15th September, 1914.

1. The Battalion is now in process of being formed. It will become a Battalion of the Duke of Cambridge's Own Middlesex Regiment. The Regiment in the Peninsular War earned for itself at the battle of Albuhera, 16th May, 1813, the glorious title of "The Diehards." It has won fame at El Bodon, in the Crimea, and in South Africa, when it saved the situation at Spion Kop. It has now two Battalions, the first and the fourth, actually in the fighting line of the present Expeditionary Force in France. It rests with Officers, Non-Commissioned Officers and men of our new Public School Battalion to uphold this reputation both in camp and the field.

2. The Organization of the Battalion will be :—

> HEAD-QUARTERS SECTION.
> A B C AND D COMPANIES.
> MACHINE GUN SECTION.

A total strength of 29 Officers, 1 Warrant Officer, 49 Staff Sergeants and Sergeants, 16 Drummers and Buglers, 1,005 Rank and File.

3. Provisional appointments have been made (see Part II orders) to the various ranks of Officers, Warrant Officers and Non-Commissioned Officers all to date from September 15th, 1914. The appointments to commissioned rank now made will require to be confirmed by the Army Council when the Commanding Officer considers it desirable to forward recommendations on the subject.

Vacancies have been left for 50 per cent. in each rank in order to enable Officers commanding Companies to submit recommendations of suitable candidates for appointments from those who have enlisted and are enlisting.

4. Lists of Companies appear in Part II. Men wishing to transfer into another Company in order to serve with friends will give in their names to the Adjutant at 11 a.m. on Wednesday, the 16th inst.

5. The Battalion strength about 10 officers, 700 men, will parade at Waterloo Station on Tuesday, 15th inst., at 11 a.m., and proceed by train from thence to Kempton.

The formation of the Public Schools Battalion. Part One Orders. 15th September 1914.

20

blocks. Officers, NCOs and men slept in tents. These were old, worn-out, bell tents of every colour from dirty white to brown to olive to green, and in every state of disrepair. It was obvious that they would be quite useless once the cold weather came. The volunteers accepted leaky, mouldering tents with good grace, still buoyed up by their initial enthusiasm. What they found less tolerable was the lack of weapons and uniforms. How could they be accepted as soldiers when they lacked the tools of their trade? Like their comrades in the Pals battalions they drilled with broomsticks, lengths of wood or gas-piping, anything that bore a superficial resemblance to a rifle. Most humiliating of all they still wore their civilian clothes. As one youth remarked, they looked more like *franc tireurs* than soldiers. The only items of uniform that could be bought privately were forage caps. (These, in the county of Middlesex colours of mustard and maroon, cost the volunteers ten shillings which was close to a fortnight's pay for a private soldier in 1914.)

Anthony Chubb joined the battalion on the 21st of September, signing on at an office in Panton Street, just off the Haymarket. Aged sixteen he was listed 'On boy's service' and given the rank of bugler/batman. He was embarrassed when his uncle accompanied him to Kempton Park the following day.

> I had only just left school and was very green. I think my parents were worried about the advertisement in the evening paper. They sent my uncle along to make sure that I wasn't carried off to a Turkish brothel.

Tony Chubb was proud of his regimental number, 871, which made him one of the 'Originals'.

His job was that of batman to the Battalion Adjutant, Captain Carey.

> Captain Carey was quite old for a soldier. A former officer of the Indian Army, he had a beautiful long Afghan coat embroidered with colourful designs. It was called a 'poshteen'. What this long suffering gentleman made of my clumsiness as an officer's servant I cannot imagine.
>
> At Kempton I met up with Mr Goodwin who had been my classics master at Christ's Hospital. Another master, Mr Forbes, came to visit him. I amused them both by telling of the tales that we boys invented to account for the limp that Mr Forbes suffered. Soon Mr Goodwin left for Officer Cadet School, as did so many of the Originals. Our RSM was a retired senior NCO of the Scots Guards who rejoined the army as soon as war started – RSM Oliver Smith. Our Drum-major was a former Grenadier Guardsman, very smart and the ideal man for the job. He taught me, and most of the other boy-soldiers, to blow the bugle and play the side drum.[1]

In a letter sent some time later Tony Chubb wrote:

> I cannot remember whether I told you the story of how we came to have a pipe band, but in case I didn't, here goes. This chap, Mackay was honorary Colonel of the Battalion until Colonel Hall took over. It was Mackay's idea that we should have a pipe band. He managed to enlist a complete band in Glasgow, consisting of some ten pipers, a bass drummer, two tenor drummers and a side drummer. I remember that they came from Cou

May 16th 1811, with the 57th Foot, later the Middlesex Regiment, taking heavy casualties from French grapeshot at the Battle of Albuhera, a seriously wounded senior officer cried out, 'Die hard 57th!'. Above is the painting by Lady Butler 'Steady the Drums'.

Caddens and the Springburn road, and that is all I ever learned about Glasgow. Mackay claimed that we earned the right to such a band at the battle of Albuhera (where, as you know, the old 57th of Foot acquired its nickname "The Diehards"). His justification was this: the Duke of Athol's Regiment was wiped out with the exception of the pipers and they were attached to the 57th. Ever since Albuhera the regiment has been entitled to a pipe band. It is a beautiful story and much too good to be disbelieved. Whether true or not, that is how I, a Londoner who had never been as far north as Hadrian's wall, found myself in the rig-out of a Highlander and playing the drum in a pipe band. Our full dress consisted of khaki anklets, Argyle and Sutherland hosetops, a kilt and plaid in Blackwatch tartan, a forage cap with red and white check round it. For ceremonial occasions the headgear was a large feather bonnet with a tail hanging down one side. We were always much in demand to play at functions; weddings, funerals, the officers' club at Queen's Parade, and of course at the weddings of Colonel Mackay's daughters.

The officers were not mean about the traditional dram, or drams, for the pipers. I remember Duke's Hill at Woldingham, where we camped early in 1915, strewn with Scottish pipers in various stages of disarray after one of these functions.[2]

The novelty of war, the wave of patriotic enthusiasm, the uniforms, bugle calls and marching men, sold newspapers. The London press was quick to hear of the novelty of a battalion of former public schoolboys. The reaction of the *London Evening Standard* is typical of the line taken by the press throughout the war.[3]

> *8th October 1914.*
>
> *The enthusiastic patriotism and magnificent spirit of the old public schoolboys of England is unmistakably shown in response to the Call to Arms. The Battalion of the Public School Boys of the Middlesex Regiment – 1500 strong – is recruited to the last man. The Battalion is encamped at Kempton Park, near Sunbury station, and amid beautifully picturesque scenery. Rows of newly erected tents, put up by the recruits themselves, were occupied yesterday, and for the first time. In a strictly preserved enclosure men from Rugby, Eton, Charterhouse, Canterbury, and, indeed, from all our world-famed Public Schools are drilled and instructed in the duties of a soldier. On every hand one sees the splendid enthusiasm that will teach the Kaiser a wholesome respect for 'French's contemptible little army.*
>
> *The commanding officer told our representative that many had refused commissions. They prefer to fight side by side. "We are Kitchener's men", said one of them proudly, "just ordinary Tommies." Sharing the tent of Corporal Norman, who is in charge, are two commissioned officers, a Captain of the Queen's Bays and a Major to the 19th Hussars. They are now merely privates. The recruits are doing every kind of work, no task is too hard or menial. They cut the wood for the fires, wash, scrub – do anything and everything that makes for efficiency in the field. "It's soldiering, don't you know?" said a recruit with an Oxford accent, "and we just love to rough it."*

The reporter knew that his readers would be interested in the athletes.

> *The playing fields of our Public Schools are greatly represented. There are enough internationals, said Corporal Norman to assemble two rugby teams and at least one association.*

Among the athletes, Private H.E. Holding, triple Oxford Blue, ran for England in the Olympic games. Holding was the guinea-pig for Professor Leonard Hill's experiments

Volunteers in civilian clothes eating lunch outside their tents. Kempton September 1914.

The stables at Kempton. These were turned into stores and Battalion HQ offices. September 1914

Tent of the 16th Battalion Pipers.

with the effect of oxygen on athletic performance.'

The newspaper continued praising the volunteers athletic achievements.

There are boxers, fencers, runners, footballers and polo-players. Strong of muscle and sturdy of frame – they represent all that is best of England's manhood.

Private George Mitchell – "Jarge" they call him in camp – is one of the heros of the camp. "He nearly beat Charpentier", declared a comrade, "and now he is going to fight with him". Private Mitchell gripped our representative's hand in his own strong palm. "We mean business over yonder." He exclaimed.

24

Merchants have left their counting houses, artists their easels, lawyers their parchments, musicians their instruments.

"All professions are represented." Said Mr Gerald Lindley, who a short while ago was playing on the stage of the Lyric Theatre. "Two of us have come from the footlights, architects are busy drawing plans for the huts. You could not name a calling which is not numbered in our ranks. By the way, let it be understood at once, that we are out for serious business. We were taught in our schools to be serious in our tasks and most of us are serious in our professions, and we shall be deadly serious when we meet the enemy."

Some six or seven volunteers are drafted away, the proud bearers of commissions, but generally the spirit is – "here we are, Public Schoolboys, above everything, Englishmen, and we want to fight. Whether in trench or bayonet charge we will show the Teuton that one Englishman is worth twenty Germans". This is the spirit of the whole Battalion of the most accomplished, most highly educated, most delicately nurtured gentlemen in England. Dukes' sons, the sons of belted earls, the man who has fallen down on his luck, all are boys together. Corporal Norman expressed this idea. ' We are born of the same race, bound by the same ties of patriotism, proud of our country, strong in antagonism to anything and everything that threatens our dominance. We are just boys together.'

The giant of the Battalion is known to his comrades as "Long Tom". He stands six foot eight inches – a splendid specimen of fine muscularity. "And the life! The discipline! They're just delightful!" Exclaimed one sturdy man. "We rise at six in the morning, do five drills a day besides parades and route marches. The life makes one fit." His eyes twinkled merrily. "Only the sergeant is a little bit rude sometimes."

Many years later Alf Damon described the early stages of the war and those of his fellow volunteers most eager to get their names in the papers.

There was plenty of loose talk at Kempton. Plenty of wind-bags bragging what they would do to the Hun once they got out there. We saw the back of the braggarts when the weather changed and Johnnie Hall took over and the training became more arduous. Some may have been as good as their brave words; others – well no doubt they found some safe rock to cling to, like limpets, and passed a comfortable war, well away from the fighting.

1. Tony Chubb survived the war and was demobilised in 1919, a veteran of four years of trench warfare and still too young to vote.

2. Wallace Grain has a slightly different account of Colonel Mackay's line of succession, tracing the roots of the pipe band back to the American War of Independence when both the Middlesex and the Atholl Highlanders carried the number '77th of Foot'. Wallace Grain gives the bandsmen's kilts as Mackay tartan. The pipe band survived to the end of the war. Three of the original pipers were killed, one died of wounds. Piper Crawford won the Military Medal. In 1918, the band was transferred to the 2nd Middlesex. Whether the Irish wolfhound went with them is not recorded

3. See the comments made by both Siegfried Sassoon and Robert Graves on the hysteria and mendacity of the press throughout the war.

Chapter 5

THE LAMPS ARE GOING OUT

The lamps are going out all over Europe; we shall not see them lit again in our time.
Lord Edward Grey. August 1914.

B ESIDE THE THAMES THE WEATHER GREW COLDER. Heavy dew soaked the bell tents. The mist rose from the river turning the early morning drill squads into grey ghosts. More and more of the original volunteers left for officer training while the flood of new recruits dwindled to a trickle. Numbers were down, well below Colonel Mackay's estimate of a thousand, let alone the *Standard's* fictitious 1,500. Colonel Mackay was replaced and reduced in rank to Major when he handed over the Battalion. He moved to a holding battalion, the 24th Middlesex. His replacement was an officer of the Regular Army whose experience included India and a period on the General Staff. Lieutenant Colonel J H Hall was a disciplinarian with a flair for organisation. One of his first tasks was to sack some of the more colourful of Mackay's officers and replace them with professionals. That experienced soldier, former member of the Sikh Frontier Force, Captain Carey, remained in place as Adjutant, promoted to the rank of Major. The new Quartermaster was Lieutenant A d'Alpuget, formerly of the East Surrey Regiment. The new Company Commanders were all experienced officers:

A Company. Captain H W Ryan, formerly Lieutenant of 19th Hussars.

B Company. Captain G C Way of the Natal Mounted Rifles.

C Company. Captain V Ward-Brown; Dublin Fusiliers.

D Company was commanded by Lieutenant F

A.C. Purnell with the Battalion Mascot, an Irish wolf hound.

26

R Hill who was formerly a sergeant in the Bombay Light Horse.

Both Captains Way and Ward-Brown had fought in South Africa and Lieutenant Hill in India. Lieutenant Townsend came to 16PSB from the Worcestershire Regiment. His must have been a QM Commission because he had fought in both the Ashanti and Nyasaland campaigns more than thirty years earlier. Another veteran of South Africa who joined the Battalion at Kempton was Captain Parnell (not to be confused with one of the originals, A C Purnell who became the Battalion bombing officer in France).

The officer commanding each company had a second in command: Lieutenant F.J. Jackson, East Yorks Volunteers; Lieutenant W H Dawson, Rangoon Volunteer Rifles; Second Lieutenants J C Clayton and R Goodman each held temporary commissions with University OTCs. The RSM, Oliver Smith, had done an outstanding job in supervising and inspiring training during the first stage of turning the Battalion from a bunch of enthusiastic amateurs into trained and disciplined soldiers. A retired Colour-sergeant of the Scots Guards, he was too old for active service. He moved to the 24th Battalion. Colonel Hall replaced him with an outstanding regular soldier, Sergeant G A Macdonald, who had recently been promoted to CSM.

One of the volunteers serving in the ranks was discovered to be a doctor. Private H Bury-Knight was appointed Battalion Medical Officer with the rank of Captain. Noel Peters said that he was a good doctor and well liked. 'He was known to the lads as "Niffy Knight" because he always doused himself with cologne and covered his hair in bay-rum pomade.'

Following the battle of the Marne, and the change from a war of movement to what was, in fact, siege warfare along a line from the Channel ports to the Swiss Alps, news from the British Expeditionary Force persuaded the more thoughtful of the Originals that the war would not be the rapid and quickly decided conflict predicted by strategists and amateur soldiers alike. Another wave of volunteers applied for commissions. Arthur Purnell, G H Heslop, R H Watts, F S Cochram and one of the Cleghorn brothers were all commissioned in January 1915. At this stage in the war a commanding officer could request that some of the officer candidates be returned to his battalion once they had completed their officer cadet training. Most of the 16th Battalion officers serving on July 1st 1916 were original volunteers.[1]

Colonel Hall's need to lead an elite unit into battle in France became close to an obsession. In his darker moments he envisaged the reduction of his proud battalion into an officer selection unit, a mere service battalion, like the 24th Middlesex. The dilemma for the volunteers of 16PSB, to apply for a commission or not to apply, was not helped by their commanding officer. Charles Lawson described the difficulties of getting an application for officer selection.

> *The CO, Colonel Hall, must have received orders from the War Office, who knew the real casualty figures amongst junior officers, so (at this stage) he did not impede those who sought commissions, but they were not popular with Battalion Headquarters who believed that those who applied were undermining the chances of the Battalion going to the Front*

as a crack unit. To apply for a commission from the ranks of the PSB you filled in a form giving details of your education, training, etc, and it had to be supported by the signature of someone like a mayor or JP. The Commanding Officer could refuse to forward it on. His only comment to me was that the Essex Regiment was taking a lot of casualties so I would get what I wanted. At that stage demand exceeded supply. No CO was pleased to see his command disappear, or becoming an OTC. My application only went forward when I brought in a recruit to take my place. This I did by going to the nearest recruiting office and giving the Recruiting Sergeant ten shillings for his next recruit. By the time I received my commission many of my fellow originals had gone the same way. Looking back, I do not feel that this stage of the war was very well managed. Many of the originals became very disillusioned with the character of the Regular NCOs who were supposed to instruct us. Some even resorted to bribery to get the instruction they felt was lacking.

Several of the originals confirmed Charles Lawson's remark that Colonel Hall did not push suitable candidates forward for commissions, seeking instead to build up a first rate fighting unit and take it to France as quickly as possible. Lionel Renton admired Colonel Hall both as a commanding officer and as a soldier. Neither Charles Lawson or Alf Damon were sympathetic to their CO's problems. Charles Lawson wrote a clear and thorough account of his CO's character.

Lieutenant-Colonel Hall was very "Sandhurst" in manner. Of medium build, not particularly impressive physically, but dignified and soldierly in bearing with a straight back and a toothbrush moustache. He was always well turned out in a conventional gabardine tunic, riding breeches and highly polished boots. He wore the old style, double braced, Sam-browne belt.[2] The double-barrelled name "Hamilton-Hall" did not appear on PSB orders. He used the name J.H. Hall until he became CO of the 2nd Middlesex in 1917. From then on his name appears as J. Hamilton-Hall.

Charles Lawson describes his CO as 'reticent and reserved' and not well liked, in contrast to the Adjutant, Captain Carey, 'who was more of a swashbuckling type with plenty of medals and a good voice on the parade-ground.' He goes on to describe his CO as a 'War Office soldier with some influence behind him which gained him his command.' He believed that the reticence and reserve that made Hall unpopular were due to commanding an officers' training unit and not leading a corps of gentlemen athletes into battle, as 16PSB was conceived in the summer of 1914.

To me, he was a man facing disappointment in all his dearest hopes, at a time when many thought that a modern war could not possibly last more than weeks, or months, at the most. He was not alone. Many of us sought commissions urgently for the same reason. Well into 1915, responsible people affirmed that the current exchange of thousands of tons of detonated high-explosive over fixed battle-lines could only result in the extermination of all the combatants within a short time. As his dream of an outstanding command faded away and the iron entered his soul, Colonel Hall became less well liked.[3]

Other volunteers, who served under Colonel Hall in Flanders, gave a different impression of their Commanding Officer. By a paradox this confirms Charles Lawson's

The 16th Battalion Pipers.

clear and perceptive character sketch. The CO changed when his luck changed and he was able to realise his dream of leading his Battalion to the Front Line. Seen from the viewpoint of the ordinary soldier, with no ambition to become an officer, Colonel Hall was an efficient commander, worthy of respect, but hard and above all, ruthlessly professional. Men feared, admired and followed his leadership, but there are no amusing or affectionate stories of the kind told about the OC of B Company, Major Way, or the Adjutant, Captain Carey.

I never heard Noel Peters speak ill of anybody, but sometimes he would poke fun at figures in authority in a gentle way,

> Colonel Hall was what we called a real War Office Colonel, not at all like Colonel Mackay who was more of an actor, or entertainer. Colonel Hall had an odd trick of speech, ending his orders with, "Do you follow me?" or he'd end with "Hwa?". Some of the fellows would put a comb on their upper lip and take off his accent to the life. "D'ye follow me? Hwa?"

Lionel Renton joined the Battalion later but served under the command of Colonel Hall until Lionel was severely wounded at Beaumont Hamel. He took a different view of his CO from Charles Lawson or Alf Damon:

> The sixteenth was a first rate unit and Johnnie Hall was a first rate CO, a tough and energetic leader. He had no time for slackers or whiners. He got rid of some of the old dug-outs brought in by that fellow Mackay, and made sure that we got first rate, keen regular NCOs to train us. I've heard chaps say that their training NCOs were no good, idle, boozers, or skrimshankers. No doubt this was true in some battalions, not all of the old sweats were good. No doubt it was true in the PSB in the early days. Some were real old

rascals who knew every dodge in the book to get out of work. But ours weren't like that. We had some of the best of the old regular NCOs.

Our RSM was Oliver Smith, who came back out of retirement. He was good but too old. He was succeeded by Macdonald, who they promoted from sergeant. A splendid chap. Like his predecessor he was a Scots Guardsman. Another Scots addition, which sat oddly on a London regiment, was the pipe band. They were always a centre of attention, and usually well looked after as far as booze was concerned. I remember a couple of dishevelled looking pipers, in kilts, vests and boots, stumbling round the camp at reveille playing "Hey Johnnie Cope". And the fellows in the huts shouting "Put a sock in it". "Go and make that racket elsewhere." "Stop that, shove off."

Slimmed down to a small select group the Originals were fit and gaining experience in soldiering. The Public School limitation was dropped and a new type of recruit replaced the 'delicately nurtured gentlemen' that so impressed the representative of the *Evening Standard*. Noel Peters remarked that 16PSB remained an elite unit and never lost either it's eccentricity or its special esprit de corps, but the snobbish quality went as summer breezes changed to the snows of winter.

The new arrivals were not like 'The Originals' but they brought qualities of their own. The only grumble, by old or new soldiers, was the lack of weapons or regular uniforms. There was no training in marksmanship because there was no ammunition. The best their musketry instructors could do was to train them to aim, using old worn out rifles. The volunteers paraded, they drilled, they carried out field exercises like soldiers, and yet they continued to dress like civilians.

At last there was a buzz of excitement throughout the Battalion. Several horse drawn carts arrived carrying cloth bales of uniforms and long wooden boxes which, by their shape, could only contain rifles. Disillusion was equally swift. When the bales were opened the colour of the cloth was not khaki but navy blue. The uniforms proved to be blue serge of the period of the war in the Sudan. The rifles were an even greater disappointment. Unpacked from their long boxes, stripped of the brown paper and thick axle grease, the rifles that the volunteers held in their hands were not the modern, short, Mk3 Lee-Enfield magazine rifles that they expected, but their ancestors; the single-shot, 1895 pattern with the long barrel. These museum pieces were so worn in the barrels and so loose in the breach that they were fit only for arms drill. Tony Chubb expressed the disgust of all ranks. 'Someone in the War House had it in for the PSB.'[4]

The Battalion could not remain long at Kempton Park. Rumours spread that 16PSB was about to move to a permanent, hutted camp at Woldingham. Tony Chubb said, 'We left Kempton Park and moved to Sutton where we were billeted for the night ready to march on to Woldingham next day. However, when we paraded in the morning, full of enthusiasm, ready to move off, we were told that the camp was not ready. Eventually we stayed there until January 1915.'

The move, first to Sutton and then to Woldingham, in the depth of winter, illustrates both the inability of the Regular officers of the General Staff to cope with the hugely

The Battalion soccer XI. Kempton. October 1914. Purnell front row, second from right.

The first issue of uniforms. Kempton. Sergeant Purnell, centre back row.

enlarged army whether Regular, Territorials or Kitchener's New Army Battalions. It also shows the efficient and enterprising way that the volunteers took the initiative. The *Surrey Herald* described the move from Kempton to Sutton.

> 24th of November. 1914.
> MILITARY INVASION OF SUTTON.
> Officer Corps billeted.
> The residents were informed it would only be for one night and few expressed any objection to doing what they could to make their guests comfortable. On the contrary they felt it an honour to show how much they appreciated the self-sacrifice of those who have come forward to serve the country in its hour of need. The Commanding Officer, Colonel Hamilton-Hall and the Adjutant, Captain Carey are staying with Sir Ralph Foster, J.P. at the Grange... Billeting allowance is 3s 4d a day for the men, quite sufficient to pay their keep, but some of the residents are entertaining their guests so handsomely that it is evident that the question of money had not entered their calculations.

The weather was colder than usual and the move a foretaste of what the volunteers could expect in France. The men marched. At this stage in the war the Battalion had no transport of it's own. The ASC was over-stretched in France and had no vehicles to spare in England.[5] The only answer to the transport problem was private initiative. Luckily 16PSB still had enough wealthy young men in its ranks to provide private motor vehicles. So, first Kempton and then Sutton witnessed an extraordinary and un-military exodus. A column of civilian motorcars ferried backwards and forward, carrying kit and equipment, training aids, bedding and cooking pots. Motorcycles carried large parcels and bundles strapped to petrol tank or pillion, or resting in sidecars. The bulk of the kit and bedding, and that museum-like collection of useless rifles arrived in a pantechnicon hired from a removal firm, guarded by two men with sporting rifles, the guards supplying their own ammunition.

In a letter from Tasmania, Alf Damon described the arrival of the first men at what was supposed to be a winter camp at Woldingham. His account differs from others about the dates. There is a simple explanation for this. The Battalion was scattered. Some officers and men were billeted in Sutton, others in nearby villages. Alf was unlucky because he was one of a small body of men picked for advance guard. One hundred men left Sutton to make ready the winter camp at Woldingham. Alf makes plain his contempt for both the War Office planners and the local builders that the General Staff had hired to do the job. Not only had the construction of roads and huts been dilatory during the relatively mild weather of autumn, but now that the weather was bad and the huts needed with urgency, the builders used the weather as an excuse to delay construction still further. The advance party had to shelter from the cold as best they could in the half-built huts, builders' store sheds or what crude shelters they could construct for themselves. It was fortunate for the contractor that his fate did not lie in Alf's hands. Private Damon would have placed the profiteer against one of his uncompleted walls and shot him.

Advance party 16MX march from Sutton to Woldingham. January 1915.

The official account describes the 16th (Public Schools Battalion) of the Middlesex Regiment as comfortably installed at Woldingham Camp by the end of December 1914. Nothing, in fact, was so clear cut. Alf remarked that the official account of the arrival of 16PSB is typical of most of the official accounts that he encountered throughout the rest of the war. It was, he said, an account of what was planned to happen, and all being well, should have happened, but did not happen. Seldom, if ever, did plan and report tally with what actually took place.

'Our man, Johnnie Hall, was a master of the type of report that the gentlemen in Whitehall liked to see.'

1. By the end of the year 1914, 16PSB had supplied 360 NCOs and men for officer training, of whom 36 were selected for Sandhurst.

2. Later in the Great War this pattern was only worn by officers of the Light Infantry. This lasted through both World Wars and into the National Service period through the nineteen-fifties.

3. Charles Lawson was commissioned in the Essex Regiment in May 1915 and, leading his platoon, went over the top, as he put it 'on the infamous 1st of July.' 'In our Battalion (1st Essex Regiment 88th Brigade) as in the PSB, the carnage was appalling,'

4. Some of Arthur Purnell's photographs show 16PSB drilling with these antique rifles, some volunteers in navy blue serge, others still in their civilian clothes.

5. The ASC became a Corps of the army during the South African war, but had its foundation in the Wagon Trains devised by John Churchill, Duke of Marlborough. At the end of the war of 1914-18 it became the Royal Army Service Corps, or RASC, later re-named the Royal Corps of Transport, today the Royal Army Logistics Corps.

Chapter 6

FROM THE EMPIRE

Men came from all over the Empire, from India, Egypt, Ceylon, the Malay States and Argentina.
Noel Peters.

THE PRESS WAS QUICK to coin such phrases as, 'The mother-land calls her sons home to defend her shores'. There were many references to 'sons of the sea' and to the superiority of the Royal Navy. For once, this was not totally inaccurate. Like every well-brought-up English boy Lionel Renton knew that British Imperial supremacy depended on the Two Fleet doctrine. This argued that the navy must be maintained at such strength that it could defeat the fleets of any two nations in combination. So successful was this policy that the Royal Navy had not fought a major battle for close on a hundred years. Perhaps the admirals and captains had grown complacent and lazy because the British force in the Pacific was outmanoeuvred and outgunned by a smaller German fleet off the coast of Chile.

Holland was neutral. The captain of the three masted barque, like many Dutch people, sided with the Boer Republic during the South African war. Holland remained neutral so the captain had no pressing reason to return to Europe where, if anything, his sympathy lay with his German neighbours. Whatever his planned course the last person he would confide in was an English youth who had only just received his seaman's ticket. The barque's course took it straight through the centre of the Battle of Coramandel. Lionel Renton remained mystified that the crew of the barque neither saw

Wagon with timber for barrack huts. Woldingham January 1915.

Digging trenches, Woldingham. (Part of the outer defences of London) early 1915.

nor heard any sign of the first sea battle of the Great War. Crew and captain remained in ignorance of the battle until the barque reached Holland seven weeks later. Lionel immediately took the Hook-of-Holland to Harwich ferry and hurried to London to enlist.

He joined 16PSB after the Battalion moved to Woldingham, in the miserable conditions of the winter of 1915. Woldingham Camp was completed but the huts were built in a hurry and with slovenly workmanship. The volunteers of the PSB, an elite fighting battalion, trained to a peak of readiness, were employed as labourers. Week in week out, in snow, sleet and rain, they dug trenches. An added irritation was frequent inspections by staff officers (invariably called Brass-hats) who were more interested in turnout and attention to minute details of dress than in soldiering.

'Generally these inspections gave them yet another excuse for not sending us to France.' Charles Lawson said,

One inspecting officer noticed one or two dirty fingernails, which, he said, he did not expect to find in a regiment of this type. The season was mid winter and we were digging trenches to form the outer defences of London. Washing facilities were inadequate; it was impossible to get all the grime off our hands. We were not training to serve at table in London restaurants.

What the soldiers of the Great War called 'Spit and polish' and a later army called 'Bullshit' reached a high art form:

Polished boots and buttons were believed to be passports to the Front. Neither were any use when we did, at last, get there. Nor was it possible to keep fingernails manicured, much as the Brass-hats desired it.

As the icy weather set in and the news from France became more desperate and dispiriting, many of the originals thought of Indian summer at Kempton with nostalgia. 'I was thinking of the happy state of the boys at Kempton Park.' Alf typed on his old Olivetti:

I well recall Major Way doing a music-hall turn one evening in the marquee. He'd had a few, just enough to make him merry and he recited "If my mother could see me now", to roars of applause from the crowd. We also had an amateur boxer who had stood up to Charpentier for five rounds without being knocked down. One evening a famous singer performed for us at the Coliseum. We paid ten shillings a head for transport up to London, the show and back to Kempton. She sang various marching songs including one that had been written specially for us, 'The Public Schools Battalion'. This brought the house down as you may imagine.

I heard the other day that the old camp at Woldingham is still there, at the top of the hill. Here we were drilled by our new RSM, Macdonald was his name and he had been a Scots guardsman. His voice carried a great distance and he was respected by all who met him as a real gentleman. Heaven help those he caught stepping on his square, off duty. At last, at Woldingham, we had proper uniforms, regimental numbers (mine was 963) and were divided into companies and platoons. I was in 6 Platoon, commanded by Lieutenant Sholto-Douglas, which was in B Company, commanded by Major Way. Both were experienced soldiers and good men. I am sorry to say that both were killed soon after we got out to France, blown to bits by a shell, along with the runner, Dick Bird. This happened within days of our first going up to the line at La Bassée.

Alf Damon remembered a song that they sang at Woldingham, as they dug into the clay and chalk and carted mud by the ton in baskets and barrows.

> *Why did I join the PSB?*
> *Why did I join the army?*
> *To be buggered about in the mud all day,*
> *I must have been bloody-well barmy.*

Every soldier, NCO or officer was desperate to get out to France and see action. Many blamed their commanding officer for the delay. This was unjust. No one was more ambitious to embark for France than Colonel Hall.

A section in their hut with their bread ration. Woldingham 1915.

Chapter 7

THE FIGHTING COOKS

It was the sight of those fellows, marching down Piccadilly, that made me decide to join up, young as I was. I couldn't bear to be left out of all the excitement.

Noel Peters. In July 1915

LORD KITCHENER began his second great recruiting campaign. Noel Peters signed on at the Panton Street recruiting office and joined 16PSB at Woldingham. Like Tony Chubb, Noel signed on as a boy soldier and was originally allocated to the band. But someone in Battalion HQ read through his application form and realised that here was an unexpected asset. Private Peters was a trained cook.

Noel became a soldier almost by chance. There was no work for him when the household returned to London from Scotland, so he moved to another job. He entered the service of the Rt Hon Talbot KC, who had a practice in the inner temple, with his residence in Wilton Crescent, Belgravia. It was a good job for a lad, Noel said, and enlarged his experience of preparing food, cooking, storage, and the purchase and preserving of food. Despite this useful and congenial position Noel was restless. He tried to join up at Christmas but the recruiting office would not take him. He was too young and looked his age.

That spring the family moved down to Mr Talbot's country house at Three Bridges in Sussex, leaving the KC in London, with a small staff to look after him. The butler, the cook and a ladies maid all moved to the country and took Noel with them because Mr Talbot had a large family. Hever Castle, near to Three Bridges, had been turned into a hospital. Patriotic families with large houses converted them to care for wounded Belgian soldiers. Some of the lightly wounded came over to the Talbot house for the day as guests. They still had traces of Belgian mud on their uniforms.

Life might have continued peacefully, in the lush Sussex countryside. But after a month Mrs Talbot decided to return to London. The family moved back to Wilton Crescent. Noel found London much changed. The city resembled an armed camp; an exciting place to live with new sights of martial display every day. Soldiers and horses were everywhere. Volunteers drilled in Hyde Park with pieces of wood for rifles. Green Park was full of horses: horses of every size and shape, from smart riding horses and hunters, to van horses and big Suffolk drays, all tied to the park railings. The War Office commandeered every horse that was not on essential service, and, Noel said, most of the poor beasts ended up in France where many perished.

Noel was sent on an errand, collecting a parcel for Mrs Talbot from a shop in Piccadilly. The London Scottish Territorials marched past. En masse they were on a route march through the streets of London. Young girls were waving at the Territorials,

I couldn't bear to be left out of all the excitement.

men cheered, small children ran along beside the marching boots, businessmen raised their bowler hats as the soldiers in kilts marched past. There was an intense feeling in the air; great excitement. Patriotism was running very strong.

'It was the sight of those fellows, marching down Piccadilly, that made me decide to join up, young as I was. I couldn't bear to be left out of all the excitement.'

For two days Noel queued through his off duty period. Each time he had to go back to Wilton Crescent just as his section of the queue neared the recruiting officer's desk. On the second day he was walking away, down the Mall, when he passed a recruiting sergeant, easily recognised by the red, white and blue cockade on his uniform peaked cap. 'Are you trying to join up son?' the sergeant asked Noel. Noel told him that he was. He wanted to join the Royal Artillery. 'You don't want to go and get mixed up with a rough lot like that,' the recruiting sergeant said, 'a smart young lad like you. I can picture you in infantry uniform, smartly turned out. And I have just the regiment that will suit you. It's a regiment for gentlemen's sons and respectable lads. None of your common riff-raff.' Together they walked to Panton Street, just off the Haymarket.

When he returned to Wilton crescent he received a wigging from the cook. 'This isn't like you to be late on duty Peters.'

'I've joined up,' Noel said.

'What you want to do a silly thing like that for? Ain't you happy here?'

Cook was distressed. Within the year Noel realised that the good natured cook had more prescience and sense than most of those who shouted and cheered as the soldiers marched by.

Fellows think that being a cook is a cushy number. Not in the infantry it isn't. You've a mass of hungry fellows to feed. It isn't easy serving up hot grub in flooded trenches. You do the best you can. That's all you can do.

Chapter 8

ESCAPE FROM THE TAR FACTORY

Edward Catchpole and Sons. Tar distillers and manufacturers of Naval Varnishes. Coal-tar. Naphtha. Grease and Asphaltum.

THE STORY OF THE TWO CATCHPOLE BROTHERS was told to me by their youngest sister, Fanny. The two brothers joined 16PSB at Woldingham in the winter of 1915. Both enlisted under the name of Tennant. The Catchpoles were a large and prosperous family who lived at 'Ravensdeane', a solid Victorian brick house that stood in its own grounds at Grove Park, outside London, in Bromley. Mrs Catchpole died when Fanny was born leaving her husband, Edward, to care for three boys, a small girl and a newborn baby, as well as the management of his tar and varnish business in the London docks.

Edward Catchpole was a tough and thrifty businessman. He did the best for his children, hiring a housekeeper-cum-nurse to look after them. He employed the usual kitchen and garden staff found in middle-class homes in the London suburbs. Fanny remembered their childhood as a happy one, mainly because the children had each other. Edmund, the second son, was the one to devise imaginative games for the little ones. The death of his young wife made Edward withdrawn and severe, absorbed in his business dealings and the management of the tar factory. Albert, the eldest boy, grew up to be very like his father and followed him into the family business. There was little affection between the father and the two younger boys, and, as they grew up the clashes of wills became more frequent and more distressing for Fanny and her sister. Edward intended that, like Albert, both of the younger boys would enter the family business when they left school. Both received a good education; Edmund at Cranleigh and Philip at Eltham Naval College. At Cranleigh, Edmund showed a talent for acting and drawing and none for the subjects necessary for a business career. He remarked, even as a young boy, that he had no intention of wasting his life in the reek of tar and asphalt. Edmund was generous and charming, liked by everyone who met him. He showed no interest in money, distributing it generously, whether it was his own or family money. Philip was six years younger than Edmund, equally talented in the arts but without his brother's confidence and drive. Albert, the oldest and most reliable of the three boys, was most like his father both in his virtues and his faults. He alternated between moods of pride in Edmund's achievements and exasperation at his mercurial and imprudent temperament.

Fanny remembered one infamous family row when Albert had to attend a board meeting at the factory, chaired by his father. Going to the cupboard for his best overcoat he found the coat hanger bare except for a pawn ticket that indicated where the coat had gone. Albert accused his brother of theft. Instead of hanging his head in shame, Edmund roared with laughter. 'I didn't steal your wretched overcoat, only borrowed it. You've got the ticket. You can get it back from the pawnshop any time you want.'

This and other similar incidents, tried his father's patience to the limit. On Edmund's suggestion he agreed to pay his son's passage to Canada. Edmund was happy in Canada and earned his living by working at a variety of hard outdoor jobs until he reached the age of twenty-five when he inherited money from his mother's estate. Edmund immediately returned to England and became an actor, changing his name from Catchpole to one that he thought was more romantic, that of Tennant. As Edmund Tennant his first debut as an actor came at the Duke of York's theatre with Mr Lawrence Irving's company. The next opportunity was touring with the Alexander Marsh Company. Early in 1914 he set off on a tour of theatres in the West Indies and Panama with the Glossop Harris Company.

The actor Edmund Tennant before the war. (The brothers' real name was Catchpole.) They used Edmund's stage name when they enlisted in 16 PSB in late 1914.

Edmund's younger brother Philip was a gifted linguist. This aptitude was noted while he was at Eltham College. Edward Catchpole had good contacts in the City of London and obtained a post for his son in the Foreign Exchange office of the London and South Western Bank. The life of a trainee banker in the City did not suit Philip. He was not happy. Unfortunately, he did not have the confidence of his mercurial brother and could see no way of breaking out of the position in which he found himself. Like many of his colleagues, he might have remained in a job that bored him for the rest of his working life had the war not given him the escape that he needed. Despite this he had more patience than his brother and waited until Edmund returned to London in the winter of 1914.

In a spirit of euphoria, Edmund and Philip looked through the recruiting advertisements in the London evening papers, discussing and arguing over which regiment sounded the most exciting and which they should join. The title 'The Public Schools Battalion' caught the imaginations of both brothers and they agreed to join at the Panton Street recruiting office. Edmund was twenty-seven and Philip twenty-one, they signed on using Edmund's stage name of Tennant. So the two brothers Tennant completed basic infantry training after which their company commanders recommended that each should go forward for officer's training. Both refused, believing that they would get out to France quicker by remaining in the ranks. The winter weather found the Tennants digging trenches in the mud at Woldingham.

NOTE
Edmund and Philip's youngest sister, Fanny Catchpole, trained as a nurse and served with Queen Alexandra's Nursing Corps through the Second World War in North Africa and Italy where she met and married Sergeant O'Donnel an Irish professional soldier. He died about a year before I met her. An energetic, perceptive and lively person, she told me the story in the sitting room of her house in Guildford. She also lent me letters, written by Edmund and Philip and photographs to copy, a very generous and trusting action. Her grief at the early death of her talented and lively brothers was still apparent.

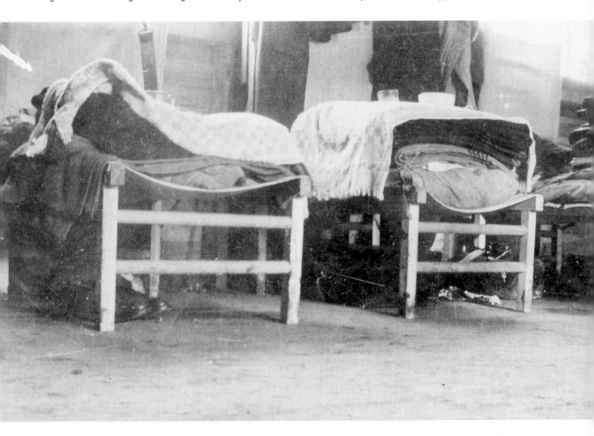

Barrack hut. Woldingham. Early in 1915. (Compare the amateur layout of bedding and kit with later regimental kit layouts).

Chapter 9

FAEX ROMULI

THE DUTCH SAILING SHIP, on which Lionel Renton was a deck-hand, reached Rotterdam in March 1915. His first choice was the Middlesex Regiment. Lionel was educated at Highgate school, the parent unit for whose OTC was the 7th Battalion of the Middlesex Regiment, based at Priory Road, Hornsey. He was disappointed to discover that both the 1/7th and the 2/7th were fully recruited. Travelling on a tram to the centre of London he ran into a school friend and told him of this bad luck. 'Why don't you join us? We're all Public School chaps.'

A number of volunteers came to 16PSB by way of the 24th Service Battalion. One of them was Laurie Barrow who wrote to Alf Damon nearly sixty years later:

> *I joined the 24th, a feeding battalion for the 16th. I joined up at Harrow where I lived. Of course I knew that it was Public School. I had only a secondary school education, but that didn't matter at that stage in the war. A pal of mine was in the 16th so I wanted to serve with him. Bill Martin was his name. He was killed with the bombing party on 1st of July.*[1]

Albert Edwards joined by the same route:

> *I was born in the Earls Court Road and went to school first in Kensington then to Hurst-Pierrepoint College in Sussex. By 1914 my people had moved to Wimbledon. I shared digs in town with a young chap called Gerald. His name was Hahn. He enlisted under another name because there was a lot of anti-German feeling about. We both worked for Maple and Co in the Tottenham Court Road. Gerald had been in the cadet corps and he found out that the 24th were recruiting, so we joined them. Gerald transferred to the 16th and I followed a month later. By this time he had corporal's stripes up. We were so proud to belong to 16PSB. I met with two other friends, the Miller brothers. Bert Miller stayed with the Middlesex Regiment, though not with the 16th. Gerald Hahn was killed when we first went up to the line, at La Bassée. A sad job.*

John Wilson joined up at Horseguard's Parade a year after the outbreak of war. From the 24th he transferred to the 16th who were at Woldingham, then moved to Nottingham.

> *I was quite young, enlisting under age out of a sense of duty that was, perhaps, misled. I was full of enthusiasm when we first went out to France, ready and eager to go out on patrols or bombing raids. Then, as casualties increased, some good friends amongst them, and I became aware of the dangers, my enthusiasm waned. I still have memories of two close friends killed out there. I realised then that one's lot is decided by fate.*

By the time Noel Peters joined the Battalion 16PSB was stationed at Woldingham and the snobbery and social elitism of the first few months at Kempton had almost disappeared to be replaced by a new professionalism. The volunteers no longer took pride in the exclusive nature of the Battalion, nor was it possible to do so after recruitment opened up to any suitable candidate regardless of class or lineage. Pride now was in the individual's qualities as a soldier and, collectively, in the quality of 16PSB as a fighting unit.

Nonetheless there were those who regretted the changes in class and looked back in nostalgia to a more gracious and mannered time. One of these was the poet Arthur Graeme West.

Arthur Graeme West was born in 1891 and was a pupil at Highgate School where he won a scholarship to Blundells School, Tiverton. He was clever, introverted, loved books and was fascinated by insects: none of these qualities designed to inspire popularity in an English Public School. His biographer, C E M Joad, who was his tutor at Oxford, tells us that West was classified as a 'worm'. Joad writes:

> Being a worm at Blundells meant that no one thought of asking your opinion on anything of importance and no one went out with you except other worms.

In 1910 West won a scholarship to Baliol College, Oxford. Joad describes him as a solitary, self-sufficient young man, with a passion for literature. Despite his intense dislike of his Public School, some of its Spartan conditioning must have rubbed off because he always kept himself fit by exercises and long hikes, usually by himself. The outbreak of war, when he was on summer vacation, left him unmoved. He barely noted it in his diary and returned to Oxford in the autumn of 1914 intending to spend a fifth year in research. West had a small private income, so small that a more gregarious graduate could not live on it. He lived for study in the manner of an earlier age, almost monastic.

Oxford must have been a strange place during those first years of the war. The American writer, Lafayette Young, visited the city and compared it to the road to a tomb.

Streets of Oxford were bereft young of men, as were many other cities and towns throughout the country.

The streets of old Oxford are like the pathways in a cemetery. I have no doubt that Cambridge is the same. Great Britain may not be sending many millions (to the war) but she is sending her best blood and brains... A Rhodes scholar from Tennessee told me that all his chums and room-mates had gone and that a majority of them had been killed. He found himself almost swallowed up by the war spirit ...This is a scientific, machine-made war. The battles amount almost to suicide. There is no escape.

The exact reason why West joined the army is not clear, an organisation that he detested from the day he joined to the day of his untimely death. West was a scholar inclined to internationalism rather than patriotism in the crude sense. He was immune to the flag-waving jingoism that propelled so many men to enlist. West makes no attempt to explain this abrupt change and Joad does not know why his former student suddenly abandoned his careful plan of study to join the army. Did some fervent young girl present him with a white feather? This too was a powerful spur to put on uniform. In many cases a rash decision is taken in the emotional rubble of a collapsing love affair. We know that West was a man with a great interest in, and an affection for women. Whether there was a young woman in Oxford who was responsible for his rash decision to exchange a life of culture, and comparative comfort, for the cold, filth and intolerable stench of the trenches remains a mystery. It was not the danger that concerned him, he was brave and assertive both in the ranks and as an officer, it was the ugliness and coarseness of army life that both enraged and depressed him. All we know is that, like the American Rhodes scholar, he was swallowed up by the war spirit.

West first applied for a commission through the University OTC, and then applied again to the county regiment, the Oxfordshire and Buckinghamshire Light Infantry. Both turned him down for the same reason; poor eyesight. He joined the 16th Public Schools Battalion, as he put it 'more or less by a ruse'. He paid a private doctor to pass him fit for service, thus by-passing the recruiting office medical officer. He joined 16PSB as a private soldier and, once again, put his name forward to apply for a commission. Colonel Hall refused to forward his name.

By the time he joined the Battalion it had experienced great changes and though it was true that not all the originals had gone to become officers, (Alf Damon, Lionel Renton, the Tennant brothers all remained in the ranks, quite deliberately the sooner to get to France) West's companions in the barrack hut more closely resembled recent recruits in any other battalion of the Middlesex than they did the 'Public School men enlisted to train and serve together' of the recruiting poster of September 1914. The young men who enlisted in 1915 were, in West's eyes *Faex Romuli*.

The first week of basic infantry training comes as a shock to the most sanguine of young men. West had neither time nor inclination to write his diary until later in the year.

The earliest events of 1915 have to be put down from memory, in the briefest way, because I bought no diary, money being rare at the time. Lacking the stimulus to energy given by an allotted space to be filled daily, I never wrote. A perpetual undercurrent of search for a commission was the main thing, though the surface of life seemed much as usual.

The first and chief way in which these experiences offended me was by their irredeemable ugliness. This was horribly intensified, after some month and a half, towards the end of which I was often happy, by five of the "Faex-Romuli" coming into the hut and crowding the number to over thirty.[2]

On Sunday too began an indefinite period of isolation for measles and we were thrown together more. Marches, in which these five were within one's vision or smell (not perhaps that they impinged so unpleasantly on that sense by the uncleanliness of their persons as by the rankness of their cigarettes) stirred in me such a spirit of fermenting malignity that I would have killed them. I never hated army life so much. Their thick necks, whose lines were so graceless, that seen from behind there was a continuous unbroken sweep from base of the neck to crown, their big flapping ears, the inveterate curl under their hats, their insolent leering expression, or their vaguely wretched stupidity was stirringly noisome, after the faces I was growing accustomed as my own surroundings. I used to walk alone, or I did this day – beside H... or C... who had left their positions to come by me, while the air, soft as milk and as sweet, came past tainted by their vile cigarettes. The landscape, that seemed almost to complain that such as we three could not visit and praise it as it deserved, being further dishonoured by these ugly presences, the companions of our constraint. If any more of these creatures come and no change of huts can be made, they will rise, like H.G. Wells' Morlocks in The Time Machine, from their position of excluded ugliness and possess the

Left: Cambridge University men building their own huts. These upper-class men had to become accustomed to living and sleeping alongside working-class fellow recruits. (Note the bow ties.)

Below: Shoulder to shoulder, recruits carry out their ablutions. Some from the Public Schools found this difficult to adapt to.

house. The attitudes of the former hut dwellers is universally hostile at present, and some of those whose own social position was, perhaps, not very well assured, are foremost in the underhand campaign of indignant protest.

What was this change in the Battalion that roused such loathing and contempt in Graeme West? His view at the time is so different from that of those writing forty or fifty years later. In the case of the survivors it is inevitable that a certain amount of nostalgia is bound to creep in. As Edith Piaf sang, *'Les morts sont tous les brave types'*. No survivor speaks ill of his dead companions.

C E M. Joad edited and published West's diaries as a tribute to his former student and he is generally approving. But in this case Joad condemns these 'snobbish strictures'. Graeme West's diary, written during, or immediately after events, is a valuable check against the recollections of survivors written decades later. In West's case the changes that so upset him were the changes brought about by the end of selection by schooling. The Battalion opened up its ranks to anyone who was both physically and mentally suitable to serve in 16PSB, regardless of schooling.

Even as late as forty years after the end of the Great War class consciousness was still entrenched in the British army and navy. This was much less marked in the RAF, being a recently formed service. Alongside birth and money, antiquity makes the third leg of the tripod of regimental pride. Though the origins of the Middlesex Regiment dated back to the 57th of Foot in the Peninsular War, the traditions of the 16th Middlesex were instant traditions and customs dated back to Colonel Mackay at his famous meeting at Harrow-on-the-Hill. The Irish wolfhound, the pipe band, the Battalion song, all were concocted. Military purists were bound to look askance at them. (This, no doubt is part of Robert Graves vendetta against the Public Schools Battalion. See Appendix 3.)

Even as late as the Cold War period the guest from a line regiment dining in a Guards or cavalry mess had impressed upon him, immediately, his status as a lower being in the social hierarchy. This class-based trilogy of breeding, wealth and regiment was more obvious at the start of the Second World War, and even more extreme at the beginning of the Great War. The slur 'A temporary officer and a temporary gentleman' was common between the wars.[3]

West's distaste is less that of class, the poet could not be described as an aristocrat, more an intellectual superiority, of a type that was endemic in Oxford. With 21st century hindsight it is easy to censure Arthur Graeme West. One thinks of the numbers of brave, idealistic and thoroughly admirable young men buried at Beaumont Hamel, indeed all along the twenty mile strip that is the site of the first day of the Somme battle, and one feels embarrassed by West's harsh comments. That said, anyone who experienced an Aldershot barracks or the stinking lower decks of a troop ship, will have some sympathy with Graeme West's irritable and intemperate outburst.

January, February and early March 1915 were the worst months that 16PSB experienced during their training in England. Indeed there was no time for the training that the volunteers needed and desired.

In fact digging trenches for the Training was supposed to take about a year to complete, but the surprising thing was that we novices did as well in those few months as did a peacetime recruit in twice the time. By the time we reached Clipstone we had some first rate NCOs to train us.

This respect was mutual. RSM Oliver Smith wrote of his time at Kempton and Woldingham, 'I have never met a better lot in my life and that is saying a good deal.'

Drill and physical training were part of each day's routine. These, like strenuous route marching, were part of the Battalion's training from the first days at Kempton because they could be done in civilian clothes and without rifles. These increased from five miles a day to twenty miles in full kit. Colonel Hall boasted that his men could march under any conditions and out-march any other unit. Men who were not fit were transferred to 24th Service Battalion. One of the physical efficiency tests was clearing a six foot wall carrying a rifle and full equipment. The recruit ran from a twelve yard line, put one foot on a four by two inch wooden rail, gripped the top of the wall, hauled himself over, dropped to the other side in an upright position, and carried on running.[4]

Many of the recruits had some experience with the Lee-Enfield rifle gained in their school cadet corps. Those that had none began their training with a rifle clamped to a tripod. Each man practised until he could line up the back-sight and foresight on the bull's eye. Next he got used to taking the correct trigger pressure. Ammunition for training was scarce, so he only learned to shoot at a target when his instructors were satisfied that he had mastered the handling of the rifle. The aim of the weapons' training instructors was for most of the Battalion to reach the same standard as the regular soldiers of the BEF, to fire ten rounds accurately and rapidly.

In 1915, as in 1900, the army gave great importance to training with the rifle and bayonet. In the first exercise the recruits charged suspended sacks, bayoneted them and ran on. In the second the target was an experienced instructor with a six foot pole. This had a loop of rope at one end and a padded ball at the other. Finally the recruit passed on to close quarter fighting using the bayonet and the brass butt of his rifle. Alf Damon wrote that there was very little equipment to train with

How to aim at a target. Training with a rifle clamped to a tripod.

in the early days of the war. There were no machine guns issued to infantry battalions in training and, initially, no grenades. They practised throwing stones at a target area. Later they were issued with canister grenades. These were fitted with an igniter, while the grenade thrower had a striker strapped to his wrist:

Striking this started the fuse. The timing was unreliable so you threw the damn thing as fast and as far as you could. Throwing the canister was an ordeal, rather like Russian roulette. But most of us made the grade. The first of the Mills grenades weren't much better. One of the best of the Originals had an accident with a Mills bomb which put him out of the war.

Finally the recruit passed on to close quarter fighting using the bayonet and the brass butt of his rifle.

Once trench warfare became formalised officers and NCOs came back from the front line to teach the new techniques for dealing with what was, in effect, siege warfare. They pointed out that hand grenades were a vital tool in trench warfare.[5]

The German stick grenade resembled a large can with a handle. The fuse was ignited by pulling a wooded knob on the the handle whose stick-like shape enabled an experienced grenadier to throw it for a considerable distance. The French army too developed a grenade; much smaller and shaped like an egg. The British General Staff, whose experience was gained in a rapid moving war in South Africa, believed siege warfare to be a tactic of the past and, in August 1914, there was no efficient grenade. Officers and NCOs improvised with a variety of home made bombs that they threw, or catapulted, at the enemy. There are many stories of these products of private enterprise, both comic and tragic. Alf Damon's story concerned a grenade accident, not with one of the jam tin bombs at the start of the war, but in 1915, when the army in France had been issued with the first pattern of the Mills grenade.

In the early days at Kempton Park we had an excellent amateur boxer known to all as "Jarge". He came from Bradford and once paid £500 to go into the ring with Charpentier. The last time he boxed was at the Croydon Empire. We all went up to watch and to cheer Jarge on. This was a variety show and the band had a bald headed drummer. As Jarge came out of the ring he seized the drum sticks and beat a tattoo on the drummer's bald pate.

Alf continued:

Jarge was one of the early group who went for commissions. This he duly got and was

Clipstone camp, Notts. Church parade. 16th MX, 17th MX and ASC. On parade. July 1915. (Note Mine winding gear top right.)

> *posted to another battalion. While he was in France, he was instructing his platoon on throwing the new Mills grenade. One exploded as he threw it. Mitchell survived but it took his arm off. This put him out of the war and out of the ring.*[6]

The move, so long anticipated, came at last, but it was not to the south coast but further north to Clipstone Park near Nottingham. George Jones-Walters gave a clear account of the move. George was another of the boys who enlisted giving a false birth-date.

> *The Public School qualification was relaxed when I joined in 1915 or I could not have joined. My school was more public than Public School. 16PSB split up soon after I joined at Woldingham, A B C and D Companies went to Clipstone Park, commanded by Colonel Hall. E and F Companies remained at Woldingham to form a reserve battalion commanded by J J Mackay. This later became the 24th Service Battalion. We in the 24th remained in touch with the 16th throughout the war, providing replacements and taking their convalescent men. When the 16th ceased to exist, the 24th remained a service battalion.*

1. L/Cpl William Cecil Martin. Killed 1.7.1916.
Two lance corporals and two privates all named Martin were killed on the first day of the Somme battle. Cpl Stephen and Pte Charles Martin were killed in 1917.

2. Faex-Romuli. The editor of Graeme West's diaries, C E M Joad, rather politely translates *Faex-Romuli* as 'The dregs of Romulus' knowing that the authorities would not permit publication of the book with its real meaning, which is 'Romulus shit' or in this context, 'Romulus little shits'. See *The Diary of a Dead Office*. Ed C E M Joad.

3. For an amusing description of the snobbery of the 'OK people' in an officer's Prisoner of War camp in Italy in 1943 see Eric Newby, *Love and War in the Apennines*, Pp. 38-43. Hodder and Stoughton 1971. 'Before the war I had rarely spoken to OK people, let alone known any well enough to talk to.' P39.

4. One of these walls, though rather taller, was still in use at the Middlesex Regimental depot at Mill Hill in the early sixties.

5. With their usual efficiency, the German army staff foresaw the importance of defensive positions and defensive warfare. The infamous Schlieffen Plan depended on a rapid moving hook through Belgium, sweeping down towards Paris. To do this the generals in the field relied on a 'hinge'. This meant a strongly defended position, to the south of the advance, that could not be broken by an attack by the French army. As a guest observer at German manoeuvres several years before the war Douglas Haig reported on the number and ingenuity of devices for trench warfare that he saw, from drainage pumps to smokeless cooking stoves to trench mortars. Not least, a reliable hand grenade. Though behind in the development of a reliable grenade the British army caught up. Captain Arthur Purnell was appointed bombing officer after the Battalion moved into the front line. He suggested improvements to the fuse on the Mk one Mills grenade. These were later taken up by the War Office. First issued in the spring of 1915, 33,000,000 Mills grenades were issued during the Great War. Variants of the Mills remained in service through the Second World War and into the Cold War. The 36 Mills Grenade was still used in Korea and Malaya in the nineteen-fifties. Refs: Douglas Haig: *The Educated Soldier*. John Terraine. *World War 1: Trench Warfare*. M Houlihan. Ward Lock Books. London. 1974.

6. Many soldiers remembered that trip to the Croydon Empire, including Noel Peters.

NOTE ON LOCATIONS.
Woldingham lies between Caterham and Westerham, close to today's M25. Clipstone is north of Nottingham, between Mansfield and Ollerton, lying between the river Maund and the edge of Sherwood Forest.

Noel Peters in marching order. Note earlier pattern of Lee-Enfield rifle (Mk1) and leather equipment. 16PSB were issued with Mk3 SMLE and with webbing equipment when they embarked for France.

Chapter 10

MEN WHO MARCH AWAY

What of the faith and fire within us?
Men who march away
Ere the barn-cocks say
Night is growing gray.
Leaving all that here can win us;
What of the faith and fire within us
Men who march away?

Thomas Hardy. 'Song of the Soldiers'. September 1914

LF DAMON WAS PLAGUED by the obstinacy and vicious character of mules throughout his long and varied service through the war and the advance to the Rhine. 'Did you ever have anything to do with those no-hopers? Take my advice: don't.' Before moving to Clipstone the Battalion received an issue of horses and mules. Alf knew one of the volunteers responsible for the mules:

> *There were three tough characters who came from the Argentine to enlist: Allen, Ramsay and Vibart. They were chums, all wild men, and Vibart was the wildest of the three. After the Battalion received its allocation of mules we won a bit of money on Vibart. He'd been a muletiero in the Andes, in Chile, and was immensely strong. One of the muletiero's tricks was to lift a mule and throw it. We had several other battalions brigaded with us at the time and we took bets that he could do it. In fact we bet heavily on him. We all went onto the parade ground and Vibart got his back under the mule's hindquarters, you know, and lifted the astonished beast up in the air and threw it. Later on Vibart was made up to transport sergeant and became more respectable, but early on he was a holy terror. While we were at Woldingham the cookhouse usually stayed open quite late. If you'd been out, and were pally with the cooks, you could usually get some tea or soup or something left over. Well I suppose Vibart had a skinful, or one of the cooks was a bit stroppy because one night they got into a fight. It took four of us to get Vibart off and drag him to the guard room.[1]*

The Battalion left Woldingham and moved to Clipstone Camp on the 9th of July 1915. The solicitor, turned Orderly Sergeant, Wallace Grain, gives Clipstone only a mention in passing. He was mainly concerned with 'The inclement weather'. He records 'Intensive training varied by occasional visits to "The Black Boy" in Nottingham.' In contrast the brief stay in Nottinghamshire made a great impression on Alf Damon. What made Clipstone memorable was neither the forest, nor the city of Nottingham, but a young woman. Her name was Lily Shelmardine. Lily and her sister worked in one of the big canteens that were opened and run by local charities, not only for the county regiment, the Sherwood Foresters, (King's Royal Rifles), but also admitted the Londoners temporarily based at Clipstone Park.

The Misses Shelmardine were the children of a wealthy Nottingham family and had recently left school. In normal times they would have completed their education at a finishing school for the improvement of young ladies in a genteel spa town, like Matlock or Bath. But there was a war on, and everyone, man, woman or child, had to do what he or she could for the war effort. The Shelmardine girls chose to work in a soldiers' canteen. They were unusually pretty with dark hair, dark eyes and glowing complexions, ruddy with health. They had that surface shyness that covered an inner self-confidence typical of middle class young women of the time. Many months later, when Alf returned to England on a stretcher, he learned that Lily's father was a wealthy Nottingham manufacturer and had been the city's mayor before the war.[2]

Two years earlier, serving private soldiers with sausage, egg and mash, or selling chocolate, biscuits, yellow dusters or boot polish, would have been unthinkable for well brought up young ladies. But times were far from normal, nor were these early soldiers. Throughout every part of the country Kitchener's New Army volunteers were generally better educated, and of higher intelligence than the unfortunates who joined the regular army before the war.

Being a modest person Lily said nothing about her family when they met across the canteen counter, or later when they were 'walking out', as the phrase was then. They liked each other. Alf made her laugh. Nor was Alf shy about asking her to accompany him to the cinema, or a tearoom of her choice on Saturday afternoon. The following evening, after consulting her sister, Lily Shelmardine agreed. It was obvious that Alf, a soldierly, self confident and jolly young man, made a good impression on Lily. As for Alf, the memory of her shy smile, her neat presence and her gentle voice, stayed with him through the freezing mud of Flanders and the concussion, noise, dust, heat and slaughter of Picardy. Time was short, guard duties, orderly room duty and cookhouse fatigues, many. Alf and Lily met, but always in the evening when she was on duty. Each time they arranged an outing in Nottingham on a Saturday something happened to prevent the meeting. And then, in the autumn, the Battalion moved south. The long awaited preparation for France had begun. Alf was reluctant to say good-bye to Lily but he was not the type to be cast down for long. The excitement, the certainty that, at last, they were heading for France, drove everything else from his thoughts.

Perham is a windswept open stretch of downland on Salisbury Plain. Here the 16th were reunited with 17th and 18th Middlesex, joining 100th Infantry Brigade in the 33rd Division. The 33rd was known as the 'Domino Div' because of its black and white divisional sign. Final training before embarkation included intensive shooting practise on the Bulford Ranges, platoon and company exercises and marching both by day and by night. Alf remembered one night march in particular because it was exceptionally cold.

Perham Down camp.

> *My section stopped for a rest, sheltered from the biting wind by a high wall. We huddled together for warmth. To our great surprise we heard female voices singing. This glorious sound reached us through the frosty air. The great wall enclosed a nunnery and the nuns were singing midnight mass.*

The General Staff was dominated by cavalry generals. Understandably, Douglas Haig and his colleagues dreamt of restoring the war of movement, with which they had become well aquainted during active service in the Sudan and South Africa. Preparing for the day when the British army would break through the enemy line, the infantry battalions exercised with the Divisional cavalry. At the conclusion of the 33rd Divisional exercises, Queen Mary inspected the Division. After the infantry marched past it was the turn of the cavalry. Noel Peters described the horsemen from Tidworth massed on the skyline. On the order they charged. The infantrymen watched them plunge by

Perham Down camp, (Noel Peter's hut extreme left. Marked with an X).

The Pipe Band. Perham Down. Aug 1915: Lance Segeant Pipe Major Charles Stewart 1152; Piper John Grant 1144; Piper William Sloane 2188 (wounded Somme October 1916, died June 1974); Piper Fred Carruthers 1154; Piper Norman McDonald 1148; Piper Dugald McFarlane 1150; Piper Henry Mitchelson 1154; Piper Thos Latham 1157 (killed Somme 1 July 1916); Piper James Gilchrist 1930; Piper John Kerr 1153; Piper Corporal Thos Gibson 1149; Drummer William Sloane 2530 (killed Somme 1916).

down the slope in a thunder of hooves and yelling riders, sabres and lance-points flashing in the pale winter sunlight. 'We saw cavalry in France,' Noel said. 'But always behind the line. We never saw anything like that again.'

1. Seven soldiers named Allen were killed on July the first 1916.

2. Canteens were set up all over the country by a variety of charities. They were usually attached to churches. Some combined religious indoctrination with tea and buns; others were more tolerant, viewing their role as providing home comforts for young men far from home. These were the fore-runners of the NAAFIs and Union Jack Clubs of the Second World War and National Service periods. In view of the different way that young women are treated today – and the way that young women behave and talk in the 21st Century – it is important to point out the immense difference in the way women and girls were treated in public. My Mother-in-law, Kitty Maher, spoke of her childhood in Walworth during the Great War. 'We had some real villains in Walworth, very rough men, but even the lowest of the low would never have used the sort of language in front of a woman that you hear all the time today.' Young women working in canteens in both world wars were treated with a respect that today is unimaginable. Survivors of the religious clubs could still be found in Aldershot in the nineteen-fifties, for example the Church of Scotland Club whose raisin scones were generally considered to be supreme.

Chapter 11

GOODBYE PICCADILLY

It's a long way to Tipperary it's a long way to go
It's a long way to Tipperary to the sweetest girl I know.
Goodbye Piccadilly, goodbye Leicester Square,
It's a long long way to Tipperary
But my heart lives there.

Alf was sad to say goodbye to Lily Shelmardine, but life at Perham Down had its compensations. Those of 16PSB not on guard or other duties received weekend passes. London was Alf's home and easier to reach from Hampshire than Nottingham. Even on Salisbury Plain, and with the advantage of a free rail pass, wartime travel was not easy. To get to Perham Down, by early morning working parade, the revellers had to leave London before 10pm, reaching camp at four in the morning. Despite the knowledge of the move to France known to all ranks (and, no doubt, known to the enemy equally quickly) there was that delay inseparable from any army in any time. At last each man was given a travel warrant to his home and a pass for two weeks' leave. With it came a warning of the dreadful consequences should he fail to return from leave on time.

Embarkation leave is a strange time, from a social, perhaps even a psychological viewpoint. At no other time is the gulf between the civilian world and the enclosed and alien world of the army more marked. For the former Public School boy, or the former Borstall boy, the break is less painful than for the boy who has always lived at home, but it is painfully familiar. Throughout his short life, it seems, he has ridden this uncomfortable, cold, dirty train, reeking of coal smoke, returning to school or to camp. He is leaving the relaxation, the comfort of home and the kindness of women for the world of men. Hard beds, cold dormitories, bad food, rough language and behaviour. He returns to the coarseness of men, the smell of men, cigarettes, foot-rot and flatulence. And yet with all these irritations goes a comradeship, a shared purpose and a sense of adventure that cannot be found in the routine of civilian life. On his two week embarkation leave the soldier is separated from his unit, his comrades and the ethos and protection of the male tribe. In returning to the civilian world he returns to a world that is both familiar and at the same time unreal. He is on loan. He is on borrowed time. For the first time, perhaps for the last, the youth is forced to stand alone and contemplate the possible results of volunteering. He sees his past clearly: what he has done and what he has left undone. The future is a blank wall in which is set a single iron gate. Whatever happens to him beyond that wall and that gate, nothing in his life will be the same again and he knows that he will never again be able to explain the changes to his nearest and dearest. 'Out there' will always be a barrier between those who went and those who stayed. At the same time there is a sense of destiny, of the rightness of wearing harness. Whether in train, or ship, or barracks, this is the fate of the men of his family. This is what a man does. Traversing that iron gate is part of the process of becoming a man.

Lionel Renton returned to see his family in Surrey. Alf travelled to Waterloo and thence to Lewisham, by tram and by omnibus. Edmund and Philip Catchpole (alias Tennant) spent their leave with the family in Bromley. Noel Peters returned to Kent, or so one might suppose. Noel's descriptions of the houses of the gentry in which he worked before the war are exact. His memories of events in Flanders, or above the Somme, were clear and informative. But never once did Noel talk about his childhood or his family, except to remark that he was a man of Kent.

In his diary, written in camp 7th November, Arthur Graeme West described the end of his leave:

> As I began my journey through the raw November night, returning to camp from this, the last weekend of leave, it pleased me to picture all those other Saturdays and Sundays from early spring to late autumn that I had spent when my station had been at W... C... or S... It chanced as I lifted the blind for a last sight of London, the towers of Westminster sprang into clear outline from the indistinguishable mass of mean buildings between them and the railway, and so moulded my yet vague memories definitely to the journey from Victoria to North London. I remembered in an orderly, detached way, as it were another's experience I was contemplating, the thrill of first contact with London as I emerged from Victoria station into the open square, looking for a northbound bus. True I never felt free, never dreamt for a moment that the old days were back again, myself and the city, too deeply stained by war, but I gained here a comforting security that the possibilities of my old life were being preserved, held in trust against the day when I should be able to resume them all.
>
> The shops, the advertisements, the people hurrying about the streets were evidence of the vitality of the former way of things. And it was thus that the women pleased me especially, by their brave show of other concerns than the war. How delightful it was to mark the spreading of a new fashion, and how kindly one felt to this one or that who, with the new skirt swinging high above the ankles, gave assurance of bold prodigality, an open loyalty to a code which many affected these days to despise.

THE ROAD TO FLANDERS.

We were so desperately keen to get to the Front. Lionel Renton said:

> It's very hard to recapture that feeling now. So many terrible memories blot it out. After seeing so many botched up actions, so many of one's friends killed, it is hard to imagine that spirit. We were so afraid that the war would be over before we got out there, you see. Even when we saw the Front Line; the mud, the mess, the dreadful state

56

everything was in — because there was no properly organised trench line early on you know, not properly made like they were later — all that was obscured by a tremendous excitement. We were out there, in France, at the Front.

Moving a division is a ponderous business. First to go were the Divisional Pioneers, the 18th Middlesex who reached Le Havre 14th November.[1] On the eleventh of that month signs came that the move had begun. The men of the 16th Middlesex handed in their stiff peaked caps and were issued with soft caps with a narrow peak and ear-flaps. For the first time, hair was clipped close to the scalp as a protection against trench-lice. A N Russell wrote in his diary: 'On meeting civilians one felt quite nervous about taking one's cap off, people stared so. At the same time, one felt genuinely labelled "Active Service".'

At Perham Down the camp was a bustle of packing and preparation. The smell of paint and stencil ink hung heavy in the air as heavy equipment was boxed and labelled. Officers, looking anxious, hurried about consulting lists. NCOs bellowed and cursed. On the 15th Russell wrote in his diary, 'Still hanging on! We expected to go off today and were all packed up last night. We were given respirators and each man given his ration of ammunition. But nothing further happened.'

Fond 'good-bye' said countless times.

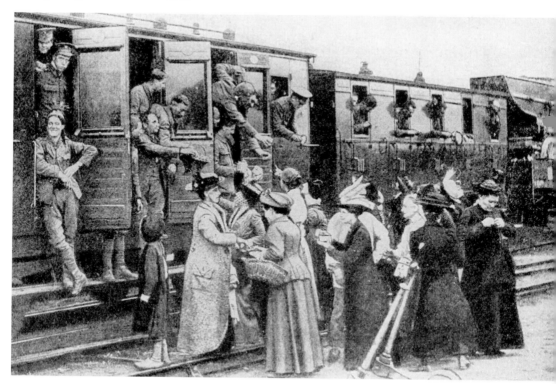

The Battalion experienced a temporary split. The main party travelled eastward to Folkestone, while a smaller group that included the transport and all heavy equipment, headed west for Southampton. With them went the irascible Sergeant Vibart and his even less amiable mules.

Assigned to the Transport section A L N Russell listed in his diary:

4 Officers. 122 Other Ranks. 21 Horses. 43 Mules. 4 Machine guns. 19 Vehicles and 9 bicycles left camp for France. [Russell meant mule-drawn transport, infantry battalions were not issued with motor vehicles, either in England or France.]

16 Nov 1915. We got up at 5.30 this morning and had an unprecedented good breakfast of bacon and sausages. Then we paraded at 7.15am and marched to Ludgershall, all of us glad it was no further. Greatcoats were worn as well as any extra clothing, scarves, cardigans etc, this being the only means of carrying them and the results pretty tent like. Spent the night on Southampton docks and on the morning of the 17th embarked on the Monas Queen and arrived at Le Havre on the 18th November.

Less interested in statistics than Russell, Alf wrote of the remainder of the Battalion:

That night, our last in Blighty, some silly fellows wrecked the canteen. We were paraded and told off by the CO. Those not present in the canteen, as well as the guilty, would have to pay for the damage. I did not drink at that time so never went to the wet-canteen. But it was our last night so I did not grudge the money.

The main party entrained early on the morning of 17th November. A section of the rear-guard formed up in slovenly fashion. Major Way leant out of a carriage window and shouted at them to smarten up. As he bellowed, his voice was blotted out by a sudden roar of steam from the engine. The ranks preparing to entrain saw his mouth opening and shutting but heard no sound. As the steam died away the reply came to the Major in a great chorus. 'If my mother could see me now.'

The main party of the Battalion travelled in carriages of panelled wood that had once belonged to the South Eastern and Chatham Railway Company and they arrived in Folkestone on a blustery, cold afternoon. The ancient carriages spilled their load of jostling, tumbling khaki onto the quay. The men dragged webbing belts and cross straps, rifles and boxes of ammunition with them. They adjusted their webbing and puttees and collected their large packs and blankets. Already feeling the cold wind from the sea they found what shelter they could on the dockside and settled down to wait.

There was no hot food, not even a mug of tea. The volunteers drank from enamelled steel water bottles. Some nibbled dry biscuits, which was the only food that they carried. The queasy feeling in the pit of Alf's stomach was increased by the sight of French torpedo boats bouncing on the waves beyond the breakwater. The wind increased and grew more penetrating as the winter sun disappeared behind clouds. Outside Folkestone harbour the swell increased, wind and waves pitching the little torpedo boats this way and that, as they followed their zigzag courses, throwing white plumes of spray against the dark sky.

As darkness came, at 4.00pm, the troopship manoeuvred alongside the quay for

Paddle steamer commandeered by the Admiralty for use as a cross-Channel ferry (similar type of pleasure steamer to the **Monas Queen**).

embarkation. Despite her grey paint, blue RNR ensign and Admiralty title, 'Transport 062', her origin was clear. This was a little old paddle steamer, more fitted for summer excursions down the Solent than crossing the Channel in a winter gale. The Royal Navy and Fleet Auxiliary pressed into service every steam-ship that could carry men, horses and guns across the Channel to France.

Laden with kit and weapons the men climbed the wooden gangplanks to the deck of 062. As the sun began to set the wind was worse and white water broke against the harbour wall. Rumours of mines and submarines passed between the sections.

As soon as he was on board 062 Alf climbed to the upper deck to gain a better view of the French anti-submarine patrol. As each patrol boat passed she turned, heeling over deck under water, upper-works and quick firing gun drenched in spray. As the light faded the French boats turned and headed home. The torpedo boats' presence was not reassuring. Talk spread around that either a torpedo or a mine sank a supply ship earlier that day. This rumour was confirmed as Paddle Steamer 062 cleared the harbour wall and approached the Channel. Amongst the white-crested waves the sea showed less turbulent patches. These were slicks of oil on which floated lifebuoys, broken boxes, timber and dark bundles of khaki. These dark shapes resembled corpses but were, in fact, bundles of uniforms and blankets. They were sucked towards the paddles and scattered in the wake as the blacked-out steamer pitched and wallowed her way across the 20 miles of water to France. Alf remained on deck to avoid the stench of sweat, cheap tobacco and vomit below. The funnel trailed sulphurous coal smoke. From the engine room hatches came fumes of soot and engine oil. Decks were littered with cold, unhappy, vomiting soldiers.

The main party of the Battalion disembarked on the quay on Boulogne harbour at 7.15 on the morning of 8th November. Platoons and companies formed ranks and marched out of the docks, pushing their way through a cheerful crowd of dock workers and their wives who were selling fruit, and fresh bread rolls.

'This sounds attractive, Alf wrote. 'But most of us had left the meagre contents of our stomachs in the channel and were not yet ready to risk food at that time in the morning. So the kindly and business-like ladies had little success.'

The sky clouded over behind the town as they marched up the hill on the Calais road. Rain fell as they approached Osthove camp, which was built by Royal Engineers on the cliffs above the small seaside resort of Wimereux.[2]

The Quartermaster and cooks preceded the Battalion out of Boulogne to the camp. Here Noel Peters and his colleagues prepared tea, heating dixies of water over charcoal fires that they tended in hollows and sand pits in the downs. Noel remarked that they had no other means of cooking because the field-cookers had landed at Le Havre and were travelling north-east to Flanders. Noel burnt his hand. He had no salve or ointment so he covered the burn in axle grease, wrapped it in a dishcloth and carried on. During the two days and nights that the Battalion spent at Wimereux Noel did what he could to make the food appetising. This was not easy. Preparing dixies of tinned stew, heated over fire trenches fuelled by charcoal in the open, needs resourcefulness and application. But, Noel said, it prepared the cooks for worse conditions to come.

Soldiers soon recover their appetite and even the most sea-sick were now ravenously hungry. To Alf's delight, the commercially astute ladies of Boulogne anticipated this need for food and walked or cycled up the steep cobbled road from the port to the camp on the downs. They carried hot coffee in metal cans wrapped in straw, and baskets wrapped in clean linen. The baskets carried fresh bread, hot from the baker and pats of Normandy butter. They exchanged food for francs, shillings or anything of value that the soldiers could barter.

If life at Osthove camp was preferable to either the deck of steamer 062 or the docks at Folkestone, it was no Streatham Locarno. To the men and boys of 16PSB the camp rapidly became familiar and boring. Colonel Hall made sure that his men were not idle. To prevent brass buttons, badges, shoulder titles and buckles giving away their position to the enemy the Battalion was ordered to paint them with brown shellac as soon as it was warned for active service on Perham Down. At Osthove Camp the CO decreed that all brasses must be restored to their former glory. The volunteers spent their time at Wimereux picking off every trace of shellac and polishing the brasses with 'Soldiers Friend', small cakes of metal polish.

As the Company sergeant-majors and RSM MacDonald inspected the buttons of each platoon, Sergeant Vibart and his mules, the General Service wagons, field kitchens, machine guns and personnel of the Transport section, travelled by train from Le Havre to Thienne in Flanders. A.L.N. Russell wrote in his diary:

We got into big horse boxes and luggage vans, each holding 40 men, or in our case, mules and supplies. It is not a comfortable way of travelling. The journey was planned to take three and a half hours, but in fact it took seven. The countryside was dreary, most of it flat fields divided by irrigation ditches. These were enlivened, to some extent, by lines of trees planted at regular intervals. Sometimes the train passed close to a small village of brick built cottages and farms. We saw very few people. Rain fell and the grey afternoon

*light faded to the darker grey of dusk. At last the train stopped and we scrambled out to
form up beside the railway line. We had no idea of our whereabouts and were still sore and
confused by the journey. But gradually our ears took in a dull noise sounding
continuously in the distance. And slowly we understood that this was the sound of the
guns. It was rather weird and thrilling arriving like this, in the dark, in an unknown
place, within the sound, for the first time of what lay ahead of us.*

*We harnessed the animals and marched beside them and the GS wagons for about an hour
and a half until we reached a village. The other side was a slovenly looking, dirty farm and
here we and the horses and mules were distributed to barns, stables,
sheds and other farm buildings.*

Battalion transport included not only the GS wagons but also the
field cookers and their limbers. These waited for the main body
to arrive.[3]

Paraded at Osthove Camp, the 16th (Public Schools Battalion)
of the Middlesex Regiment awaited their Commanding Officer's
inspection. With the RSM two paces behind him Colonel Hall
pronounced the shining brass-work up to regimental standard.

The morning was dry; the sky bright but there was a chilly
wind blowing in from the sea. With drums beating and pipers
sounding the Battalion marched from Wimereux downhill into
Boulogne. Their route turned away from the sea and followed the
railway line. On factory boards, and the end walls of houses, there
were posters attached. As the volunteers grew accustomed to
France these would soon become commonplace, but that morning
they were still strange and exotic. The largest showed the image
of a heroic *poilu* turning to point out the enemy and the way
forward to his comrades. '*En les aura!*' Other posters warned of
the dangers of careless talk and enemy spies. '*Taissez vous!*' '*Mefiez
vous.*' These became more numerous as they followed the lower
road into the industrial part of the town and approached the
marshalling yard and rail-freight yard. At one corner of this
gleaming network of steel tracks a train was being assembled and
made ready. Lines of freight vans were pushed into place and
coupled together. Each had its permitted contents stencilled on
the side. '*40 Hommes. 8 Chevals.*' Alf remarked that not only were
the horses more valuable than men and that no sensible horse
would put up with conditions endured by soldiers.

The business of entraining the Battalion was supervised by a
disparate group of officials. Rail Transport Officers of the Royal
Engineers conferred with French officials of the '*Syndicate National
des Chemin de Fer*'. Sitting in the steel doorway of one of the trucks

*On factory boards, and the
end walls of houses, there
were posters attached.*

Alf Damon, Laurie Barrow and Arthur Kent enjoyed the drama as a stolid red-faced, elderly Sapper officer was assisted, or more often hindered, by volatile Frenchmen in baggy overalls in sky blue wearing wooden clogs on their feet and black oilskin caps on their heads. One official blew into a brass cow-horn trumpet; others ran about like poultry emitting high-pitched squeaks. Arthur Kent remarked that the sole qualification for admittance to the French railway service appeared to be castration. At last, like the finale to a grand opera, an immense locomotive made its entrance at the slow pace befitting its bulk and presence, steam hissing, oiled pistons thrusting, wheels of vast diameter turning inch by inch. Even Alf was impressed by this glistening mass of machinery with its black cylinders, polished steel connecting rod and writhing mass of copper piping. As this monster passed, its weight shaking the ground like the entry of the giants in Gotterdamerung, the driver seized a lanyard and the whistle gave a high pitched peep-peep.

For Alf, Arthur and Laurie, their first experience of French railways was a novelty. This novelty soon became commonplace and then lacked any vestige of charm once each platoon was inside a van, the doors closed and the journey started. The trucks lacked any form of springing or suspension. Every kink or fault in the line was transmitted through wheels and axles to the floor of the wagon. The men were packed tightly and the riveted steel floors gave no comfort to aching buttocks, thighs and spines. From time to time the train stopped, allowing the men to stretch their legs, empty bladders and contemplate the unfamiliar and dismal landscape. As soon as the train stopped one man from each truck ran to the locomotive, mess tin, can or bucket ready to catch the boiling water that the driver released from the boiler. The runner dropped a packet of tea into his can and ran back to his mates. At mid-day Noel and the other cooks handed out packets of sandwiches that they prepared the night before leaving Wimereux.

After a long slow journey, interrupted periodically by halts in sidings to allow a priority traffic to pass, ammunition or wounded, the train stopped for another tea-break on yet another flat, monotonous plain. But this time the atmosphere was different, though it took a few moments to identify where the difference lay. Then the soldiers could hear, faintly but unmistakably, the sound of the artillery bombardment. As Alf described it, the sound resembled that of surf on a shore far away. Their rail journey ended in darkness, in a nondescript hamlet untouched by war. It consisted of very little; some farm buildings and outhouses, a row of cottages and a station building with a bar at one end labelled 'Hotel de la Gare'. Beyond it stretched a large and recently built rail yard where a few British sappers and pioneers still laboured on its shining rails. This was Boeseghem and here the Battalion was re-united with its transport and the cooks with their fieldcookers, limbers and mules.

The unyielding and sordid steel wagons were left behind, but this was not journey's end for 16PSB. In the rail-yard the Battalion was re-united with part of 100th Infantry Brigade. Of their Middlesex comrades, the 17th were waiting for them, while the 18th

Pioneers were ahead of them at Bethune. The two battalions marched to La Miquellerie. Alf lost track of the number of days that they spent marching. Mile followed mile traversing flat farming land. Farm followed farm, village after drab village. At night they slept in cowsheds and barns, if they were lucky, or in the open if they were not. The nights were cold and the marching men looked forward to hot stew, bread and tea at the end of each day's march. They were not disappointed; the cooks did not let them down.

For the cooks each day's routine was the same. Each morning Noel Peters cleaned and loaded the cookers and then prepared sandwiches for the Battalion mid-day halt. Riding on the mule-drawn field cookers the cooks overtook the columns of marching men and set up their temporary kitchen area well before nightfall. The surface of the paved road (pavé) was uneven before the war; after sixteen months of military traffic the pavé was deeply rutted and full of pits. On the final day of that tiring march, approaching Bethune, the coupling pin on Noel's limber sheered off. The pin connected the cooker to its limber. Unsupported the broad cylinder full of food tipped backwards spilling the steaming stew. The cooks were engaged in scraping the precious liquid off the pave when the leading ranks of the Brigade came round a bend in the road and caught them at it. The sight of their supper, scraped off the road and put back into the cooker, mixed with mud and worse, caused great ill feeling. By good luck, and the prudence of the cook sergeant the limbers carried spare tins of bully beef. He had also obtained onions, bartered at one of the farms where they rested. This resourceful NCO

Mobile cookers designed to feed a battalion on the march and in the field.

set a group of men to work pulling up turnips from a frozen field. With this the sergeant (an old soldier and veteran of the war in South Africa) made up the loss. When the exhausted platoons reached their billets at La Miquillerie farm, on the far side of Bethune, each soldier had a ration of fresh bread and a mess-tin full of hot stew ready for him.

More than half a century later Noel said.

When fellows are really up against it they don't dream about girls, or booze, or even about home, they dream about food. An army marches on its stomach as General Haig said. Or was it Napoleon? Well you're a clever fellow who knows things like that. It's common sense. An army marches on its stomach. He knew a thing or two about soldiers, did Haig, Napoleon or whoever said it.

1. In view of Robert Graves' allegations, that so enraged Lionel Renton, it is worth reiterating that Graves' battalion, the 2nd Royal Welch Fusiliers, the 16th (Public Schools) Battalion and the 18th (Public Works) Battalion, the Middlesex Regiment, were amongst other battalions of other regiments as part of the 33rd Domino Division at the time of going to the Front Line. It is equally important to note that 16PSB were no longer in 33rd Div during and through the Battle of the Somme, but became a part of the 29th Division. See Appendix Two.

2. Where the huts and tents of Osthove camp once stood the visitor to Boulogne now finds more permanent reminders, memorials to a later war. These are the massive gun turrets and concrete bunkers that housed, or serviced the long-range guns that bombarded Dover and formed part of Hitler's Atlantic Wall, built by the German engineers between the summer of 1940 and that of 1944.

3. Russell does not give the name, but the village was Boeseghem. Boeseghem and Thienne are roughly two thirds of the journey from Boulogne to Bethune. These two small villages lie west of the forest of Nieppe and east of the Neufosse canal. This connects the La Bassée canal, via Bethune to St Omer and, eventually with the North Sea at Gravelines. The strategic importance of these broad canals that criss-cross Flanders hardly needs stating.

NORTHERN FRANCE RAIL LINES AND ROUTE

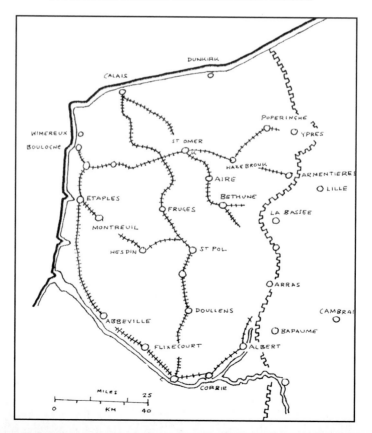

PART TWO

Chapter 12

TOWARDS THE GUNS

On the blue and lulling mist of evening, proper to the nightingale, the sheepbell, and falling waters, the strangest phenomena of fire inflicted themselves. The red sparks of German trench mortars described their seeming-slow arcs, shrapnel shells clanged in crimson, burning momentary cloudlets, smoke billowed into a tidal wave, and the powdery glare of many a signal light showed the rolling folds. The roarings and cracklings of the contest between artilleries and small-arms seemed to lessen as one gigantic burst was heard. We watched with murmured astonishment and often Charlwood would say, 'Hope to God we don't go south of the Canal'.

Blunden.[1]

O N A DULL, WET EVENING AT THE END OF NOVEMBER, 100 Infantry Brigade reached Bethune, marched through the town and out the other side. On first acquaintance, many thought it a dreary place where not only the churches and city walls but the houses were built of rough cut grey stone which oozed icy water. To Alf and B Company, the town's importance lay in the hot meal that awaited them when they reached the farm. The battalion followed the line of the canal and that too was lined with the same massive blocks of grey stone that built up the walls and flood-dikes. The roar of artillery was much louder here, a continuous rumbling sound, but by this time the novelty had passed and the marching volunteers were too tired to pay any attention to the distant sound of cannon.

Bethune. French postcard. Pre-war (Noel Peters).

The marching columns passed the last of the factories and brick-works that marked the edge of town and then divided. B Company turned left, away from the canal-bank towards a complex of buildings that stood dark and isolated surrounded by wet fields that shone like polished steel in the last rays of the winter sun. Barns, stables and store sheds surrounded a courtyard in the middle of which steamed a malodorous pit filled with dung. By this time, Alf said, they were too tired to care where they slept or what it smelt like. Through the vast open doors of the barn he glimpsed the cooks busy at work. B Company ate their fill that evening. No one commented on the mishap on the road. Stewed bully-beef mixed with turnips and onions never tasted better, even though some of it had been scraped off the pave. A generous ration of bread was washed down with hot sweet tea, and the cooks managed to scrounge fresh butter and

Bethune. A battalion on the move.

chocolate to make amends for the incident of the linch-pin on the fieldcooker. That was a good night, B Company slept well, bellies full, sheltered from the wind and at ease on soft, clean straw.

Alf woke refreshed in the clear pink light of a fine dawn. But then his sense of well-being and rightness with the world was disturbed. So was the entire company. Like his comrades, Alf discovered the first and most persistent fact of Flanders' life. The straw, on which they slept, was not changed, merely added to layer upon layer. The transient battalions of soldiers played hosts to countless numbers of tiny permanent residents. Dawn found B company tugging at tunics and breeches, scratching, cursing and attempting to dislodge the mites that had attached themselves during the night.

If Bethune was a relatively pleasant place the area that lay between it and its neighbour, La Bassée and south of the Canal, was, in 1915, one of the least comfortable stretches of line anywhere on the Western Front. It was here, in what was titled the Bethune sector that 100 Brigade received their first training in the realities of trench warfare and experienced their first period of front-line duty. Alf Damon, Noel Peters, Lionel Renton, the Tennant brothers and Arthur Graeme-West all served with 16PSB at Bethune in late 1915 and early 1916. They all left records, either in verbal, diary or letter form. There is no record that they knew each other, or if they did, it was as passing acquaintances. At this stage in their lives Alf Damon, Lionel Renton and the Tennants must have been remarkably similar; adventurous, cheerful young men with a sanguine, slightly cynical view of the world and its follies. Noel Peters was different because he was a dedicated professional to whom the war merited less attention than the task of perfecting his metier. Noel was the best, and most dedicated, sort of skilled craftsman, an artist without any trace of egoism. The great majority of young men left no record and great numbers were killed before they could develop any distinct personality. All of those who survived were changed by the war. Lionel, for example, was an adventurous youth, a boy seaman before war broke out, but, under the stress of war, he changed from an adventurer and amateur soldier to a professional. Arthur Graeme-West defies any easy categorisation. Where the others accepted the army and took the rough with the smooth, Graeme-West loathed army life with an unmitigated hatred. His tutor, the philosopher C.E.M. Joad wrote:

> West enlisted convinced of the rightness of his cause, feeling it was his duty to help his country, but disliking, as intensely as any man who put on khaki, the work he had set out to do. To such a man the army came to seem a thing of evil.[2]

In Flanders, on 30 November, West wrote in his diary, recording an impression of a route march. 'The bare trees against an almost colourless sky were exquisitely beautiful.' He was a man who noted the beauty of natural things more than the character and idiosyncrasies of his companions. Their fate moved him as little as his own. His thoughts concerned the beauty and fitness of nature and the ugliness of man's destructive and aggressive works. He did not start to describe the landscape of war until the Battalion moved out of Bethune and into the front-line trenches.

Bethune. Caserne Montmorency. Pre-war French postcard (16PSB shared Montmorency barracks with a smaller number of French troops) (Noel Peters).

Alf Damon remarked that, once they reached Bethune, the men thought less about the Battalion and more about their company, as a unit. Both the regimental history and the slim history of 16PSB recorded events as they were planned to happen to the Battalion.[3] Wallace-Grain records events as he found them in the Battalion War Diary and this unwittingly distorts the truth. For example Wallace-Grain states that the Battalion began front-line training on the morning after the men marched to their billets and he describes the Battalion moving from La Miquelerie to Bethune. According to survivors, they had more than a week to get sorted out and the Battalion was split up. B and D Companies remained out of the town at La Miquelerie farm, while HQ Company with A and C Companies moved into Montmorency barracks in Bethune. These minor distortions, which are innocent and well meaning, are of little importance. But they become important once the Battalion went into the line and began to take a steady haemorrhage of casualties.

Alf Damon and Lionel Renton, both serving in B Company, commented on the dispersal of the Battalion. Men that they knew well in training in England rapidly became strangers. Then too the Battalion suffered its usual loss of experienced men through posting. After a few weeks in Flanders, to Colonel Hall's intense annoyance, another batch of NCOs and privates returned to England for officer training. They were replaced by new men, who 'apart from their cap badges and canary yellow epaulette ribbons one would not have recognised as members of the same Battalion'. As Alf said, he also remarked on their changed social status:

> *Being a member of the BEF raised a man's esteem in the eyes of the English civilian population, but out here he was just another Soldat Anglais, of little worth. The warm welcome extended to General French's small regular force in 1914 had long since cooled. The French population had endured too much for too long. A year is a long time when the war is in your backyard. Families that did not have husbands, sons or grandsons at the front were both fortunate and rare. Amongst the farmers, craftsmen and labourers only the old men remained, and these did not waste words in greeting. To the Tommy's mumbled attempt at politeness, 'Bon jour, Mussir' the peasant raised a gnarled hand in acknowledgment.*

Alf remarked that the reception of B Company at the farm was no different to other companies or battalions training or resting behind the line anywhere in France. The peasants showed no interest in the war, except when it affected them or theirs. The myth grew, between the wars, that British soldiers disliked the French on whose land they fought. This was not true of the survivors of 16PSB who wrote, or told, of their experiences in France. Each man showed an intense sympathy for the French civilians who suffered so much during those years of war.[4]

La Miquellerie farm was built in a square with two wooden doors, strong enough to keep out intruders and big enough to admit a hay wain fully loaded. They stood open to allow marching troops to leave or enter. The central yard was paved with granite blocks almost six inches square, with the cesspool in the centre from which rose a thin haze of ammonia-laden steam. The barn was immense, large enough to house B Company. It was divided into three sections, each partition fixed to stout posts that supported the hayloft and a smaller attic-like storage area above that. These posts were cross-braced with yet more strong timbers to support the weight above.

Each day's exercises, or working parties, began with a mug of coffee and a biscuit at 6.30am, followed by physical jerks in the farmyards. Duties varied after this warm-up, ranging from hard physical labour, to a route march wearing full kit, carrying a rifle and bandoleers of ammunition, descending in severity to some relatively light fatigue duty if the soldier was lucky.

Once they reached France, every member of the Battalion unpicked the black domino shoulder flash, that was the Divisional sign for the 33rd (New Army) Infantry Division. For security reasons the domino was painted over on all GS Wagons, hand carts, field cookers and stores. Each battalion in the Brigade retained its coloured ribbon. 16PSB renamed themselves the Yellow Peril.

From Bethune to La Bassée the road runs parallel to the canal passing through a dismal landscape, part mining, part industrial, part agricultural.[5] This is a flat plain with areas of cultivation between factories or mines. Here are the small-holdings consisting of vegetable plots or fields with chicken runs, a few pigs, or a cow or a horse on a field of poor soil. Today the visitor can motor a well-made road, though the sad landscape is little changed. Lines of British graveyards mark the spot where once the front line cut this road. At this point a dead zone was created between the two market towns. From this point, and stretching away to either side, nothing mortal could walk upright and survive. In late 1915 the road out of Bethune deteriorated rapidly and then vanished. Its presence was marked only by displaced cobble-stones and broken bricks. Here and there a bullet-riddled signboard or enamelled sign advertising 'Suze', 'Ricard' or 'Pernod' protruded from the mud. Old, foul trenches cut the path that had once been the road and the route forward was impeded by black water-filled shell holes and remnants of barbed wire. As the carrying party approached the canal, they saw the sandbagged parapet of that makeshift, baled-out ditch described on the map as the Front Line.

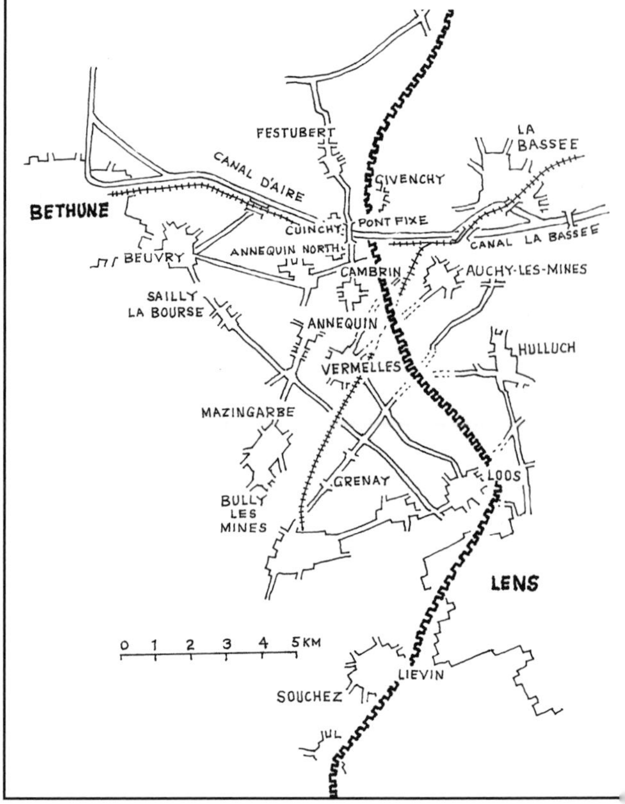

Map 2. General map of the Neuve Chapelle, La Bassée to Loos sector of the line. Late 1915. (This was the old Loos battlefield.)

Fortunately for the 33rd Division the General Staff had learnt something from the previous year where disastrous mistakes followed each other in quick succession. The most painful lesson was the battle of Loos which took place in this very section of the line. The staff no longer sent inexperienced divisions straight into the line, but rotated the novice battalions, platoon by platoon, into the line under the tuition of an experienced unit, a Regular Army battalion if possible. Even Regular battalions were now diluted because of the terrible losses in 1914. The all-regular force, that was the first wave of the BEF, was followed within a few months by the Territorials. They, in their turn, took heavy losses. They were followed at the battle of Loos by the first of Kitchener's New Army battalions.

Writing of life at La Miquellerie farm Alf made caustic comments about the lack of realistic training. The CO relied on marching as the best training to make his men fit to fight. 'Our man, Johnnie Hall, liked to boast that his Battalion could out-march any other. The quickest point from point A to point B is on two legs, was his favourite expression. Our man himself travelled comfortably on four.'

Both Alf and Lionel Renton give the impression that, in B Company at least, the Company Commander and the Platoon officers travelled on foot with their men. In contrast to his remarks about his CO Alf admired his Company officers, from the energetic and ebullient OC of B Company, Major Way and his 2 IC, Captain Sholto Douglas, to the platoon commanders of whom the most outstanding, in those early days, was Lieutenant Heslop.

Route marches took them out of the farm gates along the straight, poplar-lined road, through mile after mile of flat, monotonous fields of beet or turnips with less frequently a grassy field feeding cows or goats. The slippery cobbled pave made marching resemble a form of torture. This was made worse when there was a thin layer of ice on the cobbles. Alf wrote 'Hob-nailed boots are not the best footwear for this polished, uneven greasy surface. We ended each march with bleeding toes, blistered heels and soles that resembled raw steak.'

Returning to the farm at dusk, B Company cleaned themselves, their rifles and bedding, not forgetting that fetish of the British army, their boots. The volunteers scraped, burnished and polished, the CSM demanding that they should return to a parade-ground shine. He knew as well as they did that such an ideal state was a pious hope rather than a realistic goal in Flanders.

Lionel Renton could remember when he first went up to the line.

> I can remember what it felt like but not the day. The reaction amongst us boys, and we were mere boys, was excitement. Does that sound stupid to you? It's true. We nearly lost a couple of young fellows who wanted to see what Fritz looked like. A shot from a Prussian sniper soon discouraged them from such foolishness. You could see nothing except the wall of the trench. So your ears and imagination had to supply the rest – that and your sense of smell.

16PSB first came under the tuition of one of their own regular battalions, the First Middlesex, later on that of another London regiment, the Royal Fusiliers. Praise for their front line hosts was universal. Lionel Renton said that he, and many others, had reservations about the old sweats that they first encountered in England or later in such detested places as the Bull Ring at Etaples. 'Dreadful old lead-swingers, scroungers, drunks, bullies and thieves.' But for the NCOs in the line he had nothing but praise. 'Their kindness, patience and above all, their helpful tips for staying alive made one value the best qualities of the old Regular Army.'

The Battalion diary gives us an idea of the rotation of companies during that first tour of duty.

> Dec 3. 1915. A and B Cos marched to Le Hamel.
>
> C and D Cos moved into Chambord barracks, Bethune, whence fatigues were sent daily to assist in mining operations near Pont Fixe.
>
> Dec 4. Two platoons from Le Hamel to trenches at Festaubert with 1st Middlesex.

The British front line in 1915. French Postcard. (Note that the breastworks are built up of sandbags because of flooding and the Tommy is wearing a cap. This was before steel helmets were issued to the army in France and Belgium.)

Dec 6. C and D Cos from Bethune to Annezin. The platoons in trenches on 5 Dec returned to Le Hamel

Dec 7. A Co Le Hamel to Annezin. Two platoons to trenches with 1st Middlesex – as above.

Dec 8. Two platoons to trenches as above.

This routine, rotating platoons into and out of the line, continued for nearly a month. Arthur Graeme West was in one of the platoons that moved up to the front line on December 4th. He recorded this memorable 24 hours in his diary.

7th December 1915.

Parade 3.30am. Haversacks, waterbottle, groundsheet and leather jerkin for the trenches. Raining hard, wet already across the old trenches for nearly a mile. Meant to go by communication trenches but they were so full of water that we had to go on top. Mud and water worse than anything we had ever met, many went up to their necks, and all of us soaked over the knees. We passed support and reserve trenches with fires and braziers and many dugouts draped in groundsheets. In the support trench men were sleeping here and there outside, sitting on firing platforms on groundsheets. The trenches were tolerably wet but boarded at the bottom...

Broken bits of trench, the whole parts of which we held in groups of five... very bad place, about fifteen inches of sandbags but the tops had been knocked off, no backs to the trench at all and the water was deep. Nothing but a few sticks to stand on. At first we were quite amused and laughed at the position, but the prospect of twenty-four hours of endurance of it, our isolation and exposure, cooled us down and we sat still and dripped and shivered. Flares went up continuously and occasional machine-gun bullets whizzed and snipers shot.

Sent to post No 5. Wet again but change worth it... shelter of corrugated iron which covered about 6ft space, though water lay underfoot in the trench. Bombs, ammunition stored in a recess.

Phillip Tennant described a similar trench in one of his letters to his family in Grove Park.

They are very wet. In water up to our knees. The weather has been cold and sheepskin jerkins and anti-frostbite fat were issued. We brought our blankets up this time and it is in a nice mess now; blanket, overcoat, sheep-skin coats and ourselves all wet and mixed up with mud. We get a 'don't care' spirit and just suffer it all, with mud thick to our waist and up to our elbows. Never mind, some day it will be all over and we will feel proud and glad that we have done what we have, and we shall call them good times and wish we could have just one of those trench meals again. No meal we could ever have is enjoyed as much as our trench breakfast; we look forward to it all night. We make a fire and boil a mess tin of tea and cook our rasher of bacon, and usually eat the whole of our bread ration. If we have any cheese we toast that in with the bacon fat. It is generally mixed up pretty well with dirt, but we do enjoy it.

The fatigue parties took another route to the line. They carried dry soil and timber to the sappers mining under the German line. They followed the old towpath, sheltered by the railway embankment, past the last estaminet, its door pitted with shell fragments, past old trenches and gun pits.

'The railway is unrecognisable.' Philip Tennant wrote in another letter. 'The telegraph wires brought down and tangled in thick coils on the railway bank and their poles leaning at angles this way and that. The insulators look like teeth and the rails, curving in the air, like snakes.'

Little remained of Cuinchy station and around it lay the shattered remains of heavy mining machinery and derelict factory buildings. The towpath and canal bank were broken and foul with pools of mud and water. The La Bassée canal, unused and unregulated, was stagnant, deep and black, crossed by the skeletal remains of Pont Fixe which had been broken and bent in the middle by the impact of a large shell. This area,

The La Bassée canal, unused and unregulated, was stagnant, deep and black.

named on trench maps as 'Cuinchy Keep' came under constant shell fire, the German gunners using the destroyed bridge as an aiming mark.

The Pont Fixe was a place of special horror and ill omen. Many soldiers comment on it in their letters home or diaries. Philip Tennant wrote in a letter.

> *At one spot a steel bridge spans our position, beneath it and beside the canal is a large pool in which stagnant water has collected. The railway line stretches on either side overgrown with weeds that flourish between the sleepers. The enemy trenches are only about 40 yards away so it is impossible to cross the railway line which is under fire from snipers constantly. Some ghastly remains of earlier fighting lie in the stagnant pool, best left to the imagination. The dead have lain there for months and to try to get them out for decent burial is to invite certain death. When the rain pours down, as it does most of the time, we search for what cover we can find. Some under old sheets of iron or huddled in dug-outs, while some crouch under their groundsheets.'*

He ends his letter, 'We try to make the best of it. My companions are a cheerful crowd and make little jokes to hide their cold and fatigue.'

1. Edmund Blunden. P16 *Undertones of War.* OUP 1928.

2. *The Diary of a Dead Officer.* Arthur Graeme West. Editor C E M Joad.

3. *The Middlesex Regimental History* by Everard Wyrall.
History of the 16th Public Schools Battalion by Wallace-Grain. An example of the minor discrepancies between the official version and the diaries or recollections of those who were with 16PSB at the time, concerns the Battalion's arrival at Bethune and the date of the first platoons moving up to the trenches. That the Battalion marched through Bethune at night on Dec 3rd and sent some platoons up to the Front line early the following morning is absurd. In fact 16PSB reached Bethune on the 25th November and had more than a week of general training before they began to rotate platoons into the front line. Everard Wyrall was a military historian and professional writer of Regimental histories. Wallace-Grain was a solicitor who served with 16PSB in the early days. It seems unlikely that he went to France with the Battalion. The style or 'voice' of the narrative changes after the Battalion embarks for France. The most probable sequence of events is that, through no fault of his, Wallace-Grain was amongst those older men who were transferred to the 24th Battalion. The story is culled from official papers through 1916 to the disbandment of 16PSB. We can begin to see, even in these early accounts, an acceptance by the writers that those in authority know best and that senior officers are always honest, unbiased and reliable sources. In practice, accounts written by those who experienced the full violence of a battle and its aftermath frequently give a totally different account to that printed in the official version.

4. See Appendix Two. Robert Graves remarks about French civilians do not tally with the recollections of the survivors of 16PSB.

5. Two canals join at Bethune. The main canal runs north of Bethune and south of La Bassée, joining the Canal de la Deule at Bauvin, then behind the German line.

Chapter 13

A CUSHY ENOUGH TOWN

DURING THIS PERIOD OF TRAINING, when the Battalion was becoming acclimatised to trench warfare, Battalion HQ and HQ Company moved to what had been the headquarters for the Bethune garrison before the war, Montmorency barracks. Platoons rotated between the front line or support line areas around Cuinchy Keep, and either La Miquellerie farm or Montmorency barracks near the centre of Bethune.

Before the war Bethune was the market centre for the mining villages and vegetable gardens of this flat region. Its strategic importance had not changed over the centuries. Bethune had been the seat of the counts of Flanders and, like Arras, the town was fought over repeatedly during the Spanish conquests of the Low Countries. In the 17th Century its mediaeval walls were re-designed and reinforced by the master of military architecture, Vauban. By 1915 Bethune had become the main rail-junction and supply centre for the British army in Flanders. Though it was within range of the German guns the town had suffered very little war damage. When 16PSB first arrived there was a rumour that the General Staff on both sides had an unofficial agreement: the Germans would not shell Bethune if the British did not shell La Bassée, which served as a base behind the German line very much as Bethune did for the BEF. True or not the pleasant historic town suffered little damage at that stage of the war.[1]

Once the cook sergeant, Noel and his fellow cooks knew their way around Bethune and the surrounding countryside and could set up their cookers in relative calm and

Vermelles. Ruin of the church 1915. French postcard.

stability, then the food improved and was served hot, more often than not. Noel was fortunate, his sergeant shared his enthusiasm for food and the provision of the best meals possible under difficult circumstances. The cook sergeant sensed an apprentice worth teaching. Though La Miquellerie was far removed from the spotless table at one of the Right Honourable Talbot KC's dinner parties at Wilton Square, Noel was no novice when it came to preparing food on a large scale. The key to giving a modest variety to the evening meal was ingenious scrounging and at this the old warrior, the Cook Sergeant, was a master worthy of emulation.

Fellows grumbled, of course they did. That's the way with the British soldier. But it was a contented grumble, if you know what I mean. I'd have been worried if they hadn't, it wouldn't have seemed natural. Though maybe they wouldn't have grumbled if they'd known what was in store for them – what was waiting for all of us – in the next few weeks.

At this stage in the war, and with the trenches and ground surrounding Cuinchy Keep semi-flooded or deep in mud, no one on the staff considered it possible to supply the men in the front line with hot food, other than what arrangements they could make for themselves. In contrast, the evening meal was a good one and life was pleasant enough in the evening, for those not serving their twenty-four or thirty-six hour stint at Cuinchy or Hamel, or else on guard, or on picket duty in the town. Some evenings had to be devoted to cleaning kit, but others were spent in one of the many estaminets that kept open in, or near Bethune. In almost every case the patron and his sons were away in the army, or had been killed early in the war. The estaminet was maintained and ruled by Maman and her daughters. Alf described these businesslike Flemish women as bearing no resemblance to,

The strumpets and temptresses conjured up by religious zealots in England. These stolid Flemish working girls were suspicious of all foreigners, soldiers in particular, and they kept themselves to themselves except for serving up the beer and taking in the money.

They were very good at that. These young ladies were far removed from the 'Ooh La La, French seductresses' seen on the saucy postcards that the lads bought later in Amiens or St Omer. The Flamandes were a marked contrast to the young ladies of Picardy or Champagne who he met later in his service in France. The latter were far more vivacious and attractive.

In the steaming estaminets of Bethune the soldiers drank thin, onion smelling beer. 'I did not drink alcohol at that time, Alf said. 'So I stuck to coffee or a Jus de Fruit, which were better value. Some of the lads drank all sorts of over-priced sickly liquids – Creme-de-menthe; Creme-de-cacao, or else vin blanc or vin rouge.'

The Provost-Marshal's regulations allowed only officers to drink whisky or cognac and an estaminet could be closed down if it was proved to have sold spirits to Other Ranks. But old soldiers found ways round the regulations. As Alf said, 'Spirits could be obtained if personality, charm, telling the tale, bribery or other skullduggery were exploited to the full – and they often were.'

'There was very little opportunity to spend money once we were in the line, as we were most of the time, or close to it. It was stupid to carry surplus cash in one's pockets. If one was wounded it would be pinched.'

A private soldier's pay of seven shillings a week converted to 10 francs. Pay parade was held fortnightly at Bethune and once every three weeks once the Battalion moved into the line. Married men received only five francs, half their pay being sent home to their wives. The remainder of the soldier's pay was credited to his account. He could draw on it when home on leave. Not one of the volunteers who wrote, or told me his story, received money from home. We know that Arthur Graeme West had a private income, but a very small one. The Tennant (Catchpole) brothers received a supplement to their pay sent out by their father. Fanny told me that Albert was generous with parcels of food and warm clothing.

Officers could enjoy the sophisticated pleasures of Bethune. In late 1915 the town was still unspoiled by battle or occupation. Cafes, wine merchants, pastry cooks and banks all catered for the more affluent of the British officers. Edmund Blunden describes a fine old mahogany table in the Banque de France that was lent to the army field cashier 'During his temporary tenancy'. Here the young officer could cash a cheque. He could eat in one of the restaurants reserved for officers or visit one of several shops that prospered through this invasion of young officers with money to spend. Book shops or antique shops where '...delicate white fingers turned the pages of fine volumes or displayed pictures of one's choice'.[2]

Then, as ever in the British army, the difference between the life of the officer and that of the man in the ranks divided along class lines. On the other hand, all those who spoke or wrote an account of life in the ranks of the PSB remarked that the Tommy was far better cared for, once out of the line, than was either the Poilu or Fritz on the other side of the wire. The French received a generous ration of Pinard, a coarse red wine, but not much else. The British received soap, cigarettes, tobacco and rum, which came up with the food supplies and was rationed out weekly.

Noel Peters said that there was no system like NAAFI, that became practically universal during the Second World War and the period of the Cold War, but that there were a few canteens, such as the YMCA and the Salvation Army, but he said that these were well behind the lines, usually close to Divisional or Army headquarters, and so they were useless to Brigade troops who rarely, if ever, went back that far.

During the entire length of the war no attempt was made to cater for the comfort or relaxation of forward troops, or those immediately behind the line. This occasioned some bitterness, as you may imagine.

1. The German artillery smashed Bethune to rubble during their final desperate attack of March 1918. With great energy and skill the citizens restored it through the inter-war years. Luckily, it suffered little damage during the German Blitzkrieg of 1940.
2. *Undertones of War*. Edmund Blunden. OUP 1928.

Chapter 14

THE LA BASSÉE CANAL

IF ONE IGNORES A FEW MINOR BENDS and kinks, the front line from Neuve Chapelle to Loos ran north to south, bisecting the La Bassée canal which runs east to west, from La Bassée to Bethune. The infamous Pont Fixe was in Allied hands in 1915 but under constant shell fire by German artillery. The land around Loos is flat, as it is in most of Flanders, but where there were minor ridges the Germans had made sure that they held them. The highest points were the spoil heaps from the mines, these too were in German hands and invaluable for their artillery spotters. (See map.)

The section in which 16PSB experienced front line training and in which they spent their first period of front line service covered a little over five miles of the line, running from Le Hamel, which is close to Festubert, southward through Givenchy and then, continuing south of the Canal at Cuinchy it ran through the shattered mining village of Annequin to Vermelles. This, the extreme south of 100 Brigade area, was the old Loos

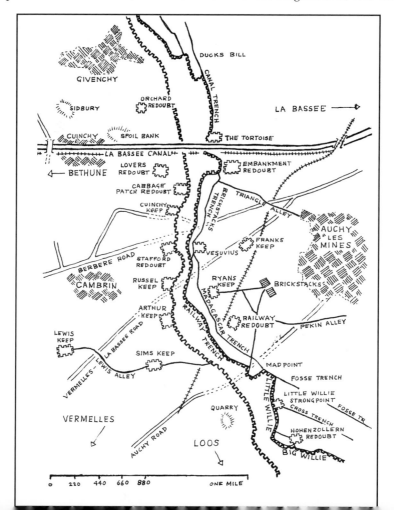

The remains of the attackers still lay unburied in No Man's Land, or hanging on the German wire.

battlefield. The German line had been very strong at this point, using slight ridges to advantage, and it still was well defended. Behind the line the Germans were constructing a formidable second line of defence. The remains of the attackers still lay unburied in No Man's Land, or hanging on the German wire; a reminder of the failure of the first mass attack by Territorial and New Army Divisions.

Alf Damon wrote of the grim lesson of Loos.

This point that we held in the line, near Vermelles, was the position where Scottish Territorials went over, and many of them stayed out there. If you fixed your shaving mirror to your bayonet at the correct angle you could see what was left of these brave fellows in the mud or on the wire, their ragged kilts flapping in the wind. It was a sight to sober even the most bloodthirsty and imprudent. One awful sight haunts me. A giant of a highlander was caught up on the wire not far from our forward trench. Decomposition had bloated his corpse still larger. When the breeze lifted his kilt his huge naked arse was exposed. This was not the artists' impression of heroic death for King and Country that civilians back home liked to peruse in cheap magazines.

Lionel Renton loathed the old Loos battlefield as much as Alf did.

What a place that was! The Brickfields, Vermelles, the Quarries, Annezin. You'd never believe it but the first casualty in our company was drowned; the mud was as bad as that. The Germans with their usual eye for ground, had picked out the best positions. Not that anywhere was much higher in that dismal plain, but where there was a ridge or spoil heap, they took advantage of it. To add to our miseries, they pumped their trench water onto the slope and it ran down into our forward trenches. We had to move up to a line of breastworks above ground and Jerry kept knocking the sandbags off so that we had to replace them at night as best we could. The old French communication trenches had become canals and the shell holes ponds. The only consolation about the softness of the mud was its effect on shells. They plunged in so deep that their explosions did little damage, merely sending up a great spout of mud and water into the air to rain down on us. The duds must still be there, I suppose, quite a problem for the farmers. Digging in was impossible anywhere along that part of the line. The lines were so close together at the Brickstacks that neither side could shell the other. On the other hand you could lob a grenade from one of the saps into the trench opposite. If you were on watch in the sap and you heard boots thudding along the duckboards, you got the hell out of it, because you guessed that the fellow was about to chuck a 'Potato-masher' at you. Jerry had good grenades. Ours were not very good until the Mills bomb came along. At first we had the old percussion stick grenades complete with streamers to guide them in flight. They were splendid grenades in the open but dangerous in a trench. Once you'd set it from 'Safe' to 'Fire' you only had to knock it on the back of the trench to blow yourself up.

Jerry sent over some big shells from time to time. We called them Jack Johnsons after the boxer. One of these would make a hole as big as a room, which would fill up with water very quickly. These, and the flooded trenches, were a hazard going up to the line at night. We tried to stick to the duckboards but that wasn't easy in the dark.

When we first got to the trenches we made the mistake of marching in Christmas tree order; greatcoat, large pack, small pack, water bottle, full webbing, tin hat and 200 rounds of ammunition. The whole lot must have weighed 100 pounds. Then sometimes we carried shovels, picks, sandbags, extra ammunition, grenades or flares. Your greatcoat slowly filled up with water while the mud caked up on its skirts and on puttees and boots. We had a bugler lad with us going up to the line. I suppose he was exhausted because he fell to the back of the section. We didn't miss the bugler until we'd covered some distance. Someone said that he heard a plop, which might have been a dud shell. by the time we set off back along the duckboards to find him he was dead. He'd fallen into one of the big shell holes and couldn't get out. This was before the days of the quick release clip on your webbing. The belt was broad and it tightened through the brass buckle. There was no way of removing it in a hurry. The wretched bugler lad must have sunk straight to the bottom.[1]

The Battalion began to take casualties, a few wounded at first followed by two deaths. Then the number of wounded increased and so did the narrow escapes. That the area immediately behind the line was as dangerous as the line itself is shown in a near miss experienced by a small party from B Company, described by Alf Damon.

We were just nearing the end of the road, where our communicators started, when a shell landed behind and slightly to the right of us. A piece of iron struck my rifle butt. As one man we dived into an estaminet, which was open for business right close to the line. The beer was terrible, as usual, but we felt that we needed it. The only thing to be said for it was that it was cold, but that wasn't so remarkable. Madame kept it outside in the winter weather.

All ranks loathed the canal. It, and the bridge across it, seemed particularly ill-omened. Beside the canal stood Cuinchy Keep which resembled a small fortress dug into the ruins of a mine building. Trenches ran behind massive stumps of walls. Underneath

A German 5.9 inch (15cm) howitzer with a six-man crew in the winter of 1915.

them deep dugouts were connected by tunnels beneath the ruins. The bridge still hung over the canal, despite many direct hits, connecting the trenches to the north to those on the south of the canal. The side of the bridge facing the enemy was covered in hessian, to allow men to cross, balancing on its naked girders, hidden from enemy snipers. Nothing of any size could cross this way, so all heavy equipment had to be unlimbered, or partially dismantled and then ferried across the canal on pontoons. This was a risky business because the pontoons came under fire from fieldguns and trench mortars. Field kitchens were heavy equipment so Noel Peter's first impression of the hazards of front line life was not the flooded front line trenches, nor the much knocked about breastworks, but ferrying the cookers across the canal. Even when the ordeal of crossing the foul and much shelled water was over the cooks had no time to congratulate themselves. The siting of these large wheeled cylinders was crucial. Too close to the line was senseless, and yet they could not be placed too far back. 16PSB must have been among the first battalions to attempt to supply their men in the forward trenches with hot food. Noel did not know whether this was an enterprising experiment that was purely local, or whether orders for this came from a higher level. The Quartermaster and cook sergeant achieved a compromise by siting the cookers in Annequin. Noel described Annequin as a ruined mining village, under which the miners had employed their skill to construct shelters for their families that were proof against anything but a direct hit from a Jack Johnson. Cellars and tunnels connected the trenches in front of the village. Even in late 1915 many French families clung to what remained of their homes rather than take to the road and an unknown future. They depended on the soldiers for scraps of food. Noel's field cooker was protected on one side by the massive remains of a mill wall and by sandbags on the other three. He said that everyone had to be extremely careful not to draw attention to the village. If the Germans' artillery spotters saw any sign of movement they called down a barrage of shells. The first whistling rush of a shell, heralding a bombardment, sent everyone, soldier or civilian, running and scrambling for the cellars. Women, children, soldiers, old men all huddled together underground until the pounding ceased. One barrage went on for hours, Noel remembered, 'As though these gunners held a special grudge against us and were determined to erase Annequin off the face of the landscape.'

When the shelling ceased the cooks emerged, blinking into the light and went in search of the tools of their trade. The cooker, with its limber with tins and sacks of food, was buried under a wall that had collapsed, destroyed by the blast from a large shell that had fallen close by. They dug through the rubble, salvaged the food that was still edible, recovered those dixies and pots that escaped unholed, repaired the battered but intact cooker and carried on preparing the evening meal.

At Annequin, behind the line, the problem was shelling. At Cuinchy Keep and at the Brickstacks the menace came not from artillery but from snipers. The Prussian guards appeared to have recruited especially deadly marksmen who shot at anything that moved, and they rarely missed. North of the line, at Givenchy, the line was held by

Saxons who Noel described as 'decent fellows'. Lionel Renton and Alf Damon said the same thing, Arthur Graeme West remarked in one of his poems that the Hun was a man very like he was. At different times Noel cooked both north and south of the canal. He much preferred Givenchy where the front line soldiers, on both sides, had a civilised arrangement. This was an unofficial truce at breakfast time. On both sides of the line cookers belched smoke as the cooks hurried about their work. Sufficient time was granted for everyone to eat a peaceful breakfast and then both sides set about their day's work: each trying to kill the other. Alf, who had no love for staff officers, said, 'You may be sure that the Staff knew nothing of this little custom. Had they suspected it, one side or the other would have put a stop to it, while they tucked into a lavish meal, well out of range of the guns.'

Lionel Renton spoke of these little local truces and arrangements to rescue wounded men or bring in the dead.

This did not happen everywhere of course, but in the old Loos sector conditions were so foul and the trenches so close together that we tried to help each other, when we could. One of these local arrangements operated at Givenchy. Life in those flooded holes was miserable for both sides. Fellows needed a moment to enjoy their grub and both sides respected that. Neither side sent over mortar shells or grenades at breakfast time. The regiment opposite us were Saxons, decent fellows. The trenches were so close that we could hear them talking or singing. Jerry was a great one for singing and the Saxons set up little impromptu choirs. One of these choirs was so talented that he always earned a round of applause from our chaps.

At Cuinchy Keep and at the Brickstacks the menace came not from artillery but from snipers.

The German artillery smashed Bethane to rubble during the final desperate attack of March 1918.

> *You see in 1915 the ordinary soldiers in the line treated each other with respect. The further you got from the line the more bellicose and bloodthirsty people became. Civilians were the worst, their heads filled with the propaganda that they read in their newspapers and magazines. We treated prisoners well and they did the same.*

Alf confirmed this view of the Loos sector.

> *The Prussian Guard were an elite. The Saxons at Givenchy were ordinary fellows, like us. Some of them could speak English and we exchanged messages, particularly about prisoners; how they were, who was wounded, that sort of thing. We had a keen Lieutenant called Salmon who enjoyed night patrolling. Salmon did a very foolish thing. He chucked a grenade when he was close up under their wire. This gave away his position. The Saxons*

opened fire with machine guns and killed the entire patrol. Next day they hoisted a placard to let us know the position where our chaps were buried. When the Saxons moved out they put up a notice telling us to be careful because the Prussian Guard were taking over their section of the line. There was no chance of a truce with those monkeys.[2]

Noel was concerned by the fate of the civilians. He slipped them scraps of food when he could, particularly the children. Unlike the Somme battle area, later in the year, where the civilian population was deported, this part of France supported a large civilian population. The citizens of Bethune and Beuvry carried on their normal business. Even in villages that were close up to the line, like Annequin, some of the population made a brave attempt to ignore the fighting. A few families remained in what was left of their cottages, repairing roofs and walls during lulls in the fighting, taking refuge in their cellars once the shelling started. Some cottages still maintained their small vegetable gardens. Noel was moved by the sight of flowers in the tiny front gardens and vines curling round shrapnel-pitted doorways. 'They tried to cling to something from normal life. I admired that.' Of those who stayed most were the families of miners. The mine-owners, knowing that the war would not last for ever, paid some of the supervisory and maintainance staff to keep an eye on the mine-shafts, water levels and pumping gear, or what little survived. Two great slag heaps overshadowed Annequin. One of them still showed the remains of a trolley-tip at its crest. Not only the miners kept their eyes on this area. The Germans sited artillery spotters, dug in on the mine tip, to direct their guns. Counter-batteries shelled the mine tips at regular intervals and sometimes these shells fell short, hitting their own lines.

Many of those hit were civilians, killed by the shells fired by both sides. Noel described the pitiful sight of the bodies of civilians: miners, market gardeners, women in black dresses. These women ventured out during a lull in the firing to get a little food for their families and were caught in the open when the bombardment resumed. There were lulls, some of them prolonged, but they were deceptive and could end in violence at any moment. Sometimes, Noel described, it was possible to imagine a time of peace. The wind moved through the reeds, the smell of the evening meal from a miner's cottage, even the flight of mallard rising from the marshy ground beyond the canal. Then the dreadful orchestra would begin again; the whizz and crack of low angle guns, the slow tumbling ascent of *minenwerfers* followed by the dull boom of their explosion, and then the rattle and rapid clack of rifle and machine guns joining in the concert.

Alf Damon wrote of that time in the line beside the canal.

My apprenticeship began beside the La Bassée canal. For some time we were kept behind the line, in the reserve trenches. We took a few casualties from shells. But my first experience of the front line was at this place Cuinchy. A group of us were ordered to report to the sappers who were shoring up tunnels set in the line. We carried planks along a communication trench. A sapper officer came the other way, along the duckboards. I pulled up and saluted him, shifting the heavy plank as I did so. "This is war" he said, as though I needed reminding, "Do not halt and stand to attention, Jerry can see that plank sticking up and welcome your signal." He was a pompous man, but he was right. Sure enough, as

The Germans sited artillery spotters, dug in on the mine tip, to direct their guns.

he spoke, a shower of small trench mortar bombs came over. Luckily they were not well
aimed.

This area was a warren of old mine tunnels that ran under both lines, Jerry's and ours.
There were rumours of spies coming and going through the tunnels, some plausible and
some far-fetched.[3]

When we had delivered our planks we were at the disposal of the sappers. My job was
a miserable one. I was put to work in a soaking wet cubbyhole about five feet by five feet
and told to stay down there for five hours. My task was working two hand pumps, one
sending down air into the mine-shaft, the other extracting carbon monoxide. The others in
my detail had the job of carrying sandbags full of spoil and dumping it further back. I
suppose that the sapper officer forgot about me. Only when the candles in the shaft began
to gutter and go out did they send someone to find out what had happened to their air
supply. They found me collapsed over the pump handles. That ended my stint for that
night.

Alf described his life as one of constant movement from one dreary part of the line, to
reserve trenches, briefly to the relative comfort of La Miquellerie and then back to the
line again. Alf, and indeed the majority of 16PSB, experienced what every other infantry
battalion learned, that the war of fixed trench lines had become a war of constant
movements for both individuals and individual platoons. A division moved to another
sector of the line, brigades changed position, battalions rotated within the brigade and
companies and platoons changed places within the battalion. As a former staff officer
Colonel Hall interested himself in the logistics of constant movement. It is probable that
the Battalion's new adjutant, Captain Cochram, did too.

'Haig was a master of the railway timetable, wrote A J P Taylor and he did not intend
to be complimentary.[4] A brief study of the map of northern France and Belgium reveals
the enormous strategic importance of the sophisticated network of lines, both full sized
and narrowgauge, that spreads throughout Flanders and Picardy. Both sides depended
on rail transport to an extent never seen in war, before or since. The fact that a
commander in defence could move his reserves faster than his adversary could move

his attacking brigades forward was one of the many factors that put defence in advance of attack, speaking both strategically and tactically. This was one of the reasons why the British suffered such heavy losses as the General Staff planned attack after attack with little to show for it.

The men in the line knew nothing of the unprecedented feat of logistics that moved men, ammunition, food and trench supplies of all kinds, from the Channel ports to camps and supply points out of range of all but the largest of the German guns, and, from there, moved up to the line. The men in the line had little time to contemplate such niceties, nor did they care. Cold, wet and exhausted, the infantryman could only think about fulfilling the next task while concentrating on not making that momentary mistake that would end his life. He could hope for nothing but some hot tea in the morning and, if he was lucky, some bread and bacon. If he was even luckier he might get something hot to eat in the evening.

The period of mining fatigues came to an end. This was followed by periods rotating into and out of the line.The reserve trenches, a short distance behind the line were scarcely more comfortable than the front line trenches. Here, in reserve, the platoon was employed either on fatigue parties or engaged in repairing trenches and breastworks, carrying revetting materials, or wood, rations, ammunition or water. Whenever a rocket went up the platoon stood-to, ready to reinforce the line. The signal for a German attack was a red, green and white flare. The weather became worse. Conditions in the line were both miserable and dangerous, particularly at the Brickstacks, a natural defence which both sides contested with ferocious and usually futile attacks. At Cuinchy the trenches were ill-made and, being so close to the canal, subject to flooding. There was little anyone could do to improve life in the front line or reserve trenches, but Colonel Hall and his company commanders did what they could to make life more comfortable when the platoons were out of the line, back at Bethune.

Even before the Somme battle there were battalions in France where the men detested most, if not all, their officers and senior NCOs. Here and there in such a large army one found sadistic martinets who inflicted a discipline that was unnecessarily harsh. There were battalion COs and brigadiers who combined a ruthless expenditure of their men's lives with toadying to the staff at division or GHQ, thus ensuring rapid promotion. There were mysterious accidents where an officer of particular loathsomeness earned a shot in the back of the head, at close range.[5]

16PSB was not one of these unhappy battalions. Even if one makes allowance for nostalgia in the survivors, the letters and diaries lent by relatives of dead soldiers prove that the Battalion maintained a high morale and was both humanly and efficiently administered and commanded. All the men that I spoke to (or corresponded with) spoke of their company and platoon commanders with affection, or at least with respect. Tony Chubb and Alf Damon described Colonel Hall as 'a cold man'. He was a regular officer of his time, a disciplinarian, but everyone remembered him as a fair man who cared about his battalion and never asked of his junior officers, or men, tasks or dangers that he would not face himself.

When the Battalion moved out of the front line and back to Bethune Noel Peters was posted to HQ company where he saw a lot of his commanding officer. Noel told me that the CO rarely showed his feelings and so appeared reserved, but that he cared about the welfare of his soldiers and tried to find ways of making life better for them. Noel believed that the experiment of attempting to take hot food up to the men in the line was due to Colonel Hall's initiative. Though it was often interrupted by shelling, or other misadventures, the men understood the reason why the food was cold or not up to the usual standard. They grumbled and cursed the cooks, but it lacked the bitterness found in some units. There is no doubt that the provision of decent food was one of the factors that kept the morale of 16PSB above the average through the bitter winter of 1915-16.

1. The first fatal casualties suffered by 16PSB were Private Andrew Cadmore who died on the 9th and Private Albert Biggs on the 12th December. One of these unfortunates was the bugler but there is no indication which. (Ref: Everard Wyrall.) Alf Damon and Lionel Renton mention helmets in the list of kit carried. In fact both men are confusing these first periods in the line with later experiences because helmets, usually called 'Tin hats', were not issued until 1916.

2. Alf mistook the name. The first officer of 16PSB to be killed was 2nd Lieut Bowman, killed on patrol on the 2nd January 1916.

3. Paul Fussell comments on trench myths. Chap 4. Fussell. *The Great War and Modern Memory*.

4. *War by Timetable*. A.J.P. Taylor.

5. An example of a sadistic officer who rose to high rank is Captain, later Brigadier, F Percy Crozier of the 36th Ulster Division. Crozier condemns himself by his own writing, boasting of his harshness in his autobiography *The Men I Killed*. His loathsome book includes detailed descriptions of many of his crimes. Not the least odious was the court-martial and shooting of a battle-shocked young soldier 'of good family' shortly before the Somme battle. The firing squad was made up of the youth's companions from his platoon. Deeply disturbed by the injustice of his sentence his comrades fired wildly. To Crozier's ghoulish interest he had to be 'dispatched by a second volley'. News reached Belfast of Crozier's brutal treatment of the Irish soldiers under his command. Many acquaintances refused to speak to him and cut him dead when he returned to Northern Ireland.

Chapter 15

CHRISTMAS 1915

A FEW DAYS BEFORE CHRISTMAS the pipes and drums of the 16th (Public Schools Battalion) of the Middlesex Regiment marched out of Montmorency barracks with their mascot, the large, shaggy Irish wolfhound, with his dog-handler in the lead. The band marched to the square in the centre of Bethune and played for more than an hour to the amusement of Flemish citizens and soldiers from many parts of the British Isles. The only exception were a few purist Highlanders who could not understand how a London regiment, that was not the London Scottish, acquired a pipe band. The story of Major Mackay and the foundation of the Battalion did little to placate them. 'We were proud of our band, said Alf. 'But, to be honest about it, as puzzled about its authenticity as the Scots lads were.'

For a North London battalion to possess pipers and drummers, in kilts and bonnets, commanded by a sergeant piper was a rare eccentricity. All who served with the Battalion, whether Public School, university, clerical, artisan, or working class lads from Tottenham, Enfield or Kilburn, remarked that 16PSB was never an ordinary infantry battalion.

B Company came out of the line. They were placed in close support in some shell marked barns from which they could be rapidly brought forward to the reserve trenches. Alf Damon wrote.

> *We rested in some neglected and draughty barns. Christmas Eve approached and number 24 Section of 6 Platoon decided that they wanted something better to celebrate Christmas than the plonk sold in the estaminet. Only one could speak schoolboy French and he was nominated. Timing was crucial; the bottle of Scotch or Cognac must be*

Cuinchy. The ruins of the Chemist's shop. Heavy casualties from shelling suffered by troops passing this spot as they moved up to the line led to a rumour that there was a spy nearby who was signalling to the Germans.

procured on Christmas Eve and not before. A soldier found with a bottle of spirits in his kit might well be court-martialled. Madame kept her prizes behind the bar, in front of the mirror. In the weeks before Christmas no suitable bottle was seen. Only the most outrageous optimism pushed the odds to three to one against our nominee's success.

The Boche was punctilious in observing the festive season so we expected little activity from him; our own staff were less predictable. The unfortunate C Company moved up to the line with A Company in support. On Christmas Eve parades finished for the rest of us at noon and there was little work for the next thirty-six hours. We spent the afternoon cleaning kit, boots and brasses, but no one worked hard. We went along to the estaminet after the evening meal; inside a pleasant fug brewed up, which made a change from the freezing wind blowing along the canal bank and through our draughty barn. We never did get our bottle of Cognac. Arthur Kent emulated the Saxons opposite us and got together an impromptu choir. I had no idea that Arthur could sing until that Christmas Eve. He had a fine tenor voice.

Christmas day itself was not remarkable, Alf said, Number Six Platoon, B Company spent Christmas day trying to keep warm, their only entertainment watching two elderly and very drunk farmers fighting on the straw until they fell asleep still clawing and scratching.

Christmas 1914 saw a remarkable and spontaneous truce. Officers and men ceased firing and walked forward into No Man's Land to shake hands with their enemies, and even exchange little presents and arranged impromptu games of football. Such an expression of common humanity displeased the staff on both sides. No such fraternisation was permitted on Christmas day 1915.[1]

Accounts vary on which side opened fire first at various points along the front line on Christmas day 1915. Concerning the La Bassée sector, Alf Damon, Noel Peters and other survivors of 16PSB agreed that it was the British artillery that fired first and the German gunners retaliated immediately.

It was this counter-barrage that caused casualties. Several men from A Company had a narrow escape from death and five of them were wounded. It happened at a notorious crossroads called, with irony, 'Windy Corner'. Though little remained to show that this had once been a junction on the Bethune to La Bassée road, the crossroads was marked on the German artillery spotter's maps. It was overlooked by one of the larger of the spoil heaps and the spotters could call down a barrage whenever they saw any sign of movement. A photograph shows the site of Brigade HQ, which was very close to Windy Corner, but there are no clear features in the photo, merely stumps of walls and piles of rubble.

Corporal A E Slamin described his lucky escape on Christmas day in a letter home.

A shell dropped not far from us and a piece hit Sergeant Burnett on the left leg. I was blown over. I remember getting up and finding that everyone had vanished except for Burnett and he was in a bad mess. I did what I could for him and carried him some distance down the trench (at least it seemed a long way, shells were still coming over). When I came to the doctor's dug-out I met others and we took him in. Dr Edmunds dressed his wound – it was ghastly. There is no doubt he would have bled to death if prompt action had not been taken. The doctor was wonderful. I held Burnett's leg while it was being dressed. Burnett would have me go with him, with the stretcher bearers to the first aid post. Lieutenant Usmar (a very fine officer, very popular with the platoon) sent me down with him. We came out of the line (on Boxing day) and very much to my surprise, I was made temporary, unpaid Lance Corporal.[2]

Noel Peters was close behind the front line on Christmas day, attached to A Company. Though a repeat of the fraternisation had been forbidden, the platoon, whose feeding was Noel's responsibility, expected a peaceful day. The cooks worked hard and imaginatively to prepare a special Christmas stew. All was calm on both sides of the wire. Noel could see the smoke from the German field cookers and hear the Saxons singing sitting at ease in their trenches. In the A Company support line the cooks had dug a series of saps into the trench wall, each big enough to contain a charcoal fired brazier on which sat a dixie of stew.[3] Then, without warning, the British artillery opened fire. After a brief pause the German batteries responded. A whistle blew and the platoon took cover as a *minenwerfer* shell came over. The trench mortar struck the sap and blew it, Dixie and brazier to pieces. Fortunately no one was hurt. Noel's Dixie was undamaged. Though this depleted the ration, the cooks made sure that each member of the platoon got a mouthful of hot stew, fresh bread, a mug of tea with a tot of rum in it.

Germans loading a 24.5 cm **minenwerfer** *(trench Mortar) in the winter snows of 1915.*

When A Company moved out of the line Noel returned to Caserne Montmorency. Though the barracks was old and draughty, life there was preferable to life at the Brickfields or Cuinchy Keep that cold winter. Alf too spent periods of his service in Flanders at Montmorency. Each man commented on the primitive plumbing at the barracks. To well-brought-up lads used to the sophistication of London, the French hole-in-the-ground privy was primitive and indecent.

There was a long slab of cement with several holes in it. Each hole had, cemented beside it, a bent piece of iron pipe that you could hold onto while you squatted. The wind whistled round and up the hole, so you didn't linger over your morning motion.

B Company shared Caserne Montmorency with a battalion of French infantry. Both Alf and Noel commented on the miserable conditions in which the French conscripts (known as *les Poilu*) lived. There was an extreme contrast between the romance and glory of army life, depicted in the posters on the barrack wall, and the neglect suffered by French private soldiers in real life. While their officers and senior NCOs were relatively well paid and uniformed in good cloth, the private soldier's pay was meagre, his clothing thin and of poor quality, food appalling, compensated only by lavish rations of Pinard. 'Small wonder that the poor devils mutinied in 1917,' Alf said.

In theory, and on paper, the Battalion now enjoyed a rest period, divided between La Miquellerie and Montmorency. In practice duties were only a fraction less arduous than front line duty. Platoons were employed on fatigues, of which the most common was repairing and maintaining trenches, most of which flooded almost as soon as they were drained. The advantage of Montmorency was the Anglo-French concert party, the 'Roosters', which included part of 16PSB band. These gave ribald and scurrilous performances at the barracks as rehearsals between visits to other brigades and to Divisional HQ.

Noel spoke, many times, of the importance of both food and rum in maintaining soldiers' morale: but he meant separately. Early in the new year Noel was moved to HQ Company, which was based in Montmorency barracks. Here he enjoyed the luxury of a proper kitchen in which to perfect his art. The French, he said, cared little about sanitation but were strong on cooking and cooking equipment, even if the other ranks never saw the benefit of well made ovens, cast-iron pans and sophisticated implements. Young though he was Noel was now, unofficially, the senior cook. The Cook Sergeant and the Quartermaster knew that he would do the best he could for the men that he had to feed. The same could not be said for some of the others who saw cooking as a means of escaping the worst of front line duty.

Noel received an order that D Company were moving into the barracks. The company had been in support trenches filling sandbags, digging out fallen trenches, and repairing parapets and breastworks. Noel knew how much they looked forward to a hot meal, hot tea and a rest. The Commanding Officer looked in at the kitchen to see how Noel and his assistants were preparing the meal for the exhausted men. The Company was expected to return at 10 pm. Colonel Hall asked whether the food would be ready in time. Noel assured him that it would be. 'And hot, Peters? Wha?'

'Yes sir, nice and hot.'

At this moment the Colonel was called away. He returned looking very angry. Orders for D Company's rest period had been countermanded at Divisional level. They had to return to the trenches immediately.

At this point in his account Noel put in a gentle reminder. Colonel Hall, he said, was Sandhurst and War Office through and through. To criticise an order from a superior officer went against his training, caste and philosophy. No hint of blame passed his lips but his disappointment was plain to see. The CO marched out of the kitchen and returned a few moments later with a rum jar under his arm.

'For the tea, sir?'

'No time for tea. Put it in the stew.' Colonel Hall said and walked out of the kitchen. Noel thought that he must have misheard the Colonel and ran after him to check. 'You heard what I said, man,' Hall said. 'Rum in the stew. Are you deaf? Hwa?'

The rum would ruin the taste of the stew. Noel anticipated the angry comments of the men of D Company. He conferred with the other cook and they decided to put half the rum in the stew and put the rest aside in a basin to give to the men in their tea when they returned, after their second stint in the trenches.

The fatigue party returned and ate their supper with no complaints, apart from a couple of sarcastic remarks about the odd taste of the stew. Then they set off back to the flooded trenches. Noel took the empty rum jar back to Colonel Hall's office and left it with the orderly sergeant. Then he called for his mate to help him clear up the kitchen. There was no reply. Suspicious of the silence Noel searched the kitchen. Cook and basin had disappeared. Noel found the cook wedged in a corner of a store room in a drunken sleep, the empty basin beside him. Noel carried him to an empty part of the stable and hid him under the straw. Neither the orderly officer or sergeant found him and he suffered nothing worse than a bad headache.[4]

For Alf the relatively comfortable period in Bethune ended as B Company moved up to the trenches at Annequin to relieve the 18th Royal Fusiliers. The changeover took place at night, in cold, drizzling rain. Despite the poor visibility the German artillery spotters must have heard, or sensed something. A barrage of shrapnel shells caused casualties both amongst the Fusiliers and the Middlesex men. The platoon commander, Second Lieutenant Seager and two soldiers were wounded by shrapnel balls. On the following night the Company sent forward a raiding party under the command of Lieutenant Bowman. Bowman was one of the 'Originals', a good officer, Alf reported, and keen to get to grips with the enemy. Unfortunately he was not as cautious as he should have been.

Wrecked bridge on the La Bassée canal.

93

The defenders spotted the raiding party and opened fire. Bowman was killed. Early in January the rest of the Battalion moved forward to join B Company. Casualties came in a steady dribble of ones and twos, some wounded and sent back to aid centres and casualty clearing stations, others killed. This, Alf commented was 'what some sanguinary general, from his château well behind the line, described as the normal wastage of trench life.'

1. For a description of the way GHQ put an end to all truces on the front line see pp 207-212 of *Christmas Truce*. Malcolm Brown & Shirley Seaton. Pub Leo Cooper 1984.

2. A.E. Slamin was a modest man who did not mention in his letter that he was also wounded, nor that he was recommended for a decoration. The following year he was commissioned and rose to command a company of the 2nd Welch Regiment. He saw much action in France and was wounded at St Quentin in 1918.

3. The dixie was the ubiquitous cooking pot used by cooks in the British army through both world wars. It contained two gallons of liquid, (stew, soup or tea) and had a lid that was used for frying food. The dixie probably went back to earlier wars, South Africa and Sudan, and it was still in use well into the nineteen-sixties.

4. The rum jar became an icon of the Great War as the Jerry-can became one for the Second World War. Stories about rum and rum jars were common currency. My neighbour in Putney, Albert Mills, told a long and involved story about the German offensive in the spring of 1918. The Battalion retreated leaving a jar full of rum behind. Albert knew where it was, hidden in a dug-out. During a lull in the fighting he slipped away from the others and went forward to retrieve the jar. Unfortunately, returning to his own line with the rum, he met a party from another battalion under a very green Second Lieutenant who promptly surrendered to a German patrol. The Germans got the benefit of the rum and Albert nursed a grievance against that British officer for life. Many jars have been unearthed intact on the Western Front and are valued by collectors. Some were found on the Gallipoli battlefield after the fatal bush fire of 1999. Ancient shells and rifle cartridges were exploding all over the peninsula. Once the fire died down the Turkish army sent in conscripts to search the ground for any remaining shells. These young lads found cap badges, shoulder titles and buttons, Turkish, Australian and British, which they sold to a small museum close to Cape Helles. They did not know the value of the rum jars so they smashed them. I found the remains of one, clearly recently broken, close behind 'Johnson's Jolly' trench. The name of a Glasgow pottery was stamped on the base.

Chapter 16

THEY SHALL NOT GROW OLD

Look for the Sixteenth Middlesex always in the casualty list now.
Philip Tennant.

A FEW DAYS AFTER CHRISTMAS PHILIP TENNANT wrote a letter to his brother Albert, who was now assistant to his father in the management of the bitumen and varnish factory in Rotherhythe.

30.12.15
Dear Albert,

Thank you for your two letters, also for the £1 note enclosed, which has been very useful. We didn't know that we had such valuable clothes; please thank Daisy for such a masterly stroke of business. Also we received letters from Mildred and Rose. Daisy's parcel turned up alright, about the 20th, and was very welcome. We always appreciate bullseyes in any quantity, as well as coal-tar soap, though some of the family might not think so. Mamie sent us two fine parcels which reached us the day before Christmas. They were the only ones we got just then and were tremendously acceptable and made us feel quite festive. Since then we have had a parcel from Aunt Mabel and two first rate rifle cases from Uncle Sam. We wrote to him for them. They will save us a heap of work. Any letters from home are worth a lot, and we get quite excited over such details as whether Rose has a gas stove in her bedroom or not and what Mildred ate for breakfast. We also note that there is a special parcel to be expected from Madge and you.

Since I last wrote to you we have had two days in the trenches. Of course we went in on Christmas day. We got up in the middle of the night and put on all our war-paint and went by motor bus to within about four miles of the firing-line. We had to carry all our rations up extra, and while you were having your dinner, we were marching over a bad, muddy road, full of shell holes, carrying over 100lbs of stuff each and swearing terrifically. We got up without trouble, and went into support trenches, about 600 yards from the Germans. There were quite nice little dugouts, about 12 feet by 6. There were nine of us in mine, and a charcoal brazier, so we were quite warm, when we had covered up the door. The trenches there are built up out of sandbags, as they can't dig in because of the water. We did a lot of comic things for practice and tried to repair the parapet in the middle of the night. We hadn't been up a minute when Fritz turned a machinegun onto us, but no one was hurt.

We had no extra Christmas rations, but we are all pretty good cooks now, and I fried steak and bacon in my mess tin and made a wonderful good meal. I will give a

Corporal Philip Tennant.

demonstration when I come back. On Boxing day our artillery was giving the Germans hell, and we watched our shrapnel throwing their trenches into the air all afternoon. They were replying, about one shell to our salvos. They were hitting about a quarter of a mile to our right and I got a fine view through glasses. I was in charge of rations again and had to take our party in the dead of night to villages behind the lines. You never meet anyone but one or two sentries. It is pitch dark and you have only a vague idea of where you are going, and the road is full of shell holes full of water, some of them three or four feet deep. You go through villages all smashed up by shell fire. (I shouldn't like to go through too many of them at night – there are such a lot of graves in them.) If you are lucky you find the stores, or a soup kitchen in a ruined house with a ray of light screened. On Christmas night I went out for stores and the Germans sent three Whizzy-bangs after us, but missed by quite two hundred yards. The funny thing about those shells is that they explode before you hear them coming. You can hear all the other shells whizzing through the air before they reach you. The second night I went for soup. Coming back we had to cross a bridge across a trench. I was carrying a dixie, or rather, half of it, and as I stepped on the bridge it fell right in – so did I, about ten feet down, up to my waist in water, and got a lot of hot soup over my head, the first hot wash I have got over here. Still, not all the soup was spilt, which was a good job for me.

We wore the new long waders which are awful in mud because they tug right off and make you sit down in the mud constantly. In water they are excellent. There was a very thick, rich grey mud in our trench, about a foot of it. Our officers made us shave and wash on Boxing day, so we all adjourned, in batches, to Jack Johnson holes behind the lines. The water was not at all clean, and I thought it was a bit risky to wash my delicate complexion in it. We are always knocking our hands about and then the mud gets in and they poison. I have got my right hand poisoned in two places. We came out on Monday and then had to march ten or twelve miles to our billets. You can't imagine what real anguish it is to cover that distance on coming out of the trenches after being short of sleep for two nights. We had a lot of men fall out. We had been very short of water for two days, as all the water is brought up to us in petrol cans and we were nearly done up. They gave us all a rum ration on empty stomachs and we were all a bit dithery, and sang as loud as we could. Without the rum we would never have got back to our billets, as the march took over six hours.

We rested for two days and today marched to a new one (our tenth in France) and are quite comfortable in a big girls' school about three *miles behind the line. Look for the Sixteenth Middlesex always in the casualty list now. But perhaps you have seen us there already. We shall go up again in a few days, but are enjoying a blessed, blessed treat at present. Edmund and I went into the big town near us yesterday and went to the pantomime, for soldiers only. Very topical and very broad. We are both quite well and eager to do a bit of strafing on our own account and have got over the habit of referring to 'The Dear Old Strand' ten times a day. Any letters thankfully received and parcels ditto. We are getting paid regularly and don't eat any more of the army food than we can help, hence our good health. I hope Father is going strong, and is going to business regularly now.*

Best wishes for New Year to everyone.

Yours Philip.

On January 10th 1916 the platoon in which Philip and Edmund were serving was withdrawn from the line to close billets. They were first reserve. Edmund was corporal in charge of one section which rested in a barn close by a trench named 'Harley Street' in the Hamlet of Cambrin, at about five kilometres distance from the canal. The section were fully dressed with their rifles and equipment beside them ready to move out at a moment's notice. Some men dozed, others played cards. The Tennant brothers started a sing-song and several other men joined in. They were disturbed by the screech of a stray shell. It was a large one and it passed through the roof and exploded on the floor of the barn. Eleven men from that platoon were killed instantly and another twenty-four seriously wounded.

Four of the dead came from North London: George Brown; Albert Curtis; Walter

Piper, Bertie Kempley; all of them private soldiers. The seven others killed came from South London and news of their deaths reached their loved ones by the *South London Press*:

Pte Stanley Allen; Pte Duncan Bruce: Pte Nelson Heath; Pte Edgar Mathews; Pte Frank Springfield; Cpl Edmund Tennant, aged 29; and L/Cpl Philip Tennant aged 23.

The Tennant brothers' youngest sister, Fanny, told me of that terrible January afternoon when the news reached Bromley.

We knew that it was possible that one of them might be killed. During a war one gets used to such a horrible thought. But we never imagined for a moment that they might both go at once.

Fanny returned from school, which was not far from 'Rosedean'. It was late afternoon, almost dark, and the gas lights were shining. Her elder sister, Daisy, opened the door, tears running down her face. She said, 'The boys have been killed.'

'I can remember every detail of that afternoon,' Fanny told me. 'I can remember the shape of the brass knocker. The colour of the paint round the door. I looked at the view down the hall as though I had never seen it before.'

Corporal Edmund Tennant.

Soon after the tragedy the family moved from Bromley. Her Father had been overworking and had not been well. The news of his son's deaths broke his spirit. The brothers' Company Commander wrote to their Father:

It is very sad and their loss is regretted by the whole platoon and I shall never replace them. It may be some comfort to know that they were doing their duty in every sense of the word.

Fanny's Father changed from a vigorous, rather choleric person to an old man that afternoon. He handed over the factory to Albert and moved to Kent with his youngest children. Fanny never returned to 'Rosedean', the house in Bromley where she lived as a child.

'Look for the Sixteenth Middlesex always in the casualty list now.'

This sentence in Philip Tennant's last letter to his family held a terrible prophecy. Two more tragedies struck the Battalion before the end of the month.

Three days after the shell destroyed the barn at Cambrin and many of those within it, the Battalion returned to Caserne Montmorency for ten days of comfort, not in the sense found in the civilian world, but compared to the extreme discomfort and tension of the trenches. Here they rested for ten days before the Battalion was ordered to Annequin once again.

The Germans completed a series of strong-points, or *stutzpuncten*, that made up their second line of defence. Their line was strong, particularly so along the line of the old Loos battlefield, that notorious area south of the Canal. Not only had they completed a line based upon logical and scientific calculations, but they had built up great reserves of ammunition, stockpiling it over a period of months.[1]

On 26 January the Germans mounted a ferocious attack across the old Loos battlefield. Battalion HQ received an urgent call to re-enter the line immediately. Two

Temporary graveyard at Cambrin. Graves of the men killed in the barn by one shell. These include the two Tennant brothers.

companies of 16PSB moved forward to reinforce the King's Royal Rifles. Alf Damon described the tragedy on the morning of the 28th.

We had been heavily shelled about stand-to, but the shelling appeared to have stopped. There was a shortage of shells on our side. Each gun had to hold some ammunition back in case of an emergency and the remainder worked out to about five shells per week. This meant that our counter-batteries could not retaliate so Jerry had it pretty much his own way. Our Company Commander, Major Way was walking along the trench to our position with Captain Sholto-Douglas and his runner, Dickie Bird. Following the OC, and at a little distance along the communication trench, came Captain Heslop with a party of men, roughly a platoon in strength. Whether the spotters on the mine tips caught on that there was a large party on the move, or whether it was sheer bad luck, is impossible to say, but suddenly Jerry dropped a heavy bombardment on the front and support trenches. A shell dropped into the trench right on top of the leading party.

Alf told the macabre end of the story. A well known man in 6 Platoon had the horrible job of sorting the scattered and dismembered remains of several men. He was Grimwade the stretcher bearer. Grimwade and Lieutenant Ionides had to carry the remains back to Battalion HQ. Or as old Tom Pottinger put it, 'They buried the three of 'em in a Bully Beef tin.[2]

Alf said that the death of Major Way and Captain Sholto-Douglas was a severe shock to everyone in B Company, and the Battalion as a whole. Both officers were well liked. Alf, and other Originals, had known them since the first day at Kempton racecourse. The ordinary soldiers killed in that unlucky bombardment were also popular men. Private Frederick Arthur Bird was killed by the direct hit, while Privates George Craxford and Stanley Evans were killed by shell fragments at a distance to the explosion. Captain Heslop and fifteen Other Ranks were wounded by the same blast.

Alf wrote: 'So died a very popular Company Commander, formerly a Captain in the Natal Mounted Rifles, an experienced soldier of the South African War, and Captain Sholto-Douglas another experienced and respected officer, and their runner young Dickie Bird.'

No doubt many others, as well as Alf, thought of that evening back in the autumn of 1914 when Major Way, who'd had enough to drink to make him very merry, sang 'If my mother could see me now'.

The Battalion's third tragedy in the month was also B Company's loss, but it was of a different kind and the Company felt the shame of it. One of B Company's platoon sergeants was sentenced by drumhead court martial. Divisional HQ ordered the Brigade, plus an extra battalion, to march to Beauvry to witness the sergeant's humiliation. Alf guessed that this was done to serve as an example to all ranks. The wretched NCO was Lionel Renton's platoon sergeant.

He was tried by courtmartial for being drunk on duty. He was an old soldier, India, South Africa, and he was too old for active service life. Lack of sleep, fatigue and constant shocks were sapping his nerve. Maybe the tragedy of the shell landing in the trench was the last straw. We were in the front line at the time of the incident, which made it worse. We'd noticed him going downhill well before Christmas, and his drinking habits. But being young and inexperienced we did not know how bad his condition was. In the trench he managed to get hold of an extra rum-ration or two and he became fighting drunk. Too many men saw it to hush it up quietly and send him back to some useful job in England. So he was tried and sentenced. It was the only time that I saw this depressing ceremony.'

The scene made a big impression on the youthful cook, Noel Peters.

The 16th Middlesex were drawn up on the playground of a girls' school that we used as a parade square. On our right was the 17th Football Battalion, Middlesex and on our left the Argyle and Sutherland Highlanders. The prisoner, a sergeant in the 16th Middlesex, was marched on with an escort, through a passage in the ranks, onto the square. An officer of the 16th Middlesex stepped forward and read out from King's Regulation 24688. The prisoner was found guilty of being drunk and disorderly and of insubordination to a superior officer. He was reduced to the ranks.

The 16th Battalion RSM drew his bayonet and cut the sergeant's stripes, first one arm and then the other, and threw them on the ground. We learnt afterwards that the stripes had been loosened before the parade. This was reduction to the ranks and was performed in an awe inspiring and ceremonious way and there was a dreadful silence as the prisoner and escort marched off the parade square. All you could hear was the sound of the guns. The trenches were only four or five miles away and we could hear the bombardment further down the line, towards Arras.

The pathetic figure of the old soldier, ex-sergeant, was marched off to prison and disgrace. Lionel Renton's platoon had a new sergeant, Sergeant Bill Cairns. Lionel Renton described him as 'an excellent Sergeant' and Laurie Barrow 'such a nice fellow' Sergeant William Cairns was killed on the first of July that year.

Walking in his well tended vegetable garden in Portsmouth Noel Peters said.

I never forgot that dreadful ceremony. Which is odd when you think of all the frightful things that happened through the war and all the good fellows killed. Memory is a funny thing. Some things you remember and some you don't. After the war it was a long time before I went back to France. I was in service, you know, looking after a series of different families and wealthy gentlemen, and I was raising my own family. Sometime after the Second War we passed through Beauvry on a British Legion trip. The girls' school and its parade ground were still there. I could remember that awful day as well then as the day it happened.

Fn1. The reasons why the German defences were planned more thoroughly and intelligently than either the French or British lines (with the exception of Verdun) is considered in the chapter on the reasons for the failure of the British offensive on the Somme. One of the key factors in this was the failure of Haig's Intelligence staff, under Charteris, to appreciate the strength and depth of the defences and their resistance to intensive artillery bombardment.

Fn2. After the war Pte Grimwade, the stretcher bearer, became Managing Director of Grimwades Fine Paper Co. Old Tom Pottinger appears in several stories of 16PSB. Despite being always referred to as 'Old', Tom Pottinger must have been young enough and fit enough to be passed for active service or he would have been posted to the 24th Service Battalion, MX, with many of the older, or less fit volunteers.

Chapter 17

THE BRICKSTACKS

IF THE WAR SEEMED BAD AT ANNEQUIN before Christmas, it entered a new, more degraded and vile phase after the New Year and the drumhead court martial of the elderly sergeant. The Battalion rotated with the Fusiliers moving between Beauvry, in reserve, and the front line at the Brickstacks. The Brickstacks was detested by everyone, not because the trenches were any wetter, muddier or more battered than those north of the Canal, but because this sector of the line faced the old Loos battlefield with all its unburied horrors and the stench of the Scottish and English dead. Territorials or volunteers, all were the victims of Sir John French's incompetence, all rotting in the mud. The stink and taste of this vile grey mud corrupted all that it touched.

'Everything tasted the same,' Noel said.

That was one of the worst things at the Brickstacks. We carried clean drinking water up to the line in old petrol tins. The taste of petrol and paraffin got into everything. Then there was the chloride of lime that they tipped onto the corpses and the Lysol, used as a disinfectant. In the background was that smell, that dreadful stink – all the time. I don't have to tell you, you can imagine it for yourself. A horrible sweet smell. I suppose after a time you cease to notice it. You lost your sense of smell and your sense of taste.

You'd make a dixie of tea. Or you'd take a lot of trouble to make a composition stew taste better. Maybe you'd scrounge some vegetables, real vegetables not the tinned kind, steal some onions and potatoes. Or sometimes you could get hold of some real steak. Now and then I'd scrounge a little curry powder off the Indians up the line at Festubert. Or there might be a few herbs that had survived the shelling in one of the little neglected gardens behind the miners' cottages. Anything to give it a taste.

You'd get the grub up to the line somehow, dodging between shells and diving into dugouts when the whistles blew. At last, with a bit of luck you'd reach the line. Some stout fellow would have a brazier going nicely and you'd put the dixie on to warm. And finally you'd serve it out into their mess-tins. And then, after all that you'd hear one of the fellows say, "It all tastes the same".

Sometimes I'd get a notion to make a special dessert, to give them a treat. Tinned fruit spiced up with some rum and then add some apples and plums that I bartered for a couple of tins of Bully Beef, and then make some custard to go with it. When I got it up to the line still intact the lads would say, "It all tastes the same".

In mid-January Battalion HQ received orders by field telephone, to reconnoitre and then make a bombing attack on a German strong-point known as 'Mad Point'. This, like the infamous 'Duck's Bill', north of the Canal, was a small sharp salient thrusting into No

Looking across No Man's Land towards the German-held village of Auchy les Mines.

Man's Land. To the staff this irregularity on the map was an affront to military order and must be bitten off at the first opportunity. The Battalion officers who had to plan the attack knew that the operation would prove far more costly to the attackers than to those in defence. But orders are orders and so three patrols set off into No Man's Land to reconnoitre. They were commanded by officers: Lieutenant Cleghorn, Second Lieutenant Samuel and Second Lieutenant James. In this new version of siege warfare, fighting from shell holes and flooded trenches, Sandhurst training was no great advantage. Regular, Territorial or Temporary officer, all were amateurs at this new style of warfare, learning a new trade. Some young officers, like Cleghorn, took to this individualist fighting immediately, others never would. Night patrolling demanded a cool nerve and the instincts of a hunter.

Patrols served various purposes ranging from a special task, such as taking a prisoner for intelligence, reconnoitring a position or testing the strength of the enemy's wire, to a tactic known as 'Aggressive Patrolling'. This aggressive spirit was a special favourite of the General Staff. Like morale, senior officers wrote many pages of reports and memos on the subject. Their object was peculiarly British. 'Dominating No Man's Land and keeping our chaps busy and on their toes.' Neither their French allies nor their German opponents saw any need for this show of aggression, as Alf Damon recorded of the period when he was attached to the French on the Champagne front late in 1917, between major attacks each side left the other's trenches alone. The high casualty rate of young officers and NCOs, which meant a high wastage of the best and fittest men, did not seem to trouble the staff back at St Omer.

Such patrols could only take place at night. Balaclavas and woollen caps were worn; equipment and weapons were muffled with cloths to prevent clinking or rattling; faces and hands were blackened with burnt cork. The units holding the line on either side of the point where the patrol would return were warned of their presence by a code word. As night fell the three sections went over the top of the trench, under their own wire, which had been temporarily lifted or cleared, and out into No Man's Land. Almost as soon as they had gone out an order came from Brigade HQ cancelling the attack. It came too late.

In one of his poems Arthur Graeme West describes just such a night; the clinging mud, the obstacles, tangles of wire, old abandoned equipment, the mounds of ration tins that threaten to fall with a clatter, the foul stink of the unburied dead rotting in broken trenches and water-filled shell holes. He describes the moment of intense anxiety, caught in the open as the landscape is lit up by flares and star-shells.

This was exactly what happened at 'Mad Point'. An alert sentry heard a sound and, at once, the sky was brilliant with parachute flares: their bright light descending gently to earth, illuminating the broken and fouled landscape in a cold white light. Searchlights traversed the ground while machine guns using tracer criss-crossed the open ground, firing from the German front line and from 'Mad Point' itself. Each man lay still in whatever cover he could find. Frequently this meant feigning dead in a pile of decomposing corpses. At last the tracer bullets ceased their lines of fire above their heads. After several hours in freezing darkness, Cleghorn gave the order to withdraw. The NCOs and men made their way back to their own trench as silent and as cautious as possible. One of the three patrols was detected before they could reach safety. They attracted a savage and concentrated fire of machine guns and trench mortars. The cost of this unnecessary and fruitless adventure was an officer, a sergeant and four men. They disappeared into the swamp of No Man's Land and were never seen again. The officer in charge of this unlucky section was listed as missing. He was Second Lieutenant Samuel, later listed killed in action. Lionel Renton knew him well.

> Sammy was a conscientious officer and well liked in the company. He was one of the 'Original' volunteers, so I knew him from the early days. Sammy was a non-orthodox Jew, one of the well-known Samuel's jewellery family I believe.

The dead sergeant was Lance-Sergeant Edgar Henman and the soldiers Privates Sydney Upfold, Tom Jones, Clement Keatinge and Sid Laws.

Orders from Divisional HQ stressed the importance of constantly harassing the enemy, to dominate No Man's Land. On 3 February a second order for a night attack was passed down by Brigade HQ. This would be a much larger affair and aimed at three craters at 'Mine Point'. The units involved would be the whole of D Company with the addition of thirty-two bombers supplied by Brigade, the attack being under the command of Lieutenant Cleghorn.

> 'A group of lads from D Company went over from our section of the trench,' Alf Damon
> said. 'The lads told us the code word as they were going out, so that we wouldn't shoot
> them coming back. That was the last we saw of them.'

Once again the men moving into position across the mud and broken ground were spotted by alert sentries on the other side of the wire, and once again up went the parachute flares and star-shells. Caught in the open Cleghorn signalled his men to take cover and lie still. He managed to get them back to the Middlesex line before dawn without losing a man, though he and three soldiers were wounded. Cleghorn's party had a bad time but at least they were able to crawl back to their own line in darkness. Far worse was to come.[1]

Despite the first pallor of dawn in the sky, Brigade ordered a second attack. When Colonel Hall queried the order it was repeated, the attack was to commence immediately. For this attack the officer commanding was Captain F R Hill, supported by Second Lieutenants James and Tanqueray with a second large party of bombers and riflemen. With the sky growing lighter the danger to Hill's group increased with every minute of delay. To add to the illumination, the Germans, now thoroughly alert, fired flares and rockets into the air. The ground was strafed by trench mortars and traversed

Shattered wire, both British and German. Night patrols had to cope with these obstacles to attack the German trenches. Note the cluster of corpses directly in front of the German wire.

by machine-gun fire, splashing into the mud and shell holes in which the Londoners had taken cover. This local fire was immediately followed by an artillery barrage. Shells fell on No Man's Land and the Middlesex front line trench.

There was no explanation given for the idiotic decision to send in a second party after dawn, most probably it was a mistake at Divisional HQ, of an order misunderstood somewhere down the chain of command. The only real surprise about this aimless attack was the small number of those killed either out in the open or caught by the shelling of the forward trench: Lieutenant Hopwood Corporal Stuart Monks, Privates James Shearer, Bernard Doyle, Murdo Macauley, George Blaxendale, Harold Holstead and Edmund Houghton.

A private soldier was killed on the night of the first patrol. He was not one of those killed in No Man's Land but in the trench, close to Alf Damon. By an odd coincidence both Alf Damon and Arthur Graeme West knew him and were standing close by when it happened. The oddity is the difference in their viewpoint of the dead man, but this may be because the two witnesses had a very different view of both life and death. Alf wrote:

> *After the deaths of Major Way and Captain Sholto Douglas, B Company suffered another tragedy, this time at dawn stand-to. In our company were three brothers Rieu. They had originally enlisted in the French Foreign Legion, but then transferred to the 16th. (I never discovered the reason for either move because they were half French.) One brother, Henri Rieu, was on watch in pitch darkness before dawn, a few feet from where I was sitting on the fire-step. He turned to talk to one of his brothers and received a shot in the head which killed him instantly. This was sheer rotten luck, undoubtedly, because no sniper could see him, the light was too poor. His brothers, Alfred and Charles, carried him away, overcome with emotion, as one can imagine, being French. With some misgivings, I took his place as look-out.*
>
> *They were an unlucky family; Alfred Rieu was killed on the first of July and Charles a year later.*

It is possible, though not certain, that the death of the sentry described by West is that of Henri Rieu. West calls him 'the Tab', which is Oxford slang for a Cambridge student.

> *An estaminet. Feb 12th 1916.*
>
> *Dear Lad,*
>
> *I had your letter this afternoon and set myself to answer it at once. We have had a rather bloody – literally – time of it. The Tab I had met at Woldingham was shot in the head and killed instantly one night standing next to me, and you may have observed that we have lost several officers. We had an extraordinarily heavy bombardment. Also I had a rather exciting time myself with two other men in No Man's Land between the lines. A dangerous business and most repulsive because of the smells and appearance of heaps of dead men that lie unburied where they fell, on some attack or other, about four months ago. I found myself much as I expected in the face of such happenings: more interested than afraid, but more careful of my own life than anxious to approve any new martial ardour. I become, I assure*

you, more and more cautious, though more accustomed and easy in the face of the Hun. For the moment, thank God, we are resting, and the certain knowledge that I shan't be killed anyhow for a day or two is invigorating.

The spring is manifest here, in young corn, and in the very air and strong winds: and even here I react to it and find myself chanting verses from 'Love in the valley' as I did last year in Surrey. I have an odd feeling, though very insistent and uplifting to me, a feeling which I probably vainly unfold to you, of being so integrally a part of, and so thoroughly approved and intimately associated with all these evidences of spring, that Nature herself will not suffer me to be killed, but will preserve unharmed a love so loyal and keen-sighted as myself. We shall see.

I got a 'Spenser' from T... and am now travelling through the Faerie Queen *with the chaste Britomart. Yes, by all means send me* Tom Jones: *these long things I can manage very well here, when we are back from the hellish trenches, where I find it hard to read, though I can manage to write letters, more or less.*

I believe I shall get leave – if I am not killed or wounded first – certainly in about two months' time and possibly before. It is bruited about that the Battalion starts leave in a day or two. My God! What heaven it will be while it lasts, and what awful hell going back!

However, I live so utterly in the moment that I can easily shelve the last few hours till they come. I hope it arrives when the spring is farther on. I will bear witness to all that I can to keep you out of the Army: I am intensely pleased that you have not got forced in yet, and I hope you will escape. How bloody people in England seem to be getting about peace and peace meetings. I suppose they are getting rather Prussian in the country, but are all peace meetings always broken up by soldiers (who've probably never been here at all?).

I have contracted hatred and enmity for nobody out here, save soldiers generally and a few NCOs in particular. For the Hun I feel nothing but amiable fraternity that the poor man has to sit just like us and do all the horrible and useless things that we do, when he might be home with his wife or his books, as he preferred. Well, well, who is going to have the sense to start talking of peace? We're stuck here until our respective governments have the sense to do it.

Send me Tom Jones *then, if you please.*

I must really stop, dear lad.

A G W

Arthur Graeme West's thinking about the war and the stupidity of national governments was unusual and way ahead of his time. What he wrote on peace and the Hun pre-dates Siegfried Sassoon's sudden conversion by more than a year. West would appear eccentric in any gathering, in the army in 1916 he must have seemed quite extraordinary.

Lionel Renton commented on the different reactions shown by his fellows in the face of fear, disgust, extreme tension and lack of sleep. First he described an adventurer, one of Vibart's companions who returned from South America to enlist. This man was a professional tough-guy, ready to fight anyone on any pretext, or none. He was a brave

The old Loos battlefield. The dead remained in No Man's Land.

The reason why the men of 16PSB detested this sector of the line. The bodies of Scottish Territorials killed during the Battle of Loos still lay where they fell in No Man's Land.

man, Lionel Renton said. He liked to show off his courage and tempt fate. He was always last man in from a wiring party, or a patrol, walking erect on the parapet at first dawn light, when others would hurry to the protection of the trench.

One dull, evil morning, with patterns of shells throwing up fragments of wire and sandbags, with the rotting remains of the dead all mixed and thrown up into the air with great spouts of mud and water, his nerve broke. His section corporal found him on the duckboards, crawling on all fours, howling and slobbering like an animal in pain. When the shelling eased two men tried to lift him. He gripped the slats of the duckboards yelling. His screams were having a bad effect on everyone around him. At last an officer gave him an injection of morphine and two NCOs dragged him into a dugout.

At this stage in the war no one thought of a case like that with sympathy, as we do today – understanding it as a mental breakdown. Such failures of nerve were judged as cowardice by everyone, usually called 'funk' or 'windpup'. What happened to him? I don't know. They did not tell us and no one asked. Either he was shot or he spent the rest of his life in a lunatic asylum.

Lionel Renton contrasted this unfortunate shell-shocked man with another of his companions, a countryman, good-natured and uncomplicated. He was a postman who was never heard to utter threats or curses against the Hun, the Staff, or anyone else; a most un-warlike man. During one of many bombardments at the Brickstacks, Lionel Renton had to deliver a message, when anyone who could sought cover in a dug-out. He was hurrying along the front line trench when he came on the postman contentedly sitting on the fire step, eating a sandwich.

'You seem happy enough despite the bombardment?'

'Oh I'm happy enough sir.' replied the postman. Though equal in rank with Lionel, he addressed everyone with an educated voice as 'sir', whether officer or in the ranks. 'You can have a bombardment any time, sir,' he said, 'but it is not every day that you get a cheese sandwich.'

Alf Damon explained that mining and countermining went on all the time, partly because there were so many pre-war tunnels under the lines and plenty of Flemish miners who were unemployed and were happy to help the sappers – on either side. From time to time one side or other would explode a mine under the other's trench. 'The race would be on to take the rim and then drive a sap out to the crater. The side that reached the crater lip first usually held it.'

On the 16th of February the Germans exploded a mine. It was the largest quantity of explosive detonated in that sector at that stage in the war. Lieutenants Dawson and Wilson held onto the lip of the crater with a small party of men armed with rifles and a couple of Lewis guns. The enemy replied to their fire with mortars and heavy machine guns. The Middlesex party held their position until relieved by the 21st Royal Fusiliers. The courage and tenacity shown by this small group commanded by two junior officers is recorded in several places and yet there were no gallantry decorations issued nor was the event even mentioned in despatches.[2]

For the rest of the month the Battalion followed the now familiar routine: a period in reserve at Beauvry, followed by reserve positions at Annequin north, and then back into the line at Brickstacks. A few days in the mud and stink of the front line and then back to the reserve position. This dreary cycle might have gone on in this way for months had not someone on the staff had other plans for 16PSB. Someone in the Map room at Saint Omer looked at the lists and maps spread out on the long mahogany table, matched this brigade to that, considered the balance of divisions, and eventually decided to detach the 16th Middlesex from 100 Infantry Brigade in the 33rd Division and attach it to Headquarters Command.

Knowing nothing of this, nor of the decision taken far behind the line, the junior officers, NCOs and men of 16PSB marched back to Bethune. In the familiar surroundings of Montmorency barracks they were given a few hours to clean themselves, their uniforms, webbing equipment and weapons and get on parade. The Battalion paraded in companies on the drill square at Montmorency barracks, inspected by their platoon sergeants, CSM, and company officers. Finally, under the fierce eye of RSM MacDonald, they were inspected by Colonel Hall.

On the 26th of February 1916 the 16th (Public Schools Battalion) The Middlesex Regiment (The Duke of Cambridge's Own) marched from the barracks to Bethune station, drums beating and pipes wailing. Here they boarded the steel trucks coupled to the wheezing locomotive that would take them westward to Saint Omer.

1. Lieutenant Cleghorn was later awarded the Military Cross.
2. See Wallace-Grain p36.

Loos. The Tower Bridge. This landmark could be seen for many miles along the La Bassée line.

Chapter 18

SAINT OMER
THE VIEW FROM THE CHÂTEAU

I N MARCH 1916 SAINT OMER remained the General Headquarters of the British
  Expeditionary Force in France and Belgium. That spring the newly appointed
  General Officer Commanding the BEF, Lieutenant General Sir Douglas Haig, was
engaged in moving his headquarters to the small town of Montreuil, beside the river
Somme, half way between Boulogne and Amiens. It was at that moment, as GHQ staff
were moving their files, maps, and statistics from Saint Omer to the Somme that the 16th
Middlesex marched into camp at Quiestede, a small village close to the outskirts of the
town, not far from the forest of Nieppe.

Saint Omer is an old, pleasant town that has survived two world wars. The town was
bombed in 1940 but the ancient centre, the Cathedral and the Hotel de Ville repaired
with such skill that one can imagine Saint Omer as it was early in 1916. On the western
edge of the town is an old airfield. Up until only a few years ago it looked very much
as it did when it was the principal airfield for the Royal Flying Corps, and the RFC
Headquarters in France. It was here that the GOC suffered his worst moment of
humiliation, and potentially, the greatest setback to his career. Late in 1915, a few
months before 16PSB moved from the La Bassée front to Quiestede, King George V
visited Saint Omer on a brief tour of inspection during which he fell from one of Haig's
horses. He suffered no damage but spent the next two days in bed. Haig felt the
disgrace of this incident keenly and it preyed on his mind for a considerable time.[1] The
beginning of March 1916 found the 16th Middlesex in a hutted camp at Quiestede, half-
way between Saint Omer and the small town of Aire-sur-Lys. Aire was a railway
junction town and a line ran from Hazebrouk in the north, through Aire, St Pol and
Doullens to Amiens. Both Flanders and Picardy were well served by railways before the
war and these had been extended and enlarged through 1915 to serve the camps and
huge supply dumps that dwarfed villages and covered fields from the junction and
supply base at Hazebrouk to Bethune and Saintt Omer parallel to the front line, and
stretched all the way back to the Channel ports along lines running east to west.

The reason for the abrupt change of scene was to select potential officer candidates,
which would not have taken more than a week, but by an odd trick of fate 16PSB spent
two months at Quiestede. Two months out of the line was no mean reprieve. The reason
for this good fortune was an epidemic of German measles, a disease that the army
medical authorities took more seriously in 1916 than they would today. These crucial
two months led to a change of divisions. 16PSB transferred from the Domino to the
Bottle of Bass Division.

Though it is hard to believe, considering the numbers of officer candidates that left the Battalion during its eighteen months existence, records state that 16PSB forwarded another 250 candidates during its stay at Quiestede. This shows that the Battalion continued to attract volunteers with a high standard of education long after the exclusive Public School stipulation was removed. Once again some of the Originals refused to apply for commissions, preferring to stay with the Battalion in France. Once again these included Alf Damon, Lionel Renton, Laurie Barrow and several others.

The demands made by trench warfare forced the army to change its procedure both for selecting and training officers. In this new type of warfare, losses of young officers reached unprecedented levels.[2] Colonel Hall and the Adjutant, Captain F S Cochram, selected potential officers between the 11th and the 24th of March. The candidates would have been sent back to officer selection boards immediately, but the outbreak of German measles postponed this move.

The potential officers were split into smaller groups, known in the army as 'cadres'. These groups were billeted in farms just outside the village. Each had an experienced NCO in charge and its own cook. Noel Peters moved to one of these cadres with a set of cooking equipment.

With a cynicism that was unusual for Noel, he commented that rations improved the further one got from the line. Being close to GHQ meant that he had much better material on which to practise his art. Alf was less tactful. He loathed all those stationed behind the line and hated the Commissariat worst of all. Many of his spicy letters thundered against those planning and supplying food to the soldiers in the front line. 'Dirty skunks lining their own pockets' was one of his milder insults. In fact, by the early months of 1916, and certainly by 1917, rations improved and both senior catering officers in France and academics in England were working to improve the soldiers' diet starting from both a practical view, at trench level, and a scientific level.[3] For the first time in British history food became a proper subject for scientific research. New words like 'diet' and 'calories' came into common use. For the first time catering officers received training on the techniques to provide their men with a balanced diet and not to merely fill them up with carbohydrate. This ideal was not always possible, as Noel was quick to point out. Ration supplies were erratic, sometimes providing good material for the cooks to work on, sometimes so bad that they were forced to barter, borrow or steal extra food. Noel had one minor satisfaction: the German cooks fared worse. German front-line soldiers named 1917 'The year of the turnip', but in fact the blockade on German ports by the Royal Navy began to affect their rations earlier than that. 'An army marches on its stomach,' Noel said. 'And Jerry's belly was emptier than ours.'

One of the potential officers was Arthur Graeme West. I asked Noel Peters whether he remembered a poet amongst the candidates. He did not. West was an unusually talented and perceptive man, and the record of his impressions and thoughts on the war is unlike any other. Many soldiers became disillusioned after the Somme disaster and

Cooks preparing food.

lost that blind, childlike faith in their leaders in which spirit they volunteered, but it was most unusual for a soldier to see through the charade of bogus patriotism as early as West did. And yet, attempting to see Graeme West as the boy cook as Noel Peters might see him, Graeme West would not stand out. His diary reveals him as intelligent and sensitive but far from sociable or chummy. He was not an athlete and singer, like Arthur Kent, nor a muscle-man like Vibart, nor an actor like Edmund Tennant, nor a sharp-witted sharp tongued character like Alf Damon, nor a natural leader like Lionel Renton. Graeme West had no sociable talents that Noel might remember, and yet his voice speaks to us clearly, a mind ahead of its time. He writes like a contemporary, an eccentric university friend transported by H G Wells *Time Machine* from our world to the mud, stench, filth, lice and horror of the winter of early 1916.

The potential officer cadre, to which Noel Peters was attached, occupied a thatched farmhouse a little way out of the village of Quiestede. Life became much pleasanter. The weather improved, there was less rain and the wind was less cold. The men slept on clean straw and there were tubs of clean water so that the candidates could clean themselves of the vile mud of the old Loos battlefield. A horse-drawn fumigation unit moved from cadre to cadre disinfecting uniforms and greatcoats to kill off the lice. (Though Alf remarked that the fumes killed the lice but did nothing to attack their eggs so, within a week, they were all lousy again.)

The cooks were able to prepare regular meals, rising at five to prepare breakfast and working late into the night. Noel never complained about the long hours; cooking was his vocation, food his passion. He scrounged fallen bricks from a derelict pig-stye and enlarged and rebuilt the chimney and fireplace so that he could set two dixies on the fire instead of one so that everyone could receive a generous helping of hot nourishing food at the evening meal. He grinned. 'They weren't grateful, my customers complained about a monotonous diet of stew. Not that I expected gratitude. Cooking is what I do and I did the best I could.'

Noel's culinary experiments were hampered by lack of an oven. He wanted to give the lads roast meat as a special celebration meal before they went off to England and officer cadet school. He remembered seeing a spit in an old house and decided to cook the meat over the fire as they did in the Middle Ages. He persuaded the armourer to make up a set of irons that would take the weight and a steel pin with a crank handle on the end of it. For several days he skimmed fat off the stew and saved it to baste whatever fresh meat he could beg or barter. At last he got hold of a whole sheep. With the aid of a volunteer, an officer candidate who shared Noel's interest in food, he spitted the carcass and turned it over the fire, basting it with the fat, catching the extra fat as it dripped down in the lid of a dixie.

The evening was fine. Noel sat outside the farmhouse preparing vegetables and enjoying the afternoon sunshine. Occasionally he re-entered the house to see that his apprentice was basting the roast meat as he should. His customers approached attracted by the scent of roasting mutton. Someone noticed smoke pouring out of the thatch.

Noel climbed onto the roof with a bucket just as the chimney caught fire. At first the water appeared to spread the flames, but more men ran up to form a bucket chain to pass water up to those on the roof. Soon the flaming chimney and smouldering thatch were under control. As the group was enjoying a roast dinner the farmer arrived, summoned by neighbours. He threatened to sue Noel, the Battalion, General Haig or the British government. A French speaking cadet calmed him down while Noel presented him with tins of Bully, sugar and tea. The farmer calmed down. His house suffered no permanent damage. They remained on good terms, keeping the farmer in tinned food for the rest of their stay at Quiestede. But, Noel said, all good things come to an end. The domestic interlude was over. The MO declared that the epidemic had run its course. The last cadre of officer candidates marched away and Noel rejoined the Battalion at the railway siding at Aire. The Battalion entrained for Doullens, the railhead behind the left flank of the Somme sector of the line. They were to join an all-regular division, the 29th Division, known as 'The Incomparable 29th' fresh from the Gallipoli campaign.

1. An honour guard of Headquarters troops were drawn up on parade on the airfield for inspection. Haig was both a cavalryman and a personal friend of the King's and so he lent King George one of the prize horses from his stable. The cavalry mare was specially trained, groomed and every last leather strap and brass buckle polished and re-polished. All went well as the mounted royal party trotted onto the parade ground. Unfortunately the cheer that went up from the pilots and aircraftsmen on the adjoining field startled the mare. The King lost his seat and fell. Entries in Sir Douglas Haig's diary show a marked contrast between his reaction to the King's tumble from Haig's horse and the disaster on the Somme. Haig refers to the former incident several times and is clearly worried about its effect on his career whereas he refers to July 1st 1916 as 'a day of ups and downs'.
2. Comparison of officer casualties in the two world wars demonstrates this. During the war of 1939-45 casualties of officers below Field rank were about equal: losses of captains and lieutenants being roughly equal to second lieutenants. But through 1914 to 1918, the deaths of second lieutenants ran at a ratio of five to one. During major battles like the Somme or Third Ypres these figures became more dramatic; a ratio of about ten to one.
3. From the middle of the war onward experiments and research into nutrition and mass catering became an area of study in the Department of Social Science at the University of London. The author's mother, Marguerite Hawes, aged 18, was a student in the department through the fatal influenza epidemic of 1918-1919, when skills learned in war had to be applied in the first months of peace as a matter of urgency.

Soldiers enjoying the labours of their cooks.

Chapter 19

LEAVE

SPRING 1916

OFFICERS WERE ALLOTTED TEN DAYS' LEAVE every eight months, the Other Ranks considerably less. Some soldiers had no leave during eighteen months in France. Leave depended on rank and on where you were stationed. For those on a permanent staff job in England getting home for a weekend leave was not difficult to wangle. This added to the bitterness of the men in the line. Like many other survivors of the Somme battle, Noel had no leave until the winter of 1917:

Leave was the luck of the draw. You'd hear fellows belly-aching: "when are we going to get leave, when we going to get leave?" There were always rumours of leave, then just when you thought it was all set you'd hear, "all leave postponed" or "leave cancelled".

Alf was one of the lucky ones. To his surprise and delight he was handed a leave pass and travel warrant to South London.

When we marched from Brickstacks to Bethune we were told that several of us would

Le Havre to Southampton was the route taken by the hospital ships. Germans were sinking hospital ships claiming that when empty they were being used to transport ammunition.

be going home on leave. At that time it was 'first come first served' which meant that it was between the old originals who joined in September 1914, and there weren't many of us left. I was lucky and found myself on a train bound for the coast. We crossed from Le Havre to Southampton, which was the route taken by the hospital ships. We were held up at the docks and there was a rumour that a hospital ship had been sunk at the mouth of the Seine. Jerry claimed that our hospital ships, returning empty to France, carried ammunition instead of medical stores, which was why he sunk several of them. Our press denied that we would do such a dastardly deed, but you have to be realistic and not blinded by patriotism. In the docks we passed a large cargo boat with about ten feet blown off its bow section. Not the most inspiring sight as you head out into the grey Channel.

We hung about from dawn until evening waiting to sail. Apart from some bread rolls, bought at Le Havre station that morning, I had nothing in my pack except some Fortnum and Mason's partridge paste, which I ate on hard compo biscuits. So I was not surprised when I was mal de mer *when the ship hit rough water. I was glad to reach Southampton and find a canteen on the dockside serving hot tea and buns. After many hours on one harbour dock side or another, we crowded onto a troop train and went our separate ways when we reached Victoria.*

One thing sticks in my mind about that journey. My route took me by the Inner Circle underground train. I admit I was looking a bit muddy and dishevelled, but I was not prepared for the remarks one civvy made to another, loud enough for all the passengers to hear. 'I wonder when the authorities will supply a special carriage for those fellows, instead of permitting them to rub their dirt off on passengers.'

Conditions at Cuinchy Keep had not allowed me a bath or a change of clothes for a week, so he was right, he and his fellow passengers stood a good chance of sampling the trench lice that we experienced all the time.

The de-lousing session started as soon as I arrived home; in a copper full of boiling water. By good luck some of my cousins were home on leave and we made up a big family party to see The Maid of the Mountains. *That was a good outing. On another day I got out my bike, put it on a train to Bromley and went cycling through the Kent countryside. Kent was called the Garden of England in those days. It seemed to me just like a garden, clean and green and well ordered, after the black mud of Flanders.*

We were a happy family. I enjoyed my childhood. My family worked hard and played hard and enjoyed life. Most homes had a piano in the front room (whether anyone could play it or not was another story). We made our own entertainment and Sunday evenings we'd get round the piano and sing. I can still sing the songs we sang together.

Alf's comment on his first sight of London since embarkation the previous year was that it was a different world.

Even our families had no idea how we lived out there. I never tried to explain it. I was home to enjoy myself not to belly-ache, and besides I've no time for those fellows who waste energy moaning about their lot. We are what we are and we have to make the best of it.

The gap between the civilian world and the world of the trenches was widening month

Alf Damon. Home on leave from France, March 1916.

by month. 'Business as usual' was the catch phrase in London and, on the whole, Alf remarked, business seemed pretty good. The demand for uniforms, for arms, ammunition and for trench stores of all kinds created prosperity. Soldiers in training camps, transport drivers and factory workers were better fed and better clothed than they had been before the war. The voracious demand for shells opened up old factories and created new ones, drawing both skilled and unskilled workers onto the production lines. The changes in Britain's cities came as a shock to many soldiers coming back from France on leave. 'Leave was not cheap. Prices had risen in London and everyone seemed to have stacks of money to spend. Except the Tommies home on leave.' In Woolwich the good-natured munition workers, young girls known as 'Canaries', insisted on treating the Tommies on leave from France. In Woolwich, as in Manchester, Liverpool or Glasgow the soldiers' girls no longer worked meekly at some form of domestic service. They no longer smelt of flour and soap, but of the picric acid that coloured the munition workers' skin yellow as canaries. Or the young woman spent her day conducting a bus in the reek of petrol fumes.

The so called Canaries earned as much as £4 a week, including overtime. Before the war a skilled fitter earned £2 and 10 shillings. A private soldier earned a shilling a day and there was no pay rise until 1917. Some old biddies in South London moaned about the Canaries, their lack of morals and their spendthrift ways. But I saw no harm in them. They earned their money the hard way and many died making it.

In France we talked about leave all the time. We looked forward to leave and talked of all the things that we'd do back in Blighty. There was a lot of joking and teasing. But in the silence of our hearts we knew that those ten days back at home would

Time to return to the front.

make life back at the Front even harder to bear. The moment of going back was the worst. The dreadful moment at Victoria station. Those great masses of khaki, many of them noisy, some of them drunk, trying to put a hearty face on their fears. Others, very quiet, saying good-bye to mothers, sweethearts or wives. And when the guard waved his flag and blew his whistle then our friends and dear ones receded, smaller and smaller until the line curves out of the station and the train crosses the river, steam gusting past the carriage window. And then, somehow, that life was gone. Chaps got out fags and passed them round. Some ate, some slept, some whistled tunes heard on leave. We were back in the army and civilian life forgotten.

His London leave opened Alf's eyes to the gulf between life on the Home Front and life in the Front Line. And yet Alf was not embittered or disillusioned. The great mass of soldiers still believed that their cause was just, still believed in their leaders and still viewed the war as a job that had to be done.

My leave passed all too quickly. I reported to the RTO on the other side of the Channel and was kept kicking my heels on a freezing dockside. There appeared to be some sort of muddle so they sent me to the transit camp while they tried to find out where 16PSB had got to.

Alf, like every one of his comrades, developed a very low opinion of transit camps. Le Havre camp, he admitted, was not as bad as the notorious Bull Ring on the sand dunes outside Etaples.

These places were staffed by the worst type of old regular NCO; lead swingers, bullies, scrimshankers and drunken old sweats. The rationale behind the transit camp was to make life as uncomfortable as possible for the soldiers passing through so that they would beg to be sent back to their battalions at the front.

At last I was given a movement order. The RTO told me to entrain for somewhere called Doullens, on the plateau above the Somme. From there I was to make my way as best I could to a village called Mailly Maillet. That was the first I heard of the change from the Domino division to the Bottle of Bass.

120

PART THREE

Chapter 20

THE GOLDEN VIRGIN

THE MARKET TOWN OF ALBERT-SUR-ANCRE is the nearest town of any size to the Somme battlefield. Albert lies on the Roman road from Amiens to Cambrai. The road appears as straight as a ruler on the map, but in fact it undulates over the chalk downs so the first sight of Albert is gained from above the town as the walker or cyclist reaches the top of a gently curving ridge above the valley of the river Ancre. The Virgin, restored and regilded, shines in the early morning sunlight above the river mist and the smoke of small factories and brick dwellings. She stands out as a landmark, unmistakable and poignant. The Basilica, built early in the twentieth century, was formed of ostentatious red and yellow brick. If not a thing of beauty, it was at least well constructed and strongly built. This was a factor that would save the lives of many sheltering in the crypt of the Basilica, whether terrified civilian or wounded soldier.

Albert was captured during the rapid German advance of 1914. The town was recaptured by the French and badly damaged by artillery fire from both sides. From 1914 to 1917 the town was within range of the German guns. The railway station and most of the principal buildings lay in ruins, town houses, and terraced rows of artisan dwellings, roofless, fire blackened and broken. The German gunners took advantage of the gilded statue as an aiming mark when they fired their salvos of shells into the ruined street of the town. One shell struck the spire so that the Golden Virgin hung forward over the town square, 'as though casting her infant into the flames', as one soldier described this pathetic symbol. A legend grew up that Albert would only fall when the Virgin fell.

The Basilica and the Hanging Virgin at Albert.

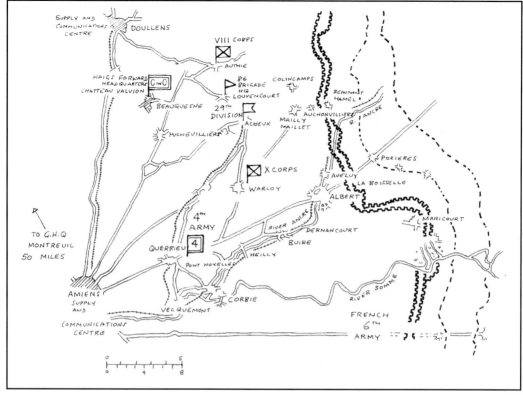

Map 4. The Fourth Army chain of command as it effected 86 Brigade.

In the spring of 1916 everyone posted to this section of the line knew about the figure of the Virgin, hanging in chains over the shattered town, her child in her arms. Some of the officers of the 16th Middlesex may have visited Albert, though they were more likely to cadge a lift into Amiens for an evening's relaxation. It is unlikely that either Alf or Lionel Renton got the chance. Noel may have travelled this far along the line on one of his foraging expeditions, but if so he did not mention it. He may also have cadged a ride into Amiens, a city that he knew well at a later stage in the war. The Roman road connected Albert to Amiens, twenty miles behind the line. Amiens is the capital of Picardy and it was this historic city, growing outwards on either side of the Somme with its seven canals, its railway sidings, its factories and repair yards, that became the main supply centre for the battle of the Somme. Before the war Picardy was a fertile and prosperous agricultural region. Industries grew up in its small towns to serve the farms. Those in, or close to, the Somme valley were typical. Albert, Corbie and Doullens each had its agricultural engineers, its local transport and its mills. In addition Albert had a bicycle factory and a railway repair yard. The area was exceptionally well served with railways, both full sized and narrow gauge. The Picardy countryside, with its chalk downs and woods above the broad valley of the river Somme, was as different from the marshy plain, mines and spoil heaps of Flanders as any soldier could imagine.

The Brigade Diary recorded the change of scene.

24 April 1916. The 16th (Public Schools) Battalion of the Middlesex Regiment, commanded by Lieutenant Colonel J Hamilton-Hall, entrained for Doullens to join 86 Brigade, 29th Infantry Division, relieving the Munsters in the front line at Beaumont-Hamel.

(From the War Diary of 86 Brigade.)

The 16th Middlesex detrained in the station yard at Doullens on the evening of 24 April 1916. Doullens was the last town of any size untouched by war before one reached the area of trenches leading to the Front line. The agricultural areas of northern France resisted change longer than anywhere comparable in southern England. Maybe it was the size of the country, or the German occupation of 1940, or maybe it was sheer conservatism, but Doullens changed very little for sixty years after the battle of the Somme. Today it is a busy centre for light industry, circled by wide roads and concrete housing estates; in its ugly conformity it resembles any small town in any part of Europe. Twenty-five years ago Doullens had been spoilt neither by the violence of war nor by the official vandalism of peace. It was easy to see it as the Middlesex men saw it as they climbed out of the cattle trucks, collected their kit and formed up in the station yard, ready to move off. I saw it very much as it was in 1916, a tiny market town in a wooded valley, where a mill-race flowed through an old flour mill. A sleepy place where

Middlesex marching behind the line.

carts were still pulled by dray-horses and the smell of dung was stronger than the petrol fumes. Nothing much had happened to, or in, Doullens since its moment of glory, when, for a few days, the town was the centre of the world stage. In the spring of 1918, the Germans made their last desperate gambler's throw, bursting through the British line, throwing every counter they had onto the board, aiming for the Channel ports. At that moment this small town became the temporary headquarters of the Allied forces in France and Belgium under the overall command of Marshal Foch. Foch's HQ looks, as it always did viewed from the valley, a grandiose château on a ridge, partly screened by mature trees that never suffered shell fire, its shuttered windows glowering down on the town.

The Battalion marched along this road, up the steep hill and onto the downs. From here there is a choice of two routes to Mailly Maillet, both easy going. The northern road goes by Courcelles and Colincamps; the southern via Engelbemer and over the downs. The marching column of 16PSB could use neither route. An infantry battalion on the move, with its mounted officers, horse-drawn carts, mule-drawn ammunition limbers and field kitchens, and, not least for 16PSB, its pipe band, is an impressive sight. It is also not an easy spectacle to conceal. Moving a battalion is neither silent nor simple, even in time of peace. These downs were ranged by the German artillery spotters. The least sign of a movement of a large number of troops, or a supply column, and the spotters could call down a line of shells on the road. Colonel Hall took the wise course, the hidden route along steep valleys and wooded roads through Bertrancourt.

'Bags of swank, now lads, bags of swank,' the RSM bellowed as the marching column

Mailly Maillet showing the ruined church in the foreground.

A battalion on the move with the supply and equipment wagons in the rear.

left Mailly wood behind and followed the long line of the stone wall that masks Mailly château. The 16th Middlesex entered Mailly Maillet shortly after midnight, drums beating and pipers playing. The ranks checked their dressing, straightened their backs and marched with heads held high. Partly this was pride and partly the knowledge that there was a hot meal awaiting them. Early on the march, as they reached the crest of the hill above Doullens, the mules trotted past them towing the field cookers, the cooks riding on the limbers. Noel Peters was glad of a brief rest, jolting and precarious though it was, with the knowledge ever present that the mules might turn temperamental. Once the cooks reached their destination Noel was too busy chopping vegetables, apportioning quantities of rations, coaxing flames from the charcoal packed inside the field cookers, and later, too exhausted to notice details of the Battalion's arrival.

Others remembered the arrival in a more romantic light, Alf Damon and Lionel Renton amongst them. Indeed the moment stayed in their memories; one of those moments frozen in time. It was the last time that the Public Schools Battalion, as they knew it, paraded together. As the column swung into Mailly the band changed to the marching tune of the Middlesex Regiment. In that little shell-pocked town the Brigade Commander and his staff stood on the steps of the Hotel de Ville to take the salute as the Battalion marched past.

Though Mailly Maillet was sheltered from unfriendly view by the ridge on which the church spire of Auchonvilliers made such a prominent mark, it lay within range of the German guns. Shell-fire had smashed most of the fine old trees both in the centre of the village and the avenue beside the château wall, breaching the wall in many places. The Gothic church, with its strange, sensuous, almost Celtic carvings, was protected by wattle and straw mats. But the spire and the roof had gone, destroyed by direct hits. Several large unexploded shells lay rusting in the wreckage of the nave. Noel wondered whether they were still dangerous and why no one had bothered to remove them.

Chapter 21

OCEAN VILLAS

T HOUGH LIVING ON OPPOSITE SIDES OF THE WORLD both Alf Damon and Lionel Renton made the same negative comment about the landscape of the Somme. Each remarked that he saw nothing of the landscape until the morning of July the First and then, as Lionel observed with grim humour, there was not much time to admire the view or the beauty of the morning.

Soon after they moved into the line at Auchonvilliers Lionel Renton made use of his shaving mirror and bayonet once again to make a primitive trench periscope. He described the view at ground level admitting that he could see very little,

An unruly overgrown field with a few shell holes and the spoil heaps from some ancient trenches. Thick rank grass, brambles, here and there a bright red poppy. There was masses of wire, of course, like a rusty stain all over the field, some of it old French wire, some of it our own; rusting ration tins, there were always lots of those, one of many hazards if you were out patrolling at night. But generally it looked good. It was so much better than we were used to at La Bassée. So on arrival, no complaints. Of course we had no idea what was in store for us.

Noel Peters had a similar first impression.

When we arrived at Mailly we thought, we're all right here, this is a nice quiet sector. We went in and out of the line between Mailly and Ocean Villas (Auchonvilliers). *Eight days in and eight days out. To be honest, at that time we were better off in the line because there wasn't much going on, apart from the Hun sending over the odd shell or two. Behind the line Brigade grabbed us for fatigues, or if it wasn't Brigade it was the sappers, moving trench stores and mining gear, or it was the gunners needing a whole lot of big shells carried up to their gun pits. Of course cooking was easier out of the line, cushy really. But even up the sharp end it was a lot easier than the Brickstacks. Ocean Villas was a destroyed village when we got there. It was so close to the line that not a chimney was left standing, nor a roof tile in place. Despite that it seemed like a serene, peaceful place, at least that's how it remains in my memory. There were roses growing over the wreckage and masonry.*

Deep, well made trenches in this section of the line allowed some movement in daylight, the evacuation of wounded, for example. But most activity took place at night. 'At night the whole place came alive,' as Noel said. Relief by battalions or companies and all movement by ammunition and supply parties took place at night.

The 16th Middlesex relieved the Munster Fusiliers the night after they arrived at Mailly Maillet. The companies entered the communication trenches in the valley between the villages. From that point on soldiers saw nothing except the walls of the trench, the revetting material that kept the trench shored up and the pack and helmet of the man in front of him. These communication trenches were not mere roadways below ground, they had their own society. As the Middlesex men moved up to the line they passed many shelters, recesses and bunkers, either of the old French timbered type or new ones whose roofs were reinforced with heavy gauge corrugated iron, steel angle sections, sandbags and earth. Here lay stores of every kind, from medical to entrenching tools; every type of ammunition from the heavy spherical Stokes mortar bombs, known as 'Toffee apples' to case upon case of .303 rifle and machine-gun ammunition. Rockets and flares stood in recesses in the trench wall, ready framed. Nightfall saw the specialists hard at work. Here were signallers and telephone linesmen repairing breaks or reeling out new lines. Sappers were busy with pumps, earth-moving trolleys or mining gear.

'Most things were done at night.' Noel said:

There was tremendous activity at night. The ASC would dump sacks of food in the fields behind the line and it was up to each Quartermaster sergeant to move it forward from there. Imagine – sacks of loaves, sugar, tea, tinned vegetables, big tins of Bully beef, jam, beans.

He paused, thinking of all that food and of the carrying parties taking it forward to the QM stores and the field cookers.

Of course the stuff that the fellows really disliked was the heavy stuff, the ammunition. Shells, trench mortars, rifle ammunition or grenades, all came up at night. The things that they hated most were the gas shells. They were heavy and dangerous. Of course Jerry knew what was going on and, from time to time he'd send over a barrage of shells. The ASC muffled the horses' hooves but you could hear the wagons creaking. The little petrol tractors they had on the railway were noisy and the big tractors that pulled the heavy guns were worse. There was movement at night, constant movement. You could hear this racket for miles on a still night. At night the whole area came alive. Like ants moving. [1]

Colonel Hall with Battalion headquarters occupied a cellar in Auchonvilliers while the rifle companies moved forward to 'Second Avenue' and spread out to man the front line that was dug in either side of the valley road. The dug-outs in the line and in the village gave protection against shrapnel and indirect fire but, because of the thin brick and skimpy timbering they provided none against a direct hit.

Noel Peters returned to his vocation; food:

Cooking was easier at Mailly, of course, because it was further away from Jerry's guns and out of range of the trench mortars, flying dustbins and flying pigs, that made life in the line a misery. But even Ocean Villas wasn't too bad. The village was flattened long before we got there. There wasn't much standing, but the Munsters had dug tunnels and trenches under the ruins so it was cushy enough. Every French house had its cellar, so we cooked in cellars or dug-outs. Jerry had the range, of course, and he had a clear view of where his shells were dropping, so every so often he'd decide to knock the village about a bit more.

Viewed from Redan Ridge, or the Bergwerk, the village of Auchonvilliers stands clear

128

A fatigue party and field kitchen behind the lines on the Somme.

of the skyline, the slender spire a clear landmark. The spire, roof and upper structure of the church had gone by April 1916, but if one imagines the small village in ruins and the spire gone, its position on the ridge still remained clear to the German artillery spotters. Luckily for HQ Company the centre of the village was masked by the remains of large barns, hedges and few broken, but hardy, trees. Most of the farm buildings, cottages and one poor estaminet, had been reduced to mounds of bricks and timber. Noel reported that one or two survived, tilted at strange angles, like card houses. The timbers supporting one cottage had given way, dropping the thatch neatly over the cellar, 'like a bird's nest'. Nettles, cow-parsley and hemlock grew thickly over the broken gardens; brambles and rose thorns ran wild over cellars and trench parapets. In Auchonvilliers, Noel said, all labour, fatigues, movement, shifting of stores, or cooking took place underground, mostly in the stout brick lined cellars, called caves by the French. Some of the old French dug-outs were useable, but in most the timbers were rotten, or the walls too damp to be much use, even for storage. The Munsters dug new shelters, but the roof protection was not thick enough and they gave protection only against shrapnel balls and shell fragments.[2]

The communication trench that ran from Auchonvilliers to the 86 Brigade front-line trenches ran parallel to the Auchonvilliers to Beaumont road. It drops down a gentle slope from the ridge and crosses a flat meadow before it enters a shallow valley whose sides become progressively steeper as it approaches the ravine in which Beaumont Hamel was built, which leads down a steeper slope to the valley of the river Ancre and the railway line and Beaumont/Beaucourt station.[3] A glance at the aerial photograph shows that both village and station had gone before July the First, marked only by patches of pale rubble. The trenches show more clearly because of the chalk piles thrown up by the trench diggers. The disposition of the enemy trench lines, the communication trenches and even the forward supply dumps were known to the British General Staff at Montreuil because the RFC and the French Air Force gained command of the air well before the summer of 1916.[4] But, as both Noel Peters and Lionel Renton remarked, the infantry in the front line could see very little except at ground level, even using the box-like trench periscopes that officers and the more enterprising ORs bought in London while on leave.

Reaching the support trenches that ran at right angles to the road the fatigue party. or group of replacements, would approach the front line trench through a maze of subsidiary communication trenches. Turning northward the front line trench followed a

Aerial view of part of the Somme battlefield looking northeast up the valley of the Ancre. In the foreground are German trenches opposite the British lines in front of the village of Hamel.

cart track behind a bank, ascending gently to 'White City'. (To the French this track is known as Le Chemin Vert.)[5]

Retracing his steps to the mouth of the communication trench, and continuing along it to the front line, the newcomer crossed the flat meadow and reached the shelter of a bluff about ten feet high. This bluff, or *remblai*, changes direction forming almost a right-angle. One face parallel to the road was exposed to German machine-gun and rifle fire from the Hawthorn Redoubt, while the other face of the bluff turned and followed a sunken road that passed in front of White City and pointed in the direction of the downs and the village of Hebuterne. This track was called Le Voie des Chenes. This angle on the bluff was important as a sniper's position and observation post from which to watch the activity on the Hawthorn Redoubt.[6] The bluff was important to the Brigade battle plan because it was the start line for the advance on the infamous Sunken Road. This, the field beyond it and the *remblai* that lies close to the German position at Redan Ridge, assumed great importance during the attack. The sunken road lies 250 yards from the British front line and 200 yards from the German. This lane leaves the road along the valley bottom, climbs Redan Ridge where it rises to the level of the fields and becomes a cart track. The sunken area is broad, nearly twelve yards across. It is protected on the nearer side (that closer to the British line) by a bank rising to ten or twelve feet. On the side nearest to the German line it is barely six feet. This feature looked like a useful protection for the attackers, seen on the maps of the planners. It was, in fact, far from a safe jumping-off point. Not only was it exposed to machine guns firing from Hawthorn Redoubt, but its width and low protecting wall made it vulnerable to mortars firing from the Redan. German patrols measured the distance and their mortar officers had it ranged with great accuracy. This area was so dangerous that it could only be entered by night. Both sides patrolled it and sometimes ran into each other, which always generated a lively exchange of firing and grenade throwing. About a hundred yards closer to the German line lay another hazard; a second *remblai* of flints dropping ten feet to ground level and exposed to fire from the Redan directly in front and on higher ground. This trap could not be seen from the British line but patrols from 86 Brigade had explored, measured and mapped it. The attackers would have to check their advance, scramble and slide down the loose bank of flints, exposed to fire from the defenders who were well dug in on the opposite slope.

Some of the 16th Battalion officers knew of the strength of the position that they would attack. Both Captain Purnell, the bombing officer and Lieutenant Cleghorn patrolled and reconnoitred the valley. They did not hide the truth from their CO. The Adjutant, Captain Cochram knew and so did the RSM. Fortunately for their peace of mind neither the junior officers, NCOs nor men knew. Certainly neither Noel Peters or Alf Damon had any idea of what faced them. Lionel Renton knew no more of the hazardous ground than the others did but, he told me that he knew something was wrong when he observed the peculiar behaviour of the elderly Divisional commander, General De Lisle. The majority had no premonition of what was ahead reassured by the confidence of the Munsters, the regular army battalion that they relieved. These experienced soldiers described the sector as 'cushy enough'.

Though it might appear to be a cushy sector, the steady wastage of men continued. Three men were killed during the first four days in the line. One was killed in a road accident while two were killed by the explosion of a shell in a communication trench, fragments of which wounded several other men. The dead were Privates Heburn, Bond and Honiatt.

Despite reservations about Kitchener's volunteer army in general the regular soldiers of 29 Brigade were impressed favourably by the officers and men of the 16th Middlesex. When their ten-day stint in the line was over the Battalion pulled back beyond Mailly woods for re-training. There they cleaned themselves up, paraded and were inspected by the commander of 86 Brigade, Brigadier General W.de.L. Williams. The Brigadier took the unusual step of writing to Colonel Hall on the turn-out and keenness of his Battalion.

1. The light railway constructed right up to the support trenches were the revolutionary 'Deceauville' system. The track was pre-fabricated in sections and could be brought forward and bolted together rapidly. For towing the trucks full of ammunition or trench stores the Allies used either small petrol driven tractors or steam locomotives. Up until quite recently the latter could be found in Francophone countries in parts of West and North Africa and in South America, exported to the French colonies in the early nineteen-twenties. The author found one of these historic locomotives in Iquitos, in the Peruvian jungle, one in Tunisia and several still running in France.

2. On July the First even the crypt buried under the rubble of the church, was not sufficient protection against sustained and well-aimed shell fire. On the 1st, 2nd and 3rd July this stone vault was the dressing station and collection centre for the seriously wounded. Many wounded men died there with the nurses and orderlies when a large shell penetrated the roof and exploded inside the crypt.

3. This is the valley landscape of A P Herbert's moving and evocative poem 'Beaucourt revisited'.

4. For a clear account of the air war over the Somme see Cecil Lewis, *Sagittarius Rising*. Pub: Peter Davis 1936. Penguin Books 1966.

5. White City. This was an important position both as a redoubt and as a supply dump. White City lay to the north of the valley road dug into a ridge a short distance behind the line. The entrances to the dump are clearly shown in the well-known photograph. Both 29th and 36th Divisions claim this picture. Noel thought that it was takenbefore the battle, others that it was taken after. Both Noel Peters and Major Dick Smith recognised the Colour Sergeant in the foreground and some of the men in the photograph.

6. Since the battle this insignificant spur at the angle of the bluff has become famous because it was in this sandbagged position that Malins, the war photographer, set up his cine-camera. From this point he took the film both of the explosion of the great mine under Hawthorn Redoubt, of the attack by part of 29th Division, and the retreat by a small number of survivors of that attack, withdrawing to White City. In 1976, when I spent several days mapping and making topographical sketches of the valley and the sites of the German defences, this bluff and the track 'Le Voie des Chenes', had changed very little in the sixty years that had passed since the battle. The meadow behind still showed clear ridges and indentations of the communication and support trenches, on whose grassy remains Friesian cattle grazed peacefully. The ridges of the parapets and the depressions showed clearly the Greek key pattern. Twenty years later the field had been levelled and ploughed. No trace or marking of a trench showed. The bluff, from which Malins directed his camera, was unchanged since my first visit, in fact a tangle of rusted barbed wire on which I tore my trousers, was still lurking in the grass.

Chapter 22

LANDSCAPE WITH FIGURES

THE LANDSCAPE AND COMPOSITION OF THE SOMME and Ancre valleys and the nature of the downs above them had a direct effect on both the planning of the battle and its tragic outcome. This included not only the surface geography, the tributaries of the main river, the small streams cutting through steep-sided ravines, the rolling uplands and the dense woods; but in the composition of the land itself.

The surface of the earth was fertile loam, tended and cultivated for thousands of years before it was ploughed and pitted with high explosive, cast away into the air to drift away as dust in summer and turn to thick grey mud in winter. Below this topsoil lay a mixture of clay and flint, and below that hard, even chalk. The flints, that the farmers raked and carried, formed banks and terraces, known as *remblai*, in the local *patois* (dialect). Chalk was an ideal medium, both for trench digging and for tunnelling. Its nature was well known to the local inhabitants who had mined it and quarried it for hundreds of years. The caverns, tunnels and caves, left by these early miners, had been used as refuges since the first wave of invaders swept through this much invaded region. This vital property of chalk was well known to company and battalion commanders in the line. It was equally well known to the sappers on the General Staff, as their meticulous and well drawn geological surveys show. Time would show that the firm, hard chalk gave each side an advantage. The German military planners had the intelligence to make full use of it. The British did not.

The downland heights above the Ancre valley have a similar appearance and characteristic to the Chiltern Hills or the Berkshire Downs. They are mostly open country with smooth undulations marked here and there with sudden deceptive hollows, dingles and small cliffs. Some of these are natural, some caused by ploughing. Centuries of cultivation have produced ridges (*remblai*) or sunken tracks, walled by piles of flints. These are most noticeable between Serre and Beaumont Hamel and were to become a natural defence.

In 1914 the German advance took Cambrai and swept on through Albert to spread out along the escarpment known as the Ancre heights. The French re-captured the town almost immediately, perhaps as a matter of honour, but they failed to capture the cliffs above the little river Ancre. Outstandingly successful at using the nature of the ground to aid their defence, the Germans drew the line that would soon become their forward trenches, across the dusty road that connected the villages of Beaumont Hamel and Auchonvilliers. This country lane, where neighbours visited, where farmers exchanged produce and gossip, and where lovers strolled on summer evenings, became a zone of trenches, dense thickets and coils of barbed wire, saps and machine-gun posts. Here, in

this dead zone, nothing moved above ground, except stealthily and at night.

The German occupiers took full advantage of the captured territory. As many British officers noted in their diaries, or wrote later in memoirs, 'The Boche had a good eye for the lie of the land, usually took, or withdrew to the high-ground, and built his defences in the most advantageous position.'

Unlike the British, who had to consult their allies (and hosts) over every detail affecting the civilian population, the German General Staff subjected both the land and its population to a ruthless military logic. Nothing was allowed to interfere with military necessity. The area behind the line was cleared of civilians and reformed to provide supply, dispersal areas and training grounds. The inhabitants were conscripted for labour on defence works. Great areas of forest were felled to provide timber props for bunkers and gun pits, or to provide fields of fire for second or third line defences. The actual fighting zone stretched from the front line to the rear for five or six miles. Within it the Field Security Police maintained a culture of secrecy and draconian discipline.

'The Boche has a predilection for burrowing,' one young officer remarked. That predilection cost the British dearly. Parallel to their development of siege howitzers, firing shells of great size, the Germans developed the science of defence against such shells. The answer was reinforced concrete of sufficient thickness and, the small forts that they called *Stutzpunkten*. On the Somme front this was not necessary. Provided that the German army engineers dug deep enough, the nature of the chalk protected their soldiers against even the largest British shells.

Digging deep, German engineers burrowed into the ground on the Somme.

134

Chapter 23

THE MASTER OF RAILWAY TIMETABLES

ITH HIS PACK ON HIS BACK, gas cape folded to regulation size, ammunition pouches and enamel steel water bottle full, his shrapnel helmet on his head and his rifle slung, Lance Corporal Alf Damon set off across the rolling downs of Picardy in the direction of the village of Acheux. He put all thoughts of leave behind him and concentrated on the present. His leave seemed set in a different world and a long time ago.

In fact it was quite a long time since he left Victoria station because of a series of problems with RE Movements Control. From Le Havre he was sent to Etaples. Where he endured a frustrating and humiliating wait at the Bull Ring while Movement Control tried to discover why 16PSB were no longer at St Omer, at last they established that his unit was no longer part of the 33rd but was now in the 29th Division and he gained his travel warrants and movement orders and entrained for Amiens and thence to Querrieu. Walking across the downs he was overtaken by a horse-drawn ASC wagon which took him to the headquarters of the 29th Division at Acheux. From there he had to walk.

Alf's first sight of the downs above the Somme valley reminded him of a fairground, but a fairground on a colossal scale. The tents, the lines of tethered horses and mules, the steam traction engines and artillery tractors, the parched grass, the horse dung

View of British transport lines on the Somme.

flattened into chalk ruts, had the oddly festive atmosphere of a country fair. The air was full of white dust thrown up by vehicles, horses or marching feet. The dust covered every machine, weapon, tent and pack. It settled on the grass, on water, on food, it entered the moving parts of machines, into eyes, mouths and noses. Everywhere within the orbit of this huge army there was the same stale smell compounded of old food, refuse, petrol, cordite and excrement. With the lingering smell came clouds of flies which, like the all pervading chalk dust, clung to everything. The flies settled on rubbish, on animal dung and open latrine pits and then flew on to feed on the food in freshly opened tins, mess-tins and dixies.

Alf passed railway lines being constructed, both 'Deceauville' trench-tramways and full-scale tracks. Small steam locomotives passed towing flat-bed trucks loaded with artillery ammunition. Petrol and diesel tractors towed yet more supplies. Steam lorries dumped ballast for road construction while steam rollers rumbled backwards and forwards compressing the hard surface. This, Alf thought, bears no resemblance to the makeshift and unplanned existence of the damaged and flooded line opposite La Bassée. Alf, whose view of all organisation was sceptical, not least the army, was impressed despite himself.[1]

On his journey he passed a brigade training for an attack, exercising over white tapes that represented the enemy fortifications. He passed horses and more horses. Some

General Sir Beauvoir de Lisle addresses a battalion of his division on the eve of battle.

were tethered, some being exercised, some led to canvas troughs to be watered. Sturdy gun horses pulled 18 pounder field guns with their limbers. In the distance he saw a line of huge draft horses towing a howitzer. Crossing the ground lay many temporary water hoses leading to stand-pipes or horse troughs. Alf was surprised by the number of guns that he passed. As for the heavy artillery he had never seen guns or howitzers of this size before. To feed these monsters, as well as the medium and field guns, lay dump after dump of shell of every calibre and type. Some were being stored in bunkers but much of the ammunition was stored in the open. At one place he came on an orderly pile of heavy shells and a 'Ruston Bucyrus' steam crane to move them. He guessed that these would be fired from one of the huge 15" Naval guns. Later, when he was in hospital, it came as no surprise to Alf that one of the largest ammunition dumps had exploded.[2] For a moment his spirits sank as he remembered the muddle and the

stupidity at the Bullring and wondered how he would ever find 16PSB in this vast and chaotic landscape. But then his natural resilience and common sense re-asserted themselves. He discovered that every crossing or track junction had its forest of signs. Boldly painted boards with a variety of symbols, numbers and letters. Some pointed to camps or dumps of ammunition or supplies, others to divisions or brigades. Following the red and yellow 'Bottle of Bass' symbol Alf had little difficulty picking out the direction to Mailly Maillet.

On 5th May the 16th Middlesex paraded for inspection by the Corps Commander, Lieutenant General Sir Aylmer Hunter-Weston, a jolly and ever-optimistic Scot. The parade took place on the downs behind Mailly Maillet and it was an affair of considerable importance to the officers and considerable nuisance to the men. They were now officially welcomed into the 29th Division of VIII Corps.

General Hunter-Weston.

During one of my talks with Lionel Renton, sitting on the verandah of his pleasant house outside Guildford, he mentioned the Third Army. With some embarrassment I picked him up on this.

'Excuse me saying this. You were there, I wasn't even born then, but weren't you in Fourth Army? The line was drawn just north of you. They were Allenby's Third Army. Surely you came under Rawlinson?'

'Did we?' he replied. 'Well there you are you see? You know that because you've studied it. Buggered if we knew, or cared. We knew our battalion, that became almost like family, and we knew the fellows that were in the trenches on either side of us. So, in a vague sort of way, we knew our Brigade. We knew our division because we were proud to wear the "Bottle of Bass" shoulder sign, but when it reached the levels of Corps or Armies, well, we didn't give a damn for them.

The main impression at the time was that we had joined an all-regular division and our Brigade, the 86 Brigade, was an elite Brigade, absolutely first rate soldiers who could have trained, or stiffened the conscript divisions who came into the line in 1917. But these fine fellows were thrown away at Gallipoli and the Somme. Gallipoli left a dent in the morale of 86 Brigade. There was a rumour that we relieved the Munsters because they had a feud with the Dublin Fusiliers. After Easter the Dubs in turn hated the Lancashire Fusiliers.'3

In common with the other volunteers Alf Damon was delighted to join a regular army division.

The Divisional sign was a wide-based red triangle with a yellow border, hence the name 'The Bottle of Bass Division'. Before Gallipoli the Division was made up of regular battalions serving in India. But they'd lost a lot of men, they were cut to ribbons in Gallipoli, so there were a lot of replacements amongst both the officers and in the ranks.

The 29th Division had been an elite before it was sent to the Dardanelles, and would be again, but morale was not at its highest during the spring of 1916. General Hunter-Weston commanded the 29th in the Dardanelles campaign where he picked up a serious illness, like so many of the men under his command. By 1916 he had recovered his health and his habitual bounce and optimism. He was promoted to command VIII Corps and was delighted to include the 29th Division as part of the Corps. Nicknamed 'the jovial Hunter-Bunter' he may be the model for the General in Sassoon's bitter poem 'Plan of Attack'.4 Hunter-Weston's extrovert personality was the opposite to his fellow Scot, Sir Douglas Haig. Haig, the dour type of Lowlander, was said to have a superstitious prejudice against anyone involved in the Gallipoli disaster, as though they carried bad luck with them. This is not so surprising as one might think. Outwardly a modern, well educated and rational soldier, in fact Haig believed that his orders came from God and engaged in nightly conversations with the Almighty. The only belief that the two Scottish Generals shared was a faith that the massive attack on the Somme must succeed.

If Hunter-Weston was optimistic, the Divisional Commander was not. Major General de Lisle was described by Noel Peters as a 'nice old Gentleman'. De Lisle was promoted to succeed Hunter-Weston in Gallipoli, in command of the 29th, when his superior officer was taken ill. He was much liked by his men, both in the Dardanelles and in Picardy. Lionel Renton, a shrewd and unemotional observer who survived two world wars, described General de Lisle in tears as the Brigade paraded for the last time before the attack on the Somme. 86 Brigade was commanded by another Gallipoli veteran, Brigadier General W de L Williams.

Lionel Renton said, 'We only saw one senior officer close to the line and that was General de Lisle. He was pessimistic I remember, which made a change from all the talk of a "Walk-over".' Alf Damon remembered the same inspection of the Brigade by the Divisional Commander.

He arrived on his horse, with his staff and an escort of Lancers. We paraded on three sides of a square in a hollow on a grassy meadow behind Mailly woods. He was straight with us, I'll say that for him. He told us that it would be a hard attack, fiercely resisted, and that many of us would not return. You may find this hard to believe. I am not imagining this or gilding the lily, but this was General de Lisle, commanding the Bottle of Bass division. He wished us luck and as he did so many of us saw the tears plainly on the old gentleman's face.

The Divisional Sector, described from right to left, ran from the 36th Division's line on the Ancre valley at Hamel to a point on the ridge to the north of Auchonvilliers to Beaumont road where the 4th Division sector began. (The line that divided Rawlinson's Fourth from Allenby's Third Army came further north, at Gommecourt.)

None of these hierarchical matters were on Alf's mind as he walked across the downs, his uniform and equipment now covered in a layer of chalk dust. Reporting to Brigade HQ at Louvencourt he was told that he had been promoted to full Corporal and that he must go forward immediately to Mailly Maillet. When he reached Mailly he found the Quartermaster, comfortably settled in the village. The Quartermaster told him to move up to the line at Auchonvilliers. The old soldier gave him a word of advice. 'Watch yourself approaching Ocean Villas. They get some nasty whizz-bangs coming over.'

The Battalion was taking casualties; the usual steady haemorrhage of front line duty. In May Lance Corporal Albert Everet was killed by a shell burst together with Privates Bowskill, Denis George, and Private Johnson. All were killed by shell-burst or shrapnel, two more were seriously injured. One soldier was deranged to such a degree that the MO, 'Niffy' Knight, certified him 'Shell-shocked in action' and he was invalided home.

Shell exploding on a British trench.

He had the coveted Blighty wound, but at a terrible cost.

Alf did not need reminding of the need for caution. All thoughts of the pleasant life on leave was gone. The old trench-wisdom reasserted itself.

> *The route to Ocean Villas led through woods up to the ridge where I entered a deep communication trench. There was no such practice as following tapes to your positions or hopping over the bags, as we used to do at La Bassée. At Ocean Villas we entered the communicator and kept our heads down to evade snipers. In very dangerous spots there was usually a sign "Beware of snipers". In very wet places there were similar warnings telling the new arrival to stick to the duckboard, or warning him to turn right or left. It was all very orderly and controlled compared to the mess and chaos of Flanders.*
>
> *I recall one dark, wet night following the Company Commander along the trench and mistiming my step. He hauled me out of a sump hole wet to the chest in cold, muddy water. You got used to that sort of mishap. It was the luck of the game.*

The game was easier in moonlight but more dangerous. Men spoke of a 'sniper's moon'. Alf said that he became more cautious at night after the death of Henri Rieu. On a moonless night the patrol moving forward into No Man's Land had only the stars for illumination, or the light of flares sinking gently to earth. Sentries could see little from the front line except the parapet and a tangle of wire. Sentries were ordered to put their heads above the parapet every so often and young officers stood on the fire-step to encourage their men. Alf remarked that this frequently had the reverse effect when the foolhardy young man took a bullet in the head.

When wiring parties went out the sentry could see a huddle of dark shapes and hear the clink of spades and picks. Unfortunately the enemy could hear this noise too, often with fatal results. Alf described the process of re-wiring a section of the trench. In the early days the wiring party used wooden posts and large wooden mallets (usually described as a 'beetle' or a 'maul'); the key man of the group was the wirer who wore thick leather gloves to twist the wire round the post and tighten it while the others drove in more posts. By 1916 a sapper had invented the screw picket, a steel stake shaped like a corkscrew with a round eye at the top. Two men put a stake through the eyehole and 'waltzed round and round it', as Alf put it, screwing the stake in while stepping over the wire. The wirer tightened the wire six inches above the ground, then a foot, then eighteen inches, and so on.

Alf remarked on the amount and variety of nocturnal activities. Night fatigues were more frequent on the Somme front than in Flanders. By night the front and support trenches were as busy as the rear areas were by day. Unlike the French, who used African or Vietnamese forced labour, the British did not establish a civilian labour corps until late in the war. Sappers and labour battalions dug new jumping-off trenches, extended saps, made a second set of communication trenches to allow a two-way flow when the day came, built or enlarged dug-outs. Safe shelters, hollowed out into the chalk, housed regimental aid posts, ammunition stores, signallers, or battalion or brigade staff. These secret activities could not be kept secret and did not go unnoticed by the defenders. Any noise in No Man's Land attracted the attention of the German sentries. If the flares showed any activity then the defenders would lay down a barrage of mortar shells or traverse the ground with machine-gun fire.

Before first light the working parties slipped back through gaps opened in their own wire, glad to be under cover and looking forward to hot tea and, if they were lucky, a little rum and a brief rest. Platoons in the firing line stood to arms. Along that extended battle line, from the Belgian coast through Flanders to the Ypres salient, through Artois, Picardy and Champagne, through the Argonne to the bloody salient at Verdun, across the Vosges to the Swiss border, men of many corps, armies and nations stood-to as the first dawn light sharpened the blurred edges of stakes, wire, sandbags and all the myriad junk and wreckage of No Man's Land.

Alf, like many infantrymen on both sides of the wire, commented on the less than glamorous hazards between the lines: the broken fragments of wire that snagged the trousers and puttees of the men on wiring fatigues. They spoke of the sleek rats that thrived in this uninhabited area, or the shock and disgust when one's boot slid over a half-decomposed corpse.

The distance between the lines at Auchonvilliers had its advantages; the range was too great to be bothered by either hand grenades or rifle grenades. Sniping was still a danger but less deadly than at the Brickstacks. Unlike the former industrial area around the La Bassée canal, the lines in rural Picardy were far apart and the newcomers saw little sign of the enemy except a brief glimpse of grey uniform in the distance. Even at this distance putting one's head over the parapet was unwise so the only glimpse of the enemy line was through a trench periscope, or Alf's trick of attaching his shaving mirror to his bayonet. To the right the sentry could make out a greenish grey patch of overgrown and broken ground, with the dark red shading of distant wire as the slope turned away. To the left only the earth and chalk banks of the parapets showed, rising to Redan Ridge.

Because of his proximity the enemy was a known figure at La Bassée and the survivors spoke of him in familiar, almost affectionate terms. Alf spoke of the enemy as the Boche, Hun, Jerry or the Alleyman. But the enemy was remote on the Somme sector and several accounts describe him as a more sinister figure. Before the artillery barrage began, that preceded the attack, on still nights the Middlesex sentries might hear German spoken, or even the sound of singing from the German dug outs. Patrols reported singing even after the defenders had been subjected to bombardments of unprecedented severity for many hours. As Alf said, 'Mr Fritz was fond of singing, and very good he was too.'

If the greater width of No Man's Land had its advantages it also contained two major disadvantages, first, and most obviously: the attackers had to cross a considerable distance before they reached the enemy's wire; second: the German artillery could safely bombard the area around Auchonvilliers without any danger of shells falling short and hitting their own line. The greatest pest, all the survivors agreed, was the trench mortar. The Germans developed a number of these early in 1914, they ranged in size from the 76mm trench mortars to the *minenwerfers* of 250mm calibre. Until the British introduced the Stokes mortar they had nothing to match their opponents. Alf referred to the enemy mortar bombs as 'Flying pigs', 'Rum jars' 'Flying torpedoes', while the Stokes mortars were re-named 'Toffee-apples' or 'Plum puddings'.

'Jerry was well equipped with mortars and howitzers, ranging from the small kind, dug in behind Beaumont Hamel village to the giant Krupp guns,' Lionel Renton said. Alf Damon was impressed by their artillery. 'They had plenty of Five-nines, we used to call the shells whizz-bangs. All you could hear was just a Shh-sst before the explosion. The gun fired at a low angle so that was all the warning you got. A howitzer was a different matter, at the height of its trajectory the shell would turn over, wobbling in the air. If you were lucky you could hear the sound of it falling and get out of the way. Jerry had a 210 millimetre gun that threw a large shell. We called them Jack Johnsons, after the black American boxer, because of the tall black plume of smoke from its explosion.'[4]

Alf and Noel remembered the early summer of 1916 as an easy period and, despite the shelling, they spoke of Auchonvilliers as a 'quiet sector'. Noel called it 'Cushy enough'.

1. *Materialalienschaft.*
After the Battle of the Somme the German General Staff referred to the Great War as 'Materialalienschaft', or war by machinery. From the mid summer of 1916 onwards many front line soldiers wrote of the war as a killing machine that was out of human control. References in letters and diaries to the 'Slaughterhouse', the 'Abattoir' or the 'Meat-grinder' become common from the beginning of 1917.

2. Andruicq. A lucky bomb, dropped by a German pilot, scored a direct hit on the ammunition dump at Andruicq. 9,000 tons of HE shells exploded. Naturally this news was not reported and the civilian public knew nothing about it. An explosion that could not be hushed up was the massive explosion at the Silvertown ammunition factory in the East End of London.

3. Gallipoli.
On April the 25th 1915 the 29th Division was the main striking force landing on the beaches at and around Cape Helles. 86 Brigade, then commanded by Brigadier Hare, attacked beaches at Sedd-el-Barr. The Lancashire Fusiliers took appalling losses on 'W' Beach. The Munsters, the Royal Hampshires and the Dublin Fusiliers all lost heavily, under Turkish machine-gun fire, during the disastrous landing from the sally ports cut in the sides of the steamer '*River Clyde*'. Towards the end of the Dardanelles campaign the GOC of 29th Division, Sir Aylmer Hunter-Weston, became exhausted, worn out by overwork and lack of sleep. Seriously ill with dysentery 'Hunter-Bunter' was sent back to England and General de Lisle took over his command. Many of the officers serving with the 29th Division, who had gained a great deal of hard-won experience at fighting on the Gallipoli peninsula, believed that Haig was prejudiced against Hunter-Weston and not only disliked de Lisle, but everyone who had served in the Dardanelles, for reasons that were close to superstitious; as though the 29th were 'bad luck'. Through the first days of the Somme battle Haig persistently assumed the worst about the men under Hunter-Weston's command. Haig's remark on the night of the First of July, the '8th Corps appears never to have left their trenches' is incomprehensible.

4. Trench Mortars.
Early in the war British mortars were so ineffectual and so notorious for betraying their position that many company commanders refused to allow them to be fired from their trench area. Once the efficient and deadly 'Stokes' mortar became operational in 1915, the British had an answer to the *minenwerfer*, and infantry companies had an effective tool for reducing the enemy trench parapets. The 'Stokes' mortar continued to be used up to the start of the Second World War. Its use by both sides in Spain 1936-39 is one example.

Chapter 24

LE GRAND TROU

Everyone will be entrenched in the next war: the spade will be as indispensable to the soldier as his rifle.

Ernst Bloch. Polish banker and economist writing in 1897.

S IR DOUGLAS HAIG LAID DOWN AN ORDER that fighting troops should not be exhausted either by labouring or by heavy fatigue duties. Lionel Renton remembered this as an order honoured more in the breach than the observance. Noel Peters and Alf Damon spoke of the period before the battle of one of constant carrying fatigues. They spent a lot of their time, when the Battalion was out of the line, either carrying ammunition, mostly artillery shells, or labouring for the sappers and miners who were digging a shaft under the German strongpoint on Hawthorn Ridge. This fatigue was described to me partly by Alf Damon and partly by John Wilson who wrote:

> *The 16th Middlesex were well acquainted with Beaumont Hamel, if only from a distance. We manned the trenches opposite well before July the First. When we were relieved by either the Lancashire or Dublin Fusiliers, we were often employed by something called 'chalk fatigue'. This meant carrying sandbags full of chalk out of, and away from,*

Before the battle. Wiring party preparing to go out on a night wiring detail.

the entrance to the mine-shaft. Royal Engineers were tunnelling a shaft through the chalk to a position where they could place a mine under Hawthorn Ridge.[1]

The carrying party joined the miners at one of the mouths of the shafts that were hollowed out of the sides of the support trenches. These shafts led down steps to a gallery from which the miners had hollowed out chambers used as stores or sleeping quarters. No one spoke when on chalk fatigue and boots were muffled by sacks. The only light came from candles set into niches in the walls of the tunnel. It was hot and there was very little oxygen. What air there was smelt earthy, damp and unhealthy. Before they entered the tunnels for the first time the Sapper officer in charge warned them of the dangers underground and explained why there must be no talking or noise. The Germans also dug tunnels in the chalk. They had listening devices and were skilled at countermining. Danger came from many directions, not only from counter-mining and lack of oxygen but from mine-poisoning. As the fatigue party made their muffled way along the tunnel they passed smaller tunnels that led off to left or right. Here sappers sat in recesses in the walls, headphones on their ears, listening to geo-phones for the slightest sound of enemy movement within the chalk. The danger of detection by geo-phone was so great that no one moved beyond the collection point but the miners working barefoot. Here, at the extreme end of the tunnel, they cut into the chalk with bayonets and entrenching tools, laying the chalk spoil in ammunition boxes which other miners carried silently to the collection point.

Deep within the main shaft the carrying parties picked up their loads of sandbags filled with chalk and carried them to the surface and a welcome lungful of clean air. At this point another carrying party took the sandbags to the woods or to quarries to disguise the tons of white powder. The final load for the carriers was box after box of

The mine tunnel. Least favourite of the fatigues allotted to 86 Brigade before the attack.

ammonal, carried down to the gallery from which point the miners carried them up to the chamber under the German position, Hawthorn Redoubt.

There were three other tunnels dug from shafts in the 29th Divisional area. Two of these were 'Russian saps', tunnels that were dug out at sufficient depth to remain undamaged by either German or British shells. Each of these rose, close to the German line. A small charge would blow the exit hole at the moment of attack. The third tunnel ran close under the surface and had a concealed exit door in No Man's Land, hidden in the long grass.

The second fatigue in order of unpopularity, was carrying gas cylinders. Each one of these had to be carried by two men up to the bunker excavated to receive them. The cylinders were heavy and not designed for carrying around the bends in communication trenches. Carrying these there was always the danger of striking the valve at the cylinder neck against the wall of the trench, or a shell fragment sheering it from the cylinder. In either case the gas, escaping in great volume, would be fatal for the two porters.[2] Next in order of dislike came artillery ammunition. As 'Z' Day approached more and more guns, of every shape and calibre, were brought forward to their gun pits. Each of these guns and howitzers had its reserve stock of shells that had to be replenished.

By early June the newly arrived Battalion knew the back area around Mailly Maillet as well as they knew Bethune, or better. The weather was warmer and the countryside unspoilt. There was general agreement that Picardy was nicer than Flanders, and the girls (on the rare occasion that they saw them) much prettier. When the Battalion was in support Alf Damon and Arthur Kent walked the five miles to the villages close to Divisional HQ where the landscape was peaceful and undisturbed.

'I got to know this area well, thanks to a bit of luck,' Alf said. 'I put my name down for a course and my number came up, and I suppose training as an engineering apprentice before the war helped a bit. The course trained us in the art of firing the Lewis gun. How to dismantle it, clean it, and, even more important, find any faults and rectify them, all with eyes blindfolded. The Lewis gun was a well designed weapon and the first batch were well engineered. But as the war went on and demand for these guns increased the machining of the moving parts became less accurate. All such automatic weapons had their faults and depended on meticulous accuracy of manufacture. Lives depended on the speed with which the Lewis gunner could remedy the fault and bring the gun back into action. The course took place in Acheux and I grew to like the villages around there and made friends with some of the local families. Later, after the course was finished, Arthur and I used to walk over to Bus-les-Artois or Longueval for a meal. It was so good to get away from the army routine, even if only for an hour or so. We made the journey as often as we could afford. Omelette and chips was our usual fare, cooked by Madame Fourcroy. Sometimes she would give us a piece of fruit tart or some cheese without adding to the bill.[3] If we were in luck we might have a cup of coffee after our meal, or a glass of wine. I didn't drink spirits in those days, but we used to buy rum or eau de vie, a local spirit that the

farmers distilled. This was forbidden to all Tommies but we could buy it from Madame because she knew that neither Arthur nor I drank and so wouldn't get rowdy and give the game away. We used to take the spirit back to the lads in the platoon; as a present if we felt generous. Other times, if we were short of cash, we'd sell it at a profit. I came from a pious family who were all teetotal. I neither drank nor smoked. Naturally, I did not blaspheme or use obscene language. I will explain the significance of this later.

A few weeks before the battle, General Haig entertained King George the Fifth at his forward base, 4th Army HQ at Querrieu. The cavalcade toured the divisions, both Royal and General Staff mounted on splendid horses, with Haig's escort of Lancers polished to perfection. They inspected the 29th Division but I did not see this splendid exhibition. I was down in the usual place – the hole in the ground – not my favourite abode. His Majesty must have seemed a bird of ill-omen to our French friends, because all the civilians living in the villages behind the lines were ordered to move out. The Foucroy family had to abandon their farm. Madame Foucroy made no complaint simply blaming it on "La salle guerre". Unfortunately others blamed 'les Salles Anglais'. Some used language of much worse nature, which showed just how low their ally had sunk in their esteem. What hurt them most was having to give up their cellars. This was worst for the shopkeepers and farmers who had built up a collection of fine wines, Calvados, rum and eau de vie over many years. In the month before Haig's big push one could buy a bottle of Champagne, or a very good table wine for a franc, or less. The Provost and the Military Police assured the local residents that their property would be respected, but the French had seen armies through Picardy in 1870 and 1914 and they knew better.

Noel Peters confirmed Alf's account of the forced migration of the farming families and villagers.

Soon after his majesty came to inspect us the army moved the civvies back from the country immediately behind the line. It was a shame to see them go. Most of them had relatives nearer Amiens, so I suppose they were alright. It was not like 1918 when they had to drop everything and run – just like we did. This was all quite orderly and well organised, but they didn't like it. Who can blame them? Now it was not like La Bassee any more, with civvies living right up close to the line, so we could barter eggs and some decent grub for tinned food or sugar. Luckily for us cooks there were other farmers, further back, who still carried on a brisk trade. We had to travel further and pay more, because we were in competition with others more favourably placed, like gunners and ASC lads. We used to trade a bit with the Wagonners too.

Back behind the Divisional HQ the farmers carried on their business and farmed their land. I got on alright with the farmers and their wives. Maybe they could see that I was only a lad. I picked up enough of the language to get by and barter. Once the civvies were moved back, out of artillery range, we were at our wit's end what to give the lads that would vary the menu. So we swapped tins of Bully or Maconachies stew for eggs, fresh vegetables, olive oil, onions, a drop of wine, sometimes fresh meat, if we were lucky. It gave the boys some fresh grub. If one of us could get a lift with a GS wagon there were plenty

146

of farmers selling food in the back areas, towns like Amiens or Doullens. I've thought since that Jerry must have had his agents in the towns behind our lines. That didn't occur to me at the time, of course, but some of the officers and senior NCOs spoke rather too freely. No doubt Jerry knew as much as we did, maybe more because fellows in the line didn't know much of what was going on. You talked to the civvies or the base-wallahs to find out the latest rumour. I liked the French. I learnt a lot about cooking from some of those farmers and their wives. I was an eager pupil I suppose. Some fellows said they didn't like the French, but all I can say is that they were alright with me. Some of the farmers' wives would say that us boys were too young to fight in the war. "Oh les pauvres garcons!" they'd say, or, "La Guerre est triste. La salle guerre". Or "Malheur, malheur, les pauvre soldats". It made you feel good to know that they cared, but it didn't do you no good in the long run. All that "Malheur, malheur" just made you sorry for yourself and that doesn't do anybody any good. We had a job to do and we took it seriously, making sure that the lads had some decent grub.

Alf Damon.

Shortly before the battle we were taken off mining fatigues and sent to Mailly woods to cut withies to make hurdles and trench ladders. We took turns on this fatigue, spending some time in the woods and some time in the line. I had charge of a gang of lads. Sometimes a subaltern came along too, not because he was needed, just because it was a pleasant way to escape worse duties. We took a sandwich lunch and filled our bottles with watered lime juice. We had the odd shower of rain, but most of the time the weather was warm and the

NCOs and men of 16 MX at the entrance to White City Dump. This photo is labelled as taken after the attack of July 1st. (Noel Peters refuted that. He recognised several of the NCOs in the picture. He named some of them and the men who were killed on July 1st. Noel claimed that the picture was taken in late June.)

work pleasant. This was more like a picnic than serious army duty. It was a relaxed time that we all enjoyed. Then, after nightfall, we took the hurdles and ladders up to the line to be stored ready for the big push.

Whether it was the spies in Amiens, that Noel mentioned, or simple observation, the preparations for the attack had not escaped the Germans' attention. The Wurtemburgers defending Beaumont Hamel hoisted placards on their wire, carefully lettered and in English: 'WELCOME TO THE 29th DIVISION' and 'COME ON TOMMY WE ARE WAITING FOR YOU'.

When the British guns opened a breach in the wire the Wurtemburgers hung red cloths either side of the opening with a large arrow. 'THIS WAY TOMMY.'

'After General de Lisle inspected us, and made an emotional speech, some of the lads called the 16th "The Suicide Mob", Lionel Renton said. *'But of course they meant it as a joke. I suppose one or two faint-hearts were troubled by his words, but if they did they didn't admit to it. I never met anyone who showed any lack of confidence.'*

Both Noel Peters and Alf Damon confirmed this view:

We were told that it would be a walk-over and we believed it. We weren't silly or ignorant of Jerry and his fighting capabilities, but we saw the artillery preparations, and then, we heard the guns, like thunder, a continuous drumming noise. Nothing can withstand that, we thought. Our officers told us that there won't be a mouse left standing after the guns stop. It will be a walk-over to occupy and hold the Boche trenches. Well, our officers were wrong and we were wrong, and old General de Lisle was right. He should not have said what he did, but he was right. Maybe it was lucky for us that we didn't know how right he was.

---

1. The men doing this skilled and dangerous work were the Yorkshire and Northumberland miners of 252 Tunnelling Company Royal Engineers. Both John Wilson and Alf Damon described this arduous and unpopular fatigue. Though the former made his home after the war in West Yorkshire and the latter in Australia, their accounts of the preliminaries to the battle match up in every detail.

John Wilson joined the 24th Holding Battalion at Woldingham a year after Alf joined the 16th. John Wilson was put on the first draft of replacements sent out to the 16th in France. He joined the Battalion early in 1916 when it was attached to GHQ at St Omer.

2. On July the First the wind was not in the Allies' favour, so the order was not given to release the poison gas.

3. Alf Damon wrote: 'I often thought of the Foucroy family. Madame Foucroy was still attractive and she had two pretty teen-age daughters. They were in my thoughts when the Boche broke through our lines in the spring of 1918. I worried about what happened to three women on their own. I am glad to say that the family survived unhurt. Monsieur Foucroy came back from the Champagne front. After the war I wrote to Armandine, the oldest of the two sisters, to ask if I could purchase two finely sewn, very graceful, little aprons, such as she and her sister wore (are they still fashionable?). One was white silk lace, the other was green silk lace. One for my mother and one for my sister. The aprons arrived safely and were much appreciated.'

Chapter 25

NOW THRIVE THE ARMOURERS

D ARK SMOKE AND WHITE CHALK DUST rose over the German lines. Where there had been a village the haze turned pink with brick dust. The village of Beaumont Hamel was hidden in the ravine, but its position could be estimated by the rising dust from the buildings reduced to powder by the bombardment. Noel Peters said:

The guns opened up a week before the attack. The weather was bad. The bombardment started in the rain. The noise bounced back off the low cloud. Soon there was a tremendous thunder of a thousand guns all firing together. First the eighteen pounders started, then the six-inch and eight-inch howitzers. They didn't stop, day or night. The guns kept on until the sound grew like some great machine, like a great wheel turning round and round. They said that people could hear the sound of the guns back in England. We could see the dust and smoke rising into the sky behind the ridge like a great cloud. We thought nothing could live through that. We thought we could simply walk over and take the Jerry line.

Noel continued,

There was a huge, long-barrelled gun in the woods, near our camp at Mailly. It was one of the sights that the lads went to watch. I don't know the exact size of the shell; somewhere around twelve or fifteen inch I should think. It had a light railway track to bring up the shells. There was a small crane with an arm and a block and tackle to lift the shells to the breech. The noise was terrible. The gunner would shout "Ready to fire". We'd clap our hands over our ears, but even then the sound when she fired was enough to deafen you. All the tree-branches would open up – like that – when she fired. The bombardment was

Large calibre British gun.

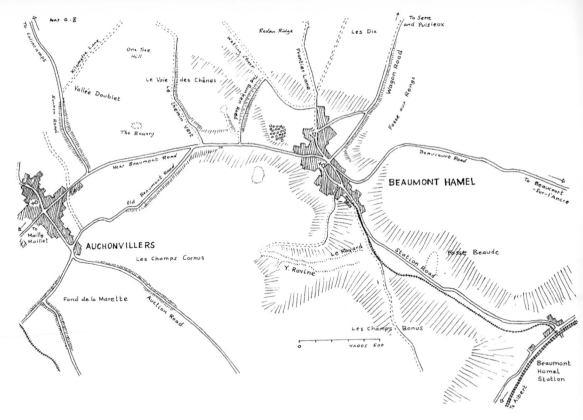

Map 5. The Auchonvilliers to Beaumont road (The Valley road) before the war.

the most fearsome thing I'd ever seen or heard. Some of the gunners went deaf even before the war was over. At night we went out to a field beside the tents. We couldn't see the Jerry line, of course, but we could see the glow along the horizon and reflected off the clouds. It flashed along the entire front, like sheet lightning. You never heard a gun, just a continuous roaring sound, like a heavy sea breaking.

The officers had a special dinner to celebrate the start of the battle. I wasn't a Brigade cook, but I helped them to prepare the meal. That would be the night of 24 June. The guns started that morning, as we began to prepare the meal, and they went on day and night up until the attack on the First of July.

Alf Damon said that the first orders for the attack were issued about that time and they were told that the bombardment would continue for four days. Soldiers that survived the battle remarked on the quality as well as the volume of the bombardment. Several said that the bombardment left an indelible impression. They fumbled for words.

Like an orchestra. An endless mass of sound without individual sounds; all part of a great rolling mass of sound. At first we were triumphant – the old Alleyman's catching it now, there won't be much fight in him after this lot. But then, after several days, one began to pray that it would stop, this terrible drumming, thundering roar. God knows what it did to those fellows at the receiving end.

'I don't fancy Jerry's chances'. We almost felt sorry for the bleeders. We had no doubts we'd beat 'em this time. Once we'd punched a big hole through his line then Jerry would throw in the towel. That's what we thought. Now we know different, of course.[1]

Both the British and French High Commands had learnt lessons from 1915: the need for guns and more guns. The number of guns, the size and duration of the bombardment, sounded impressive, but many gunners realised, at the time, that they did not have the right tools to do the job. Most of the guns were of small calibre and many of the larger ones were old and worn out. At the planning stage Rawlinson (GOC 4th Army) was promised more than enough heavy guns for the task ahead, but that promise was never met. Heavy guns, and particularly heavy howitzers, were in short supply.[2]

'Being hindwise is a foolish kind of wisdom,' Alf Damon said. *'We know today that the whole thing was a disaster and that the General Staff had not a clue about the strength of the enemy defences. We know that now – with hindsight. We didn't know it then. I suppose one or two bright fellows knew something was amiss, but that didn't do them any good, did it? They got shot up like everyone else. So I don't pretend I had any premonition or fore-knowledge superior to anyone else. But, looking back, I can see that there were a few signs, had we the wit to see them. There were rumours of some of the big guns wearing out, and shortages of shells. Some bright spark even spotted that the majority of our guns were throwing quite small shells – the mass of 18 Pounders for example.*

We were told that it would be a walk-over, and we believed it. We were told that Jerry's morale was shattered by the ferocity of the bombardment – and we believed that too. We should have known better. The Hun was a tough fighter. I'll tell you something that illustrates my point.

Shortly before July the First we were issued with mirrors, about five by three inches, which we could clip onto our bayonets. They were less obvious than the usual type of box-periscope. We could get some idea of what the shelling was doing to the Boche forward trenches, not that anyone could see much because there was some ground that was a little higher than our position. I saw very little. Almost as soon as I raised my mirror above the trench, glass spattered everywhere. Jerry had some talented snipers at Beaumont Hamel and this one shot out several of our new trench mirrors. An officer of another battalion was passing with his runner. "Let's see how good he is with a tin hat," he said and hooked mine up with his walking stick. The sniper responded to this challenge immediately and my tin hat spun to the trench floor with a large dent in it. The officer took my bent tin hat and gave me his in exchange. I often wondered what tale of daring-do he told. And in what place of honour my hat ended its days? But you get my point? If that sniper's morale was damaged then it didn't impair his aim.'

German snipers, machine-gunners and light mortar crews were active during lulls in the bombardment. Officers and men of 86 Brigade commented on the speed with which they returned to their front line positions once the British barrage lifted. It was not the German practice to pack their front-line trenches in the way that the British did. The Germans minimised casualties by manning the line sparsely, with mobile reserves ready to reinforce the line at the moment of attack. This depended on thorough training and discipline, as well as deep communication trenches and tunnels. German prisoners, captured at Beaumont Hamel by raiding parties sent out by 86 Brigade, showed by their regimental titles and broad Schwabian accents, that the defenders holding this section of the line were Wurtemburgers of the 119th Landwehr Regiment (Princess Olga of Wurtemburg's Own). A piece of body-armour picked up during a raid had a red Maltese cross painted on it; the Wurtemburg emblem. Landwehr meant reservists. These were not young kids but experienced, seasoned fighting men. If any regiment could keep up its morale and will to resist it would be the defenders of Beaumont Hamel.

1. Sergeant Quinnell MM. Royal Fusiliers. Conversation at the Royal Chelsea Hospital. 1975. Albert Mills. Royal Fusiliers. Conversation Putney 1975.

2. See Appendix One, at end of book. The diary and sketch book of Major Ynr Probert.

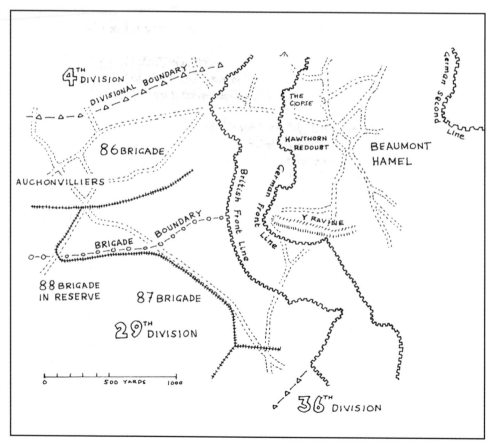

Map 6. British and German front lines at Beaumont Hamel showing Divisional and Brigade areas.

Chapter 26

OVER THE BAGS

'VIII Corps have sent out no patrols.'
Sir Douglas Haig

ALF DAMON DESCRIBED PATROLS earlier that summer, designed to seize prisoners or harass the enemy. This was not the aim of one of the last patrols before the big push. On the night of the 27th/28th June Lieutenant Cleghorn led a raiding party from the 16th Middlesex along the shallow valley to the left of the Auchonvilliers–Beaumont road. The men's faces were darkened, grenades and weapons taped and muffled to prevent rattling. The jumping off point, in the centre of 86 Brigade front, was manned by Lancashire Fusiliers. The Middlesex patrol entered the communication trench at Auchonvilliers. At one of the support trenches a shielded torch blinked to guide them. The worst hazard, on a patrol, was noise. But on this night noise was not one of Cleghorn's worries. The guns sited behind Mailly had temporarily lifted their sights to bombard the village and the tunnel entrances cut into the cliffs in the ravine. The noise of shells exploding on the enemy rear positions masked all lesser sounds. A small group of Lancashire Fusiliers appeared above ground, against the starry sky. They had cut and rolled back their own wire and laid white tapes. It was their job to guide the patrol back to their own trench.[1]

Cleghorn's mission that night, was to discover the condition of the wire facing 86 Brigade line and report on how much damage the shelling had done to the German front line trenches. The small group climbed out of the Lancashire trench on short ladders and crept along the valley avoiding overgrown shell craters, broken earth and trench debris. From time to time a whizz-bang crossed the British barrage or the bright spark of a *minenwerfer* fuse described a slow trajectory. A magnesium flare wavered in the sky descending to earth on its miniature parachute. The patrol froze, caught by the sudden bright light. For one member to move or panic would betray the whole group. Passing the start of the sunken road, and leaving the *remblai* to their left, the patrol reached a point where the ground rises towards the German line around Redan Redoubt, the trenches stepped, one behind the other. Despite the evidence of fresh craters, still reeking of the fumes of high explosive, the wire remained uncut. It was not even damaged. Cleghorn wriggled along, parallel to the German line, to try to find a gap. He found none. Time was short. Leaving most of his patrol in No Man's Land, Cleghorn took two men with him and they cut and crawled their way through the wire entanglement to drop into the Wurtemburgers' front line trench. The trench was deserted, marked by shell fire, but not seriously damaged. The trench had that foreign smell, a mixture of damp woollen cloth, leather, pickled cabbage, garlic sausage and a scented soap sent by German charities to front-line soldiers. (Alf described it later on in the war, when his unit reached the Hindenburg line.)

Cleghorn had the additional task of bringing back a prisoner, if one could be found, but there was not one to be seen. By this time they were accustomed to the guns. Maybe this made them careless because a sentry spotted them. A stick grenade splashed into a mud-filled hole nearby and exploded. It was followed by the flashes of unheard explosions on either side. Crawling back under the wire was hazardous but they regained the rest of the party without a casualty. They sensed, rather than heard, the impact of the bullets hitting the earth around them. On the return journey two men were wounded by machine-gun bullets. Lacking a prisoner, but with useful information, they set off for their own line, dodging from hole to hole, dragging the two wounded men with them. After what seemed like a lifetime they reached the tapes and the hole in their own wire. From the Lancashire trench hands reached up, eyes shone in the bright light of the flares. As Cleghorn's patrol slid and stumbled into the trench the Wurtemburgers opened up with machine guns and trench mortars along the whole of the 86 Brigade front. The cost was two men wounded badly enough to be sent back to the dressing station and one man, a young Irishman, with a wound in his arm.

Lieutenant Cleghorn reported first to his CO Colonel Hall and then to Brigade HQ. The essence of his report was this: The wire was twisted and knocked about but not damaged enough to reduce its effectiveness as a barrier. The trenches too were knocked about, but could be repaired or even used as they were by determined defenders. The bullets and grenades lavished on the patrol showed that the defenders were far from cowed by the bombardment. This was not the response of defeated or shell-shocked men. The Wurtemburgers' morale was not broken, nor even dented.

Cleghorn's was not the only patrol out that night. Small groups set off along VIII Corps' front, testing the German defences from the Kentish Caves, in the Ancre valley, to the bald slope approaching Serre. They all reported the same condition. In the early hours of the morning of the 28th Colonel Hall was unaware of Haig's decision to postpone the attack. One wonders what the CO of 16th Middlesex made of this report from Cleghorn, who he knew to be a reliable and level headed officer. Hall confided in no one, nor did he keep a record of his thoughts either before, during or immediately after the attack.

Many officers commanding battalions and companies must have known the true state of the German defences that night, and had a clear idea of what their men would face when they attempted to cross, *en masse*, the open ground to the wire. Few believed the 'walk-over' assurances of their superiors, and yet very few recorded their fears. Battalion commanders were seasoned, regular soldiers, many with experience of active service in India or South Africa. They followed the Sandhurst code 'Never complain never explain'. They knew, all too well, the effect on the career of an officer if the General Staff believed him to be 'Windy' or 'Cold-footed'. Battalion COs decided not to pass on this adverse information, or if they did, it was ignored and the issuer of the bad news censured.[2] Despite a sense amongst the officers that all was not as it should be the orders for the attack were issued to company and platoon officers unchanged. Orders had to be learnt by heart and then burnt. For the first time the officers of 16th Middlesex learnt that only 23 officers would go into action.[3]

Alf Damon said that his platoon were not only ordered to leave the wounded and not to stop to tend them, but were told that the Military Police had orders to shoot on the spot anyone who turned back, for any reason. The orders concerning the battle police and the wounded revealed the lack of confidence that the regular officers on the staff had in the volunteer soldiers, and it caused great offence. This was the first moment of serious disillusion with their leaders. Resentment was to persist among the survivors long after the battle. That night Haig decided to postpone the attack to the First of July to allow more time for aircraft spotting and further bombardment of the enemy front-line and support trenches. This was not influenced by reports from the patrols that had not yet reached divisional HQs, let alone corps or Fourth Army HQ. Haig could not postpone for more than a few days. The Fourth Army, with the French 6th Army on its right, and the British Third Army as a diversion on its left, could be viewed as an orchestra brought to a peak of readiness. It must either proceed or be disbanded. Turning back was not in Haig's nature.

The new date of attack became known in the trenches within a few hours. Many who served in that area at that time believed that the news rapidly reached the rear areas. In turn it was carried to Amiens by ASC wagoners and drivers and by RE railway transport staff. There were individuals in the city with a special interest in the information.[4]

1. Lieutenant Cleghorn, enlisted Sept 1914. Pte C.R.Cleghorn. number 61, B Coy. Appointed 2/Lt. 28.1.1915. Won the MC when acting Captain. He was not serving with 16PSB at its disbandment. Captain Cleghorn survived the war.

2. The case of Colonel Sandys of the 2nd Middlesex, an all regular battalion facing the German strong-point at La Boiselle salient. Sandys reported from the Ovilliers sector that German morale appeared undamaged by the bombardment. Patrols from the 2nd MX could hear them singing in their bunkers. The order went out to all battaion HQs from Rawlinson's 4th Army HQ that any defeatist report would 'rebound on the head of the sender'.

3. 4th Army orders stated:
'Company 2I/Cs and 2 sergeants per company will remain with the first-line transport until ordered to rejoin the Brigade'. The orders continued:
'BATTLE POLICE. Their duties will be to see that no one, except linesmen, use the new communication trenches across No Man's Land from the German side. They will prevent any NCO or private leaving the German lines who is not wounded. They will direct men who have lost their way and messengers and carrying parties.
LOOTING.
Most extreme disciplinary action will be taken in the case of any officer, NCO or private found in possession of any article from the dead.
TENDING OF WOUNDED.
All ranks are forbidden to divert attention from the enemy in order to tend wounded officers or men.'

4. See conversation between Henry Williamson and George Fullard at Chelsea Arts Club shortly before the death of the latter in 1973. Fn8. Chapter 41.

Chapter 27

THE LAST DAY

THE 16TH MIDDLESEX WAS RELIEVED from trench duty by the Lancashire Fusiliers. They filed out of the dripping communication trenches into open ground behind Auchonvilliers ridge, formed up in column and marched by companies to Acheux Wood for final training for the attack. Their route took them through the busy assembly areas where woods and copses were still intact and the trees in full leaf. The long, ricketty ladders of artillery observers led to camouflaged hides in the top branches. As well as artillery OPs the woods concealed brigade signals sections, stretcher bearers and regimental aid posts. The fields beyond were covered in ammunition dumps, hidden in any rough shelter, dug into banks or covered with logs and packed earth. Sappers assembled light, trench tramway systems that would be used to push ammunition forward and convey wounded men back after the first assault. Guns of every calibre were camouflaged beneath the dripping trees. There was a brief lull in the bombardment and gunners brought up more shells or made rapid and temporary repairs to troublesome parts of their guns.

'I've never seen so many guns,' said one of Alf's platoon. Most said nothing, thinking of dry billets and warm food as they marched in the pouring rain, water sluicing from the rims of their helmets, trickling down the necks of rubberised canvas gas capes, soaking puttees and finding its way into boots.

On the following day they started training for the attack. Once again it rained. Alf took a jaundiced view of this training.

It wasn't possible to hide knowledge of the Big Push from Jerry. He knew all about it. Each brigade had a place to train that was based on the place we were supposed to attack. The staff laid out white tapes to represent the Jerry trenches and we practised on this training ground like performing monkeys until we could go through our tricks to their satisfaction. Jerry could see much of what was going on and, no doubt, there were a few obliging farmers still around who could fill in the details for a few hundred francs. Despite the dominance of the RFC in the air, a few of Jerry's observation planes got through, while in some places along the line his observation balloons overlooked our positions. With their own high powered Zeiss glasses the Bosche observers could see many of our training grounds and see the battalions practising. You can bet that it wasn't very difficult to put two and two together.

The tapes were supposed to be Jerry's front line trenches and behind that we built a replica of Beaumont Hamel church out of sandbags, complete with the church steeple. Of course the steeple had gone by then, and so, as it happened had the rest of the church, smashed to pieces in the final bombardment. But that didn't stop the staff planners

'I've never seen so many guns.'

demanding that we use the steeple as a landmark. I don't think that any of the staff had a notion of what faced us. They lived in a world of their own, which had little or no connection with ours. I never saw a Brass-hat anywhere near the line until three days before the attack. Then, and only then did a white haired old general arrive on his horse with his staff and an escort of lancers. That was General de Lisle, commanding the Bottle of Bass Division. I told you about his depressing speech. Well, I should say that it might have been depressing if we had taken any notice. We'd been told so often that it would be a "walk-over" and we'd seen and heard the force of the bombardment that we didn't believe the old general and treated the whole thing as a joke.

Lionel Renton was a little more charitable about his superiors, but confirmed what Alf said.

We only saw one senior officer close to the line and that was General de Lisle. He was pessimistic, I remember, which made a change from all that talk of a 'walk-over'. We saw Hunter-Weston once, when we were well behind the line. He seemed a cheerful, optimistic sort of officer and earned a reputation for courage under fire at Gallipoli. Regulars who served under him in the Dardanelles liked him.

Both Alf Damon and Noel Peters said that they and all their mates were optimistic about the attack. Lionel Renton disagreed.

We were told that it would be a walk-over, but we took this with a pinch of salt. We knew that the German line was not cut and that their trenches were damaged but still useable. Battalion Commanding Officers, like our man Johnnie Hall, did not report the bad news brought in by their patrols for fear of being Stellenbosched. We'd seen enough of the war by then not to believe all we were told.[1]

157

You see an ambitious career officer, like Johnnie Hall, would never complain, that would be against his code. Rawlinson sent out an order that any defeatism or criticism of superior officers would rebound on the critic's own head. That was clear enough. A pessimistic officer would be Stellenbosched, he would be sent back to command a supply dump, a transit camp, or a base workshop and that would be the end of a promising career. An officer suspected of being windy would go nowhere up the ladder of promotion.

We never saw Haig or Rawlinson anywhere near the line. Their headquarters were miles and miles back. That's not a criticism. To expect a commander to control an army of that size from the front is preposterous. Haig learnt that in 1914. By the way, some of the staff officers were ambitious skrim-shankers, but no one ever implied that Haig or Rawlinson lacked courage. They proved that both in South Africa and during the retreat from Mons. We had no idea of their problems, and certainly they had no idea of how we lived in the line.[2]

Lionel Renton was moved from B Company to A Company some time before the build-up for the attack. He remembered that the officers of A Company appeared confident.

Or if they weren't they put up a good show of bravado. Our company and platoon officers were first rate. Many joined with the Originals in 1914. On the day of the attack, A Company was commanded by Captain Watts, for reasons that I will explain in a minute. My platoon officer was Mr Tuck, of the postcard family, Raphael Tuck, another platoon officer was Mr Ionides, I don't know what became of him. Captain Purnell I knew well,

A dump for shell cases, an evidence of the massive bombardment falling on the German trenches.

he was one of the Originals and led the Brigade bombing party. In those days the Company was commanded by a senior captain with a junior captain as his second in command. The Company commander was known as The Mounted Captain, because he rode while the rest of us walked.

While we were at La Bassée A Company was commanded by a regular soldier, a very decent fellow from the King's African Rifles. Years of service in Africa had given him a sallow, ill look. He suffered from recurring malaria and his nerves were bad. By the time we reached the Somme he was hitting the bottle and his hands shook all the time. The noise of the bombardment was the last straw. He was relieved of his command and sent home. His junior, Captain Watts, took over command of the Company.

Two things stuck in the minds of every survivor: the noise of the bombardment and the rain. 'The day before the attack it was wet,' Alf said.

Rain poured down. We were issued with a green envelope for a personal letter form, which we were told would not be read by the censor. I wrote a long letter home, but later tore it up. The padre held a brief service in the tent with the rain drumming on the canvas. I went to it and then spent the afternoon playing poker. We had an advance of cash and I lost the lot. I've often wondered since, what idiot on the staff thought of giving us an advance before the battle? Where did he think we would spend it and on what? Mine went as quickly as it came, win or lose the job ahead.

One of the poker players was an Irishman named Murphy, a lad of about my own age. He had been wounded in the arm and had no money on him. He borrowed heavily, promising to pay it back the next day. He had been out on patrol with Mr Cleghorn's section the previous night. "It was all quiet out there," he told us. "And I would have been all right if it hadn't been for my bloody bayonet. I fell on the bloody thing. But 'tis nothing serious and I'll be with you lads in the morning, so I will."

Later that evening we learnt the truth from him. His great desire to go forward with the attack grew out of a need to dig up his cash. When the patrol was close to the German wire, a star-shell went up, lighting every detail of No Man's Land. As soon as the tail of the rocket arced across the sky every man threw himself flat, which was when Murphy landed on his bayonet. He was convinced that the Germans had seen the patrol and so he buried his cash with his entrenching tool. He spoke as though he was about to stroll down to the post office. 'I'll see you right with the money. I know where it is and I'll pick it up when we go over in the morning, sure.'[3]

Morale was high that afternoon. No one in our little group of card players showed any visible sign of fear. I believe that most of us were confident that it would indeed be a walk-over, as we had been told.

That evening we marched to the line by way of Mailly woods. Darkness fell, the night was unhurried and the evening was warm. As we approached the ridge the noise increased. A nine-inch naval gun was concealed in the woods. It fired every few minutes. The muzzle flash lit up the whole area so that, for a fraction of a second, you could read a newspaper. The noise was deafening. Behind the roar of the nine-inch you could hear all sorts of bangs

159

and thumps and a staccato rattling in the background, an endless drum-fire as countless batteries ranged onto their targets. In pauses between this racket you could hear fragments of the gunner officer's orders, quite distinct. "Battery X.." or "Five.. Ten". Whatever. In front of the naval guns and howitzers we came on the field batteries. To see them in action, at such close quarters was a most interesting sight. Especially intriguing was watching the spurt of flame from the muzzle of these small guns and following the shell until it vanished in the distance. This continuous firing improved morale. Lads shouted encouragement to the gunners as the column marched past. "Give the bastards hell, boys." Or some similar greeting. But of course there was no chance of the gunners hearing us above the din. Oddly enough neither the guns nor the communicators nor the assembly trenches were shelled by Jerry that night. We went into the communicators ready for the morning. The rain ceased and it was a warm night. We slept on the fire step for some hours. I do not remember anyone being in the least jittery.

1. *Stellenbosched:* slang expression dating back to the South African war when an incompetent or over-cautious officer would be returned to the base at Stellenbosch. This would mean the end of any hope of promotion, in effect the end of the officer's career.

2. Opinions on the 'walk-over' myth by officers and men from neighbouring units.
'We were told that it would be a walk-over and we felt confident. We believed that nothing could survive that terrible bombardment.' Conversation with Mr Crosbee at Birmingham School of Art 1976. Formerly Lieutenant Crosbee, Warwickshire Regiment. Opposite Serre.
Sergeant Quinnell MM, Royal Fusiliers, told me that he was sceptical about talk of a walk-over, but that no one had any idea how bad it would be.
'I only once saw a general anywhere near the line and that was when we were training in the rear. He told us that it would be a walk-over. After the devastating power of our artillery not a mouse would be left alive in the German trenches. That's what he said, not a mouse. All we had to do was walk over and occupy their line.'
'So, you were confident that the attack would succeed?'
'We thought that it would succeed but we didn't think it would be easy. We knew what Jerry was like and we knew eye-wash when we heard it. You see, we weren't amateurs by then, we'd been in the trenches for over a year at Ypres and then at Albert. We'd seen a bit of scrapping and we knew when the staff were jollying us along. We knew that it would not be as easy as they told us it would be.'
Conversation with Sergeant Quinnell MM at Royal Chelsea Hospital. 1976. This was borne out by one of the brigade majors.
'Hunter-Weston was extremely optimistic, telling everyone that the wire had been blown away, although we could see it standing strong and well, that there would be no German trenches at all and all we had to do was to walk over and take the village.'
Brigade Major. 31st Division. Public Records office.

3. Captain P D Ionides.
       Commissioned 2Lt 15.9.1914
       Lt 15.10.14
       Capt 19.2.15
Capt D.B. Tuck. Survived the Somme. Mentioned in despatches.
DOW 30.3.1918
Pte Daniel Murphy. Number PS 2911. Killed 1.7.1916.

Chapter 28

NIGHT

THE WEATHER HAD BEEN STORMY and uncertain for several days but on the evening of Friday 30 June (Day Y2) the clouds lifted and the rain ceased. The 16th Middlesex paraded at Mailly Maillet. According to the official version, the strategic reserve was detached and remained on the edge of Mailly wood. The rest of the Battalion, twenty-three officers and 689 other ranks, left their large packs with the Quartermaster sergeant and marched to Auchonvilliers to bivouac for the night.[1]

Colonel Hall and his company commanders had a great deal of work to do during the days immediately preceding the attack; rehearsals by platoons, and by companies. He arranged lectures for junior officers, NCOs, runners and signallers. Carrying parties were listed to supply rations and water once the attack had gone over and the enemy first and second lines were taken.

On the eve of battle Colonel Hall and his officers made a thorough study of trench maps of the Beaumont Hamel area. These gave the most recent information on the German front and support lines and their communication trenches. (There was, of course, no information on the earthworks excavated by their engineers below ground.) At the last moment Colonel Hall and the company commanders checked that the platoon commanders had memorised their orders to the last detail. These included the timing of artillery barrages and lifting of the barrage; signals by Very lights to the gunners and signals by flares to aircraft and neighbouring units. All these orders had

A scene in the trenches at night in the Beaumont Hamel area.

to be learnt by heart and then destroyed.

Along the twenty-two mile line of attack each soldier and junior NCO was burdened with a great weight of kit. The reasoning behind this came back, once again, to the walk-over assumption. The staff assumed that the threat from the Germans would take the form of a counter-attack, once the attack had gone over successfully and the German front and second lines were taken. As both Alf Damon and Lionel Renton remarked, the weight was equivalent of the load he might take on a camping trip, before the war. The soldier could walk but he could not run, certainly not over a distance of 200 yards.[2] In contrast to this foolishness the dress regulation was a sensible precaution, some officers wore private soldiers' tunics and puttees, others wore service dress with Sam Browne belt and polished knee boots or gaiters. The former stood a better chance of survival. German snipers were skilled at identifying the officers. 'Shoot the ones with the thin legs.'

Each man wore a broad webbing belt with bayonet, full water bottle and ammunition pouches attached, the whole supported by web braces. He wore a steel helmet and carried a haversack on his back (known to a later generation as the small pack). The haversack contained mess tins, tinned food and 48 hours' emergency rations; spare socks, 'housewife' (needle and thread etc), bootlaces, two gas masks, field dressing and extra iodine. The rain had stopped so his rubberised cape-ground-sheet was neatly

Infantry followed by stretcher bearers move up a communication trench in front of Beaumont Hamel before 1 July 1916.

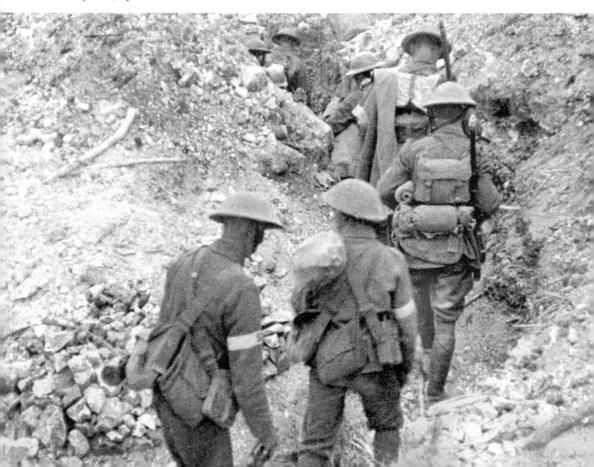

rolled and tied to the top of his pack. His Lee-Enfield rifle weighed 9 pounds 6 ounces (about 5kg) and he carried 220 rounds of .303 ammunition distributed in pouches and in a bandoleer.

Each man wore identity disc on a bootlace round his neck. The disc was made of a form of papier-mâché and carried his name, rank, regiment and religion. Some battalions had their regimental badge stencilled on the front of the helmet with the Divisional sign on the left side, while others wore their Division's colours sewn to the back of their collars. 29th Division's means of identification was a shiny tin triangle attached to the back of each man's pack.[3] A coloured tape on one epaulette indicated the battalion to which each man belonged. Alf said that the 16th wore a canary yellow ribbon above the brass shoulder title and, below this at the top of the sleeve, the red triangle edged with yellow of the 29th Division. Colonel Hall ordered that the 16th must wear polished buttons, badges and shoulder titles, whether out of or in the line and this remained the rule on the First of July.

With the exception of the 16th Middlesex the battalions that made up 86 Brigade had experienced Gallipoli. They learnt about thirst the hard way and 16PSB took their advice. Company commanders told their men to carry extra glass bottles of water. The trench tools, company weapons and extra ammunition had to be distributed amongst the platoons. These included: grenades, picks, shovels, extra sandbags, wire cutters, rockets and flares. Some carried folded stretchers, reels of telephone wire and Bangalore Torpedos, for blasting wire.

A soldier's personal kit, without the extra bottles of water, weighed 65 pounds (approximately 33kg). When water and all the extra equipment, distributed throughout the company, was added to the load, some men carried as much as 90lbs (45kg). The Brigade bombing party, under Captain Purnell, carried satchels full of Mills grenades as well as their normal load.

Noel Peters remembered the night march to the assembly positions clearly,

> The night was fine and dry. We formed up in Mailly Woods and then marched straight across country, in formation, to the assembly trenches. When our duties had been explained to us, and final orders given, we were dismissed. My job for the next day was runner to the RSM. Once we had our orders we got our heads down for the night as best we could.

Noel slept, as only the young can. Few slept so peacefully that night. The British guns reached a crescendo of activity just before dawn. Supply, transport and engineer troops worked all night. Medical officers, nurses and orderlies made their final preparations for the flood of wounded that they expected next day. Divisional and Brigade Staffs made their final checks.

From Gommecourt to Montauban fourteen infantry divisions stood-to, ready to go. At 3.00am, the majority of the battalions in these divisions moved forward to their assault positions, following tapes and hooded lanterns along the communication trenches. Once in position a few men managed to sleep in cramped and busy trenches.

So far the plans, worked out over many weeks by the General Staff, appeared to be working smoothly. By this point battalion commanders had done all that could be done. Success or failure, they believed, now rested in the hands of platoon officers and NCOs.

By this time many of these officers commanding battalions had a clear idea of what they and their men would face. They coped with this knowledge as best they could, according to temperament.

Most of these officers were young, promoted in the rapid expansions of 1914 and 1915. All were regular officers, professionals, with both thorough training and trench experience behind them. Most of them had a year's experience of leading a battalion in France or Belgium. The majority of 29th Division's officers added the appalling experience of war in the Dardanelles to their general knowledge of siege warfare. These officers knew more about the reality of trench-warfare than any of their seniors on the staff. Now they watched the men that they had trained move into position and waited for first light. Perhaps they shaved, and ate some cold rations for breakfast in the frowsty, ill-smelling headquarters dug-out.

Anyone researching the story of the 29th Division is fortunate because we have the first hand record of Lieutenant Malins. Anyone concerned with 86 Brigade is doubly fortunate. Lieutenant G H Malins was one of the first war cine-cameramen and was appointed official cinematographer to the army. His brief was to film the explosion of the mine placed under Hawthorn Ridge at Beaumont Hamel. Malins was left to choose his own position. He expected the explosion of the mine to be a spectacular moment in cinematography and so aimed to get as close to the event as possible. He was not disappointed.

Malins was one of those men who has no concept of fear, as most human beings feel it. His vocation was dangerous even by front-line standards. Such were the risks that he took and so obvious his camera to enemy snipers and mortar crews that many company commanders

Support trench. 86 Brigade. Men sleeping in the early morning before the attack. 1st July 1916.

only agreed to his presence in their section of trench under pressure from higher authority. Malins chose a sniper's sap on the edge of the Bluff on the left side of the Valley road. This is the point where the bluff changes direction and it was exposed to marksmen firing from the Hawthorn Redoubt.[4]

Malins was the guest of the 1st Battalion of the Lancashire Fusiliers, since the sap was placed slightly in front of their front line. The cine-photographer described the assembly of 86th Brigade and the final hours of the bombardment.

> *Darkness came and with it a host of star-shells and Very lights shot high in the air from German or our trenches. Rain had ceased... Batch after batch of men came gliding by in full kit, smoking and chatting.... While I was standing there hundreds must have passed me in that narrow trench, quietly going to their allotted positions. Now and again sharp orders were given by their officers. It was not long before little red fires were gleaming from dug-out entrances, and crowds of men were crouched around, heating their canteens of water, some frying pieces of meat, others heating soup, and all the time laughing and carrying on a most animated conversation. From other groups came the subdued humming of favourite songs. Some were cursing and swearing, but with such bluntness, if I may say so, that it seemed to take all profanity from the words.*
>
> *And these men were going "over the top" in the morning. The day they dreamed of was about to materialise. They knew that many would not be alive tomorrow night and yet I never saw a sad face or heard a word of complaint. My feeling while watching these men in the glow of the firelight was indescribable. I revered them more than I had ever done before; and I felt like going down on my knees and thanking God I was an Englishman. No words of mine can fitly describe this wonderful scene. And all the time men, and more men were pouring into the trenches and munitions of all kinds were being served out. The bursting German shells and the shrieks of the missiles from our own guns were for the moment forgotten in the immensity of the sights around me. I turned and groped my way back to my own shelter and, as I did so, our fire increased in intensity.*
>
> *The night was very cold. I lay shivering in my blanket and could not get warm. Shells were bursting just outside with appalling regularity. Suddenly they seemed to quieten down as if by some means the Germans had got to know of our great plans and were preparing for the blow. Presently everything was comparatively quiet, except for the scurrying of countless rats, running and jumping over my body as if it was the most natural thing in the world. I expect I must have dozed off to sleep, for when I awoke day was breaking and the din of gunfire was terrific. Innumerable worlds seemed to be crashing together, and it sounded as though thousands of peals of thunder had concentrated themselves in one soul-terrifying roar.[5]*

86 Brigade reached their assembly positions at 3.00am. The first pale light of dawn and the first birdsong came at 3.30 by which time, under cover of mist, a detachment of Lancashire Fusiliers occupied the Russian saps and slit trenches that extended towards the German line under the cover of the uncut corn. A small party entered the Sunken road while men of the 2nd Fusiliers occupied a large crater close to the Hawthorn

Shells falling on British trenches.

Redoubt. At 4.00 am a pale yellow band silhouetted Hawthorn ridge, and by 4.30 the strip was orange and the sky light enough to read by. Larks rose from No Man's Land, rising to meet the sunlight before dropping again to feed amongst the weeds and rank corn. Mist rose from the river Ancre and drifted along the valley and up the re-entrant, obscuring Beaumont Hamel and the enemy trenches.[6] The sky above the mist was bright cerulean; birds sang freely in the unnatural silence after the noise. At 5.00 the sun rose lighting up the ruins of Auchonvilliers and the British support trenches leaving the German lines in dark, misty silhouette.

Alf Damon wrote:

'At 5.00am I was part of a detail sent up to the engineers' dump at the White City.

Before we went we had a tot of rum, little more than a teaspoon each. White City dump was a sixty foot dug-out in the chalk cliffs. Here I was given a heavy waistcoat holding six, or maybe eight, mortar bombs to carry up to our front line. When we got back to the company and had delivered our load, we had some hot tea and then filled our water bottle with ready mixed lime-juice and water. I suppose I ate something, but I can't remember what we had as our breakfast.'

Not long after sunrise Noel Peters was ordered to carry a dixie of tea up the trench where B Company were waiting to go over the top. This must have been the same tea mentioned by Alf. Noel said that some of the men wanted tea, some did not, some were asleep, some joked, some knelt down in prayer. Noel wondered what they were thinking and what would become of them that morning. He gave a mug of tea to the platoon officer who was laughing and joking with his men to keep their spirits up. His nervous tension showed in the way he kept glancing at his wrist watch, over and over again. At dawn, Noel said, the hazy blue sky and the mist rising from the valley beyond the German line, showed that it would be a fine day.

At 6.25 every gun that could be brought into action opened fire in one massive final bombardment. The dull boom of the heavy guns in the rear could be picked out from the nearer thumps and cracks of medium artillery, four-point-sevens and eighteen pounder guns. The shells made a rumbling, tearing sound as they passed overhead. The crump of heavy shells falling on Beaumont Hamel added to the noise.

At 7.00am the 16th Middlesex stood-to in their assembly positions, trenches called Cripps Cut and Cardiff Street. As the sun rose and the air grew warmer a new sound joined that of the British barrage; the German heavy and medium artillery, that had

Map 7 . British and German support trenches. The assembly trenches for the attack of 86 Brigade.

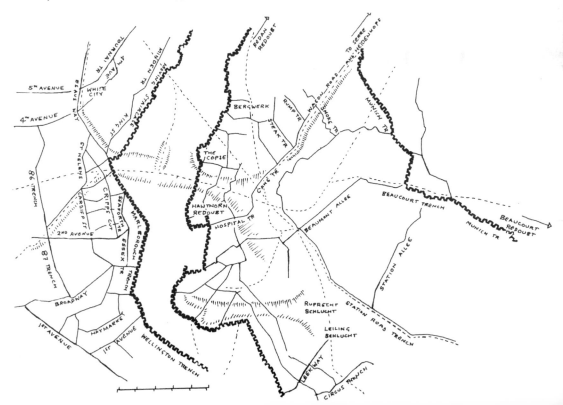

remained concealed up till then, opened a heavy and sustained fire. Shells exploded on the British front-line trenches. The assault troops crouched low, deafened by the noise and showered by earth and chalk dust. Several minutes before Zero hour the barrage lifted and, by a coincidence, the German gunners ceased firing too. For a short period all was silent. Many men, in different parts of the line, remembered hearing the larks singing above No Man's Land.

1. The 'official version' is a convenient shorthand for the version of events put together soon after the war ended and handed down to us. Some of this information does not correspond with the testimony of those who were actually there. The strategic reserve, is one example, bivouacking at Auchonvilliers another. This is explained in more detail in Chapter 41. Figures and opinions vary about the composition of the Battalion reserve, or even whether it existed. According to Regimental history, and also to Wallace-Grain, ten percent of the total strength were detached as Battalion reserve.
'9 Officers and 79 Other Ranks under the command of Major A M G Jones withdrew and camped in Mailly wood.'
Noel Peters believed that the reserve was brought forward before dawn. When I mentioned this controversy to Lionel Renton he said, 'I must say that I am very surprised that we had a reserve at all. We were so shorthanded, you see. I should be very surprised to learn that Brigade detached a reserve. But it may be so. You have to remember that everything was localised for the ordinary infantryman. One rarely knew what was going on. You knew what was happening in your trench, but had not a clue what was happening a few hundred yards down the line.'
One has to remember that neither Everard Wyrall nor Wallace-Grain was there. Each had to rely on the report cobbled together by those officers that were left in Battalion or Brigade after the battle was over and 86 Brigade was withdrawn from Auchonvilliers. Understandably, there was no time to keep an accurate record while Colonel Hall and his few officers remaining were still in the line.

2 'DRESS. Fighting order with two bandoleers of SAA; full water-bottle, mess tins, mackintosh sheet, iron rations, remainder of the day's rations, two smoke helmets. Officers will carry rifles and conform to the movement of their men. All NCOs and Privates will carry two Mills grenades, one in each side pocket, and three sandbags, with the exception of Battalion scouts.'
Noel said that each man's large pack (this webbing pack was often called a 'Valise') was stored behind the lines in a barn behind Mailly Maillet. The packs belonging to the dead and wounded were sent back to Amiens sometime in the middle of July.

3. These can be seen, clearly, in the well-known photograph of the 1st Lancashire Fusiliers in the front line trench just under the bluff to the left of the Auchonvilliers-Beaumont road.

4. By studying stills of Lieutenant Malins' remarkable and historic film one can find the exact spot where he set up his cine-camera. The remains of the sap were still clear in the summer of 1996, though the wire, munitions and trench debris that I found there twenty years earlier had been cleared away. The position of the sap is 85 yards north of the Valley road and 250 yards west of the Sunken road.

5. Lt G.H. Malins 'How I filmed the War' published 1920.

6. These would have been the perfect conditions for the pre-dawn attack that Rawlinson suggested early during the planning sessions. He was immediately overruled by Haig.

PART FOUR

Chapter 29

JULY 1ST: MORNING

TIME MOVED SLOWLY. Men noted the pastoral beauty of the morning of the First of July. 'Some idiot wrote that it rained,' Lionel Renton said. 'Rubbish, it was a hot sunny day, many of us suffered badly from thirst before the night came.' The sky was a brilliant blue, the sun warm. An early morning breeze rustled through the rank grass along the trench edge. Beyond the parapet small birds sang as though there was no war.

At 7.20am, precisely, the mine exploded under Hawthorn Redoubt. For a fraction of a second the earth shook and heaved and then a gigantic fir-cone shape rose into the clear sky. A blunt mass of earth, chalk, debris and smoke rose high into the air, like a solid form, ascending higher, and then began to break up and fall back to earth spreading a white circle of chalk. The fragmented remains of three sections of Number

The mine explosion under Hawthorn Redoubt. 9 Company of the 119th Wurtemburg Reserve Regiment were blown into the air.

Smoke and dust from the Hawthorn Mine. Photographer Malins' position was in the sap (left centre) on Moving Staircase trench. The Valley road is the dark horizontal line centre and left.

9 Company of the 119th Wurtemburg Reserve Regiment were blown into the air. The neighbouring trenches and dug-outs were blown in and buried. A German artillery observer looking through a periscope at Beaucourt ridge reported,

> *A terrific explosion which drowned the noise of artillery. A great cloud of smoke rose from 9 Company trenches followed by a shower of stones which fell from the air onto our positions.*

The shock wave, transmitted through the earth, was so severe that trench walls and parapet shook. Men on the fire-step felt their limbs shake and their teeth rattle. A young Middlesex soldier, standing with one foot braced against the trench wall, suffered a broken leg. The crater of the great mine was over fifty yards in diameter. The hillside around the point where the Redoubt had been, was covered in flints and chalk, 'as though it had been snowing'. The ill-timed explosion acted as a signal for the defenders. It removed Hawthorn Redoubt, just as the Sapper officers planned it would, but left in its place the embanked lips of an immense crater. The race was on to take and hold these new-made defences and the Wurtemburgers had the shorter distance to move. 29th

Division had not moved at all.

At 7.28 the sappers fired the smaller mines under the Redan, more mines were fired along the line, further south, at Le Tambour, at Fricourt, several small mines under La Boisselle and the giant Loch Nagar mine to the south of La Boisselle. At 7.30 the British artillery ceased fire and for a few moments silence fell upon the lines before it all started again, lifting to the German second line positions.

150,000 men stood ready along an eighteen mile front. Then whistles sounded, officers shouted and the first wave of 60,000 men went into battle. Opposite Beaumont Hamel the Lancashire Fusiliers rose from the concealed saps, crawled through the grass to the German wire and scrambled through it. The support party, to the left and the section carrying two machine guns and two Stokes mortars, were less lucky. Weighed down by their heavy equipment they struggled through the wire to reach the lip of the crater. They were too late. The Wurtemburgers on either side of Number 9 Company had closed in and set up their Maxim guns.

The first wave of attackers was destroyed as soon as it came into the sights of the defenders. The Lancashires on the right were shot down as they marched forward on the gentle slope that led to the crater. The Lancashires on the left of the Valley road were hit most severely as they advanced from the Bluff to the Sunken road. The Middlesex men, in the second wave, knew nothing of this slaughter as they waited but they could not fail to notice a new sound that added to the general noise. The German mortars were in action.

Haig's artillery adviser agreed that it was essential that the enemy mortars and field artillery be put out of action before the infantry advanced. The majority of German mortar and artillery crews were untouched by the bombardment, sheltered in bunkers

Map 8.

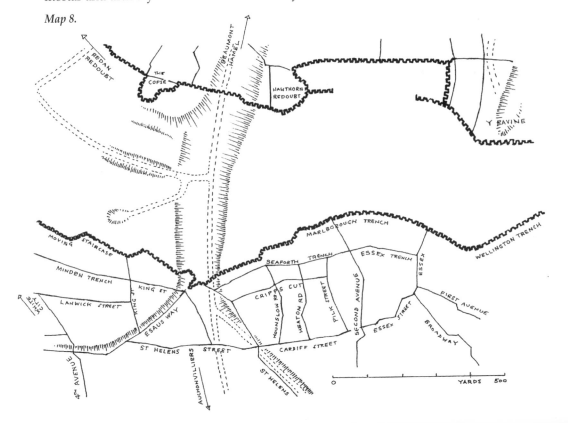

1st Bn Lancashire Fusiliers preparing to attack. 7.00am 1st July 1916. (Note the tin triangle on the collar of the man second from right. The triangle was the 29th Div recognition signal for artillery spotters.)

dug into the slopes of Artillery Road and Y Ravine. The mine explosion acted as an alarm signal and the gunners came out of their shelters at the double, hauling their pieces with them and immediately secured them to set mountings that were lined up to fire on pre-arranged targets. Further back Howitzer and Field batteries were concealed near Serre and Pusieux, protected by timber and earth shelters. Artillery observers on Beaucourt Ridge directed fire from these guns onto fixed targets as soon as the British second wave climbed out of their trenches. From behind the German second line a total of sixty-six heavy batteries now opened fire on VIII Corps' lines. Many men of the supporting battalions were killed before they left the crowded trenches.

The starting line for the 16th Middlesex, in the second wave of attack, was that drawn along Cripps Cut and Cardiff Street. These trenches were narrow and well cut into the chalk and gave excellent protection against shell fire and shrapnel. They were less good as assembly positions. Already congested they were now made worse by the numbers of wounded Lancashire Fusiliers struggling back to their own lines.

Alf Damon wrote of the period immediately before he went over,

> *No shells landed on our line until the mine went up, giving Jerry the signal. We were glad of our tin hats at that moment. A huge mass of earth and chalk rose into the air and then lumps of the Beaumont Hamel defences landed all round us; bricks, concrete, steel and rubble. Millions of small stones and chalk rained down all over us. Then the German guns opened up and we had the first sign that all was not going well. The cry of 'Stretcher bearers' went up and kept going constantly. We had few enough of them, drummers and pipers, about twenty in all, with only one first aid man to each company. There was no sign of panic, or anything like it. About five minutes after the crumps began on our assembly trenches, B Company began to move off to what we thought was our familiar jumping off point, only it wasn't. We were in a section of trench that was not familiar. We had no idea of where we were, or what to expect ahead of us. I realised immediately that we were not going to carry out the attack that we had rehearsed. I learnt later that the attack plan that we rehearsed was not used; so no wonder that we didn't know where we were. We were trained to follow the Lancashires who would take the front line and we would go over them, in a sort of leap-frog forward movement and go on to take the church. But of course there was no church. Nor was the front line where we were taught to expect it to be.*

At 7.55am the first wave of B and D Companies, 16th Middlesex, climbed their ladders, stepped over the sandbags and formed line in the open, taking their dressing from the left. The Battalion was smartly turned out. 'As if on parade,' Alf said:

> *Rifles at the port, working parts lightly oiled, bayonets flashing in the sunlight. I was one of the last over the top in my platoon, because I was carrying the Lewis gun. My number two was ahead of me carrying a case of spares on his shoulder and dragging a sandbag full of its circular magazines. Further along the trench there were two more men with sandbags full of loaded magazines who were supposed to keep close to us when we got near the German line. I never saw them again and I have no idea what happened to them.*

> *The last man I spoke to in our platoon was Lieutenant Goodwin who was our platoon commander. He shook my hand and said, "Good luck old man." And I said "The same to you Sir." Then he gave me a tap on the shoulder and went up one of the ladders that we had built earlier. I followed and had just got my head over the parapet when there was a great explosion of black smoke to my right and slightly ahead of the trench. I guess that it was a five-nine or similar sized shell. I was above the trench but still below the level of the ground where the shell burst. There's not much doubt that this saved my life. As the shell burst upwards and outwards the scrap-iron flew over my head like a fountain. Mr Goodwin and my number two must have been right in the path of the blast because I did not see a trace of either of them. It got Clutterbuck and Catley too because their bodies were right in front of me, face down, hanging on our own wire. There was no time to take any impression or to think. All one could do was to follow orders as best one could. Impressions*

came back later, in flashes, very clear, like photos. But then? No, nothing. We were higher up on the slope than I expected, so we had to go up the slope and down the slope. As I went forward over the curve I could see the line and the enemy line for the first time. I could see the bodies of the first wave strewn about, all along, some Lancashires and some were our own chaps.

Some, like my section, were hit by shrapnel as they left our trenches, but there's no doubt that the majority were killed by the concentrated burst of fire by several machine guns. Bodies lay tumbled together in lines where they fell. I remember quite clearly seeing the tin triangles glittering in the sun. Shelling had eased as our chaps got nearer the Jerry wire, but the machine-gun fire was well directed and bound to hit anyone if he stayed on his feet long enough. The luckiest thing for me was being hit before I reached the wire where my friends fell.

The section of the 86 Brigade start-line, described by Alf Damon, was well to the right of the Valley road, near the junction where Second Avenue communication trench crossed Essex Street assembly trench. The advancing lines of Lancashires and Middlesex had to ascend a gentle slope before descending a similar curve towards the Hawthorn mine crater. The line, or what little was left of it, was unable to move directly towards the Brigade's objective, but diagonally across the German lines of fire.

Hawthorn Redoubt, now transformed into Hawthorn crater, made an elbow shape, in the German line. Dug into a reverse slope position there was little to be seen of the defenders except the white debris thrown up by the explosion and the coils and webs of blackened wire. To the left, at the Redan, on the left hand side of the Valley road, the Wurtemburg trenches rose in tiers, one behind the other. The advancing Middlesex men could see grey figures moving about. As one man described them, 'Casual, as though going about their everyday business.'

To the centre and left of the valley D Company climbed from their trench, took up their dressing and advanced. Men began to fall immediately. The line thinned out but remained parade-ground straight as they walked forward a few yards. The first sight of No Man's Land and the enemy line appeared ordinary which surprised one of the survivors, John Wilson. In front stretched two hundred yards of coarse grass and chalky shell craters, with a few weed-grown patches of debris and rotten sandbags. The sun bore down on his serge tunic and heavy equipment and he thought that it would be a warm walk across to the enemy line. Then he realised that his platoon had disappeared. The batteries that had remained silent now dropped a curtain of shrapnel and high explosive shells across the valley. Machine-gunners coordinated their aim in cross ire from the Redan and the lip of the Hawthorn crater. Mortar bombs and *minenwerfers* concentrated on the British front and support trenches. These were now crowded with wounded men.

To the right Alf saw bundles of brown cloth scattered across the field:

It took a moment to realise that these were our own men, the Lancashire Fusiliers who preceded us. I had difficulty locating the enemy line. You asked me what it looked like? I

British infantry crossing No Man's Land at the start of an attack.

saw nothing of the German trenches. There was no indication of where they were, though I realised pretty quickly that he was putting down cross-fire. There appeared to be nothing ahead of us except a lot of wire to our right. All that I could see was an empty field and a lot of dead bodies. My platoon was number six. It was destroyed. The only dead I recognised were Clutterbuck and Catley, hanging on our own wire. Because I was Lewis-gunner I was carrying extra weight, plus a shovel and extra sandbags wedged into my kit. This slowed me down. If it hadn't then one of those shells would have got me too. My number two and two ammo carriers never showed up; no doubt knocked over as they got out of the trench. I walked a hundred yards or so up to the curve and along the flat. Then I started running down the incline, or I ran as best I could weighed down with the gun and all those odds and ends. After I'd travelled about a hundred yards from my starting point a bullet stopped me, going clean through my right shoulder. It knocked me flat on my back. It hit me with such force that I felt no pain, only indignation at being flattened.

Now I come to the point of the story about my pious upbringing, that I mentioned earlier. I never swore before that day, and have not made a practice of it since. When I was knocked over, ignoring the stream of machine-gun bullets and the roar of the shells, I let go with a stream of filthy language; words that would have made a Cockney Eastender blush. I suppose I must have heard all those words and retained them in my subconscious mind, because I shouted out every foul word in the book.

When B and D Companies went over the top the supporting companies, A and C, moved forward to the front trenches. Here they were not much better placed than the men in the open for the German batteries lifted their aim from No Man's Land to concentrate their fire on the attackers forward and assembly trenches. The shells were laid down in concentrated bombardment on short lengths of trench. An area fifty yards behind the line was reduced to a wilderness of shell-holes and crumbled communication trenches. During this bombardment the supporting companies climbed out of their trenches and moved forward into No Man's Land only to suffer the same

Men of 86 Bde moving up a support trench to the assembly position.

losses as the first two companies. Lionel Renton was with A Company which was commanded on the First of July by Captain Watts. His platoon commander was Lieutenant Tuck.

A Company went over directly in front of Beaumont Hamel, on level ground. I assume now, having visited the place in peace-time, that we went up the flat valley, on either side of the Valley road. Things went badly for us right from the start. We heard the mine go up with a muffled thump as we were moving into position. It was more as a vibration through the earth than a noise. That mine was supposed to knock out the strongest of Jerry's redoubts, but it made no difference to us. Moving up to our assembly positions the platoon commander ahead of us was hit in both legs by shell splinters, so that put him out of it. Our platoon officer, Mr Tuck, took over both platoons. As we climbed out of the trench into the open, Jerry opened up with machine guns from the high ground on each flank. Mr Tuck was hardly out of the trench when he fell forward dead.[1] I saw the acting Company Commander, Captain Watts, lying half in and half out of a shell-hole, his body and his head in the hole, his legs sticking out. He was dead. I couldn't see where he was hit but blood was trickling out of his mouth.[2] I don't remember when the Lancashire Fusiliers or the Royal Fusiliers went over. They must have gone ahead of us because bodies were scattered all over the flat ground between us and the Jerry wire. I ran forward about a hundred yards, and that wasn't easy with all that kit. And then I got a bullet in the groin. It knocked me over. I started to crawl for a hole but before I reached it I got two more, one through each arm. I felt one, but the other went through the fleshy part of the arm and I didn't know that both arms were hit until blood ran out of the cuff.

By the way, it's not true that wounds hurt, not straight away. They hurt later. A stomach wound hurts like hell, of course. But the one I got in the groin just felt like a kick, like the other one in the arm. Some bloody fool wrote that it poured with rain on the First of July. Nonsense. It was a blazing hot day. I had no water because I managed to get rid of my equipment and lost my water bottle with it, so I suffered badly from thirst. I lay there in a hole until it got dark. My wounds did not hurt and I stayed conscious.

Albert Edwards was wounded in the C Company attack.

Immediately we lined up the Germans opened up with a heavy barrage of shrapnel. Our company was picked off before we even got through our own wire. Our Company Commander, Captain Wegg was wounded, though I did not see him hit. My Platoon Comander, Mr Heaton, was killed.[3] Many of us crawled, or were helped back to our own trenches which were full of our wounded. From that point onwards I remember very little. I remember nothing of being moved back, out of the line, or of the RAP.

Another survivor, John Wilson, wrote:

It is now 63 years since the opening of the battle of the Somme. I have little to add to what has been said. We went over the top and advanced into No Man's Land about 200 yards, maybe a bit more. The shelling was intense and most of our chaps were hit by shrapnel. I was hit, but not seriously. My two close friends who I'd known since training were both killed that day. One was a Scot, a brilliant linguist and a very kindly friend, the

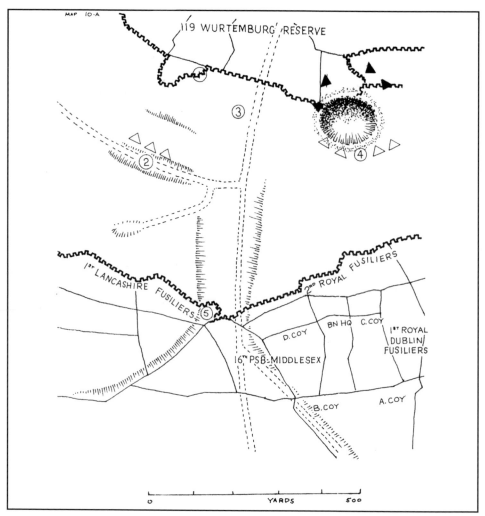

MAP 10-A

119 WURTEMBURG RESERVE

③

②

1ST LANCASHIRE FUSILIERS ⑤

④

2ND ROYAL FUSILIERS

D.COY

BN HQ   C.COY

1ST ROYAL DUBLIN FUSILIERS

16TH PSB MIDDLESEX

B.COY

A.COY

0   YARDS   500

The attack by 16th PSB on 1st July 1916. Map 9

KEY TO MAP 9. Before 7.30 am. 1st July 1916

Night 29-30 June. *16 MX patrol.* Lieutenant Cleghorn's patrol found the German front line trench empty. The dense wire in front of it was damaged but not cut and remained a major obstacle. As the patrol withdrew they came under fire from machine-guns at Hawthorn and Redan Redoubts and from the Copse. Cleghorn reported this discovery to his CO, Colonel Hall.

3.30am. 1st July. *1st Battalion Lancashire Fusiliers.* An advance party of the Lancashire Fusiliers occupied the Sunken Road position carrying Lewis guns and Stokes mortars.

6.30am. *Captain Purnell and the bombing team.* 86 Brigade bombing team, commanded by A.B.Purnell, entered the Russian Sap (tunnel) that ended close to the German front line trench to the left of the Valley Road. They were never seen again and no trace found of any of the bombers.

7.20am. *2nd Battalion Royal Fusiliers.* Immediately the mine exploded two platoons of Royal Fusiliers rushed the western lip of the crater. Their speed was slowed down by heavy equipment such as Lewis guns and Stokes mortars. Though Number 9 Coy of the 119th Regiment was blown to pieces the German platoons either side closed in. The Wurtemburgers reached the Eastern rim before the Fusiliers and a fierce fight began for the domination of the crater.

720am to mid-morning. *Lieutenant RG Malins. Official photographer.* The well-known stills showing the mine explosion, it's aftermath and the pictures alleged to be C Coy of 16PSB retreating were all taken by Malins from a sap from Moving Staircase trench close to the point where it meets Esau trench. Sixty years later the position occupied by Malins and his camera was still clear and the view of the Hawthorn crater and the field known as Les Champs Cornu little changed. Malins remained taking pictures from this position until mid-morning, exposed to the fire of trench-mortars, artillery and machine guns firing from the lip of the crater.

The moment of attack. Heavily laden troops advance across No Man's Land in the early morning of 1st July. Most of these men were dead or wounded by mid-day.

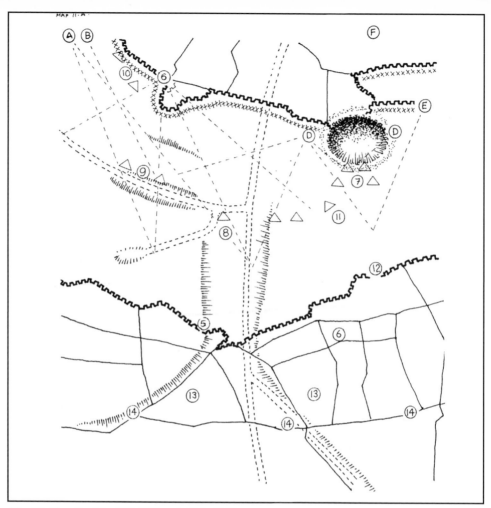

Map 10. The attack by 16th PSB on 1st July 1916.

MAP 10. Positions taken by 16PSB MX between the end of the artillery bombardment ceased and the start of the attack at 7.30am until mid-morning on the 1st July 1916

Colonel Hall. *CO 16PSB MX.* Battalion COs were under orders to remain with Battalion HQ at the start point of the attack and only move forward once the first objective had been taken.

Captain Heslop. Derek MacCullough. *D Coy.* D Company advanced towards the Hawthorn Crater in support of the Royal Fusiliers. Most of them were killed or wounded before they reached the Crater including the Company Commander. Captain Heslop. The 16PSB Adjutant, Captain Cochram went forward to re-organise the small number of Middlesex, Royal Fusiliers and Dublin Fusiliers pinned down near the Crater. Though wounded several times Cochram remained in command until this small group of wounded men became prisoners of the defenders. Derek MacCullough was also wounded several times but continued to fire at the enemy until he was shot through the face, losing an eye. He survived.

Lionel Renton. John Wilson and **George Linthwaite.** *B Coy.* The Valley Road was B Company's axis of advance. Each of these three was seriously wounded in the flat valley approximately half way between their starting point and the German front-line. Each was lucky to survive.

Lieutenant Tanqueray. *B Coy.* Many of the B Company dead are buried in the cemetery to north of the Valley Road, Lieutenant Tanqueray is one of them. Beside them lie the Lancashire Fusiliers who took this part of No Man's Land during the night. Most of Tanqueray's men were killed attempting to hold the Sunken Road. This looks impressive on the map, but, seen on the ground, affords little cover in some places and none in others. Being broad and shallow it gave no protection against mortar shells and was exposed to the machine gun on the north end of the Hawthorn Crater. The other group buried here were killed attempting to cross the Remblais or close up to the German strongpoint, the Copse.

Albert Macmillan. *B Coy.* MacMillan was one of a small mixed group of Lancashire Fusiliers and Middlesex, commanded by a CSM, who reached and penetrated the German wire. Most of them were killed or severely wounded. The survivors held out until they had no ammunition left. At nightfall the Wurtemburgers gave them the choice, surrender or be slaughtered. Albert Macmillan became a POW

Corporal Alf Damon. *C Coy.* Following close on the heels of D, Company, C Company moved up from Cardiff Street to Cripps Cut. They 'hopped the bags', as Alf put it, from the southern end of Cripps Cut where that trench joined Pilk Street trench. Alf ascended the slope of Les Champs Cornu and ran down the opposite slope in the direction of the valley road under fire from the Copse ahead of him, and from the northern rim of the Crater diagonally to his left. He was hit by a bullet and fell into a crater on the slope. Despite the wound in his shoulder he made his way back to Auchonvilliers later that day.

Noel Peters. *C Coy attached to HQ Coy.* After running an errand for the RSM, Noel Peters was ordered to the front line at Seaforth Trench close to Essex, to prepare for a counter-attack. After 8.30 am the few that were left of C Company manned Marlborough trench.

Shells falling on both front line and supporting trenches. From 7.45am German artillery and mortars targeted the assembly positions. Shell fire caused numerous casualties, first as 16PSB left the trenches to advance. Later in the morning this intense shelling killed the wounded as they attempted to find cover.

Communication trenches blocked by the wounded and dead of all four battalions of 86 Brigade.

THE GERMAN DEFENCE

The defenders of Beaumont Hamel were the 119th Reserve Regiment (Princess Olga of Wurtemburg's own) with two companies of the Bavarian Reserve Regiment.
Heavy Machine-guns firing from fixed and protected positions
   A B C D E
Mortars and small howitzers. F.

A The Redan, firing across the Valley Road and into the Sunken road.

B The Bergwerk. Positioned in concrete and steel shelters, heavy machine-guns fired on Royal Fusiliers, Middlesex and Royal Dublin Fusiliers as they advanced at a slow pace across the open field towards the Crater.

C The Copse. This bulge in the line allowed the Wurtemburg defenders to cross-fire across the approach to the Redan position and, in the opposite direction, across Les Champs Cornus.

D The Hawthorn Redoubt. The Wurtemburg number Nine company had several machine guns sited in protected positions built on the perimeter of the redoubt.Though the redoubt was blown up by the mine, and No Nine Coy with it, the neighbouring companies quickly brought reserve guns to the crater. These MGs not only fired across the Valley Road and up the Sunken Road but, to the south fired on 87 Brigade attacking Y Ravine.

E. Y Ravine. This natural feature was developed to include a mass of tunnels and bunkers that were re-enforced to protect the defenders. At it's two arms Y Ravine held several concrete and steel machine-gun posts. Some MGs fired south on 87 Brigade while others fired straight ahead or north, in cross fire with the guns on the Redan and Bergwerk positions.

F. Mortars and small howitzers hidden in tunnels in the Quarry and dug into the steep slopes East of Beaumont Hamel. These weapons lay hidden and protected from the British bombardment until the attack started. Alerted by the mine explosion the German gunners followed routine drill, rapidly brought out the guns and mortars and commenced firing from Ruprecht Shlucht and Leiling Schlucht.

XXXXXX. German entanglements of barbed wire. These were dense and well planned.The strength of German wire was something that every survivor commented on. Far thicker and of better quality steel than it's British equivalent, traces of this deadly wire can still be found today. In some places entanglements measured 40 ft (about 15 metres) in depth.The obstacles included calthrops and trip wires laid at levels of 150 or 300mm above ground level.

^ ^ 86 Brigade advance. Platoons and Sections were destroyed almost immediately each battalion rose out of it's assembly trenches.   The symbol denotes individuals or small groups of soldiers attacking the enemy line, usually without officers or NCOs. The triangle commemorates the tin triangle that each man wore tied to the back of his small-pack.

Some of the survivors of C and D Company's 16 MX retreating to their own lines after the failure to seize the Hawthorn Crater lip.

other was a Londoner. We were in the same platoon and section.

My London friend and I went forward together and found cover at the same time. Neither of us was hurt though our Scots friend was killed not long after we left our own trench. We were close to the German wire, which was dense and intact. Machine-gun fire was so heavy that we could not move forward. The Londoner and I could talk to each other during lulls in the firing. We decided that we would sit it out until dark and then get back to our lines. About 7.30 there was a heavy shrapnel barrage. A piece of steel smashed the foresight of my rifle. I called out to my friend but received no reply. I crawled over to him after dark and found that he was dead, hit in the head by shrapnel.[4]

The Adjutant, Captain Cochram, ran forward along the slope to the right of the road, to reorganise the remnants of B and D Companies, some of whom had reached the German wire almost on the crater's edge. One of these survivors was a young private named Derek McCullough who found himself alone in a shell hole. His platoon had been wiped out by machine-gun and mortar fire. He was a good shot and entered into a duel with German marksmen lying on their parapets across the valley. At about the same time a private of twenty-one was hit a few yards from his starting point. George Linthwaite was one of a section hit by shrapnel balls as they formed up beside their own wire. He was one of the lucky ones. Most of his platoon were killed.[5]

For 86 Brigade the scene was one of total confusion. With their officers dead and most of their NCOs killed or wounded, individual Fusiliers or Middlesex men crawled forward, held their ground, or advanced in short rushes. Small groups ran forward, dropped into holes or behind corpses, finding whatever cover they could before running forward again. In this individual fashion, what little was left of the 16th Middlesex reached the lip of the Hawthorn crater where they found a few live Fusiliers holding the position amongst a great many dead. To the left, what was left of 86 Brigade reached the Sunken Road. They could go no further because of the *remblai*, a death-trap facing the machine guns firing from German trenches on the Redan. On the hillside to the extreme edge of the Brigade sector, an incomplete section of men got through the German wire and reached the northern edge of the village. They held on there until they had no ammunition left. One of them was a young lad who joined the 16th only a few days before the attack. His name was Albert MacMillan.[6]

1. Lionel Renton's mistake is understandable because his platoon commander was reported missing believed killed. In fact Lieutenant D B Tuck was wounded but survived and was mentioned in despatches. He was one of a very small number of the Originals who enlisted in 1914 and stayed with the Battalion until it was disbanded in February 1918. Then Captain Tuck he transferred to the 2nd Middlesex and was wounded during the German offensive of March 1918. He died of wounds on March the 30th 1918.

2. Captain T H Watts was one of the Originals sent forward to OTS from Kempton Park and commissioned 15th Sept 1914. Made up to Lieutenant in Jan 1915 he was killed in action 1st July 1916.

3. Second Lieutenant E R Heaton was killed in action 1st July 1916. Of Captain Wegg, Albert Edwards wrote: 'I met Captain Wegg several months later at Chatham. He and the CO were doing a lecture tour in England.'
Like Lt Tuck, Capt Wegg was posted to the 2nd Middlesex when the 16th was disbanded. He was killed in action south of Peronne, near the Somme, during the German offensive 25th March 1918.

4. John Wilson wrote, 'When I left the army in 1918 I visited my London friend's parents. My Scotch friend had no parents and I could find no trace of his relatives when I visited Aberdeen in 1919,'

5. George Joseph Linthwaite of Mansfield Rd, South Croydon died in December 1981 at the age of 86. On the first day of the Somme battle he was wounded by shrapnel in the head and thigh. He rejoined the Battalion when he recovered from his wounds. He was gassed at Ypres and again on the Somme in 1918. After demobilisation he became a toolmaker. Despite Mr Linthwaite's age the coroner brought a verdict that he died of his wounds. Mr Linthwaite, he said, was 'A victim of the king's enemies.'

6. Albert MacMillan. See Martin Middlebrook, *First Day on the Somme*. Pub Norton USA 1972.

Chapter 30

JULY 1ST: MID MORNING

NOEL PETERS' FIRST SIGHT OF THE BATTLE came about the time that the supporting companies went to ground in No Man's Land. As military formations A and C Companies ceased to exist, just as B and D had done going before them. As for Captain Purnell and the Brigade bombers no trace was found of them. From the moment they entered the Russian sap to move forward to a point close to the German line they simply disappeared. Whether they were caught in the open and killed and their remains scattered in the shelling, or whether they were buried by a large shell falling on the sap, remains a mystery.

Before dawn Noel carried on with his usual duties. Shortly after first light he and several other boys carried dixies full of hot tea to the companies waiting in Cripps Cut and Cardiff Street trenches. The job allotted to Noel during the attack was to act as

The Sunken Road. German artillery and mortars had the Sunken Road ranged with great accuracy. Many of 86 Brigade attackers were killed there. In Malins' photograph two wounded men attempt to get back to their own line.

runner for the RSM. Just before the Lancashire Fusiliers went over RSM MacDonald told Noel to run back and bring up a party of men to join the rest of the Battalion. They were part of the Battalion reserve. The RSM gave Noel a chit to get past the Battle Police.

I was Sergeant-Major's runner on the First of July and he sent me back to Mailly to bring up the reserve. But when I got to the place where the reserve was supposed to be I found only the field cookers and a couple of cooks to look after them. The sergeant cook, who I knew well, told me to stay there with the others. I stayed with my mates, the cooks, for a while. No one came near us and there was no sign of the reserve.

I'd been ordered by the Sergeant cook to stay there but I didn't feel easy about it. I realised that there must have been a mistake because I could find no trace of the fellows I was supposed to bring back with me to the RSM. So I ran across the downs to Ocean Villas and then back along the communication trench.

The first wave of our lads had gone over. There was a lot of noise of rifle fire and some shelling. I expected our lot to be well past the German line and on their way to the village, as we'd been told it would be during rehearsals. But it wasn't like that. The whole thing was botched. It was terrible.[1]

Noel made his way down the communication trench as best he could. He was shaken by what he found. His objective was to find Battalion HQ, and he remembered the way well, but now the trench landscape was changed. Noel's way was impeded by shattered trenches, broken parapets, masses of dead or wounded men. The scene was one of utter confusion, heat, dust, smoke and noise. He remembered the scene as though it had been slowed down, like an unending nightmare. 'Wounded and un-wounded alike suffered splitting headaches for days.'

The supporting companies were holding the front line, their numbers greatly reduced. Someone told him that B and D Companies had been ordered back, but no one knew anything for certain. No one knew whether the runners had reached them or whether it was possible to move in No Man's Land at all through the bursting shells and streams of machine-gun bullets. Noel's company was C. There was talk that the Company Commander was dead and Noel's platoon officer, Mr Heath, killed too.[2]

The forward trenches had suffered concentrated shelling. They were broken and much changed. They were also blocked with wounded and you couldn't recognise any landmark or tell where you were. There was no chance of finding Battalion HQ or the RSM, so I stayed with C Company, or what was left of it.

Survivors of A and C Companies were making their way back, running or dodging from hole to hole. Some of the first two companies came with them, all mixed up with Lancashire Fusiliers, Royal Fusiliers and even some Dubs who went over, way over to our right and had lost their way and were trying to get back to their own lines. It was all confusion.

Some of our fellows wanted to go forward again, though the shelling was still intense. There was a sergeant called Jackson. He was either very brave or off his head. He picked up a Lewis gun and climbed out of our trench. He was barely through our barbed wire when he was hit. He just pitched forward and lay there, dead.

A series of stills from the official army cinematographer's film (Lieutenant Malins) shows part of that fatal retreat. Dark and grainy though the prints are, they show the men of the 16th Middlesex, not running or bounding forward, but walking slowly, hunched forward as though bowed by a storm. One ex-soldier described this fire as like a hail-storm of the most terrible and deadly kind.[3] Many did not receive the order to withdraw, or else were pinned down under the lip of the crater to the right or in the death-trap of the Sunken Road to the left. The Adjutant, Captain Cochram, went forward to take command of the remnants of B Company, holding the edge of the crater. He was hit as he gathered up survivors scattered over that long curved field. By the time he reached the crater the Adjutant received eight bullet wounds. He and his rapidly depleted command, held on to the lip of the crater in a tangle of wire until night-fall. Though he was losing blood rapidly, Cochram kept control of his small force and ordered the fit men to withdraw. Later that night the wounded, including the Adjutant, were taken prisoner.

Most of the men who returned from No Man's Land received wounds, of one sort or another. But some got back unscathed even in broad daylight and through that fire-storm. Noel described one lucky man.

A man came running towards us, bullets flying all round him. He kept falling down and we'd think, They've got him this time. Then he'd come bounding and limping on again and we'd shout "Get down you bloody fool". But he took no notice. He'd come on and he'd fall again. And then he took a run and a dive and landed on the parapet. We grabbed his arms and hauled him over. We took a chance, we did. You couldn't stick your head up. Jerry was sniping and spraying our parapet with machine-gun bullets. When we got this fellow into the trench there was blood all over us. This fellow was covered in blood. "Where are you hit?" we asked him. He was soaked in blood. He kept patting his legs to see where he was hit. "I don't know. I think they got my legs." But do you know what? He didn't have a scratch on him.'

1. See Footnote 1 in Chap 29 on the reserve and on interviews with Noel Peters at his house in Portsmouth. Memories of that day were still extremely upsetting for him and there were some aspects of the 1st July that he told me only when I got to know him well and he trusted my discretion.

2. Lieutenant H.J. Heath was killed in action, 1st July 1916. Shortly before the battle he was awarded the MC. The C Company Commander may have been Major Hall, who was twice wounded and reported dead, but survived. Or it may have been Captain E. Hall who was reported missing. His body was never found.

3. Noel's theory about these prints. Lieutenant Malins' set of prints show a group of men moving upright. This is captioned as the 16th Middlesex withdrawing from the mine crater. Noel Peters was not convinced that the caption was accurate. 'There's this photo showing what is said to be the 16th coming back out of No Man's Land after they were ordered back to their own trenches. I have my doubts about that picture. I don't remember men coming back in a group like that. We were in the front line all day, waiting for Jerry to counter-attack. Most of the Battalion were either killed or wounded and those that weren't couldn't get back till dark because Jerry continued to shell and machine-gun. There was a short armistice to bring in the wounded but that didn't last long. Had they tried to come in as that picture shows they could not have lived. They would have been mowed down. Those of us holding the line were all that were left of the 16th Battalion, except for one or two who made a dash for it, like the fellow I described to you.'

Chapter 31

JULY 1ST: NOON

B Y 10.30 AM ONLY TWO OF THE OFFICERS of the 16th Middlesex were still fit for duty: Colonel Hall and a junior officer with a light wound. Of the officers that were reported missing only the Adjutant Captain Cochram and Lieutenant Tuck were alive and both of them were wounded. Cochram was taken prisoner and Tuck eventually got back to his own line. The others, like Captain Purnell, were dead, their remains disappeared. 500 Other Ranks were dead, wounded or taken prisoner. The other battalions in 86 Brigade suffered a similar scale of casualties. 'We lost 79 out of 100 officers engaged,' the Brigade diary recorded at noon on the 1st of July.[1] At 10.30 the GOC 8th Corps, General Hunter-Weston ordered his staff to draw up a second plan to attack Beaumont Hamel using 86 and 87 Brigades.

'By 10.30am the English attackers were annihilated,' the war diary of the 119th Wurtemburg Reserve Regiment informs us. 'No Man's Land was covered with English dead and quantities of weapons and equipment.' The writer noted the effect of the British preliminary bombardment.

The provision of deep shelters reduced casualties to the minimum. Local commanders kept their heads, making an accurate appreciation of the points of enemy penetration, using reserves with great flexibility.[2]

By 11.00am most of the field telephone wires had been cut by the German bombardment. No Man's Land was swept by machine-gun fire, by mortars and artillery shells. The men holding their positions at the Hawthorn crater rim, and those at the Sunken Road, were under fire from the front and both flanks and losing men every minute. As for bringing up supplies of ammunition, this was impossible. Finally the remnants of the Lancashire, Dublin and Royal Fusiliers and the 16th Middlesex, were forced to retreat. 86 Brigade was now disorganised, its trenches crammed with dead and wounded men. The best that Brigade HQ could hope for was the reorganisation of the forward trenches to withstand the counter-attack that seemed inevitable. The 86 Brigade Major and a staff captain tried to reorganise what was left of the Brigade. Both were severely wounded. A second Major went forward from Brigade HQ and tried to cross No Man's Land. He was killed instantly.

Noel described the scene in the early afternoon.

I saw the Colonel, he was wounded, I think in the hand. He had it dressed and came back immediately. He was in a state, you could see that at once. The only other officer was Lieutenant Forbes. I think he was the same Forbes-Robertson who later commanded the Battalion.[3] This officer came down the line. There were so few of us that I asked him what we should do, whether we go forward to help our fellows in No Man's Land. 'You stay where you are,' he said. 'In case Jerry counter-attacks.'

The German defenders were so elated by their victory that many stood on their parapets to fire on their enemies. This was too much for the Fusiliers and Middlesex pinned down in No Man's Land who shot back. The Lee-Enfield is an accurate weapon and the 16th Battalion noted for its marksmanship so several defenders were shot down before they had time to take cover. They then began to shoot at anything that moved in the field ahead of them. The body of a sergeant lay a few yards in front of Noel's position on the fire-step in the front line. Next to Noel stood a private named Anderson. Seeing the dead sergeant's body and the Lewis gun that he held, Anderson ran forward, seized the machine gun and rolled with it into a shell hole. Noel described what happened.

Anderson was in the shell hole. He called for ammunition so two of us grabbed a box of magazines and joined him in the hole. None of our fellows were standing or moving in No Man's Land because Jerry snipers were firing, some with their heads and shoulders above the parapets. Some were even kneeling on their parapets so that they could get a better shot at our fellows. Anderson fired short bursts along their parapets to make them get their heads down. As soon as he emptied a magazine I took it off and clamped on a full one. Someone shouted to us to get back into our trench. Anderson fired another burst at Jerry while the rest of us scrambled back to our trench as best we could, tumbling on top of each other on the fire-step. When we sorted ourselves out we checked the gun, which was not damaged. Then we discovered that we had left the box of spare magazines behind. There was no chance of going back for it because Jerry's heavy machine guns were traversing the top of our trench.[4]

Looking through the trench periscope we could see them on their parapet again and we thought that they were massing for a counter-attack. We had no more filled drums for the Lewis gun so we took the ammunition from our own pouches and searched the dead men's pouches for more cartridges. And in this way we filled Anderson's magazine and a spare one that I had brought back with me. Had Jerry decided to come over we had little to stop him because there were so few of us left. We had some stretcher bearers, cooks, like me, an officer's batman and some runners and signallers. We were told to stay where we were and prepare for the counter-attack. We expected an attack any minute. As for the notion that

German shells pounding the British communication trenches.

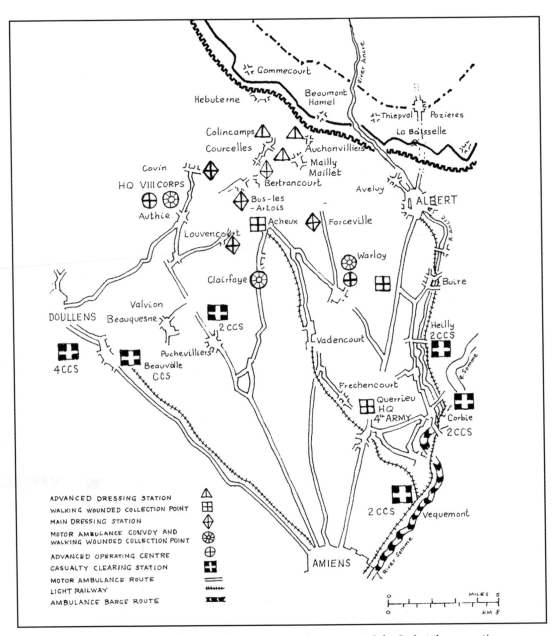

ADVANCED DRESSING STATION
WALKING WOUNDED COLLECTION POINT
MAIN DRESSING STATION
MOTOR AMBULANCE CONVOY AND
WALKING WOUNDED COLLECTION POINT
ADVANCED OPERATING CENTRE
CASUALTY CLEARING STATION
MOTOR AMBULANCE ROUTE
LIGHT RAILWAY
AMBULANCE BARGE ROUTE

Map 11. The medical plan for evacuation of the wounded, morning 1st July. In fact the evacuation was very far removed from the ideal plan due to the failure of sufficient ambulance trains to arrive immediately after the attack.

190

we could attack them, well that was plain ridiculous. We'd lost most of our men.

Luckily for us our own guns opened up shortly after mid-day. Through the periscope we could see Jerry moving back sharpish.

This bombardment was in fact, the preliminary shelling for the second attack on Beaumont Hamel; the order sent out to 86 and 87 Brigades by VIII Corps HQ. By this time Brigade HQs knew that they had insufficient troops to hold the line, let alone attack for a second time. At noon there was no communication between brigades and divisional HQs, let alone with corps HQs. Practically all telephone lines were broken within the 29th Divisional area and the few runners got through alive and unwounded. Whether by sheer luck, or the judgment of the brigade HQs, the artillery were not told of the change of plan at the local level and so the bombardment laid down on the

Wounded, Auchonvilliers.

German trenches went ahead as ordered. It dispersed the defenders but killed many men of 86 Brigade who were close up on the German wire.

With all normal communications down, junior staff officers were sent out from Divisional HQ to learn of the situation for themselves. From Mailly Maillet one staff officer walked to Auchonvilliers. His letter gives an idea of conditions in front of the village.

> *The final bombardment commenced at noon and was very severe; the noise in the village [Auchonvilliers] was terrific. The journey up the communication trench was not exactly pleasant as the enemy pitched his shells very accurately, and I had several casualties near*

Stretchering a seriously wounded man into a dug out during the afternoon of the attack.

me, *including a sergeant killed. I proceeded to make my way forward with a runner. After going a short distance, I found my way blocked by a small mixed party of Middlesex and Lancashires. The rear man told me that their Colonel was in front trying to reorganise the front-line trenches. They were unable to go forward because the attack was held up.*

Another party came up behind us. Shells were dropping all around. An officer and a sergeant-major were killed. I managed to reach the support trench and made my way forward over dead bodies and wire entanglements that had been dropped short by their carrying parties, until we reached an assembly trench a short distance from the front line. Here I met a wounded officer who had gone over the top with the third or fourth line, who told me that things had gone badly, the support companies had not got across, and the attack had come to a standstill. Together we reached Battalion HQ and found the Colonel on the telephone speaking to the Brigadier, who told him that we must reorganise our men in the trenches.[5] *Beside him was a wounded lieutenant and a sergeant-major. The Colonel said that he was going out to see what was going on and told me to stay where I was. After the Colonel had gone a short while the Brigadier asked for him on the phone, and several runners were sent out to find him but failed to do so. It afterwards transpired that he was in one of the fire-trenches organising the withdrawal of the supporting companies. The Brigadier told me to get in touch with the Colonel of the First Lancs, reorganise and attack in the afternoon. By his orders I went out and proceeded with the work of reorganisation, which consisted in sorting out the men of different battalions who were all mixed up. By the time some kind of order had been established it was well on in the afternoon, the weather was very hot and the men were exhausted. We were preparing to attack, with what men we had, when the order came from the Brigadier to stand-fast.*[6]

1. From a duplicate copy of the Brigade Diary. In 1976 this was stored in the Middlesex Regimental Archives at Mill Hill Barracks, North London. See this chapter Fn6.

2. 119th Regiment War Diary. Translation on P118 Farrar-Hockley, *The Somme*.

3. Noel Peters confused this officer with Major Forbes-Robertson who was, at this time, second in command of the Newfoundland Regiment, commanding the Battalion reserves. There is no mention of Lt Forbes in either Wallace-Grain or Everard Wyrall. 2nd Lt Ford served with the 16th when it was disbanded in 1918, but his junior rank indicates that he could not have been serving as an officer on the Somme in 1916. Major Forbes-Robertson DSO took command of the 16th when the CO Lt Col Morris was killed after only one day in command. Lt Col Forbes-Robertson commanded the 16th until it was disbanded in February 1918. He was awarded the VC in April 1918.

4. For his initiative and courage Pte J. Anderson, later Sergeant Anderson, was awarded the Military Medal.

5. The Colonel described by the staff officer is almost certainly Colonel Hall, but this cannot be confirmed.

6. The staff officer's letter, one of several 86 Brigade documents, was duplicated on pink flimsy paper similar to all the duplications of Battalion and Brigade diary entries. These were found in the 16MX file in the Middlesex Regiment Archives in the cellar of Mill Hill Barracks which by then had become the HQ of the Army Postal Service, RE for the London area.(A year or so after I visited the archives, part of Mill Hill barracks was blown up by the Provisional IRA with several casualties, some of them fatal. I am unable to discover what happened to the 16MX file.)

Chapter 32

JULY 1st: AFTERNOON

T HE ATTEMPT TO TAKE BEAUMONT HAMEL by frontal assault was over. Battalion strength was now less than a company. Colonel Hall toured the forward trenches as best he could under heavy shell fire. Noel Peters said that he looked like a broken man.

The Colonel was in a terrible state. I got to know him quite well when the 16th was in the barracks at Bethune and I never thought I'd see him like he was that day. I wonder if you can imagine what it was like? You see for young lads like me, those that were left, it was like a bad dream. We couldn't take in what was happening around us. The shock of it hit us later. But the Colonel, he had to take it all in at once and there were no officers left standing, except him and Mr Forbes. That's how it was. It was as if Colonel Hall was shell-shocked.[1]

Plans drawn up at GHQ before the battle, considered a battalion too large a unit to be controlled by one man during the first assault. Real command came down to company

Wounded man carried down a communication trench.

and platoon level. Orders stated that the CO, his RSM and headquarters staff were to remain behind until the first objective was taken. Only then would battalion HQ move forward to join the rest of the battalion and set up a new HQ in the captured trench. As events turned out on July the First this order was a wise precaution. Had commanding officers gone forward with the first, or second waves, very few would have survived. As it was some battalion commanders were so shocked and disgusted by the unnecessary wastage of their men that, against orders, they went forward with the supporting companies. Thirty senior officers were killed that day including the commander of 11 Brigade.[2]

During the middle of the afternoon both the attacker in No Man's Land and the defenders at Beaumont Hamel were relieved by a lull in the storm of shells. Noel Peters said,

> *Firing eased off a bit. We kept our heads down and only when some stretcher bearers went forward along the slope towards Serre did we cautiously look up in that direction. The shelling stopped but bullets were still coming over from the Hawthorn crater.*

For a short period there was a truce to allow the British to bring in their wounded. It also gave the Wurtemburgers a pause; a time to reorganise and bring their wounded out from the foetid bunkers and send them back for proper medical care.

There is no way of estimating how many of 86 Brigade were killed during that afternoon's bombardment by British guns close up on the enemy's wire. At last the shelling stopped. The pause made Corporal Alf Damon decide to chance his luck. Lying in a dip in the ground, which gave him a small amount of protection from the snipers and machine guns, Alf lost track of time.

> *The shelling eased, and the German machine guns seemed to have slackened off a bit, but there was no sign that anyone was coming out to help us. I began to think of getting back and whether I could risk standing up. To tell the truth I had no idea of the passage of time. The sun was broiling hot and there was no one near me left alive. I knew that I would be dead too if I waited out there much longer. I got up and set off as best I could, hobbling along, diving into a hole and then getting up and going on. Several pot-shots passed close by me, hurrying me on my way, until I reckon I set a record for the hundred yards free for all uphill sprint. In all that confusion and noise and the odd shell coming over, it was difficult to keep my footing, let alone keep to the line I had travelled on my way out. When I reached a front-line trench I jumped on top of the Lancashires, or what was left of them, who I believed well to our left. Everything was in a mess and all muddled up. A sergeant took me to a deep dug-out and advised me to stay there because our communicators were still being shelled. A staff captain had his HQ there and he was connected to Brigade by phone. Exhausted I dozed off for some time.[3]*

Derek McCullough moved, peering out from the cover of the shell hole. One of the enemy saw him, fired, and a bullet mutilated the right hand side of his face taking out his right eye.

> *I was some 20 yards from their wire. There was a lull in the shelling and four German*

stretcher bearers spotted me, one fired and hit me in the head. I wasn't quite done for and, being frightfully angry, I fired and saw one of the Germans fall. Then I feigned death. Soon after the Germans went away I received four shrapnel wounds, in the right and left shoulders and one in the thigh and one in the leg. My collar bone, shoulder blade and two ribs were broken and I had a bullet in my left lung. I managed to crawl back to our lines. That is all I remember. When I recovered consciousness I was in Hampstead.

As the firing stopped Noel Peters could see movement on the slope towards Serre and something white fluttering. He saw an extraordinary sight; one that he never saw again throughout the war. A white flag waved in No Man's Land carried by a doctor leading a small group of stretcher bearers. The party marched towards the German lines. Noel watched another doctor climb out of the trench closer to his position, near the Valley road. He walked forward steadily with one of his party carrying a flag of truce. A similar group carrying a red cross flag, approached from the German lines. The groups met on the Valley road. Each medical officer saluted and then they went about their business of caring for the wounded. Stretcher bearers came forward from both sides and, at last, some of the injured were carried away for treatment.

What happened next is not clear, and has been interpreted in various ways. What is certain is that the British artillery opened fire and that shells landed in No Man's Land. The medical teams hurried back to their respective trenches and the bulk of the wounded were left where they were. Many of the injured men were seriously wounded and needed immediate attention. The lightly wounded, unable to leave cover during the shelling, lay parched and tortured by thirst under the sun. Those who were not carried back, or crawled back, during the brief truce, lay out there until nightfall blasted by high explosive and sprayed by shrapnel balls.[4]

His energy restored, to some extent, by a brief nap in the dug-out, Alf Damon decided that it was time to get himself to the advanced dressing station before his wound stiffened or worse, became infected by the heavily manured soil of No Man's Land.

I made my way down the battered trench to Ocean Villas. The communicators were in such a mess that I soon lost my way. Luckily a stretcher bearer, coming the other way, pointed out my direction and the trench led uphill, so it seemed right. On the way, to my surprise I came on Arthur Kent. I was delighted to see him because I thought he was dead, like all the others. He sat in a hole in the chalk wall, quite dazed. A lot of blood had run down his face and neck. He was surprised that he was still alive. A bullet parted his hair, right down the middle of his scalp. The only thing he told me about it was that the impact was so great that he thought he was dead. I remember being surprised that a person's thoughts can travel at such speed between the impact of the bullet and unconsciousness.

This was not the time to hang about because both sides were shelling each other's trenches. So we made our way along the communicator towards the village, stopping to rest from time to time. Arthur had a bullet in his leg as well as the wound in the top of his head, and both of us were losing blood and pretty well exhausted. As we made our way with shells coming over I was saddened by the sight of poor fellows who hadn't made it but had died there in the trench. Picking our way over these unfortunate chaps Arthur and I were surprised by someone yelling at us. Out from his refuge in a chalk hole leapt an MP brandishing a revolver. He wanted to know where we were going. My pal's bloodstained trousers and face, and my tunic covered in gore, made it pretty obvious where we were going, and so had little trouble convincing him that we were genuine. (I heard later that two young lads, who joined the Battalion only a few days before the battle, were shot in that same trench as deserters.)

We made our way to Ocean Villas as best we could, left the communicator beyond the village and were a few hundred yards down the road towards Mailly when we met the B Company field cooker with the QM and the CQMS, Sergeant Turner and his men marching behind it. He wanted to know how far our lads had got and where was the rendezvous to get some hot food up to them in the German line. He couldn't believe it when we told him that no one had got into the German line and that the 16th was practically wiped out. I believe he thought we were doo-lally. We continued on our way, Arthur limping along. Still disbelieving the CQMS and his men marched on to Ocean Villas and his rendezvous. I often wondered what happened to all that grub, because there was no one left to eat it.

Noel confirmed that the hot food did not reach them in the trenches. On reaching

Advanced Dressing Station (ADS). Walking wounded mid morning 1st July.

Auchonvilliers Sergeant Turner could see for himself the scale of the disaster. He realised immediately that there was no chance of moving the filled dixies along the over-crowded communication trenches, and he had the good sense not to try. The cooks fed those wounded who were sufficiently recovered to eat and carried water to those who could not move.

A minority of the wounded were being treated in the crypt of the village church. Great numbers of wounded collected around the church or lay out in the open behind the village. The village suffered bombardment at regular intervals and anyone who could walk or crawl was encouraged to get out, away from the area of shell fire. So Arthur and Alf, the one with a dud leg the other a dud arm, joined the swelling column of walking wounded. As they hobbled across the downs towards Mailly Maillet, Alf noticed that the shell fire was dying down.

1. Both Everard Wyrall and Wallace-Grain comment on Colonel Hall's meticulous attention to detail, and the clarity of his explanation in the Battalion plan of battle. This is in contrast to the lack of any clear record of the actual battle. No one reading a description of either the area attacked by 86 Brigade, or an account of the wider front covered by the 29th Division, can be in the least surprised by this omission. There was no time to keep a record.

2. One of the delayed casualties amongst senior officers was Colonel Sandys, CO of the 2nd Middlesex, an all regular battalion. Sandys, who understood the true nature of the threat facing his men, went forward prematurely to join them and was wounded. Recovering in London he wrote to his Adjutant that he wished that he had died with his men then he shot himself.
Another casualty was my Mother's uncle, Captain, acting Colonel, Harold Lewis of the Baluch Horse. On the First of July he was CO of the 20th Manchesters, (5th Manchester Pals) attacking to the right of Fricourt. Colonel Lewis disobeyed orders and walked forward to join what was left of his battalion with his spaniel trotting behind him. Master and dog were shot dead

Walking wounded.

Motor Ambulance collection point on the downs above the valley of the Ancre.

by a machine gun firing from Caterpillar wood. Brigadier Prouse of 11 Brigade was mortally wounded by a shell burst while advancing after his brigade under fire. He is buried in Louvencourt cemetery.

In *The Golden Virgin* Henry Williamson describes how the Battalion CO is relieved of his command on the Somme. Williamson's semi-autobiographical series *A Chronicle of Ancient Sunlight* is fiction and has been criticised, by Robert Graves among others, because Williamson did not go over the top on the First of July. Williamson experienced the later Somme battles and was in the front line for most of the war, being wounded several times.

3. The Staff Captain described by Alf Damon may be the officer who wrote the description of the Middlesex sector of the line that afternoon.

4. There has never been a satisfactory explanation for what was a breach of the rules of war (which were still observed, to some extent, in 1916): the official account accuses the Germans of breaking the brief truce, that the German stretcher bearers were carrying off Lewis guns and that the bombardment was resumed for this reason. At the other extreme, some historians have alleged that the bombardment was deliberate policy. There is some truth in each argument. Derek McCullough was shot by a stretcher bearer, who, quite obviously, was more interested in collecting weapons than collecting wounded. On the other hand it was known to be the policy of the British GHQ to frustrate any attempt at a truce. The most likely explanation is a simple breakdown of communication. Those behind the line had no idea what was happening in front of them, and this included senior artillery officers.

Chapter 33

NIGHT
THE 1st AND 2nd OF JULY

THE SHELLING DIED DOWN FOR A TIME, allowing some of the wounded to crawl back. Then the bombardment resumed. As the British fire increased so the German artillery responded adding its contribution to the mind-destroying noise. Men lying wounded in No Man's Land or the forward trenches were killed, or received more injuries, under this barrage of shells. The forward dressing stations were hit, those at White City and Auchonvilliers church with particular severity. The former was dug deep into the chalk and its entrance shielded by sandbagged breastworks, while the crypt in the church was protected, to some extent, by the stumps of its thick stone walls. In each case it was the wounded awaiting treatment, lying in the open without any protection, who suffered horribly. Stretcher bearers too were hit as they carried their helpless loads towards Regimental Aid Centres or Advanced Dressing Stations. The lucky ones, those that could sill walk, made their way across the downs to the collecting station at Acheux. This mass of walking wounded became like a stream, growing in numbers to resemble a flood of injured and shocked men.

The survivors of the 16th Middlesex, like the Fusilier battalions, cared for their wounded as best they could aided by a tiny number of medical orderlies and sappers, transport drivers and gunners who, without orders, came forward spontaneously to help. As darkness came (about 10.00pm) Brigade staff tried to clear the wounded from the communication and assembly trenches, to rebuild damaged sections of trench and to re-organise the fit men. These officers realised immediately that the front line was so damaged and caved in that the defenders were holding on in shell holes and short sections of undamaged trench. The first continuous defensive line lay along the old support trenches. Positions at Beaumont Hamel were now reversed: the besiegers were now besieged.

In No Man's Land, the Sunken Road in particular, held a large number of Middlesex and Lancashire wounded lying amongst a greater number of dead. The embankment on either side seemed like protection but, in actual fact, proved to be a death-trap. Not only was the southern end unprotected against enfilading fire from the Hawthorn crater, but the German mortar crews had the broad track measured and ranged with great accuracy. Now those trapped in the Sunken Road attempted to get back.[1]

The mixed group holding on at the Crater's lip, Middlesex, Royal Fusiliers and Dublin Fusiliers, suffered both machine-gun fire and mortars. Most of them were wounded, including the only officer Captain Cochram, the Adjutant of the 16th. Unable to go forward or back Cochram surrendered his tiny command, the wounded remnants of more than two companies. They were picked up by stretcher bearers and carried to first aid bunkers, hollowed deep into the chalk cliffs of Y Ravine and Station Road. Here the German doctors and medical orderlies treated their wounds with as much care as they gave to their own wounded.

To the north of the village of Beaumont Hamel a group of Middlesex men, under the command of a Company Sergeant-Major, had penetrated the wire above the Redan and held out all day. Now, with all rifle ammunition and grenades spent, they found themselves surrounded and stood no chance of escape. They were in an exposed position, the majority wounded, defenceless with a heavy Maxim gun trained on them. The Sergeant-Major had no choice but to surrender. One of the men taken prisoner was Private Albert McMillan.[2]

Noel described his view of No Man's Land,

> *Looking through the trench periscope I could see our wounded and dead in No Man's Land, lying like sardines they were so close together. When it was dark our stretcher bearers went out to bring them in, or as many as they could find. Some fellows from other units went out there too; gunners, miners, all sorts. Some used sheets of corrugated iron as stretchers, or the hurdles we used to shore up trench walls, anything they could find to*

British prisoners file through a German occupied mine crater. Failure of the British to occupy and hold the Hawthorne crater was to prove disastrous.

bring them in. We wanted to go out too, to get our fellows in, but we were ordered to stay where we were, manning the line, in case of a counter-attack. There were so many wounded out there that they had to leave some of them out there. We could hear some of them poor fellows crying out all night. There was nothing anyone could do. And there was nothing anyone could do for the dead. They stayed out there in the open for months.

During the evening and early hours of darkness fire by heavy machine guns and mortars prevented any movement. At some time about 10.30pm, when firing ceased, helpers came forward from a variety of units stationed behind the line, as Noel described. Carrying makeshift stretchers along the shattered communication trenches proved impossible. The Royal Engineers bridged the trenches and speeded up the work of clearing the wounded by carrying them on trolleys and handcarts. It was almost impossible, in the darkness, to tell those seriously wounded and unconscious from the dead. Albert Edwards was one of the lucky ones. He remembered nothing, but believed that he was picked up either very late that night, or early in the morning of the 2nd July.

Lionel Renton did not lose consciousness either through the heat of the long day of blazing sunshine or through the cold night that followed. Had he lapsed into unconsciousness he would have died out there. A stretcher party found him.

I heard a search party. They were not far off, looking for wounded. I must have groaned, or made a noise, because I heard a stretcher bearer say, "There's one over here." And then he said, "Where are you hit?" I remember saying a silly thing. "All over, I think." Because that's what it felt like. They put me on a stretcher and carried me back over the rough ground to an Advanced Dressing Station. The place was in the devil of a mess, wounded all over the place. The surgeons had been at work for more than eighteen hours, they looked done in, exhausted. A Medical Officer looked me over, my breeches soaked in blood. He just nodded and said "Put him outside." I thought that he meant that I was a goner. That's what they did with chaps who were too far gone to be worth treating. I must have gone as white as a sheet because the MO said, "You're a very lucky fellow. A fraction of an inch and the bullet would have cut your femoral artery. You'd have bled to death in minutes out there. You're for the ambulance. We can't treat you here." Then he added, "You'll be all right."

In the forward trenches, Colonel Hall's first priority was to secure and hold the broken line with the small force that was all that was left of his command. He and the RSM regrouped the survivors and placed them along the line in some sort of order. The Battalion had two officers and very few NCOs amongst the 180 Other Ranks still on their feet. Many of the survivors were Battalion Headquarters staff, band-boys, runners, signallers and cooks. One of these boys was Noel.

At dusk we were ordered to stand-to. We were still under shell fire. Each man jumped up on the fire-step and fired ten rounds at the German line, then we jumped down again into our trench. We did this at dusk and dawn for four days and nights to make Jerry think that there was more of us than there was.

The line had to be held, but Colonel Hall knew well that his exhausted men needed food. He took a chance and sent Noel and three band-boys back to Auchonvilliers to pick up rations. The four boys left their rifles in a recess in the chalk and set off up the communication trench to the village. They returned some forty minutes later with a double load of cold food and bottles of cold tea, in sandbags slung on poles, two and two. The loads were heavy. Once they were safely back in the line and delivered the food they rested in a fire-bay. Noel went off down the trench to retrieve his rifle. On his way back he heard the distinctive sound of a mortar coming over and ducked down where he was. He ran back to the bay where the three boys were resting. The mortar bomb landed close to it killing all three. One was a friend of Noel's, their friendship dating back to Perham Down. Noel touched his face in the darkness. He had stopped breathing. The three boys were buried that night in Mailly Maillet.[3]

The following day, the 2nd of July, both defenders and attackers looked on the rough ground between the villages of Beaumont Hamel and Auchonvilliers, awed by the scene of death and desolation revealed in the dawn light. The ferocity of the previous day's battle had drained away and men on both sides were left in a state of shock, exhaustion and icy depression.

To the south of the battle line both the British, and their French allies south of the Somme, had taken ground and this gain was fiercely disputed. There was no pause in the fighting. But in other places, to the right of the line, the German victory was complete. Even in villages like Serre where the British had advanced a considerable distance, they had not been reinforced or re-supplied and, consequently, the Germans had driven them back and regained their old strong points.

In the trenches in front of Beaumont Hamel, in the Redan strong point and along the Crater rim, the mood of the defenders turned from exultation at the severe defeat inflicted on their attackers to awe at the scale of the destruction, and even in some cases, to pity. The Wurtemburg Regimental diary described 'The lines of English dead are like tide-marks, like flotsam washed up on the sand.' The Germans ceased firing and this

Burying the British dead.

allowed the stretcher bearers to go out once again. Some of those difficult to locate in darkness could now be brought in, many others had died during the night. The dead and wounded were scattered across a strip two hundred yards wide, full of holes and treacherous with wire and battle debris. Often it was easier to pick out the wounded from the dead by the sound of their cries of pain than by sight.

With the coming of daylight, on July the Second, medical officers on both sides resumed their un official truce, despite the breach of truce by shelling the previous day. Many wounded were carried in during that period of cease fire. It is a tribute to the extraordinary physical fitness and will-power of the soldiers in the 16th Battalion that even some of the most gravely wounded survived for a day and a night lying in No Man's Land without medical treatment.

The battalion, reduced to less than a quarter of its strength, held the line at Auchonvilliers. They held the line for a counter-attack that did not come. One of them was Noel Peters. Periodically he and a couple of others walked back to the village to pick up some cold rations, some hot tea and enough rum for a small tot for each man.

The official history states that the 16th (Public Schools Battalion) of the Middlesex Regiment was relieved from its front line position on the 3rd of July. Everard Wyrall writes. 'On the 4th the survivors of 86 Brigade were withdrawn from the lines and

Men of mixed battalions. 86 Brigade regrouping after the battle.

Medical officers on both sides dealt with the wounded.

proceded to Englebemer and Mailly Maillet woods.'

Noel Peters disputed both dates saying reasonably enough, that events that seem clear in official reports are rarely so simple on the ground, especially in the aftermath of a battle. Noel was not clear exactly how many nights they spent in the line before the Battalion was relieved. It was certainly four and maybe more than that. This was not the first discrepancy between the official report and the diaries and memories of those who were in the line. It was not the last, so there may be a simple explanation for the muddle over dates. The relieving battalion, the Monmouths, were over-stretched. They may well have kept some Middlesex men and Lancashire Fusiliers in the line for an extra day, or even two. On the other hand, Noel's impressions of those first days of July were those of a boy in a deep state of shock. His sense of time may have been distorted by a series of horrific memories, like the death of his friends in the next fire-bay, and the recurrence of distressing, and all too realistic, after-images and nightmares. Under this degree of stress three days might well seem like a week, or more.

1. The lack of cover at the Sunken Road is shown clearly in the well known photograph of two wounded men, one attempting to drag the other to safety. They are part of 86 Brigade but whether Lancashire or Middlesex men is not known. What is more of a puzzle is who was in a position to take the photograph in this terrible place at that time? Possibly Malins, though he does not mention going forward to the Sunken Road.

2. Ref: Martin Middlebrook. First Day on the Somme. Pte Albert Macmillan joined the 16th Middlesex during the last days of June and had no front-line experience prior to the battle. He spent the rest of the war as a POW, working in a mine. In 1919 he returned to his old job at Kings Cross station, as a porter with LNER. I did not meet Mr McMillan. His story is one of many recorded by Martin Middlebrook. For anyone studying the tragedy of the Somme Middlebrook's superbly researched book comes high on the list of essential reading.

3. Noel Peters was reticent about July the First. Despite eventful, arduous and dangerous front-line service in 1917 and 1918 nothing shocked him as much as the events at Beaumont Hamel. It took many visits to Portsmouth before I could begin to piece together this part of his story and often I felt guilty about asking him to recall events that were obviously painful. He said to me, several times on different occasions, 'I've stood beside their graves at Auchonvilliers many times and each time I wondered why they are down there and I'm here. It could easily have been the other way round.'

Chapter 34

A DAY OF UPS AND DOWNS

THE DAY AFTER THE BATTLE the C in C, Sir Douglas Haig wrote in his diary for Sunday 2nd July 1916:

A day of ups and downs! As regards weather, the day was fine, bright sun and cool wind, but the barometer registered a fall during the night. I visited two Casualty Clearing Stations at Montigny, one under Major Thomas, the other under Colonel MacPherson. They were very pleased at my visit. The wounded were in wonderful spirits. I saw Sir Wilmot Herringham with his coat off, setting a fine example by washing and attending to slightly wounded cases. I believe he is consulting physician at Bart's Hospital, London. Everything seems going well. The A.G. (Adjutant General) reported that the total casualties were estimated at over 40,000 to date. This cannot be considered severe in view of the numbers engaged and the length of the front attacked.[1] As Field Marshal Haig recorded the day's events, two of the Adjutant General's statistics were sleeping in a French railway carriage, totally exhausted. The train that lodged Alf Damon, Arthur Kent and more than a hundred others was waiting in a siding for clearance to begin the journey to the coast. The previous night, the 1st of July, Alf and Arthur were amongst thousands of walking wounded whose route over the downs was sign-posted to separate them from the more serious casualties who had to be carried by horse-drawn or motor ambulance.

Arthur and I walked for about a mile to the dressing station which was a marquee with a red cross on the roof, pitched in an open field. Arthur had been shot through his tin-hat, no serious damage, a scalp wound. The doctor seemed more concerned about the wound in his leg, which had become inflamed. Arthur was most surprised to find that he was still alive when he regained consciousness. I did not see many stretcher cases because our route was different from theirs. I saw the Red Cross girls driving their canvas topped Ford ambulances to within a mile of the line to evacuate the wounded. They were under fire all the time and showed great courage. In my case, and also in Arthur's, a clean dressing was all the treatment that they could give our wounds and then the MO at the dressing station sent us on our way. We walked on for a couple of miles, away from the worst of the shelling. Neither of us felt much pain and we just plodded on as best we could. There were great numbers of wounded chaps sleeping in the fields. When we saw them we both realised how tired we were and a bit sick. We slept that night on the grass without a blanket, but the weather was not too cold so no complaints about that. Also Jerry spared us a shelling.

Alf Damon was surprised to learn, many years after the battle, that his physical and mental state was predicted in the RAMC training manual for 1911.

'Immediately after an attack most men are in a high state of nervous tension. For a

variable time after being wounded this state of excitement enables a man to make his way to an ADS. A reaction, mainly due to nervous exhaustion, and, to a certain extent, to the shock of being wounded, then makes itself felt, and the wounded man is unable to proceed further without the aid of some form of transport.

Walking wounded, like Alf and Arthur, were the lucky ones. They could shift for themselves, at least for the first part of the journey, far enough to get out of the area under shellfire, shrapnel and dropping bullets from heavy machine guns. Once out of the most dangerous zone many of the walking wounded collapsed beside the road or in fields nearby. Some were more seriously wounded than they knew and only will-power kept them going. Alf and Arthur avoided the roads, crossroads in particular. These were mapped and ranged by the German artillery who aimed for ammunition lorries and limbers moving up to the front. Lorries returning empty picked up any wounded that they saw on the road. The gunners made no fine distinction between those going up and those going back.

Later, in hospital, a lightly wounded soldier told Alf that he climbed onto one of these lorries, which he found was full of men that were seriously injured. Seeing one of his mates hobbling along in the distance he climbed off again and sat beside the road to wait for him. The lorry travelled only a few hundred yards down the road when a shell scored a direct hit, killing everyone in it.

The Director of Army Medical Services (DMS) anticipated a high ratio of casualties and worked out an evacuation plan well in advance of the attack. He had the support of General Rawlinson (GOC Fourth Army) who had been adversely impressed by the failure of the evacuation plan at Loos. During the battle of Loos a shortage of

Ambulance train.

ambulances and other forms of transport caused what medical staff called Backing Up. This meant a large number of wounded in the area immediately behind the front within range of the enemy guns. Both Fourth Army HQ and senior medical staff foresaw that the problem was to maintain the flow behind the line to ease the problem of wounded being stranded at the Regimental Aid posts and Advanced Dressing Stations (ADS). Behind the line and beyond the range of all but the long range guns, each Casualty Clearing Station (CCS) was sited close to a rail line so that ambulance trains could carry the wounded swiftly to the Channel ports. In the case of the small town of Corbie, the CCS was close to the Somme canal for the medical barges. An ambulance train, complete with its own medical staff, could hold 400 wounded, while each barge held forty.

The DMS estimated that he would need seven ambulance trains and four passenger trains for the walking wounded. Rawlinson did not think this enough.[2] In the event, conditions on July the 1st and the following few days exceeded the worst nightmare of even the most pessimistic medical officer. There were too few medical staff to cope with the unprecedented flow of injured men. Surgeons, nurses, orderlies and stretcher bearers worked day and night without rest.

Arrangements for 86 Brigade wounded came under the 29th Divisional medical plan. Each battalion medical officer set up his Regimental Aid Post (RAP) with his RAMC orderlies. In Auchonvilliers Captain Knight converted the crypt into an RAP. The shelter under the church was a strong one and, in addition, Knight cleared a large farmhouse for use as an Advanced Dressing Station (ADS). This solid stone building was reinforced with sandbags and sheets of iron. Heavy casualties were predicted by 29th Division Headquarters and it increased each battalion's number of stretcher bearers from sixteen

The sight of the untreated wounded, and being forbidden to help them, haunted Noel for the rest of his life. These more fortunate lightly wounded are awaiting transport away from the front.

to thirty-two. In the case of the 16th Middlesex this included the Battalion bandsmen and pipers.[3]

The collection point for walking wounded was a dug-out beside the Auchonvilliers to Acheux road. This became a target for German guns and was abandoned, consequently, many men simply kept on walking until too exhausted to carry on.

Noel Peters said that the plight of the seriously wounded, lying untended in the open, was pitiable. Of all the horrible and pathetic sights that he saw that day the one that haunted him most was the fate of the wounded at Auchonvilliers. The village stands on a ridge. In 1916 it was both a junction point for several important communication trenches and an observation post. 29th Division staff officers, taking their lead from GHQ, worked on the assumption that the German medium artillery and heavy trench mortars would be put out of action by the four days' preliminary bombardment. This did not happen so the ferocity of the German shelling came as a rude shock. The church was both a distinctive and important target and was shelled almost continuously once the battle started. The ADS took direct hits time after time on July the First, but its shield of sandbags, baulks of timber and thick boiler-plate shielded those inside the crypt. The tragedies took place outside where the wounded awaiting first treatment Backed Up, as Rawlinson feared, lying in rows on stretchers in the fields and woods between Auchonvilliers and Mailly Maillet. Many of those who could have been saved were killed where they lay by high explosive or shrapnel shells. Both Mailly Maillet and Acheux were within the range of German medium artillery, but these were now concentrating their fire on the British batteries and their ammunition supplies coming up by road. They used HE rather than shrapnel shells, otherwise even more wounded would have been killed.[4]

At 8.30 am, one hour after the attack went over, the forward medical units treated men wounded by shrapnel in the assembly trenches. Very few men returned from No Man's Land where the attackers were pinned down. RAPs and ADSs were not overstretched. As for the CCS they prepared for the number of wounded estimated by the Divisional medical staff.

The first ambulance train had been standing in Doullens station all night. At noon it was half full with a mixed collection of wounded, including those hit the previous day, sick men and a small number of men picked up early that morning. Those wounded early in the battle and moved back along a smoothly operating medical chain were the lucky ones. The nurses were the first English, Scottish, Welsh or Irish girls they had seen since preparation for the battle began. For many, minimum medical attention, a cup of tea and a smiling female face were all that was needed to restore morale. The ambulance train set off for Amiens and Etaples in the early afternoon with half its bunks empty. Some of the wounded would be in England within twenty-four hours, the Somme chalk still whitening their boots and uniforms. The Adjutant General's complacency appeared justified; the system seemed to be working exactly as planned.

By mid-morning of July the First the CCS were filling faster than the medical staff expected but still within their capacity. They believed that sufficient number of ambulance trains would be on their way to maintain the flow away from each CCS. The first signs of strain showed themselves in the shortage of stretchers being returned from the CCS to the front. There were no beds free so the wounded men were laid out on stretchers in the open. Next came the strain on the motor ambulances and the Division's reserve was ordered forward. The system was now working at full capacity. Every CCS was full by mid-afternoon. As the numbers Backed Up so the return supply of stretchers ceased. On top of all their normal duties medical orderlies now had to construct awnings to shield the wounded in the open. Orderlies made beds out of straw to liberate the much-needed stretchers.

The reason for this congestion, the Backing Up that Rawlinson feared, was the lack of hospital trains. Of the fouteen promised by the Quartermaster General only one had

Ambulance barge on the River Somme.

arrived and that left in the afternoon. RAMC staff telephoned Movements Control officers to find that the railway staff of the Royal Engineers were as puzzled and worried as the medical staff. Later that afternoon two more trains arrived, making a total of three out of the promised fourteen to serve the whole of the Fourth Army area.

An NCO who watched the wounded returning from the morning's attack was Sergeant Quinnell MM of the Royal Fusiliers. His was one of the battalions that was waiting in Aveluy Wood to be sent forward in the second attack. (This was the attack ordered by Hunter-Weston but cancelled by de Lisle.)

> *The first walking wounded came past us, just kept going as best they could through the woods. Men without rifles or helmets, staring eyes in dirty faces, men with soiled bandages round arms or heads, men covered in blood or blackened by smoke. Most of them were silent, some mumbled or swore to themselves. Some plucked at their faces or plucked their jackets. The sight of men in that state was a shock, I can tell you, but nothing to what we saw when we went up into the line that night.[5]*

Some wounded were taken in to CCSs throughout the rear areas, others lay in sheds and barns if they were lucky; on the grass if they were not. The strain now bore down on the medical staff, working without a break, not least on the stretcher bearers. Lacking stretchers they now carried men in on anything that would bear their weight, even on frames improvised out of rifles and scraps of canvas. As darkness covered the battlefield men began to crawl in from shell holes in No Man's Land. Untreated for more than twelve hours their wounds were in a bad condition. Noel Peters remarked on the plight of those who were considered too badly wounded to be worth treating:

> *Many of those lads were in a very bad state after lying out in No Man's Land in the sun all day. The medical orderlies put them outside the RAP because Captain Knight and his men had so many to treat that they could only see to the ones who stood a chance of recovering. I had strict orders to bring food and water up to the men holding the line. I had to pass those poor fellows, the wounded lying outside. Some were delirious, some silent but still conscious, some you could see had died there where they lay untreated.*

The sight of the untreated wounded, and being forbidden to help them, haunted Noel for the rest of his life, despite everything that happened to him later in the war.

Captain Knight and his orderlies worked without rest. They were too few and the wounded too many. The medical staff had to make difficult choices and do the best that they could. Those with abdominal wounds had to be treated immediately, without surgery they would die whereas with reasonable attention they stood a good chance of recovery. Amputation of a limb too badly mangled to be recoverable was another operation that had to be carried out swiftly. Battalion medical officers had to make snap judgments, an appalling choice of who stood a chance of living and who would be put aside to die. The lucky ones were carried away from Auchonvilliers on anything that would serve as a makeshift stretcher. There was no time to bury the dead who were piled behind the barn.[6] At 10.50pm the Director of Medical services for the Fourth Army wrote in the official diary: 'Ambulance trains not yet arriving. All CCSs in southern area are full except those at Vequemont and these filling rapidly.'

Immediately behind the front of the Fourth and Third Armies, and stretching into the rear areas for two or three miles, lay 35,000 wounded men. Ambulance drivers, the men of the ASC and the young girls of the Red Cross, turned away from the CCS, searched the countryside for any kind of shelter, a barn, a cowshed or a sheltered field; anywhere the driver could leave her load of wounded in relative safety. Noel reported that stretcher bearers were now exhausted, many collapsed and slept amongst the wounded. The official diaries for most of the medical units for the 1st and 2nd of July are blank. There was no time to rest, no time to eat, certainly no time to write up the diary.

But as the Commander in Chief recorded in his diary, this was 'A day of ups and downs.'

1. The Private Papers of Sir Douglas Haig.

2. On the 14th of June Rawlinson wrote to the Quartermaster General's Department at GHQ. 'I consider it essential that means of evacuation by trains should be provided for at least 10,000 wounded per day in order to avoid over-crowding and discomfort for the wounded at CCS and other medical units. In order to evacuate this number 12 ambulance trains and 6 improvised trains will be required by this army.' The Quartermaster General, Lieutenant General Maxwell, was senior to Rawlinson on the Army List. He replied, brusquely, 'It is not anticipated that there will be any difficulty in meeting the needs of Fourth Army during active operations.' At a time when generals of every nation were noted for their lack of compassion Rawlinson's thoughts on the wounded stand out to his credit.

3. Battalion stretcher bearers were not allowed to wear a Red Cross armband, unlike the MO and RAMC orderlies. Several stretcher bearers were shot in No Man's Land by mistake.

4. In the 29th Divisional area the main dressing stations were sited at Bus-les-Artois, Bertancourt and Forceville. The wounded from 86 Brigade were supposed to be sent there but, in practice, wounded were sent back to any ADS that would treat them. Clairfaye was the base for the motor ambulance company while Authie and Warloy held Advanced Operating Centres. 8th Corps had four CCSs at Doullens, one at Beauval, two at Puchevilliers and one at Gezaincourt.

5. Sergeant Quinnell MM of the 9th Royal Fusiliers, witnessed the attack on Mash Valley, at La Boiselle, in which the 2nd Middlesex, an all regular battalion, was almost wiped out. The Fusiliers moved into a reserve position in Aveluy Wood the previous night. Their role was to attack in the second phase. 'As far as I remember the 2nd Middlesex had one officer left and about a platoon of men. The South Wales Borderers were in a similar state.' This was one of a series of conversations between Sgt Quinnell MM and the author at the Royal Chelsea Hospital and at Chelsea School of Art 1978-79.

6. Battalion Medical Officers had strict orders to treat those who stood a good chance of recovery first and attend to the most seriously wounded later. The wounded who died at Auchonvilliers are buried behind the church. This building, like the rest of the village was rebuilt in the nineteen-twenties.

7. One of the very few units that did keep up its diary was No 25 Ambulance Company ASC.
'7.00 pm Urgent demand for more stretchers. Indented CCS Heilly without avail. 8.30 pm. 36 CCS and 38 CCS Heilly closed. Choked with cases. Opened several barns for temporary accomodation.'

Chapter 35

SITTING, TRAIN OR SHIP

WOUNDED MEN IN THEIR THOUSANDS LAY IN THE OPEN. Alf considered himself a lucky man. His luck held. He woke on the morning of July the Second feeling none the worse apart from the wound in his arm which had stiffened.

Hundreds of men were lying in a large field all round us. A few were on stretchers, most of them on straw or on gas-capes. Arthur wasn't feeling too good, what with the crack on the head and the wound in his leg. My arm felt stiff and I was a bit weak in the legs, but apart from that I was alright so I set off for the CCS to see if I couldn't scrounge something to eat. The cook was a decent fellow. I can't remember what yarn I spun him, but he gave me a piece of bread and some Bully. I had an old tin I'd found so he filled that up with hot tea. I carried it back to the place where I'd left Arthur and we breakfasted in the mist with wounded all round us. Some looked in a bad way and some died in the night. After we'd eaten we still felt hungry so I set off to see if I could scrounge something else. I met the driver of an ammunition lorry. "Have you seen the doctor?" he asked. I lied and said that I had. "Hop on the back then," he said. "I have to take you lot to the railway." "Hang on

Wounded men in their thousands lay in the open.

Wounded soldiers with labels wait to board a hospial train, 1916.

a mo, I have to fetch my mate," I told him. I collected Arthur and we set off. By this time I didn't feel so good, but Arthur and I made our way back to the lorry as best we could. By the time we climbed on board it was almost full. The driver slammed the tailboard and off we went.[1]

The sun rose and it was clear to me that we were in for another hot day. There was a train waiting in a siding, a line of typical French third class carriages. The engine stood there in the morning sunshine, steam belching from its cylinders. It was connected to a line of old wooden carriages and the usual steel cattle trucks. None of them looked too comfortable, but we were glad to see it just the same. We waited. Nothing happened. Inside the carriage it was very hot. I saw one poor fellow suddenly vomit blood. Two RAMC blokes carried him off. He was very pale, no doubt with an internal injury. We waited. A very old Frenchman brought us water. He didn't say anything and never smiled, just kept coming back with bottles and jugs of water. Bless him for that whoever he was.

Then, at dusk, there was the type of commotion that always attended the departure of a train on French railways and the train moved off. There were about 400 men on that train, maybe 450. By that time I'd found a place on the luggage rack and made myself as comfortable as I could. The journey through the night took a long time and I don't know where the train went. Sometimes I'd doze and when I woke we'd be waiting in a siding while an ammunition train went past us, going up to the line. Lights flashed and I'd hear the French railwaymen grumbling and mumbling away and steam hissing from the engine. Somewhere a poor fellow started screaming and crying out in his sleep, re-living some of the things he's seen the day before, I suppose. Some of the fellows, who seemed spry *enough when we got onto the train, relieved as we were to get out of the shelling, now seemed in low spirits. They'd been buoyed up by all the excitement of getting onto the train, but now all that was ebbing away and they remembered all their mates still out there on the wire. Sometime during the night an orderly came round and attached a label to the epaulette of each wounded man. 'Army Form w3083' and stamped across it in blue letters: 'Sitting, Train or Ship'.*

Next day (July 3rd) we reached a large town and someone said it was Rouen. From there the train took us to Etretat and the coast. The hospitals were full so they put us in temporary shelters near the beach before taking us to Le Havre next day in lorries and motor-buses. On the dockside we had another long wait because two ships had collided in the harbour. Groups of women helpers carried specially marked cards which they filled in for us and sent to our homes. The same thing happened when we reached Blighty. These card workers carried on this duty until the war ended because the same thing happened when I was wounded in 1918.

By chance Lionel Renton also reached Etretat. He too spent the early hours of July the Second in a field close to a CCS, but which one he did not know.

I stayed on a stretcher until about 6.00am. It was daylight and there was an early morning mist. An ambulance backed up and two RAMC chaps put me on it, still on the stretcher. The driver was a decent chap and he asked me, "Shall I go slowly to lessen the bumping? Or fast to get you to the next hospital?"

"Put your foot down chum," I told him.

The journey was not comfortable. The poor devil in the stretcher above me had a smashed hip and was in terrible pain. Another chap's wound was still bleeding and blood dripped from the stretcher onto the chap beneath. Someone said that the trains were full and that the ambulances were driving direct to the coast. I don't remember. I suppose I

Home safe and sound and in good hands. Convalescents in UK after the Battle of the Somme.

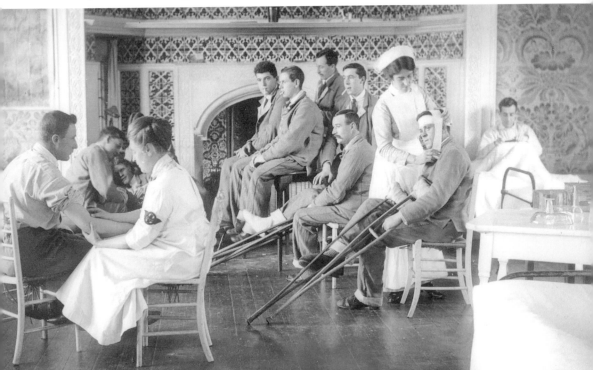

Above: A 'Netley Coach' in which shell-shock cases were transported.

Left: Inside a Netley carriage.

Below: A corridor inside Netley Hospital.

passed out. I found myself at Etretat, in a hospital where they operated immediately. The surgeon cleaned out the passage made by the bullet in my groins and patched up the holes in my arms. They gave me no further trouble, but I hadn't heard the last of the bullet in my leg.

But for the strength, dedication and courage of those doctors, nurses, drivers and orderlies, many wounded would not have survived those hot and terrible few days in July. When night came on 2 July, 10,000 of those wounded the previous day still lay in, or just behind, the battle zone. Only five trains arrived in the first twenty-four hours and carried away just over 2,000 men. After the catastrophic blunder made by the Quartermaster General's department, railway officials and RE movements control made every effort to evacuate the wounded.[2]

On 3rd July the situation began to improve. In the Fourth Army area, trains made fifty-eight journeys, moving more than 31,000 men in four days. At the end of the fourth day the Director of Army Medical Services noted that all the wounded accepted by medical units were now receiving proper care and attention.

Noel Peters remarked that another major problem now showed itself, lack of food. The problem of moving the wounded, combined with the need for extra lorries to bring up shells and small-arms ammunition, meant that ration reserves were exhausted. Noel pointed out that this was less of a problem in the front line than in the area immediately behind the line. The number actually manning the fire-steps was small and did not lack either water or food for the first couple of days. Just as they had to take the rifle ammunition from dead men's pouches, now thirst forced them to collect the water bottles. As for food there were still tins of Bully beef or Maconochie's stew, and biscuits to be found in the packs abandoned by the wounded, or on the dead.

In the area covered by VIII Corps, medical staff had a lull in which they could clean up their temporary hospitals and aid stations, reorganise, and even get a little rest, though this was short lived. For VIII Corps, in the north, the battle was in stalemate. In the south the fighting continued and wounded continued to flow in. If anything, medical units now suffered an even greater food shortage than those closer to the line. The unexpected number of casualties, combined with the length of their stay close to the front, exhausted both the daily ration and the reserves of food. CCSs were short of bandages and dressing materials, blankets, antiseptics, anaesthetics and, of course, stretchers. As for the medical staff, they were exhausted.

For the survivors of the 16th Middlesex the battle was over. Relieved by the Monmouthshire Regiment the depleted number of NCOs and men left the trenches at Auchonvilliers and formed up at Mailly woods. For the medical staff the moment of rest was fleeting. At last the ambulance trains began to move the last of those wounded on July the First. Hospital ships sailed to England from Le Havre, Calais, Boulogne and Dieppe. They landed the wounded at all the ports along the south coast, though the greatest number arrived at Southampton.[3]

The wounded received the minimum treatment in France and there was no time to clean them up. The majority arrived at a hospital in England as they were, dressed in filthy, torn, smoke-blackened uniforms, boots covered in mud and chalk, their bodies infested with lice and smeared with blood.

Vera Brittain recorded that the first of the Somme wounded arrived at the hospital in Camberwell four days after the commencement of the battle. She described, 'Immense convoys which came without cessation for about a fortnight, and continued at intervals for the whole of that sultry month and the first part of August.'[4] For over a week trains left Southampton at a rate of one an hour, carrying the wounded to hospitals all over Britain. As those in the south filled so the wounded were carried to the midlands and north. Lionel Renton needed further surgery so remained in the south, Alf Damon made a quick recovery and so he stayed in the south too. Albert Edwards was one of a train-load of wounded directed northwards.

I remember nothing about the battle, nor anything after I was shot. The first thing that I remember was my wounds being dressed in what must have been a Casualty Clearing Station. Then a motor ambulance took me to a hospital for treatment and then I was sent on to Calais and across the sea to either Folkestone or Dover. Our train went north, to Nottingham and there I met another Private from the 16th. His name was Little and we went to the same kindergartern in Kensington. I met up with him at Perham Down and saw him in France, of course, so knew him well. He was not so sure about me and I realised that the poor chap had lost his memory.

Lionel Renton remained conscious and remembered the journey from Le Havre to Southampton quite clearly. 'The first hospital train that I saw was the one that took us from Southampton docks to Netley. This was not the Butcher's Shop, thank God, but a temporary one in huts and run by the Red Cross.'[5]

The wounds in my arms healed up but the wound in my groin became very swollen and inflamed. So they had to operate again. They found a piece of khaki cloth, from my uniform, which had been carried into the wound, forced in by the bullet. It stayed there, plugging the channel so that the wound wouldn't heal properly. The surgeon took out the bit of cloth and cleaned up the hole. He left the bullet alone. He told me afterwards that it was lodged in a muscle and he didn't want to start cutting to find it. He said that it wouldn't cause any trouble where it was. I must say that he was right. It is still down there somewhere and shows up on X-rays, but it has never been any trouble. At Netley they thought that I would never walk again without a limp. But I was extremely fit in those days and, after three months, I was up and about again.

Alf Damon was lucky and recovered quickly. Though in mid 1916, luck was a matter of opinion because a quick recovery meant a quick return to France and the hazards of life in the front-line.

On arrival in Blighty, and joining a train at the docks, we were met at Victoria by yet more civilian workers who filled in more cards to send home. I thought that this was a fuss about nothing, but at that time I had no idea how bad the casualty figures were or the state of total confusion behind the line in France. In my case, and in many others, there was special need to reassure my people, as I will explain later.

Leaving Victoria station in charabancs and lorries we were surprised to find crowds of cheering civilians. Some threw roses, others cheered, young girls waved, some laughed, some cried. If you saw it on a film you'd think it propaganda or some Hollywood trash, but this was real. I had never seen anything like it before, and I never saw it again.[6] Whether civilians were sick of the lies told by press and politicians and wanted something real to cheer about, or whether they needed a victory, (because most people believed it so at the time), whether they had never seen masses of wounded before (most of us with quite presentable wounds, by the way) I honestly cannot say. In early July the newspapers told them that it was a great victory, the casualty figures did not come in until later.

The convoys of charabancs took us to a Brighton hospital and the scene was the same there, flowers, pretty girls, cheering crowds. It was amazing. The hospitals you see in the picture-papers are usually big private homes owned by Lady this or that, and staffed by her wealthy chums – 'the honourable Miss something-or-other doing her bit for the wounded officers'. These are special hospitals, special because of their rank and breeding, and they *cater for those with wounds that don't look too bad. They don't show you the other special cases, those with half a face blown away or those with severe abdominal wounds, or no limbs.*

Mine was an ordinary hospital, but I have absolutely no complaints about it. Once again I was lucky. It was staffed mainly by VADs who could not have been nicer, or treated us with more care if we had been duke's sons. The surgery was good and Arthur was soon discharged and went on convalescent leave. I followed a few weeks later.

Albert Edwards was less lucky:

In Nottingham I recovered both the use of my limbs and some of my memory. It is very strange. I remember Auchonvilliers and the trenches opposite Beaumont Hamel prior to the attack with great clarity and in detail. But the attack itself remains a blank. I can remember very little between setting off to cross No Man's Land and the slow recovery in England. The missing pieces have never come back.[7] When the wounds in my legs had been treated and I could get about, at least to some extent, they moved me to another hospital. This was still in the Nottingham area but a little way out of the town. My friend Little was there too, but he did not know who I was. I met a young nurse there. She was the adopted daughter of John Player, of Player's cigarettes. We became friends and wrote to each other through the rest of the war.

Much later, when I was fully recovered, I reported to the Middlesex depot at Chatham, where I waited around for some weeks. I expected a posting to France. By accident I was on duty one night in the HQ office and I got a look at my papers. I discovered my medical reports which were followed by a rubber stamp mark, 'Not to be sent overseas'. So that was that, I never discovered the reason.

Alf Damon wrote, 'The press printed all sorts of lies during those first days of July. Lots of eye-wash about "HAIG'S GREAT VICTORY" or "THOUSANDS OF HUN PRISONERS". It was absolute tosh.'[8]

This triumphant propaganda continued for the rest of the month. The *Illustrated War News* for the 19th of July, showed lightly wounded men at the Countess of Dundonald's country house, turned into a hospital. The text read:

'Back in Blighty: wounded soldiers at home again.'

'Heroes of the "Great Push": Somme soldiers on the roof garden.'

'Our photograph shows the cheery fellows smiling contentedly despite their array of bandages, slings and empty sleeves, all dumbly eloquent of wounds sustained in battle.'

As Alf Damon said, 'To whine about one's lot was simply not the thing to do.' So British soldiers, in photographs of any period, appear to be 'Cheery fellows', they kept their nightmares to themselves. If they spoke at all it was only to others who had shared their experiences. Some smiled and managed to learn to cope with the horror within themselves. Others could not cope and they cracked. Some never recovered their sanity. Lionel Renton described a train-load of shell-shocked wounded arriving at Netley neurasthenic hospital.

If you travel by train to Southampton you can still see the spur line going to the hospital at Netley. That hospital is closed now. In the autumn of 1916 I was walking with another soldier in the grounds. We were exercising our gammy legs to re-form the wasted muscles. We walked rather further than usual and came close to one of the other hospitals. A train came past us, along the spur line. It unloaded its wounded at the Neurasthenic hospital. I had never seen men in such a state then, and I'm glad to say that I've never seen men like them since. Needless to say, there were many more in the same state as the war went on. Some stumbled from the carriages and walked straight ahead, like sleep walkers. Others, poor fellows, were quite doo-lally; grimacing, shouting, waving their arms, gesticulating, laughing or crying like children. Some slobbered, plucked at their mouths, or picked at their buttons or tunics.

"God, what a horrible sight," my chum said. "I'd rather be dead than like that." I was too shaken to reply, but I agreed with him, I'd rather be dead.

Alf Damon discovered that he had been reported dead. The situation was so chaotic following the slaughter on July the First that many men disappeared from the Army's system of accounting. Some were never found, and all traces of their remains and identification marks sunk into the mud of No Man's Land. Others, like Alf, were reported either missing or killed in action.

There was an odd sequel to the period in hospital in Brighton. I mentioned the ladies and girls who filled in postcards to send to one's family. It was lucky that one of these arrived at my home to tell them that I was alive. The newspapers whipped up a mood of euphoria during the first few days after the battle. But then the public mood changed to one of shock and despondency when the lists of casualties began to be posted on town halls and printed in the local papers. The parents, or the relative or friend of a soldier serving on the Somme saw the long lists of a particular regiment, let's say the Middlesex, or the Manchesters, or the Highland Light Infantry, and they could gain for themselves some idea of the colossal scale of the losses. Looking through the list of the 16th Middlesex my first impression was one of intense shock that so many chums, acquaintances and our officers and NCOs had gone west. And then I received another, more personal shock. There, clearly printed, was my own name: PS 963, Corporal A.F. Damon reported dead on the Somme. Later the war office forwarded a small parcel containing the 'Dead man's' possessions. This contained articles from my pack, which I had left behind in No Man's Land. They were all useless articles, a broken fountain pen, an old belt with a few French army buttons on it. A button stick. Anything valuable had been thieved at the base in France.

There was one more sequel. A few weeks later, when I was almost recovered, I read an appeal from Miss Catley. She wrote to a London newspaper asking if anyone knew what had happened to her brother because the War Office had informed her parents that he had been killed in action on 1st July. I thought of writing, and even started a letter to her. I saw the bodies of both Clutterbuck and Catley blown up and thrown onto our own wire. I guessed that it was the big 'Jack Johnson' shell that exploded in front of our parapet that killed them both, just as the platoon formed up to move forward. But I couldn't be sure and I thought that further details of her brother's death would only add to Miss Catley's distress. By the state they were in I had no doubt at all that both men were dead.

NOTE ON THE MEDICAL EVACUATION PLAN

Eyewitness accounts are mostly those of wounded survivors of 16PSB, or in some cases, like Sergeant Quinnell, from neighbouring units. Background information, such as the plan for evacuating the wounded, and the problem of the ambulance trains, came from the RAMC college library, Millbank, London; the RAMC Museum and archives, Fleet. I also used visual information from the medical photographs that were then stored in the photographic library at the Imperial War Museum, Lambeth, London. In each of these institutions the staff went out of their way to be helpful and encouraging about the project.

1. With some diffidence, I questioned Alf about the CCS. The nearest CCS to Mailly Maillet was Puchevilliers, a distance of more than ten miles. It seems unlikely that the two wounded men could walk that distance across fields. It is more likely that the unit that Alf described was the ADS at Forceville.

2. Neither GHQ in France nor the War Office ever gave a satisfactory explanation for this fatal incompetence. During a later stage of the battle of the Somme the War Office suggested to Haig that General Maxwell should return to England. Haig would not hear of it; he looked after his own people. In 1917 Maxwell was recalled to the War Office and retired on a generous pension.

3. Hospital ships.
Two of these ships, that carried wounded throughout the Somme battles, were the large sister ships RHS *Lanfranc* and RHS *Salter*. The author's grandfather, Captain C.G. Hawes RAMC was one of the surgeons operating on wounded on *Lanfranc* in Dublin Bay during the Easter uprising of 1916. A month or so later, during the battle of the Somme, he transferred to *Salter*, ferrying wounded from Le Havre to Southampton. One foggy November night *Salter* struck a mine at the entrance of the Seine. Fortunately the ship was approaching the harbour empty rather than outward bound loaded with wounded. Visibility was poor and rescue attempts hampered by the quantity of shipping in the estuary. Two French gunboats rescued those who had abandoned the sinking ship. One carried crew the other medical staff. The first boat reached Le Havre safely. The second hit another mine. None of the doctors, nurses or orderlies survived. Captain Hawes was never found. The few bodies that were recovered are buried under the large monument to the hospital ship 'Salter' in the civilian cemetery on the hill overlooking the port of Le Havre.

4. Vera Brittain. *Testament of Youth*.

5. Netley Hospitals. Lionel Renton explained that there were three hospitals at Netley; the regular army hospital, known as the 'Butcher's Shop' where discipline was so strict that patients had to sit, or lie, to attention. The second was the neurasthenic hospital that later became the army's home for shell-shocked patients, re-named the Army Psychiatric Hospital; and finally the temporary, hutted hospital built and staffed by the Red Cross. Lionel Renton described the Red Cross nurses as much more relaxed. 'They were really kind to us. When I could limp about I used to have a cup of tea in the Sister's office.'

6. Conversation between the sculptor George Fullard and writer Henry Williamson. Williamson was wounded in France during the Great War, Fullard wounded in Italy during the Second World War. They agreed that the public rapidly gets bored with the spectacle of ambulance trains and wounded soldiers. Conversation in the winter of 1973 between Fullard and Williamson at the Chelsea Arts Club, at which the author was present. George Fullard died that summer at the early age of 50, almost certainly the result of severe wounds to the head, arm and shoulder at the battle of Monte Cassino.

7. Memory loss:
'Shell-shock' was an inexact term used throughout the Great War. At the time shell-shocked patients were divided into two categories: those whose spinal cord or brain had been damaged by the displacement of air caused by a shell exploding nearby; and those who would later be diagnosed as suffering from 'Battle fatigue', as it was called during the war of 1939-45. A great deal of research was carried out in the nineteen-sixties, particularly in the USA during the Vietnam war. Since then it has been re-named 'Post traumatic stress disorder' or PTSD. During the early nineteen-fifties the author met soldiers suffering from severe PTSD, first at the Cambridge Military Hospital in 1953, and in 1954-55 near Kuala Lumpur during the Malayan Emergency. So called 'mental patients' were still treated as though they were malingerers, and treatment seemed to have altered very little over a period of forty years. Some of these NCOs had broken down in Korea during trench warfare and under conditions of extreme cold and horror, remarkably similar to those found in Flanders and Picardy forty years earlier.

8. 'You can't believe a word they say.'
'The most bloody defeat in the history of Britain... July 1, 1916, and our Press come out bland and copious and graphic, with nothing to show that we had not had quite a good day – a victory really. Men who had lived through the massacre read the stuff open-mouthed... So it comes that each of several million ex-soldiers now reads with that maxim on guard in his mind – You can't believe a word you read.' C.E. Montague. *Disenchantment*. Pub 1922. P77.

Chapter 36

THE VALLEY OF THE DEAD

T HE EXACT DATE WHEN 86 BRIGADE, including 16PSB, came out of the line and marched to Amiens is not clear. One has to imagine the chaos behind the lines following the disastrous attacks, particularly in that of VIII Corps, where every attack had failed to gain ground. Holding their positions with only a tiny percentage of their officers, NCOs and men, neither Brigade nor Battalion officers had time to make an accurate note of the passage of time, let alone the leisure to write up the unit diary. The scene was one of broken trenches, dead and wounded men, the survivors keeping watch on the fire-step under constant shell-fire with little chance for even a brief rest. To add to this was the ever-present threat of a German attack that would find the Brigade too weak and exhausted to eject the attackers from their trenches. The question of exact recording of time was irrelevant to the reality facing Colonel Hall and his men. He expected an attack at any moment.

We know now, as no one in the British line could know then, that the Germans had their own major problems that prevented them from exploiting the weakness of their foes. They too had difficulty moving their wounded from the deep bunkers to the relative safety of aid centres behind the line. They were working at speed to re-supply the deep bunkers with food, clean water, ammunition and medical supplies. Above ground they set about rebuilding and strengthening the front line and support trenches. Not least of their preoccupations, they had to construct a complete new set of trenches to form a defensive system around the eastern edge of the Hawthorn crater. The British barrage was maintained, if nothing like the ferocity of the days before the attack, enough shells exploded to harass those digging trenches, or moving supplies, and thus ensuring a steady wastage of casualties.

We know that the attackers suffered a devastating defeat, but we know also that life, for the Germans, was far from agreeable or without care. We know this from the records that the Wurtemburgers of 119 Reserve Regiment kept themselves.

According to British soldiers taken prisoner on July the First the Germans were more practical and efficient about storing and transporting their dead than were the British. The latter, of course, were at a severe disadvantage because the greater number of their men lay out of reach in No Man's Land. One of those taken prisoner at the Redan was Albert McMillan. He was not alone in noticing the German habit of stacking the bodies in layers, one layer crossing the other, 'like cord wood' as one POW put it. The neat stacks of corpses led to one of the more audacious of British propaganda campaigns, the 'Corpse Factory' myth.[1]

Both sides, the defenders at Beaumont Hamel and the former attackers at

Auchonvilliers, were exhausted. 'There wasn't much left of the old front-line.' Noel Peters said:

> There were some short bits that weren't too bad, here and there. The rest was broken by shells, or caved in altogether. Dead men lay blocking the support and the communication trenches. Even after 24 hours there were still a few wounded men who, for some reason, were awaiting collection. We did what we could for these poor fellows, but it wasn't much because there were so few of us and we had to be on the Qui vive the whole time in case Jerry decided to pay us a visit. We did what we could for the wounded but we couldn't shift them to a safer place because we couldn't leave the line. It took the stretcher bearers three days to clear the front and support trenches.

Noel Peters described the last scene in the tragedy of the Public Schools Battalion on the Somme. The unwounded survivors of the battle for Beaumont Hamel marched from Mailly Maillet to a hutted camp to the north of Amiens to await replacements and be made up to strength. In a bare wooden hut stood a line of wooden trestle tables and on these was displayed the mail that had accumulated during the last ten days. A pile of letters and parcels containing food, keepsakes and small comforts from home, were spread out in alphabetical order. Noel remembered the scene as though those piles of post still lay before him.

> I think that was the first moment that I realised what had happened. Up until that moment, when we arrived at the camp near Amiens, we'd either been too busy preparing for a counter-attack and dodging Jerry's shells and mortars. On the march out of Ocean Villas we were too tired to think about anything but putting one foot before the other. We picked up our letters, saluted the officer in the room and marched out again. As I reached the door I turned and looked back. Most of the letters, and the piles of parcels, were still there on the tables.

In other battalions the parcels of the dead were divided up between the survivors. The men of the 16th Middlesex, by common consent, did not touch them. They picked up their own post and then stood in silence, reading the names on the envelopes addressed to their dead friends. The parcels were returned, unopened, to mothers, wives, or friends in England.

Noel's friends, the three band-boys, were not the only under-aged soldiers killed that day, or died of their wounds later. Many not only changed their ages but changed their names to enlist. Private George Iggulden of Fulham changed his name to Eldridge and his age as nineteen. Though the age is written as nineteen on the grave markers many were actually seventeen, sixteen or even fifteen. Privates Moody and Puddiphat travelled together from Mitcham to enlist. Private Frederick Tagg from Ealing, Frank Davey from Holloway, Pte Eley and Walter Hoad from Camberwell. The Irish lad with whom Alf Damon played cards on the eve of battle, Daniel Murphy came from Kellystown, County Wexford. A bullet caught him before he had a chance to dig up the wallet that he buried the previous night. Other boy soldiers came from Streatham and Brixton, Edmonton, Rotherhithe, Willesden, Enfield and Hornsey. Judging by their

The ruins of Beaumont Hamel station. Nov 1916.

The quarry and ruins of the village. Beaumont Hamel.

addresses most of these boys came from modest homes in working class districts. Many went straight from one of the Middlesex service battalions to join the 16th on the Somme. Death, on the First of July, was no respecter of age or class. A few reminders of 16th early history are shown by the graves of students who chose to serve in the ranks. Corporal Noel Hoskings of the Royal College of Music; Private Philip Osborne of Birmingham University; Private David Carlyon Vavasour of Cambridge University, died aged 36.

Then there were the foreign nationals and travellers who returned from the Empire to enlist for adventure: Corporal Alfred Rieu, the second of three French brothers to be killed. (The last of the brothers, Charles Rieu was killed in September 1917.) Pte Speranza Tremaglia gave his address as 30 Lombard Street. Pte Ellis traveled from Toronto to join the war. One of the officers also crossed the Atlantic. The American, Second Lieutenant Harold Hertslet had a young wife in Nosoton Heights, Connecticut USA.

The officers' ages vary as widely as those of their men; Captain Heslop was only 21, like the two boys Moody and Puddephat, his home was in Mitcham. He is buried close to the Hawthorn Crater. 2nd Lieut Heaton, 20, was the youngest son of a close family. At the other end of the age scale: Captain Arthur Purnell, who led the bombing party, was 36; while Lieutenant Heath was 39. Private Richard Lovett was 46. He was the son of Colonel Lovett and left the family plantation in India to enlist in the Public Schools Battalion. Pte William Levesque left a widow, Joanna, in Fulham, he was 33. Pte Sydney Shambrooke's widow, Violet Louise, lived in a terraced house in South Hackney. Corporal Bain-Kemp was 38, Pte Aust 35 and Lance Corporal James Crowden was 42.

Many wounded men who crawled, or were carried, down the communication trenches, were too badly injured to survive the journey to a CCS. Lance Corporal Hilder was too badly hurt to be moved, he died at the RAP three days later. Sergeant Harold Peakall, of West Ham, died at Mailly Maillet. Of those carried back to the ambulance centre at Louvencourt three died next day: Pte Scott aged 18; Bertie Killick of Hornsey and Pte Nichols of County Cork. Others were carried to the CCS at either Corbie, Doullens or Amiens and died within a few days. The positions in which men from different companies were found, and even different battalions within the Brigade, gives us a picture of confusion. Dead from both A and B companies were found close to the Hawthorn mine crater while men of D Company were scattered across the slopes on either side of the Valley road. (This appears to confirm Alf Damon's statement that the formation and direction of the attack on July 1st was not the one planned and rehearsed.)

But it was the parcels that remained as symbols in Noel's mind, rather than the memory of the dead men lying out in No Man's Land.

The owners would never see the things that their mums and dads, or their wives, had packed for them. I realised, for the first time, that these lads weren't coming back. We would not see our friends again. The old 16PSB was finished.

86 Brigade sorting the packs of the dead and wounded, left behind by their owners.

For five months the British attacks north of Albert concentrated on the Ancre valley and towards Thiepval. Nothing happened facing Beaumont Hamel except for routine patrolling and costly attempts to dominate No Man's Land. It appeared that GHQ staff had learned their lesson: Beaumont Hamel was too strong a position to be taken by frontal assault. To follow the path taken by 86 Brigade was to follow its battalions to the grave, which is exactly what the 17th Football Battalion was ordered to do. On the 13th November 1916, at 5.51am, they climbed out of their trenches and advanced on the enemy line. At 9.00am the Brigadier ordered the 17th back to their trenches. Of the Battalion that set off from Mailly that morning only seventy-nine men remained on their feet, with only one officer, a second lieutenant, to command them. A week after this futile attack, with its massive waste of men, Beaumont Hamel was taken from the rear by a Naval officer leading a mixed group of sailors and soldiers from several different

Scottish regiments. This was a surprise attack in darkness up the steep Beaucourt spur, which struck the defenders where they least expected to be attacked.

The capture of the Ancre Valley and the fortress of Beaumont Hamel was celebrated in the British press. In the case of the latter they had something to celebrate. If this was an asset the retention of the valley was not, as Liddell Hart commented. 'The folly of this last phase, from 25 November onwards, was that, having won the crest of the ridge and its commanding observation, the advantage was thrown away by fighting a way down to the valley beyond. Thereby the troops were condemned to spend the winter in flooded trenches. Somme mud became notorious.'[3]

A decade or so after the Armistice Noel Peters attended a British Legion dinner in London. He sat next to a retired regular officer who, as a young subaltern in the Coldstream Guards, had been in charge of the burial party sent to Beaumont Hamel. Salvage parties from V Corps took over the waste-land not long after the village was taken and were given the task of clearing it. He told Noel that very little was left to mark the attack of July the First. Rusted helmets, bent rifles, punctured steel water-bottles and a few scattered bones with scraps of webbing and khaki rags fluttering in the winter wind. Here and there they came on markers to identify individual soldiers, identity discs pounded into the mud or sodden and disintegrating pay-books. He told Noel that the remains of the 16th Middlesex were put into temporary mass graves close to where they were found, large shell holes, one close to the Crater lip, the other between the

One of several reasons why the attack on Beaumont House failed; the strength of the German barbed wire in front of the village. The Quarry. Beaumont Hamel.

Sunken Road and the old German front line. These remains were exhumed later and placed in the Imperial War Graves cemeteries.

In May 1917 a Middlesex officer, Captain H.L. Smythe, visited the place and wrote a description:

> ...there was nothing to be seen of Beaumont Hamel or Beaucourt. The whole ground is overlapping craters. All along the road, between the villages, waggons have been blown off the road. Every tree in the area is shattered. Our mine of July 1st is enormous, 100 yards by 50 and 30 and 40 feet deep. It was short of, but just caught the German front line. The dug-outs within 60 yards of it had all their entrances filled with debris and occupants buried. But the timber is intact and the shafts not blown in. They have since been opened again, possibly by the Germans, to dig out their own men. There are tunnels running from each of the two forks of Y Ravine which appear to lead to deep dug-outs in the firing line, about 50 yards away. We discovered several graves of this [86] Brigade close to the German line.[4]

Captain Smythe concluded his letter.

> I don't suppose you heard that when Beaumont Hamel was taken by the Naval Division, the remains, paybooks, etc, of some 180 Middlesex men were found in the Sunken Road, the point reached by the Fusiliers. This disposes of the suggestion that the 16th Middlesex did not get as far as No Man's Land.

1. The propaganda invention of the 'Corpse factories'. These were alleged to render down human waste to make soap, industrial greases and agricultural fertiliser. C.E. Montague discusses this myth in *Disenchantment* in the Chapter on British propaganda and the press headed 'You can't believe a word they say'. The Corpse factory story was probably invented by Brigadier Charteris, Haig's Chief of Intelligence. Joseph Goebbels was an admirer of Charteris' fertile and mendacious imagination. Invented stories of Hun Barbarism had tragic consequences twenty years later. Many ex-soldiers refused to believe accounts of the Nazi murder of the Jews because they had been lied to so many times during the Great War. One of these ex-soldiers was Henry Williamson.

3. Liddell Hart. *History of the First World War.* P331. Revised edition. Cassell 1970.

4. Smythe reports on the tunnel entrances at 'Y' Ravine and close to the Crater. Many more were found by the Naval Division in the cliffs beside the Beaucourt Road, tunnelled under the village itself and under the Redan. In 1918 French army engineers either filled in, or made permanent covers for these entrances. In the deprivation and discontent following the war the French government was fearful that they might be used as bolt-holes by mutineers and revolutionaries. Today they remain as they were though, occasionally, part of a tunnel is revealed by subsidence or excavations for building or civil engineering works. I presume that the collapse, or the unexpected opening up of tunnels must be accepted as part of normal life in the villages along the old German line because I have seen several during periodic visits to the area. Between Beaumont Hamel and Serre builders opened up a two-way tunnel railway system. They warned me, vigorously and loudly, not to enter (which I had no intention of doing). This area is still dangerous and visitors should be cautious. Near the Sunken Road a large hole opened up on the edge of a field. Inside the hole one could see one tunnel entrance quite clearly and two others that were partially buried.

PART FIVE

Chapter 37

THE AFTERMATH

It must be so – it's wrong to doubt
The Voluntary system's best
Your conscript, when you've dug him out
Has not the happy warrior's zest.
Because it seemed the thing to do
I joined with other volunteers
But well, I don't mind telling you
I didn't reckon for three years.
Though we observe the Higher Law
And though we have our quarrel just,
Were I permitted to withdraw
You wouldn't see my arse for dust.

Anonymous soldier 1917

THE SURVIVORS OF THE ATTEMPT to take Beaumont Hamel held a fragmented and badly damaged defensive line. Two of them were Noel Peters and Laurie Barrow. The number of days that the remnants of the Battalion held the line at Auchonvilliers is confused, just as the casualty figures vary from different sources. Noel believed that they remained in the line longer than the official report stated. On 4 July, in the late afternoon, the small group of men at Auchonvilliers marched to rejoin what was left of the Battalion in tents beside the shattered village of Engelbemer. After four days they moved into Knightsbridge Trench, relieving a composite group of Royal Hampshires and South Wales Borderers. When one considers that the relief took place in daylight, and in full view of German artillery spotters on Serre and Beaucourt ridges, casualties were light. Between the 8th and the 23rd of July the 16th lost one man killed, six wounded and one wounded (shell shock). The Battalion diary mentions 'Shell shock' more than once. From Noel Peters' and Laurie Barrow's accounts it is clear that practically all the survivors were suffering from post-traumatic shock to a greater or lesser degree.[1]

The entire 29th Division was withdrawn from the front line. The Division had suffered appalling losses and was completely disorganised, so disengagement was not a simple operation. Brigades, and even the remnants of battalions, had to withdraw piece by piece, until the pieces could be re-assembled. 86 Brigade left the Engelbemer – Mailly Maillet area and moved back to Warnimont Wood where replacements of officers, NCOs and men reached them from England. One can imagine the contrast between them and how hard it must have been to establish any sort of common ground. On the one side the survivors of an unprecedented disaster that had removed most of the familiar faces, shocked and dispirited wearing filthy, torn and smoke blackened uniforms. On the other side the fresh faced new recruits in their immaculate uniforms and polished brasses. One can imagine the mixture of feelings that went through the minds of the new arrivals; the bewilderment, the dread of what might come next, the embarassment of dealing with men who had been through so much, even the guilt that they had missed the battle.

One newly commissioned officer, Second Lieutenant T.W. Deeves, who joined the Battalion a week or so later, recorded his thoughts on joining the Battalion.

> *When I joined all four company commanders were 'Originals' who enlisted. All of them were exceptional men, they had to be, and all of them were killed in 1918. Apart from them the 16th were very much a mixed lot when I joined them since most of the Originals had either become casualties, or had left* [to take commissions]; *the rest of us were odds and ends used to fill the gaps. From what I heard, the ORIGINAL Battalion must have been one of the finest in Kitchener's New Army.*[2]

The 16th reached Warnimont Wood by mid-afternoon where they found all that was left of 86 Brigade. Dublin Fusiliers, Royal Fusiliers and Lancashire Fusiliers formed up for parade to be inspected by the VIII Corps Commander, Lieutenant General Sir Aylmer Hunter-Weston. The Brigade formed three sides of a hollow square on the edge of the wood. Noel remembered that a look-out was posted. There was a delay and then the look-out sighted the cavalcade approaching, and then Noel could hear the sound of horses trotting down the lane to the edge of the field. Hunter-Weston was escorted by lancers on fine horses, smartly turned out with gleaming boots, the polished wood and

The wood to the west of Beaumont | Hamel.

metal of their lances flashing in the sunlight. The Divisional Commander gave the survivors a rousing speech in his own well-known style.[3]

After he had addressed the troops, Hunter-Weston wanted to speak to some of the men who had been at Beaumont Hamel. He interviewed Noel Peters, Laurie Barrow and about two dozen others. It was typical of Noel's good nature that, after all the blunders and the carnage, after the destruction of the Battalion that had become like a family to him, Noel's only comment on the General who was to blame, in part if not for the whole disaster, was, 'He seemed like a nice fellow'.

Lieutenant General Sir Aylmer Hunter-Weston.

When Hunter-Weston, his staff and the shining lancers had trotted away, each man was given a copy of the General's speech. Other copies were sent to the wounded and the families of the dead. Then the Brigade ate the evening meal and bivouacked for the night. The following morning they set off, marching through Authie and Marieux and Beauquesne to Beauval. Camped near this unspoilt village, without trace of war or damage, they repaired clothing and equipment, were issued with some new items of uniform, such as socks and underclothes and, most important of all, had the chance to wash and clean and attempt to rid themselves of the ever-present lice.

The weather was good. On the 27th of July, cleaner, refreshed and to some extent in better spirits they marched off for Doullens. There was a rumour that a train was waiting for them at Doullens station. 'We didn't care where we went, so long as that train took us away from the Somme, a place that had become one of horror for us.'

They were marching along a country lane when Colonel Hall halted the column, took the Company Commanders aside and spoke to them privately. What happened next was described in a letter from Laurie Barrow to Alf Damon.

> *Dear Die-Hard,*
>
> *It was with great pleasure that I read your letter, as it is so nice to hear from one who went through the hoop in France. I don't suppose there are many of us still about especially as you state that we were practically wiped out on the 1st of July. I heard we came out of the line about 180 strong including HQ, transport etc. Like you I am not as fit as I was then, being 71 now and 22 then, some difference.*
>
> *I will try to give you a brief history of the remains of the Battalion after Beaumont Hamel as you would not know much about it after being wounded. We spent some time where we were in the line and then we were relieved by another Division and went back to Engellbellmer (I forget how it was spelt). Some time after we were spoken to by divisional general Sir Hunter-Weston known as 'Hunter-Bunter'. He told us we had done our best and hoped next time we would succeed. Anyhow from there we set off to march to the train. Somewhere along a country lane the Colonel halted us and passed the word along that Ypres was our next destination. We all got the wind up. Didn't we think that was a wicked thing to do to us after escaping that last lot with our lives. But it was home-from-home compared with the Somme.*

1. Because of the attack made upon the Public Schools Battalion by Robert Graves, sections of the 86 Brigade and the 16th Middlesex War Diary are worth quoting in full. (See Appendix Two.)'
 '2 Coys and Batt HQ. Proceeded to AUCHONVILLIERS, 2 Coys remaining in 88th Trench.'
'Two companies' is meaningless because the Battalion strength was less than a company, even under front-line conditions where it was extremely rare for an infantry battalion to be up to full strength. Despite this the Brigade diary entry is clear in its meaning: that what was left of the 16th was divided, half remaining where they were, at Auchonvilliers, and half moving into a reserve position to Engelbemer. From the 86 Brigade War diary. The notes below are taken from the 16PSB War diary.
 '8 July 1916: The Battalion took over Knightsbridge trench, Englebemer sector from the 2nd Hants and South Wales Borderers.
15 July: Battalion relieved by 1st Royal Dublin Fusiliers. Moved to Billets in Engelbemer. Periodic shelling of village.
18 July: Arrival of reinforcements. 134 OR.'
The Battalion remained in the village under fire until: -
'23 July: The Battalion marched from Englebemer to Warnimont Wood and proceded via Bertrancourt and Bus-les-Artois, on the Brigade being relieved from duty in front line trenches. Reinforcements of 1 Captain and 10 Second Lieutenants arrived.'
Extract from the 16th MX War diary. This was stored with the Middlesex Regimental Archives in Mill Hill Barracks, which had been the Regimental Depot. When I read the diary it belonged to the Army Postal Service, RE. About a year later one wing of the barracks was blown up by the IRA with several casualties. The Regimental museum and the archives were moved to the National Army Museum in Chelsea.

2. Second Lieutenant T.W. Deeves served in the ranks of the 15th London Regiment on the Somme. He was commissioned in the Middlesex Regiment and joined the 16th MX at Ypres, a month or so later. He was badly wounded at Masnieres during the battle of Cambrai in November 1917. His left arm was torn off by a shell and his right wounded by fragments. He had a 90% disability pension and remained in hospital until 1920. 'With only vague memories of anything in between.' He was awarded the Military Cross. See p164. Everard Wyrall. *The Die-Hards in the Great War.*
3. There is a theory that Hunter-Weston, the jovial Hunter-Bunter, was the model for the General in Sassoon's *Plan of Attack.* Hunter-Weston's message to the officers and men of 8 Corps reveals both the strong and weak points of the pre-war Regular army. This fatal combination of faults and virtues contributed to the disaster at Beaumont Hamel.

Picture of replacements joining a depleted battalion in support of the fighing at Flers.

Chapter 38

THE SOMME
WINTER 1916-1917

'Ypres was cushy enough.' Noel Peters.

IN 1916 THE YPRES SALIENT HAD AN EVIL REPUTATION with Front-line soldiers, officers and other ranks alike, and would earn an even worse one in the year to come. But for the moment the Salient was relatively quiet and both Noel and Laurie Barrow spoke of it as 'cushy enough'.

The focus of the war was on the Somme as summer gave way to autumn and then another winter of siege warfare, the trenches often knee-deep in ice-covered water and mud. Survivors of the slaughter on July the First warn us against the false wisdom of hindsight, and yet, try as one may, it is hard to see what the planners of the later battles of the Somme hoped to achieve by continuing the attacks through the winter.

Before the first massive assault on the Somme that went so disastrously wrong, the stated aim was the breakthrough. Restoring the war of movement was a sensible wish. To break through the enemy's line, to give room for the cavalry to spread out and cause chaos amongst the enemy's supply lines and store and ammunition dumps appeared to be common sense. But to continue to hope for this after the lessons of Verdun, and of the first of July on the Somme, appears more like a fantasy than the realism on which all senior soldiers pride themselves. Once the Somme battle bogged down (in both the real and metaphorical sense) then the declared aim ceased to be the 'Breakthrough' and became the 'War of Attrition'.[1]

Laurie Barrow left no further record of what happened to him, though we know that he survived the Great War and lived to a good age, so we do not know whether he moved back to the Somme with the Battalion. Luckily Noel Peters gave a clear account of the conditions endured by the survivors and the replacements during the later stages of the Somme battles. The losses of the volunteers were made up first by Derby Scheme men and then by conscripts.

It was not Noel's nature to criticise his commanders any more than he would denigrate his mates. He makes no comment on the direction or the aims of the war. His descriptions of the landscape and the atmosphere to the later Somme battles through the winter, particularly around Flers, are the more moving for their restraint and stoicism.

The village of Flers has its place in history only as the spot where tanks were used in action on the Somme for the first time. In the early summer of 1916 Flers was a small, nondescript farming village on a country lane from Maricourt to Bapaume. By the winter of 1917 it had become one of those cliches of war. A point and a name on the map,

The ruins of Flers.

which, on the ground, had almost disappeared. A section of pave, or a mound of bricks fast sinking in the mud, groups of overlapping shell holes filled with water, waterlogged forward and communication trenches, here and there the shredded stump of a tree: that was Flers. Add to that the constant shriek and concussion of shells and trench mortars, the desolate grey landscape, the wreckage of wagons, corrugated iron and rusting wire, the piles of broken ration tins, the corpses, human and equine, the rain and the cold. And over all that, persistent and all-pervading the stench of the battlefield, human excrement and rotting flesh.

I asked Noel Peters how they stayed sane through that winter.

'I don't know,' he replied. 'You lived from day to day. You didn't look further ahead, not if you had any sense. Carry on as best you could. That was the way.'

By the time we reached Ypres we had over a hundred replacements. A few were conscripts but most of them were Derby Scheme men, which amounted to much the same thing. They were nice enough fellows, but they were pressed men, they didn't have a trace of the volunteer spirit in them. The life seemed to have gone out of the old Battalion. This wasn't just because we lost so many of our pals at Beaumont Hamel, though that was bad

234

enough, but the spirit was gone. I never saw one of our fellows who was wounded on July 1st, not one. They went to other battalions or other regiments. That was stupid. Fellows fight better with their pals around them.

Flers was not recognisable as a village. Moving up at dusk Noel saw only another ridge and mounds of dirt, bricks and broken rafters with a foul track running through it. As they marched through this grim place Noel saw a flap of canvas pulled back from a hole in a shattered wall. A pair of eyes met his in the gloom. This was a battlefield grown old. Noel described it as living in a huge rubbish tip.

There was nothing to see all round but mud and useless rubbish. Broken bricks, smashed tree stumps and tins, tins as far as the eye could see. If you found a little bit of wood you were lucky. Two of us were out looking for lengths of batten or scraps of timber to make a fire. The other fellow saw what looked like a good German boot in a pile of bricks. He gave it a tug and it came away, the foot and shin bone still in it.

The support line ran through the pulverised village and here Noel did his cooking. He worked under great difficulty and danger, because the German artillery spotters were alert to any sign of smoke. Noel described the scene as though this was nothing out of the ordinary. There were no breakfast truces like those before July 1st. Smoke brought down a shower of shells. The cooks used charcoal, if they could get it. If not the food had to be carried up to the line cold. Even when they had sufficient charcoal the journey up to the line with hot food was frequently interrupted by 'crumps'.

Sometimes, when there was no charcoal and the men were cold and wet, Noel took a risk and made a fire of scrap wood in a hollow behind the line. He brewed up and hurried up the line with the dixie of hot tea before the gunners got the range of his little smoke cloud. He usually got away with it but on one occasion the gunners anticipated him and had ranged the ruined house where he built his fire. A whizz-bang landed a few feet away.

All I heard was a high-pitched SSST and then a hell of a bang, like an express train coming through the wall – there, right beside you. Splinters and rubbish flew all around. I sat there in a cloud of dust. I lost all feeling in my limbs and my ears hummed. I thought that I must be dead. Then I patted my legs and arms and I realised that I wasn't hit. Not a scratch. Miraculous, I thought.

The Battalion marched out of the line, for a rest. 'Rest meant fatigues, usually carrying things,' Noel said. 'Then it was up to the line again. At Les Boeufs the firing-step was our home.' The line here consisted of the old German support trenches that had once been well dug and revetted, but had suffered badly from both French and British bombardment.

We were forbidden to enter the bunkers, partly because they were full of water and German corpses that had been tipped down there, more to the point the entrances faced the wrong way.

As winter advanced the men had to keep moving, or banging their feet to keep them from freezing. To reach the line with rations or hot tea the cooks had to wade along flooded communication trenches, knee deep in icy water. 'We used to say, "When this is over we'll have rheumatism for life". But, do you know, those of us who survived never suffered any ill effects – except trench foot, of course.'

To be in reserve was not to be out of the war-zone. The Battalion moved back to High Wood, a terrible, haunted place, the scene of heavy fighting earlier in the Somme battle. The trees were cut short by shell splinters. Smashed branches and shards of wood lay over the crumbling trenches which were filled with broken and twisted rifles, punctured helmets, mouldering equipment. The dead had been buried but recent shelling uncovered parts of the corpses.

Then it was time to go up to the line again. The movement of so many men in the communication trenches could not be hidden and this attracted a series of crumps. Crumps were concentrations of shells, a type of moving barrage. The cry went up for stretcher bearers, men were being killed and wounded all along the trench. The platoon commander told his men to take cover in an old German dug-out which was large enough to hold thirty men at a tight squeeze. Noel and another cook-boy, Charlie Leadbetter, were carrying rations. As another series of crumps fell on the parapet they dived in after the platoon, finding shelter on the dug-out steps.

The shells sent many of us a bit doo-lally, we all had headaches and felt funny in the head, no sense of balance or time passing. I suppose that is what they call 'shell-shock' or a mild form of it. A large shell struck above the entrance. A few inches lower and it would have exploded in the bunker.

Luckily the bunker was solidly made and resisted the blast, which went upward. The concussion hurled Charlie and Noel down the steps into the platoon. It also hurled up a wave of mud and chalk, which fell on top of them, together with all sorts of debris abandoned by the previous tenants. The entrance to the bunker was blocked by the explosion. The air was full of the fumes of high explosive.

'It was hard to breathe. I thought we were done for.' Partially buried, Charlie and Noel shook themselves free and dragged themselves down the steps. A hoarse voice said 'Jerry always builds two entrances.' He was right, as the fog cleared they could see a tiny patch of light. A gallery led to a second chamber and its entrance was clear.

'No more dug-outs for me,' Charlie said. 'I'd sooner get shelled in the open.' The German gunners had this section of their old trench ranged. They moved their crumps from one section of bays to another. 'Like a cat playing with a mouse.' The Middlesex men sheltered in the bottom of the trench. If a man was hit there was little anyone could do for him. There was no chance of carrying him to the RAP until the shelling eased. Charlie sat on the fire-step some four or five men away from Noel. Some men were shivering or plucking at their faces or tunics. The shell on the bunker left them all in shock, some more than others. A shell burst on the rear of the trench. Someone called out to Noel, 'That's your mate got it, Pete.' Noel ran along the duckboard. Charlie was buried, only one arm showed above the fallen side of the trench. Noel pulled to get him out before he suffocated. His arm came away. Men dug but there was very little left of

Wiring party. Winter. Flers.

Charlie. They put his remains in a groundsheet. When the shelling stopped they laced up the sheet and dug a shallow grave, just beyond the parapet of the old German trench. Noel found some firewood to make a cross and he cut Charlie's name and number on it, hoping that someone would give him a proper burial once the battle was over and the line moved forward. Some weeks later Noel passed that way and looked for Charlie's grave. Tractors, towing heavy howitzers had rolled over trenches and mud alike. The ground was patterned with their tracks, crossing this way and that. He could find no trace of Charlie's grave.[2]

Noel's company was in the line, one wet morning early in January 1917. The cold sleety rain ceased and the landscape shimmered in a pale dawn light. Light gleamed off helmets and wet capes, sandbags and greatcoats remained dark and sodden. Like every other battalion along the front, the 16th Middlesex stood-to. As the men stood down again, looking forward to a hot mug of tea, a voice shouted down the trench, 'Pete, the Q wants to see you.' Noel picked up his rifle and small pack and made his way along the communication trench. He met the CQMS on the way.

'Peters, you're off out of it,' the Q said. Noel stared at him not understanding what he meant. 'Get your kit together,' the Q said. 'You're off out of the line. You are going home.'

In the winter of 1917 Lionel Renton, confined to the hospital in Southampton, heard news of the 16th Battalion.

'The news was bad that winter, first from Ypres and then from Flers, on the Somme.

Signalles laying telephone lines.

Those of my pals who weren't killed on the Somme were knocked out at Ypres, or back on the Somme again. Two good friends died there, Cairns and Moss. At least I think they were killed, I never saw them again.'[3]

By the beginning of 1917 the Public Schools Battalion was totally changed, and I don't mean that in any snobbish sense. The Battalion ceased to be predominantly Public School long before July 1st, but it was composed of volunteers, first-rate chaps and good mixers. Few, if any, of the wounded passed fit went back to the Battalion. As for the poor little devils who came to fill the ranks shortly before the show started, we never had time to know them or measure their quality. For most of them the big attack was not only their first but also their last. After 1916 I heard from friends that the 16th was never the same again, but that's hearsay: I never saw the Battalion again. By the time it was disbanded it bore no resemblance to the original unit. All the officers were dead, or like the Colonel promoted to command other formations. Johnnie Hall called himself Hamilton-Hall and ended the war a Brigadier. When the Battalion was disbanded in February 1918, some of the NCOs went to the 2nd Middlesex. A group of them, who survived Monchy, Passchendaele and Cambrai were posted as instructors to Barnard Castle, in Scotland.[4]

Lionel Renton was so badly wounded that the surgeons at Netley Hospital told him that he would never be completely fit and would walk with a limp for the rest of his life. He was determined to prove them wrong. He walked with a limp for many months and none of the medical boards were willing to pass him fit for Active Service. He applied for a Territorial Army commission, passed both the medical and officer selection boards and, by the middle of 1918, he was commissioned in the Dorsetshire Regiment and posted to Derry (Londonderry).

In Northern Ireland he requested two things: that he return to France and that his TA commission should be converted to a Regular Army commission. Both were granted. He took the ferry to Liverpool and travelled to Ilminster Barracks to take charge of a draft of replacements about to leave for France.

Recovered from his wound, Alf was transferred to the Machine-Gun Corps whose main training base was near Nottingham. Thus, once again, he walked out with Lilly Shelmardine who continued to write to him for the rest of the war. Unable to find a place with his old division, the 29th, he was posted to the 36th (Ulster) Division. Alf's company of Vickers guns supported the 36th Division at Ypres and then Cambrai. Then the company moved south to support the French in the St Quentin sector. Exhausted by Nivelle's wasteful attacks the French army was on the defensive, as Alf discovered:

The French Poilu resembled working men with a day's work to do, rather than soldiers. Once the day's work was done they wandered off in little groups. Marching out of the line was not their style. You'd see a little group of Poilu preparing their evening meal, putting on their sabots instead of boots and decanting the Pinard. We, that's the small number of Tommies attached to them, had the sense that these fellows had worked out a logical way to fight this war. Since the mutiny they had it their way. This was the opposite to British policy, dictated by Generals and their staffs who had never put their highly polished boots in the mud of the trenches, who never saw the line, let alone the conditions that we lived and fought in. These highly-placed gentlemen demanded constant attacks, constant shelling and the constant aggravating of the Boche opposite us.

The French Poilu and their Front-line officers had learnt how to make themselves comfortable, and reached a level of accommodation with their German opposite numbers. They treated the new arrivals as honoured guests.

Alf approved of this unexpected French practice. He had seen too many unnecessary deaths to confuse common sense with cowardice. For Alf and his new friends in the French sector the peaceful life at St Quentin was about to be rudely disturbed.

The story of Operation Michael is well known. The German High Command launched a well planned, massive attack with the aim of breaking through to the coast and seizing the Channel ports. The main thrust of the attack was against the British sector of the line, on the Somme, but the Germans mounted diversionary attacks on the French sector. Movement in the communication trenches and the reserve line of trenches was disrupted and harassed by HE and mustard-gas shells. One of these bombardments put Alf out of action. He described a near fatal wound with his usual nonchalance. 'I stopped a shell splinter in the side.'

Alf received many small iron fragments which lodged beneath the skin but did little damage. It was the large one that would have killed him but for sheer luck. When the bombardment started, and minutes before that particular shell struck close to his machine-gun position, Alf buckled on a heavy belt of leather and metal that carried tools and spares for the Vickers gun. The large shell splinter struck him, glanced off the metal and penetrated just above the hip. A horse-drawn ambulance carried him to a French CCS and then to Nancy hospital. Visiting Alf when he was recovering from the operation to remove metal fragments from his back and abdomen the surgeon remarked, in excellent English, that Alf was a lucky fellow. The largest splinter missed his spleen by a millimetre.[5]

Noel Peters was the only survivor of the Somme that I met who stayed with the Middlesex Regiment throughout the Great War. In the winter of early 1917 the scandal of the deaths of so many boy-soldiers on the Somme reached Parliament. All those who were under age were withdrawn from their battalions in the line, meeting up with others at their brigade forming a squad at divisional HQ, and finally joining a long column of child soldiers of Fourth Army, marching through Albert to a camp near Amiens.

Each boy, or his parents, had the choice, leave the army or serve behind the line until he reached the age of 18.

No figures exist to show how many boys died on July 1st, nor could they because the boys faked their ages to enlist and the recruiting offices connived at this illegality. Many parents thought enlisting a fine and patriotic act during the euphoria of summer 1914, and enjoyed a little of the reflected glory. The printed lists of casualties, as attack followed attack on the Somme, revealed army service in a different light. Distraught parents petitioned the War Office, or wrote to their MPs revealing the true ages of their children. Only when this threatened to become a scandal did the Cabinet act and the process of 'Combing out' began. Combing out, in 1917, meant the search for fit men in rear areas, or in civilian occupations, and sending them forward to the front line. The case of the boy soldiers was unique because it meant the reverse, finding the boys in the line and sending them back. Noel did not tell me anything about his home life. But he did reveal that his mum did not tell the army his age and he was puzzled how they found out. My guess is that someone in the 16th sent his name in to Divisional HQ. Just as the humane RSM sent him back to Mailly Maillet in the heat of the attack; so

Noel Peters 1917.

someone, either the RSM or the CQMS, or possibly his Company Commander, sent his name forward in the winter of the following year.

As one might expect, Noel was sent to the kitchens at Divisional HQ where the cuisine was of a much higher standard than anything required in the line. He was not to remain a cook for long, indeed he never returned to either the kitchens of an officers' mess or to a field cooker. There was another process of selection. Some boys stayed at Divisional HQ and some went to the Royal Artillery mess at Henencourt. A smaller number were selected for Headquarters 4th Army to be trained as a guard and demonstration platoon. Noel was too reticent to say why he was selected but it is obvious. In civilian life he was a neat and well organised man. Photographs serving with the 16th Middlesex show him as a smart soldier.

Headquarters of the 4th Army, commanded by General Rawlinson, moved from Querrieu on the river Halue, to Flixecourt on the Nievre, half way between Amiens and Abbeville and about fifty kilometres from the front line. The great house, park and woodland lie just outside the village. Noel always referred to it as 'The White Château.' There were two sets of guard duties, one guarding the Château, the other guarding the jute factory in the village. The most prestigious position was the ceremonial guard on the steps of the Château itself. This contained not only Rawlinson's HQ, but also senior officers' accommodation and the officers' mess. Junior officers and senior NCOs lived in the outbuildings that flanked the Château while Fourth Army school for officer training and NCOs cadres were housed partly in the grounds of the Château and partly in the jute mill.

When I asked Noel about Arthur Graeme West, Noel did not remember him. This did not surprise me because West was not a sociable soldier nor, on the surface, was there any reason why he should stand out in Noel's memory. And yet their paths crossed twice, once during the brief respite from the La Bassée canal when Noel was

Parade of boy soldiers at GHQ 4th Army Querrieu. Christmas day 1916.
These boys were under age. Those that survived 1st July were removed from the line in the autumn of 1916. Some were sent home, others, like Noel, stayed in the army returning to the front when they reached the age of 17. (See Noel's description.)

cook for the potential officer candidates, and once at the White Château.

Arthur Graeme West went forward for officer selection and endured a dreary 'Hate the Hun' filled course at an Officer Training School near Glasgow. In August 1916 he was gazetted Second Lieutenant in the Oxfordshire and Buckinghamshire Light Infantry, the county regiment that turned him down in 1914. The mystery remains about West's motives, first in joining the army, second in working for a commission. As his tutor C E M Joad remarked, 'No man was less willing to put on khaki.' The bureaucracy and brutality of Officer Training School confirmed his loathing for the army. While he was on embarkation leave he talked long into the night with Oxford pacifist friends and read Bertrand Russell's *Justice in Wartime*. He loved his close friends and shared their beliefs. In particular there was a young woman friend with whom he spent a great deal of his last leave, either on long walks in the Cotswolds or the Berkshire downs or in earnest conversation. In West's diary we know her only as J... West was far from a wealthy man, nor was he, generally, a sociable man. But thanks to Oxford, he had a circle of highly educated, close friends. There were many ways in which West could have avoided front-line service. Such an idea did not occur to him despite his loathing for the army.

'Never was the desire to desert and commit suicide so overwhelming ...' he wrote sitting on Box Station on the 19th of August 1916.

No doubt he surprised himself, as it surprised his colleagues, that he turned out to be a conscientious and efficient officer. He returned to the depot of the OBLI at Cowley barracks. The return to a disciplined, almost monastic, life seems to have calmed him. If he was not happy, at least he accepted his life and was accepted by his brother officers who he describes as,

> ...*worthy and unselfish men, not devoid of intelligence in trivial matters, and ready to carry on this unpleasant business to the end with spirits as high as they can keep them, and as much attention to their men as routine and the disciplinary conscience of their colonel will permit. They are not often aggressive or offensively military. This is the dismal part of it: that these men, almost the best value in the ordinary upper class that we have, should allow themselves to think that it is somehow necessary and inevitable; that they should give so much labour and time to the killing of others, though to the plain appeals of poverty and inefficiency in Government they are utterly heedless. How is it that as much blood and money can be poured out when it is a question of saving and helping mankind rather than slaying them? (sic)*

In September he crossed the Channel, endured yet more brutal training at Etaples and joined the Second Battalion of the OBLI on the Somme. The Battalion were in and out of the line through that month and West writes of the horrors and misery of what the Staff called 'normal trench duties'. A sentry shot beside him on the fire-step; a group of men buried by a shell.

> *A boot, a steel helmet – and you dig and uncover a grey dirty face, pitifully drab and ugly, the eyes closed, the whole thing limp and mean looking; this is the devil of it, that a man is not only killed, but made to look so vile and filthy in death, so futile and meaningless that you hate the sight of him. Perhaps the man is alive and kicks out feebly or frantically as you unbury him; anyhow here is the first, and God knows how many are not beneath him. At last you get them out, three dead, grey muddy masses, and one gibbering live one, then another shell falls and more are buried.*

On 24 September, after the battles of Flers, Morval and Thiepval, he wrote:

> *Can no peace be concluded? Is it not known to both armies that each is utterly weary and heartsick? Of course it is. Then why in God's name go on?*

And on 1 October West wrote, sitting on a fire-step.

> *... an officer here from Oxford, Nonconformist and, I think, religious, came back from a machine-gun course and remarked, half ashamedly, that he had come to the conclusion since he had been away that the war was really very silly and we all ought to go home.*

Of his own fear and his own death Arthur Graeme West wrote:

> *I found myself cool and useful enough, though after we had been shelled for about two and a half hours on end my nerves were shaky and I could have cried for fright as each shell drew near, and longed for nothing so much as to rush down some deep cellar.*
>
> *I did not betray any kind of weak feeling.*
>
> *It is merely the consideration of the fact that a shell, if it did not hit me, would either wound me or kill me, both of which were good inasmuch as they would put a pause to this existence – that kept me up to my standard of unconcern. And the more I experience it,*

the more fear seems a thing apart from possible consequences,... I feel afraid at the moment. I write in a trench that was once German, and shells keep dropping near the dug-out. There is a shivery fear that one may fall into it or blow it in.

Yet what do I fear? I mind being killed because I am fond of the other life, but I know I should miss it in annihilation.

That is not what I fear.

I don't definitely feel able to say I fear the infliction of pain or wound. I cannot bind the fear down to anything definite. I think it resolves itself simply into the realisation of the fact that being hit by a shell will produce a new set of circumstances so strange that one does not know how one will find oneself in them.

Later he wrote:

The shelling went on – this Sunday I mean – for about five hours, and we had a few biscuits and a tot of whisky about 1 o'clock.

By then the whole of the communication trench had been battered by successive shells, and we had left off going down it after each one, as the Germans had turned machine-gun fire on the levelled portion of the trench. We stood, B... G... Bl... and I, in the only undamaged bay, eating and drinking, and watching the huge columns of earth and smoke as the work of destruction went on. They had worked off this particular trench, and the men still stood all about it, but I believed for certain that they would return and smash in the only bay to which they would naturally have hoped to have driven us. I had had enough whisky to view this prospect with nothing but interested excitement, and really did not flinch as the shells fell, seemingly groping towards their mark.

Early in the New Year, Arthur Graeme West was posted to a course at the Officer Training School at Flixecourt. He had reached a balance. These entries are the happiest in the war. He had reached a new accord with his fellow beings, he liked them and they liked him. His diary, as usual, maintains a crude code but references to 'the White Château', the 'River valley' and to 'A...' for Amiens, give the location away.

Sat 10th February 1917.

The course at F... which I entered at the beginning of January is now over. About twenty of us in one mess in an inn on the Rue du Th.... were my principal companions. These were from all regiments, three or four Australians, two Scotchmen, two Guardsmen and the rest mainly North Country. Here, as usual, is the same lesson to be learned about men in the lump. They are all very nice, and couldn't understand me. ... They argue by assertions, proclaimed louder than their opponents. A gramophone has occurred during the last day and they play 'The Bing Boys'. But how I love them all....

We talk of ourselves, of our natures and moods and what we would do if we were at home: we tell one another what we were doing before the war; of our friends. R... tells me about his wife. We confide our dreams to one another: we talk of other people in the mess and of the men in our own battalions.

Out on the E... Road (l'Etoile leading to the river Somme) the whole of France lies before us; a mist is gathering over the surrounding hills and over the chimneys of the jute factory.

Little girls pass and re-pass through the crowd of officers with happy eyes. I love all the men and simply rejoice to see them going on day by day with their own jolly selves, building up such a wall of jocularity around me.

This is the last entry in Arthur Graeme West's diary. If he kept another of the small notebooks it was never found. In the spring of 1917 West's Battalion was relieved from the front line trenches and returned to a position behind the line. Dusk was coming on and the light was poor. Some distance from the line West must have raised his head above the communication trench. Quite possibly he was thinking of something other than the war. He was hit in the head by a bullet fired at extreme range. This may have been fired by a sniper, but more likely a spent machine-gun bullet dropping out of the sky. He was carried to a Regimental Aid Post but died an hour later.

1. The War of Attrition described the strategy that the British and French would kill more German young men than the Germans would kill British and French young men. Historians like John Terraine claim that the Somme was a success because it broke the German army and that more Germans were killed on the Somme than British. Historians continue to argue about the casualty figures on the grounds that British, German and French statisticians used different systems for accounting for those wounded in the battle. For a thorough and expert evaluantion of the total casualty figures of all the Somme battles see General Farrar-Hockley's *The Somme*, pp 251- 253 'The Casualties'. Farrar-Hockley sums up: 'Whatever the exact final figure, the approximate total of British/French to German was about 600,000; on either side: 1,200,000 individuals.' (He adds as a footnote that the ratio of casualties on the Allied side, British to French was 3 to 1.) *The Somme*. A H Farrar-Hockley. Batsford Books 1964.

2. When he was over seventy Noel Peters visited the Thiepval Memorial to those 72,000 killed on the Somme who have no known grave. Amongst rank upon rank of Middlesex names he found Charlie's name.
'Leadbetter. John Philip. L/16363. Pte Killed 22.10.1916.'

3. Lionel Renton was correct about the death of his friends, but wrong on the date of the death of Sergeant Cairns who was killed on 1st July.
Cairns. William Harding. Sgt PS1279. killed 1.7.1916.
Moss. Walter James. Sgt PS1834. Killed 16.12.1916.

4. Between July 1916 and disbandment in February 1918 the 16th Middlesex was in the front line, or close to it, more or less continuously. Apart from routine trench warfare, the Battalion took part in the following battles:
Arras. April – May 1917
Third Ypres. The battles of Broodseinde and Langmarck. June – October 1917
Cambrai. The battle of Masnieres. October – December 1917
Third Ypres. The battles of Passchendaele and Zonnebeke Canal January and February 1918.

5. On the subject of the hospital at Nancy, I wrote to Alf querying the name of the town. The hospitals around Paris are much nearer, whereas Nancy is south-west of Verdun. Alf was not pleased that I doubted his memory. Nancy he wrote and Nancy he meant. Though Alf sometimes forgot dates, his memory of geography and place names was reliable. At a guess, the move to Nancy was due to the disruption of the retreat; one of those freaks of movement common in war. Nancy was within range of the German guns and suffered bombardment from the ground and from the air. Alf remarked that each air-raid was followed by an eerie silence broken by the cries of the wounded. Mostly civilians, these were carried into hospital: women of all ages, children, old men, war-cripples and even tiny babies. 'That was something I hadn't seen before, even in that war, and I hope never to see it again.'

Chapter 39

THE SURVIVORS
1918

ON 7 FEBRUARY 1918 THE COMMANDING OFFICER of the Public Schools Battalion, Lieutenant Colonel J. Forbes-Robertson DSO, MC, received this letter from 29th Division HQ.

To the Officer Commanding

16th Middlesex Regiment.

On the occasion of the disbandment of the 16th Battalion, Middlesex Regiment, Major General Sir Beauvoir de Lisle, KCB, DSO, desires to express his regret at being deprived of the services of this fine Battalion.

Since being incorporated in this Division, this Battalion has seen desperate fighting, and has greatly distinguished itself, notably at BEAUMONT HAMEL, at SAILISEL, Third Battle of YPRES, and especially at MASNIERES on the 30th November 1917.

R.O. Cranfield. Lieut Colonel.

AA & QMG. 29th Division.

Nothing remained of the Public Schools Battalion except the pipe and drum band that was transferred intact to the 2nd Battalion of the Middlesex Regiment.

Noel returned to Kent for a brief spell of leave and then to the Middlesex depot at Chatham to join a draft of replacements for the 23rd Battalion which was in the line at Ypres. The 23rd was part of the 41st Division which was moved in haste from Flanders to Italy. A combined German-Austrian force had broken the Italian line at Caporetto. Fearing that the Italians might collapse Lloyd George bullied the War Cabinet to send five divisions to Italy. This was done against the judgment of both Robertson at the War Office and Haig, in France and it was to have disastrous consequences. The train took Noel from Paris to Marseilles, along the coast to Genoa and thence inland to the Italian defensive line along the Piave River. They were growing accustomed to life in the mountains, and looking forward to spring, when the 41st Division was ordered, post-haste, back to France.

Noel described Paris as a city in a state of disorder and panic, as had happened early in the war, columns of refugees crowded the streets of the capital.

There was no time to enjoy the sights. We had no idea what was going on, but a fellow who spoke French told us that the Parisians believed that Jerry had broken through.

For once, the rumours were correct. The German assault, using a combination of aircraft, tanks, massive artillery bombardment, including gas shells and, most successful of all, small groups of determined infantry with machine guns called *Sturmtruppen*, had smashed through the British line at Peronne and were moving fast

Albert Taylor in training at Chatham Barracks.

across the old Somme battlefields. The German High Command gave the breakthrough the code name Operation MICHAEL.

The 41st Division was rushed from Paris to Albert by train and then marched along the Roman road towards Cambrai. They were too late to influence the course of the battle. Noel expected parts of the landscape to be familiar but saw nothing that he recognised. The Middlesex men were told that the Germans had broken through, there was no fixed line and that the British were attempting to hold independent strongpoints. Before they set off to march the last few miles the 23rd Middlesex halted and fell out beside the road. Each man was handed a bandoleer of ammunition and Mills grenades. He was also given a green card.

'We knew what that meant,' Noel said. 'We knew we were for it. The card was a last chance to send a message to a loved one. Things looked bad.'

The 23rd reached the village of Beugny where they formed a line, occupying old trenches on either side of the road. Refugees, rear echelon troops and disorganised infantry were moving back as fast as they could. A few officers and Military Police tried to stop the flow of infantry and organise them into groups. A battery of French 75mm guns, moving against the flow added to the confusion.

The 23rd had to cover a long line with Noel's company in the centre. Noel's Platoon held the village. After a long period on watch he was relieved and took cover from the shelling in a cellar. He fell asleep and knew nothing of the battle that was raging above his head. Much later he learned that the Germans attacked in strength, pushed back the companies on either flank and swarmed into the village bombing the cellars. There was no officer to be seen and only one NCO in the cellar, a corporal. As they were debating what to do the Platoon sergeant called down the cellar steps, 'You'd better come out, lads. Jerry's all around us and there's thousands of the bastards. There's no sense in getting killed.'

As he climbed out of the cellar and laid his rifle and grenades beside the road Noel could see for himself the truth of the sergeant's remark. The Germans were everywhere and they appeared to be leaderless. They were far more interested in loot than in prisoners. Leaving two men to guard the prisoners the victorious company fanned out, searching for anything that would warm them or fill their bellies. There was a clothing dump in the village and they re-appeared carrying socks, woollen jerseys, rubber boots and leather jerkins, as well as tinned food, bread and jars of rum. The two men guarding the prisoners sulked, unable to join in the fun. They were armed with machinepistols and stick grenades. 'They did not look happ,.' Noel said. An NCO shouted at them and the guards made them line up and march towards the road. A great number of prisoners were formed up on the main road to Cambrai. To Noel's dismay their guards did not shepherd them in this direction but away from the road along the line of old trenches. They passed a huddle of khaki corpses against a wall. They were Middlesex men, their hands tied with telephone wire.

The two surly guards marched the small group to a trench and indicated that they should descend. It was an old communication trench from the 1916 battles, broken down and overgrown. More bodies lay in this trench, those of Royal Welch Fusiliers.

'Hello, this doesn't look good,' Noel said to himself. The two guards walked along the parapet above them fingering their stick grenades. 'You didn't have to be a clairvoyant to read their minds.' The end of the trench was blocked with corpses. As Noel prepared himself for death, deliverance appeared in an unexpected form. An angry shout brought both guards to attention. A figure appeared at the top of the trench and peered down at the prisoners. Noel remarked that the German officer looked like a cartoon from one of the picture papers, dressed in a long leather coat and soft peaked cap. 'A picture of the Brutal Prussian, but that fellow saved our bacon.'

The officer bawled at the guards who stood rigid with fright. He gestured to the Tommies to climb out of the trench. Then he stood, hands on hips, making sure that the two guards escorted them safely to the column of prisoners on the main road. The two guards left them there and departed, resembling two sulky, and very nasty, small boys cheated of their sport.[1]

After two and a half years as a semi-invalid, Lionel Renton was returning to the Front line. Even he had to admit that he was not entirely fit. The journey and a few days attempting to prepare his charges for what faced them in the trenches, exhausted him and he went to bed early. He woke to the sound of rioting, which he thought must be a mutiny and he reached for his pistol before peering out of the window. There came a burst of cheering and the banging of dustbin lids. Very lights, flares and rockets shot up into the night sky. Putting his head out of the window he saw an officer of his Company who shouted the news to him. An armistice was arranged for eleven o'clock the next

This Form is to be used for any candidate who is serving in the ranks of the New Armies, Special Reserve, or Territorial Force, and for any other candidate who is neither a cadet or ex-cadet of the Senior Division, Officers Training Corps, nor a member of a University.

Form $\frac{\text{M.T.}}{392}$ should be used for an Officers Training Corps (Senior Division) or University candidate, who is not serving in the ranks.

APPLICATION FOR APPOINTMENT TO A TEMPORARY COMMISSION IN THE REGULAR ARMY FOR THE PERIOD OF THE WAR.

The candidate will complete the following particulars and obtain certificates below as to character and educational qualification.

1. Name in full	Surname.	Taylor.
	Christian names.	Albert. George.
2. Date of birth.		Sept 24th 1888.
3. Whether married.		Yes
4. Whether of pure European descent.		Yes
5. Whether a British subject by birth or naturalization. (State which, and if by naturalization attach a certificate from the Home Office.)		By birth
6. Nationality by birth of father (if naturalized, state date).		British
7. Permanent address.		19 Farnham Rd, Seven Kings Essex
8. Present address for correspondence.		N-8 Platoon B Co 16th Middlesex Regt
9. Whether now serving, or previously served, in any other Government Department (Home, Indian, or Colonial). If so, give particulars.		No.
10. Whether able to ride.		No
11. Whether now serving, or previously served, in any branch of His Majesty's Naval or Military Forces, or in the Officers Training Corps. If so, state :—		Now serving
(a) Regiment, Corps, or Contingent		16th Middlesex Regt
(b) Date of appointment		Enlisted 29/5/16
(c) Rank		Corporal
(d) Date of retirement, resignation or discharge...		
(e) Circumstances of retirement, resignation or discharge A.		
12. Whether an application for a commission has been previously made, if so, on what date and for what branch of the service.		No.

Army Printing & Stationery Services.

Albert Taylor's application form for a temporary commission. Late 1916 or early 1917 FN2.

morning. All draft orders for France were cancelled.

Out of hospital Alf persuaded a medical board that he was fit. No doubt the doctors were surprised that anyone should want to be passed fit to go back to France, most wounded men had had enough. In fact many months passed before Alf ceased to feel the effect of the shell splinter in his side. Alf returned to learn about recent improvements in the Vickers gun. Not least to be re-united with Lily Shelmardine. Clipstone had changed very little but Lily had grown up.

I returned to Clipstone in 1918 and called on Lily. Even after all the changes in the country, her father still wore the tall silk hat that he wore early in the war. I forget what he did but he was obviously a man of substance and some social standing in Nottingham. He maintained the two girls at home because neither got paid for the canteen work. They stuck to the job as part of the war effort.

Alf was reticent about what passed between them, but the family must have approved of him because he was a regular visitor to the Shelmardine house.

Alf's petitions to re-join the 29th Division were granted and he said farewell to Lily and her parents and embarked for Flanders. He found the Division at Dickebusch. 'Operation Michael' had taken its toll and the Division was very short of experienced men. Despite this, everyone but Alf could see that he was not yet fit for active service. The last battle fought by the 29th Division came after they crossed the river Lys. 'Jerry must have known it was over, but he kept fighting. They made a last counter-attack. This was crazy. Our guns' fired thousands of rounds of ammunition; belt after belt, until the water in the guns cooling jackets was boiling and the dead piled up in mounds.'

After the battle a small, wet and starving mongrel bitch attached herself to the machine-gun company. Cleaned up and fed she soon became a favourite and trotted behind, or sat on one of the small carts that carried the Vickers guns.

The night of November the 10th found Alf Damon manning one of four guns dug in on a hillside in Belgium. The night was damp and cold. The gunners stamped their feet and flapped their arms to keep warm. The Company mascot barked a warning as a messenger appeared out of the mist, walking along the hillside, from hole to hole. When the messenger had moved on, their officer told them that the advance had come to a temporary halt. There was talk of an armistice. He spoke as though he did not believe the news. Nor did his men, they had heard so many wild rumours that they believed nothing.

Through the morning of 11th November the machine-gunners stayed on the ridge while the cold vapour swirled around them. They saw no senior officers who could confirm or deny the night's message. In the afternoon they resumed their march towards the German border, in mist and gathering darkness. They pulled their carts with the little mongrel trotting beside them. Not one of them could grasp that it was all over and they had survived. After an epic march from Belgium into Germany, 29th Division occupied Cologne, part of the British Army of the Rhine (BAOR).

The river Rhine played a large part in Noel's life during the last months of the war.

From Munster he was one of a batch of prisoners taken to Crefeld to unload Rhine barges. Noel experienced many misadventures at Crefeld, not least Spanish 'flu and a severe injury to his arm.

> *The hospital at Crefeld was full of wounded. After his great attack the war was going badly for Jerry and I wondered how they would receive me. But they were all right and treated me like one of their own. The corridors were full of men on stretchers and many of the wounded lay on straw in rough shelters in the yard. They were short of drugs, disinfectant and all kinds of medical equipment. The wounded were in a pitiful state, poor devils. Many were limbless, others had internal injuries and others were raving in shock or delirium.*

Noel was put on light duties for a month with his arm in a sling and then went back to unloading barges. Neither British prisoners nor German guards could see an end to the war. An epidemic of Spanish influenza infected the people of the Rhineland, as it did the rest of Europe, and it felled prisoners and their guards alike. The ordinary people were exhausted and undernourished and the disease killed large numbers, particularly the old, children, the wounded and the prisoners.

> *One day a British officer on a horse came into the camp with his escort. He was very smart, well-fed and smiling. He told us that the war was over, the British and French had occupied Germany and we were on our way home. A train was waiting to take us to Holland.*

Alf could have served in the Army of the Rhine for another year, and would have done so had he known how bad things were in England. There were no jobs for a young man with Alf's skills. Being energetic and not easily cast down he took a job in an army clothing store. Soon Alf was looking for work again. 'There was no great demand for a machine-gunner.'

Alf did not say what happened to Lily Shelmardine, but Alf was a proud man. No doubt the contrast between her father's affluence and Alf's prospects ended their friendship. Alf married and found a mundane job for two pounds a week. (Which, he said, was good money then.) His wife was pregnant with their first child when they emigrated to Australia in 1924. They settled in Tasmania where Alf went into business and the life suited them. Alf's respect for authority did not increase with age.

Like Alf Damon, Arthur Kent was wounded early on the morning of 1 July 1916. Alf believed that they were both hit by the same burst of machine-gun fire. Arthur had been an athlete before the war, as well as a fine singer. When he recovered from his wounds he took, and passed, the Physical Training examinations at Aldershot and later reached the rank of sergeant.

The train from the Rhineland camp took Noel and the other liberated prisoners to the Hook of Holland, crossing the North Sea to Hull. After ten days' leave Noel reported to the Middlesex depot at Mill Hilll and was posted to Colchester, to a German POW camp. His job was to supervise the German cooks, who, Noel said, were 'decent fellows.' In April 1919 he was discharged from the army.

Noel looked for a post with one wealthy family for whom he had worked before the war, but at the age of twenty he was considered too old to re-train. But then his sister wrote to him about a job that would suit him in Portsmouth. Noel followed his vocation, perfecting the art of cooking. He married in 1922 and bought a house in Buckland, in Portsmouth. He and his family survived the Blitz on Portsmouth dockyard. Noel was an active member of the British Legion and returned to Ypres and the Somme many times.

Noel was lucky, a very large number of ex-servicemen were unemployed.

I saw a fellow I'd known in the 24th Battalion sitting on the pavement with his cap beside him. He'd been gassed, poor fellow. At that time, once you were out of the army you were on your own. I've heard a lot of fellows open their mouths about Haig now that he's dead. If it wasn't for Haig's fund after the war many old soldiers would be in the gutter. Do you know? Towards the end, the war itself was costing four million quid a day. And yet, once it was over, Haig had to go cap in hand to ask for a million.

Alf spoke of officers, some of whom had commanded companies in France, earning a few pennies by busking. A group of former officers and NCOs hired a barrel organ and paraded through the streets. Others 'with some skill at drawing, worked as pavement artists.'

Those who emigrated to the colonies or stayed on in the army fared better. Lionel Renton exchanged his Territorial for a Regular commission, but this made little difference in 1919 when there was a surplus of officers.

After the war ended I was posted to Le Havre as Assistant Staff Embarkation Officer, embarking the Chinese Labour Corps and sending them back to China. My job meant travelling between Le Havre and the Chinese camp at Noyelles. One day my chief called me into his office. He offered me a seat and a cigarette. He was friendly but ill-at-ease. Hello, I thought, something's up. After some beating about the bush, he told me that I was about to be demobilised.

Like so many others who joined as boys, Lionel Renton knew no trade but soldiering. He took a local release, influenced by his friendship with a Le Havre girl and found a job in Paris. The couple married in 1919. The Renton family moved to England when the threat of another war became obvious in 1938. He joined the HAC, was re-commissioned when war came and was shipped out to France with the BEF. Lionel Renton served on the Divisional staff and was taken prisoner on the Somme in 1940. An unlucky coincidence, as he remarked.

Another of the 'Originals', who planned to stay in the army, was C P Lawson. He too took a Regular commission, suffered in two gas attacks and was appointed Adjutant to the 1st Essex. He later served on the Staff of Fourth Army. He applied for Staff College only to find that there were 500 names on the list ahead of his. He gave up thoughts of an army career and accepted a post in Calcutta. He sailed for India in January 1920.

Fanny Catchpole, the younger sister of the two Tennant brothers, became a nurse in London through the last terrible years of the Great War. She survived the Spanish influenza epidemic that decimated patients and staff in the London hospitals. She married one of her patients, an Irish soldier and they had a son. Both her men enlisted in 1939 and she returned to army nursing. All three survived the war.

One of the 'Originals' who became very well known after the war was Derek McCullough. Despite the many wounds received at Beaumont Hamel, including losing an eye, he managed to persuade the authorities to let him go back to France and arranged a transfer to the Royal Flying Corps. When he joined the BBC he was turned down for the job of announcer because he had a slight regional accent (West country). His recurring bouts of illness, due to the wounds in his chest, did not help. He and his wife were sent to the newly opened broadcasting station in Belfast. The damp climate of Northern Ireland aggravated the weakness in his lungs. Luckily the first General Manager of the BBC had served in France through the war and decided that McCullough should return to London. John Walsham was better known as Lord Reith after he was appointed Director General in 1927. Against the wishes of McCullough's immediate superior in the BBC, Lord Reith arranged leave so that McCullough could have his wounds treated. In all, he had more than sixty operations. The last, one before war erupted again in Europe, took place in Germany. In 1938 the BBC gave him leave to travel to Munich where a specialist surgeon took out two ribs and removed the bullet from his lung.

Derek McCullough became famous during and after the Second World War as 'Uncle Mac' of Children's Hour.

1. Under the command of Ludendorf the Germans broke through forming a great bulge in the Allied line, from Arras in the north to La Fere to the south in the French sector. They took Montdidier and Noyon and were only checked within medium artillery range of Amiens.) So rapid was their advance that the Germans took more than 80,000 prisoners, 975 guns and vast stores of war material, food and clothing. In one divisional HQ they looted the cellars of crates of fine wines, whisky and champagne. And yet this spectacular success carried the seeds of its own downfall. The attack bogged down. Ludendorf missed his target: the Channel ports. His armies were exhausted and the very quantity and quality of the supplies that they captured emphasised Germany's poverty and demoralised the advancing men. Australian and British troops held them in front of Amiens. 'Operation Michael', so brilliantly begun came to a halt at the tiny village of Villers-Bretoneux.

Chapter 40

SIXTY YEARS ON
THE SURVIVORS' VIEW

The folly consisted not in a pursuit of a goal or ignorance of the obstacles but in persistence of the pursuit despite accumulating evidence that the goal was unattainable... The question is why did the policy makers close their minds to the evidence and its implications? This is the classic symptom of folly: refusal to draw conclusions from the evidence, addiction to the counter-productive.

Barbara Tuchman. *'The March of Folly: from Troy to Vietnam'*

WALK THE PLOUGHED LAND anywhere on the old Front line, or pass recently excavated soil, and you will find fragments of bone. This strip of land, roughly twenty miles in length, resembles the site of an abattoir. A large percentage of those killed on 1 July 1916 have no marked grave. Their remains disintegrated during repeated shelling and disappeared in the mud as the Somme battle moved from summer, to autumn, and into winter. Beaumont Hamel is no exception; the names of many of the 16th Middlesex are to be found only on the memorial of the missing, at Thiepval. Of those whose remains were found, close up to the German line, some are buried near the lip of the mine crater and the rest near the Sunken Road. Others died at the RAP and are buried at Auchonvilliers. There is, too, a trail of those wounded who died soon after the battle, buried at the sites of CCSs or hospitals close to the railway and the Somme canal.

The childlike question returns: how did this monstrous folly happen? If eight people are killed in a rail-crash society demands to know why. There is a public enquiry, or a coroner's report at the least. There was no enquiry after the disaster on the first day of the Somme battle. How could there be? The war went on. Soldiers of the Great War spoke of 'The War' as a malevolent abstract being. War has its own dynamic which does not obey logical man-made laws.

In July 1966 the Allies arranged an anniversary parade and services in Albert and at the Thiepval Memorial. This was the last commemoration in which large numbers of survivors of the Somme battles marched together. Noel Peters was one of them. Noel smiled when he described the grand uniforms of the NATO staff officers in contrast to the shabby suits or blazers of the old soldiers and of the misuse that the reporters for TV or the tabloid newspapers made of the occasion. He described the scene with his usual good humour and without rancour. Complaining was not in Noel's nature.

July was unusually hot that year and there was a muddle over transport to the memorial. Sitting outside a bar in Albert, Noel and a former Royal Fusilier wondered how they would get there. A journalist offered them a lift in his car and asked if they would like to see the point in the old line from which the attack took place. Noel was disappointed that their new friend did not take them to the Auchonvilliers road. Instead the journalist persuaded the two old soldiers to pose in a preserved trench in Newfoundland Park. Once he had his pictures he abandoned them there. Noel and his friend set off to walk to Thiepval. Luckily a young woman with a car, escorting her grandfather, picked them up. The heat of the sun was so intense that Noel almost fainted when they reached the Thiepval Memorial. He and the ex-Fusilier found chairs and shelter under a marquee. They were ejected from this shady spot by a young staff officer in immaculate blue uniform, white gloves and gold braid and epaulettes. This amused Noel.

'*C'est la vie*. Some nerve we had, two old sweats sitting in the NATO officer's tent.'

The ceremony was concerned more with the prestige of NATO than honouring the dead, let alone the living survivors. Many were disgusted by it, but Noel was not one of them. 'Back in the hotel in Albert, there was a lot of fellows sounding off about the Generals, Field Marshal Haig in particular. Some knew what they were talking about, most didn't. I kept my mouth shut. What's the use of speculating after all these years? What's done is done. You can't bring back the dead.'

Alf Damon took a cynical view of Haig and his staff but Lionel Renton was charitable.

> *Take a general on the Western Front. He might have started the war as an Indian Army Major, promoted almost immediately to Colonel, then quickly up to command a Brigade and then a Division. They'd had no experience, d'you see? Half the time they had no bloody idea what they were doing. I believe that they were honest enough, according to their lights. They weren't the crooks or buffoons that writers have made them out to be. They just did not have the experience or the brains to do the job.*

Lionel Renton went on to say that the British Army of 1916 suffered from a desperate shortage of senior officers, both at Regimental and at Staff level

> *I get very bored and irritated by so much hind-sight wisdom. So many young journalists and historians judge by the standards of now without bothering to understand how it was then. Not only have the means and the weapons changed, but the whole public attitude to service, patriotism and obedience has changed.*

He looked out of the window at the garden where his wife was entertaining a niece and grand-niece from Le Havre.

> *I never met Haig. He's an easy subject for criticism. But ask yourself; what other course was open to him? He was pushed by the French, in desperate trouble at Verdun, their army approaching a condition of mutiny and by their own politicians. Haig had no choice. He was faced with a problem of two trench lines, virtually impregnable. The only tools he had to make a breach in the line were artillery and infantry. The mines on the Somme were a side-show that achieved practically nothing. Haig and Rawlinson believed that the artillery would do the job. They either believed that or they were a pair of bloody fools, and*

I don't think that either was stupid.

Amongst the survivors that I interviewed Lionel Renton's view of the Staff stands out because of its detachment. The agony of the front-line poets and artists gives their work a power that has influenced all of us, and rightly so, and yet out of these young officers have grown myths which influence our view of the generals that distort our view. Neither Haig nor Rawlinson were stupid men. To pretend that they were trivialises the argument (what Dixon dismisses as 'The Bloody Fool' theory). The mystery of the planning and execution of the attacks on the First day on the Somme is far more complex and interesting than the facile cliché 'Lions led by Donkeys'.[1]

I asked Sergeant Charles Quinnel and Captain Crosbee the same question that I asked Lionel Renton. "If both the Battalion and Brigade HQs knew that the artillery bombardment was insufficient, that the wire had not been cut and that the Germans had not been wiped out in their deep bunkers, nor their morale seriously depressed, then why did the attack go ahead?"

Their answers were almost identical.

Those generals did not muddy their polished boots. They never saw the front line for themselves so they never saw the wire. They didn't talk to the officers or NCOs who had been out in No Man's Land so they had no idea of the enemy strength.

But surely your Company and Battalion officers knew?

Of course they knew. The Company Commanders and the Battalion Commanders knew, even Brigade knew. But you have to remember that your Colonel and your Brigadier were regulars, each with his career to consider. If he passed on bad news then he'd get a reputation as a moaner, or for being windy. He'd lose any chance of promotion, or even lose his Command.

Lionel Renton repeated the theory that Colonel Hall wrote a report a few weeks after the disastrous attack at Beaumont Hamel, a report that accurately described the reasons why so many lives were lost, and why the attack was a failure. He pointed out the line in the Battalion war diary thoroughly scratched out in indelible pencil:

Many people believe that there was a truthful and accurate report, but that it was later destroyed either by Johnnie Hall himself, or at a higher level. He wrote an account many years later, by the time he had been promoted to Brigadier, but it was a whitewash job.

My own feeling, which cannot be either proved or disproved, is that belief in Colonel Hall's report is a comforter, a last relic of idealism and the volunteer spirit. The belief is wholly admirable but it is a mirage. When I searched both the Battalion and Brigade war diaries I could find no evidence that Colonel Hall wrote a candid report. Such an action is not in character. At Auchonvilliers, in the aftermath of the battle, there was no time. The CO had his hands full re-organising what was left of the Battalion to hold back an imminent counter-attack. He had as much reason as his surviving NCOs and men to be in a state of shock. Once the Battalion was out of the line and Hall recovered his habitual composure he is unlikely to have wasted time in brooding. Once he was summoned back to England to receive his DSO he then went along with the official propaganda and accepted a citation that bore no relation to the actual course of the battle. From Rawlinson to Haig and from parliament to the palace, the establishment needed a victory. Colonel Hall simply went with the flow – and, after the horrors that he had experienced, who can blame him?

Everything that can be written about the reasons for the disaster on July the First 1916 has been written. One can trawl through the numerous books on the Somme, on the generals and on the conduct of the Great War and find many different opinions, but in the end I put my faith in those who were there, in Cruttwell, in Liddell Hart and, on the survivors who I got to know in the late nineteen-seventies, in particular Lionel Renton. He had read widely and thought a great deal about what happened to him and to his friends at Beaumont Hamel, bringing to his experience as a young private soldier the trained mind of his older self, as a staff officer.

Lionel Renton's verdict was that the massacre at Beaumont Hamel resembled an accident: a cumulative error, rather than the fault of any one man. That Haig, far from being omnipotent was the servant of politicians, both in Westminster and Paris. Neither the time or the place of the attack were of Haig's making, both were decided by the French, made desperate by the losses at Verdun. Lionel Renton believed that both Haig and Rawlinson knew that the pre-conditions had not been met but that they were powerless to stop the juggernaut that they had created.

Allegations that Haig was a coward or a fool are totally misguided, he was neither. He showed courage in the Sudan and in South Africa, and a high order of courage in the early days of the Great War, particularly during the retreat from Mons and Le Catteau. No commander could exercise control from close up to the line in 1916. He could only command an immense show like the Somme from a distance. As for the idea that he was some kind of independent war-lord, that was rubbish. He was not a free agent. Firstly: the BEF was always subordinate to the French army, not least because we were on their land. Up to 1917, the French consistently took four times the casualties that we did. So Haig had to consider Joffre on the one hand, and, on the other the British Prime Minister. First it was Asquith, who was ineffectual, followed by Lloyd-George who was effective but a devious little crook.

Haig's dearest wish was to break through the enemy line and return to a war of movement. A laudable ideal, but unrealistic, as we know now with hind sight wisdom. You have to remember that Haig did not have the technology to break through, he only had artillery and infantry, an insufficient number of tanks, no parachute troops, none of the bridging equipment or landing craft that arrived on the scene in the Second War. As things turned out he did not even have a sufficient quantity of heavy guns. Luckily for our peace of mind, we did not know that at the time.

An event like that is not something one forgets. I can remember every detail of that day. Even after I was wounded I remained conscious through the day and into the night, which was when I was picked up and carried back. I can remember everything that I saw; but remembering how I felt at that age is not so easy. I suppose what I, and practically all our friends felt was confidence. We weren't green troops. We had been in France for more than eight months, much of that time under fire, so we didn't believe the 'walk-over' eye-wash. We had a great respect for Jerry as a fighter and we did not believe that it would be easy. And yet we had no doubt that the attack would succeed and that we would break through the German line. I wonder now how we could possibly believe that we would get away with it, but we did. But you have to remember that anything I deduce now is coloured by hind-sight. We know what happened on 1st July, and what happened through the rest of the war, and that alters one's viewpoint.

The causes of the disaster on 1 July are many, but the principal causes break down into four; five if one includes the excuse put about by Haig's staff at Montreuil, that the attack failed because of the inexperience of the New Army battalions.

The main causes were:

First: the strength of the German defences, both natural and man-made.

Second: insufficient heavy artillery to break these defences.

Third: despite assurances by Divisional staff, the wire was not cut and remained a formidable obstacle

Fourth: the timing of the infantry advance. The fatal pause between the lifting of the barrage and the infantry leaving their trenches. To this one can add a sub-category, the weight that each infantryman had to carry, that made any rapid movement impossible.

The argument of Colonel Boraston, and later apologists for the planners, blames the infantry at battalion level. The senior officers of Haig's staff, all of whom were regular soldiers, generally believed that civilian volunteers could not be trained up to regular army standards in less than two years. Following this logic, senior officers, from Haig downward, assumed that the New Army battalions could not be trusted to advance in small groups and so must advance in disciplined lines, as on parade. To extend this logic even further: since the plan for the attack was meticulous in every detail it must follow that the fault lay in its execution by junior officers, NCOs and private soldiers. Historians Cruttwell and Liddell Hart dispute this. Like them Lionel Renton pointed out the fallacy in Boraston's argument: that faced with the obstacles of wire and machine guns the regular battalions in the attack fared no better than the New Army battalions and suffered equally heavy casualties. As Lionel Renton said:

'When it came to this new type of siege warfare we were all amateurs, the Sandhurst officer in the trench had no advantage over the Territorial or the Volunteer.'[2]

The planning for the attack on a German line of immense strength makes a dramatic and tragic contrast to the skill and conscientious staff work of the preparations.

Haig and Rawlinson agreed that certain basic requirements should be met.

Sufficient heavy guns must be in action throughout the preliminary bombardment to reduce the German defences and to kill, wound or demoralise the defenders.

The wire must be cut.

The machine guns must be put out of action.

None of these basic aims were achieved and here lies the mystery. Did Haig and

Rawlinson know that they had not been achieved? If they did, then why did they proceed with the attack?

The French learned a great many lessons at Verdun, lessons that their British allies had still to learn. There were several factors that made the French attack more successful such as more intelligent tactics advancing across No Man's Land, but, without doubt, the most important was their superiority in heavy guns. The point where the line of the British Fourth Army met the French 6th Army lay north of the river Somme and south of Montauban. The landscape of the north and the south of the line of attack is different. There were advantages that favoured the attack to the south, whereas both the terrain and the defences in the north favoured the defenders. This study is concerned with what happened on the left of the line, in the north, specifically at Beaumont Hamel. Despite all the obstacles that had to be removed and were not, the attack might have succeeded if the first waves had taken the first line of trenches while the defenders were still in their shelters. This was proved by the initial success of the division to the right of Beaumont Hamel, the 36th Ulster Division who left their trenches and hurried forward immediately the barrage lifted. In contrast, the inexplicable muddle over the timing of the mine explosion and lifting of the artillery barrage robbed the 29th Division of even that chance of success.

At the initial planning stage Hunter-Weston insisted that the mine should explode at 3.30 am. He used the strange argument that the defenders would stand-to immediately the mine exploded, expecting a dawn attack, and then be caught in the final bombardment. Haig acted on the advice of his RE (mines) staff and compromised, agreeing on a time of Zero-minus-ten. On the day, ten minutes was all the German machine-gunners and riflemen needed. Hunter-Weston planned on a small body of men from 86 Brigade to seize the crater immediately after the explosion. This was logical enough, but he then created an even greater error. To allow the crater party to advance all howitzers and mortars firing on the German crater position were ordered to stop firing at the moment of the mine explosion. For reasons that have never been explained, this order applied not only to those guns targeting Hawthorn ridge (the crater position) but to all the guns along the 8th Corps attack. This left only the 18-pounders firing on the German line and many of these shells failed to explode. One section of each field battery was ordered to lift its fire to the German second line at Zero-minus-three. Thanks to Hunter-Weston's muddled orders, at the moment that the infantry rose from their trenches and formed ranks, only half 29th Division's 18 pounders were firing on the German front line, with no howitzers or medium guns firing at all.[3]

Communications can be described in two senses: physical and psychological.

Firstly, physical communication depended on telephone wires and runners. Most of the field-telephone lines were cut by the German bombardment. Many runners were killed while those lucky enough not to be killed by artillery or mortar fire were impeded by the dead and wounded blocking the communication trenches.

In the psychological sense, there appears to have been a marked lack of rapport and candour between Haig and his subordinate generals. Time after time a divisional commander failed to pass on some vital piece of information to 4th Army HQ, or else Rawlinson failed to pass it on to Haig. There appears to have been a failure of communication between Haig and Rawlinson, on the one hand, and Rawlinson and the GOC VIII Corps, Hunter-Weston, on the other. There is no other explanation for Hunter-Weston's incomprehensible decision on the timing of the mine explosion and lifting the artillery barrage.

Haig reveals his distrust of Hunter-Weston in his diary. His diary entry on the night before the battle is most revealing. Haig wrote that he had visited all his Corps commanders and liked what he heard of their preparations. There was one exception. The Staff of VIII Corps, Haig described as '...quite satisfied and confident.' But he added, 'Hunter-Weston and his officers are amateurs in hard fighting and some think that they know more than they really do of this kind of warfare.'[4]

'North of the Ancre the VIII Corps (Hunter-Weston) said they began well... I am inclined to believe from further reports, that few of the VIII Corps left their trenches.'

VIII Corps lost 14,000 officers and men on July 1st. The 29th Division lost 5,240 casualties. Haig's comments are interesting because they reveal the irrational and prejudiced side of his character, which was the reverse side of Haig the planner and meticulous organiser. For his part, Hunter-Weston was well aware of Haig's dislike and he wanted to prove that he could push his troops as fiercely as any of the Corps commanders. The colossal losses at Gallipoli showed that Hunter-Weston was far from being Windy, or too easy on his men. In his jovial way he was quite content to send huge numbers of his men to their deaths. 'What are casualties to me?' he is reported as saying, when in command of the 29th Division at the Gallipoli landing. Haig was misguided in doubting the VIII Corps commander's courage and zeal, but he had reason to doubt his intelligence. As for imagination, or tactical inventiveness Hunter-Weston showed no sign of these qualities.[5]

Both the French and German armies had learnt the folly of advancing in lines. By 1916 both French and German infantry had learned to advance in small groups, in quick bounds, moving from shell hole to shell hole. The only justification for the tactic used on 1st July was the 'walk-over'. This assumed that not a single defender would be left alive in the forward trenches, nor a single machine gun in action. One officer remarked, 'The battle was lost by three minutes' (reported by Liddell Hart).

Captain Edward Spears, who was a liaison officer attached to the French Army commented on the extreme contrast between the French and the British tactics of advance.

> My memory is seared with the picture of the French and British attacking together on the Somme. The British rigid and slow, advancing as at an Aldershot parade in lines that were torn and ripped by the German guns, while the French tactical formations, quick and elastic, securing their objectives with trifling loss. It had been a terrible spectacle.'

Of the British infantry Spears wrote:

> As a display of courage it was magnificent, as an example of tactics, its very memory made me shudder.[6]

Many of those who took part in the battle, or, like the poet John Masefield, visited it the following year, commented on the exceptional strength of the German defences and the way their designers and engineers took every advantage of the landscape. One of these advantages was not seen above ground but lay under the cultivated topsoil; chalk.

Chalk is an ideal medium both for trench-making and for tunnelling. Its nature was known to the local inhabitants who had quarried it and mined it for generations. Early in the war engineers noted that the compact nature of chalk absorbed and cushioned the effect of an explosion. It is hard to believe that this important information was not passed on to Intelligence Branch at Fourth Army HQ. As for the news relayed by several battalion commanders to their brigade HQs, that the German front line soldiers were safe in their bunkers, neither destroyed nor demoralised, either this did not reach the High Command or the staff ignored intelligence reports on German morale.

Like their comments on the tunnels and shelters deep in the chalk, many commented on the strength and thickness of the German wire.

Lionel Renton and Alf Damon commented on the inferiority of the wire cutters supplied by the War Office. Sergeant Charles Quinnell MM said, 'British issue wire-cutters could cut only British wire–not German wire.' Cruttwell describes the German wire entanglements on the Somme front as '... Very formidable, both in quantity and quality. The belts were at least 30 – 20 yards deep, the barbs often as thick as a man's thumb, and the posts of iron.'[7]

Shells striking the wire entanglement on July 1st exploded in the earth creating a crater. The wire suffered little damage while the crater became yet another obstacle. Major Probert remarked that the shell that would 'explode on graze' was not perfected until mid 1917. This had the improved 106 fuse that destroyed wire leaving a small crater [See Appendix One: 'The guns and Major Probert'].

At the end of 1915 the new CIGS, Sir William Robertson wrote:

> Experience has taught us that any front line can be broken. It is the depth of the enemy's defences and the power of bringing up intact reserves quickly to occupy rear lines which makes attack difficult on the Western front.

This was the official view, shared by Haig and Rawlinson and their Corps commanders. Haig's orders and diaries prove that he had no doubt about the effectiveness of the preliminary bombardment. His preoccupation, following along the lines of Robertson's thinking, lay in bringing reserves of infantry and field guns forward fast enough to maintain the momentum of the breakthrough. Haig and Birch (Chief Gunner) overestimated the power of explosive and in doing so, underestimated the tenacity and will to survive of those in the target area. Not only to survive but to emerge from their shelters with the will to fight.

During the initial planning Haig and Rawlinson agreed with Birch, Haig's chief of artillery, on the minimum quantity of heavy guns and ammunition that would destroy the enemy defences, and either kill, wound or demoralise the defenders. The quantity of heavy guns used in the initial bombardment was way below this minimum level.

Many survivors of the Somme battles commented on the inferiority of British Intelligence to that of their opponents. This criticism applied both to the gathering of Intelligence, the responsibility of GS Intelligence branch, and counter-intelligence, or Field Security.

Henry Williamson remarked that both British Intelligence and counter-Intelligence were very poor in 1916. Details of the attack, that the staff believed to be secret, were common knowledge in the bars and brothels of Amiens. Williamson believed that much of the Intelligence passed to Haig was inaccurate. Often it was mere wishful thinking. Haig's Chief of Intelligence, Brigadier Charteris became notorious for passing on information that Haig wanted to hear and suppressing anything that might question the wisdom of the plan of attack.[8]

Preparations for the attack could not be hidden from German Intelligence. On 14 June a German agent in Holland picked up the location of the attack. Despite this Falkenhayn continued to believe that the attack would come in Flanders.[9] The worst security lapse of all came when a British Cabinet Minister warned workers not to expect a Whitsun Holiday.[10]

On 23rd June a reliable German agent predicted that the offensive would be directed against Von Bullow's Second Army on the Somme.

The actual time was given away by a British staff officer. At 2.45 (Berlin time) on the morning of 1st July, a listening post at La Boiselle, tuned to intercept British telephone calls, picked up a message from a brigade major giving Rawlinson's eve of battle message. This was passed back to Divisional Intelligence at Bazentin le Petit. Though only part of the message was picked up it was enough to tell the German High Command all that they needed to know.

At 3.00 am the Regimental HQ of the 119th Reserve, defending Beaumont Hamel, signalled a general stand-to. The defenders of the village fortress of Beaumont Hamel were well supplied with machine guns and mortars which were hidden and protected by the defenders in caves or excavations into the chalk cliffs from the valley floor. The explosion of the mine acted as the final alarm. Gun crews had abundant time to leave the shelters and sight their weapons and bring them into action as the first waves of British troops left their trenches. With the firepower that the Wurtemburgers were able to bring to bear there was no chance of 86 Brigade, or any of the other brigades in 29th Division, getting into and holding the German Front line trench, let alone 'walking-over' them.

1. N F Dixon. *The Psychology of Military Incompetence*. Pub Random House 1976. See section on Haig pp 371-392.

2. See Col Boraston. *Sir Douglas Haig and his Command*.
John Terraine. *Haig: The Educated Soldier*.
Liddell Hart. *The First World War*.
C.R.M.F. Cruttwell. *The Great War* 1914-1918, p264. Cruttwell refers to this argument, 'Colonel Boraston in his unpleasing book...'

3. See Appendix One for a general description of the use of artillery along the Somme front. The guns: the diary and sketch-book of Major Probert RA. (Unpublished).

4. General Farrar Hockley commented on Haig's dislike of Hunter-Weston and VIII Corps.
'29th Division had taken part in the Gallipoli landings under General Hunter-Weston, where it had earned a high name... Haig was prejudiced against all who had joined in that campaign.'
Farrar Hockley p117.
'Friday June 30. The wire has never been so well cut or the artillery preparations so thorough. I have seen personally all the Corps Commanders and one and all are full of confidence. The only doubt I have is regarding VIII Corps (Hunter-Weston) which has had no experience of fighting in France and has not carried out one successful raid.'
The Private Papers of Douglas Haig. 1914-1919. p153.

5. A month after the attack on Beaumont Hamel the 'Jovial Hunter-Bunter' showed his less than jovial face when he sentenced a 19-year-old boy to death. John Bennett, who enlisted under age in 1914 and had endured several major attacks and many bombardments, ran during a gas attack at Ypres. Clearly his nerve broke and then recovered because he returned within the hour. He was sentenced to death but both his Platoon and Company officers recommended mercy. On review the Brigadier accepted this lenient view. Hunter-Weston overruled the Brigadier's decision, writing on the charge sheet, 'Cowards constitute a serious danger to the war effort, and the sanction of the death penalty was designed to frighten men more than the enemy.'

6. *From Prelude to Victory*. Major General Sir Edward Spears.

7. 'Staff officers wanted to know why we didn't cut it ourselves. Our wire cutters weren't up to it. The German wire was a quarter to three-eighths (of an inch) thick and we had those clumsy two handled wire-cutters, imagine the noise they made. And, you've got to remember that Jerry had look-outs on the *Qui-vive* in bays every few yards. If he heard a noise he'd send up a flare and then the machine guns would be onto you.'
Sergeant Charles Quinnell MM. Royal Fusiliers.

8. See *Henry Williamson: the Last Romantic* by Ann Williamson.

9. Falkenhayn's belief was logical. At the Chantilly conference, in the summer of 1915, Haig thought the German defences on the Somme front too strong for this to be a suitable place for a break-through. Haig favoured an attack at Messines, in Flanders. It was Joffre who demanded an attack on the Somme where the Allies could advance together, '*Bras en bras*'.

10. Arthur Henderson MP asked workers in an ammunition factory not to question the postponement of the Whitsun holiday. 'How inquisitive we are! It should suffice that we ask for a postponement of the holiday until the end of July. This fact should speak volumes.' Crown Prince Rupprecht made a practice of reading the English newspapers. He wrote in his diary, 'This fact should speak volumes – It certainly does. Sure proof of an English offensive.' See Farrar-Hockley *The Somme* p91.

APPENDIX ONE

THE GUNS

THE DIARY AND SKETCH BOOK OF MAJOR PROBERT RA

Major Ynr Probert was a professional soldier, like his ancestors who had guarded the Welsh border for generations. In the summer of 1916 he was Second Lieutenant Probert of 35th Battery RFA, attached to 37 Brigade, facing Fricourt. His battery was equipped with 4.5 inch howitzers. Not only did Ynr Probert experience the Somme battles, from first to last, but he kept both a diary and a sketch book, both of which helped him to study the effects of the bombardment when the war was over and he had leisure to do so.

Ynr Probert made drawings of the German line both before and during the Somme battles. These are detailed and carry written notes and place names, like those of a Tactical Sketcher. Before the middle of June the fields and woods look very much as they do today. The fields are green with overgrown crops. The woods in full leaf. Even the village is recognisable as a village, though the church has taken several direct hits and lost its spire. Pale lines of chalk show the German parapet, looking very like Edwardian drawings of military manouvres.

The later drawings are totally different, showing a ruined landscape.

I asked him when the rhythm of routine shelling changed to a sustained bombardment. He opened the diary on 19th June, which was a day of movement and quickening excitement. 35th Battery was sited behind a ridge, 2,200 yards behind the British front line. That day the Battery transport brought up 400 rounds of ammunition for each gun. Ynr Probert visited the 9.2 howitzers moving into position. Moving further along the line he came on the new 60 pounder and 9 inch guns registering their targets.

(Ynr Probert pointed out that the terrain to the right of the line, in the south, was different to the landscape around Beaumont Hamel, but that the artillery preparations were the same, all along the line. The quantity of ammunition fired was also similar. A note of the routine for one battery was very similar to others.)

By June the 24th the Battery received stocks of the new propellant charge 'Nitrocellulose tubular', which replaced cordite. The gunners registered the guns to check the new charges, correcting the range to allow for greater power.

Sunday June 25th. The weather improved and the clouds drifted away. For the first time since the bombardment started the RFC were in the air, spotting for guns, while others took photographs of the German defences.

60 pounder trench mortars bombarded the German line all day. Ynr Probert's 4.5 battery fired 230 rounds from each gun.

The ammunition for the 18 pounders was defective. They suffered many prematures and shorts. A shell burst close to the muzzle of one of these guns on Mametz ridge. All the crew were killed or seriously injured.

26th June. Gas shells (code name 'Peter') were fired at the enemy at 11.20am.

At 4.30pm the French artillery, across the Somme, to their right, began a violent bombardment that lasted until 7.30 pm. Smoke from the French heavy shells drifted across the front obscuring the view.

27th June. Number 35 Battery started a heavy bombardment at 7.30am and continued until evening. After 7.30pm the guns kept up a slow rate of fire which lasted all night. At 5.30am they changed to red-phosphorous smoke tins with five-second fuses. Each gun fired 880 rounds that day.

Wednesday 29th June. 'Y' Day of the bombardment. Guns fired at a slow rate all night. By day the guns fired at long range, 4,400 yards. The barrels had to be elevated to the limit to get the range. One shell hit the roof of the dug-out in which the gun was hidden. Providentially it went through and burst outside. No one was hurt, nor was the howitzer damaged. The German garrison sent up red rockets and soon afterwards we were shelled by salvos of 500mm shells.[1]

30th June. 'Y'2 Day. A comparatively quiet night. The bombardment started at 8 am. This time targets were registered by RFC aeroplanes. Number two gun suffered a premature, the gun was damaged but not one of the crew hurt. German artillery fired many rounds at the new railway loop, which has just been completed. (This supplied the guns with ammunition. On 5th July it earned its place in the history books: this was the line that carried the first tanks to be used in battle.)

Beside the track Lieutenant Probert picked up one of the new fuses used by the German gunners, 'Doppelsunder', meaning 'Time and percussion'.

Sixty years after the battle Major Probert and I sat with his diaries in his farmhouse on the Welsh border. The targets for his battery lay in Fricourt and Mametz. I asked him whether conditions were similar in his section of the line to those at Auchonvilliers? He replied that the bombardment was standard, all along the line. My second question was whether the defects in the guns, and their ammunition, were as bad as accounts reported?

Ynr Probert replied, 'We had a lot of trouble with faulty ammunition, especially prematures which caused many casualties and much damage. Prematures were caused by fuses 100 and 101. These were imported from the USA and probably sabotaged. A fault in the guns was the design of the Buffer-springs which were always giving trouble. I don't recall any serious troubles with the Buffers themselves. The French recoil system was better than ours. This was the type that they used on their Soixante Quinze field guns. Their recoil system was nitrogen filled and a great advance in design on ours.'

Most of these defects were caused by the hasty expansion of the munitions industry.

Some of the steel was sub-standard and developed hair-line cracks when turned on a lathe. Pressure on the shell from the propellant charge cracked, and sometimes detonated, the shell in the barrel. Other premature explosions happened because the fuse came off, exploding as the gun left the barrel. The worst record was held by the 18 pounder shells. During the bombardment preceding July 1st, one third of all 18 pounder shells failed to explode. This can be appreciated, if not accurately checked. In 1976 I counted 25 shells on the edge of a field near Beaumont Hamel. Of these 3 were large and the rest all 18 pounders. At a scrap yard in Dernancourt a pile of 18 pounder carcasses stood over six feet high and this was only one of several piles. Aveluy Wood was full of little piles of 18 pounder shells, minus nose-cap and driving band. The local farmers had removed the copper and brass scrap from 'Les petits obus' which they treated with contempt. On the other hand they had an immense respect for 'Les grands obus' which they left alone, or, if one was unearthed by a plough, carried to the edge of the field to be collected by a salvage squad of engineers from the French Army.

Proportion of heavy guns on each front.

British: 467 to a 16 mile front. (Including 40 heavies lent by the French.)

French: 900 to an 8 mile front.

Of the total British guns, 60 percent were 18 pounders assigned to wire cutting. 75 percent of the 18 pounder shells were shrapnel, almost useless for cutting thick German wire. A high proportion of 18 pounder shells had defective fuses and failed to explode.

(Information supplied by Major Ynr Probert.)

1,738,000 shells were fired in the preliminary bombardment 'but during the latter stages of the battle stocks were very seriously diminished'.

(Cruttwell pp 260-261.)

'Rationally it seems inexplicable that the bombardment should have been counted on to leave nobody alive in the opposing trenches... Rawlinson... spread his limited artillery evenly along the front 'without regard to the strength and importance of any particular part', with the result that 'their fire was necessarily so dispersed that many strong points and machine-gun posts were never touched'. Moreover, a large proportion of the heavy guns were of obsolete pattern and poor range, while much of the ammunition was defective. Thus the shells could not penetrate the dug-outs in which the German machine-gunners were sheltering – in waiting. Yet it is only on the assumption of potentially overwhelming bombardment that we can understand at all the tactics adopted by the British command.'

(*The First World War*. Liddell Hart. Pp312-313.)

---

1. Major Probert remarked that the Germans employed very large guns that could out-range anything with which the Royal Artillery was issued. These long-range guns were mounted on solidly-constructed, flat-bed rail trucks and were based out of range of British counter-bombardment batteries. Moved forward along normal rail-lines, the guns were fired and then moved back out of danger. These guns were a great nuisance to camps' dumps and rail-heads in the rear areas, and, especially to British medium and heavy batteries. Later in the battle the French brought up more heavy guns to help the British counter-bombardment.

APPENDIX TWO

ROBERT GRAVES AND THE LIBEL OF 16PSB

Lionel Renton phoned me, very angry. He asked if I had read Robert Graves' book *Goodbye to All That?* Lionel Renton said that Graves had libelled the Public School Battalion. I re-read my copy and discovered that Graves appears to have a personal spite against what he calls 'The Public Schools Battalion in our Brigade'.

Graves first of all says that the PSB is ill-trained and useless. There is worse to come: he describes the major battle in High Wood and accuses the PSB of cowardice and being totally disorganised in the face of an enemy attack.

Most, if not all, of this diatribe against the Battalion is sheer nonsense and not worth taking seriously, but Lionel Renton was seriously upset by the book and so I promised I would find out what I could about it.

What is one to make of Graves' account of the incident in High Wood? Firstly: that 16PSB was nowhere near High Wood at the time Graves alleges that they ran away. More damning against Graves' libellous story, the Battalion was reduced to less than a company in strength, having lost three quarters of its officers, NCOs and men at the battle of Beaumont Hamel. The story is complicated by the fact that, in Flanders, 16PSB had been in the same division as Graves' Battalion. But the 16PSB was transferred out of the 33rd Division first to Headquarters and then to the 29th Division in the spring of 1916.[1]

Since, quite obviously, the story is rubbish then why did Graves go out of his way to emphasise what he perceives as the failings of this mythical battalion? My first guess was that there must be some other battalion, in another regiment that had the title 'The Public Schools Battalion'. Graves is correct when he says that the beginning of the war, and Kitchener's call for 100,000 volunteers, saw the recruitment of several Public Schools battalions, but the 16th Middlesex was the only one to get out to France and serve in the trenches.

Looking through the Regimental histories of all the Battalions serving in the same Brigade as Graves' Battalion, the 2nd Royal Welch Fusiliers, in the library of the Imperial War Museum I could find no front-line infantry Battalion that Graves could have mistaken for the 16th Middlesex. Then I thought I had found the answer. When the 33rd Division left England for Flanders it included not only the 16th (Public Schools Battalion) of the Middlesex Regiment, but the 17th (Football Battalion) and the 18th (Public Works Battalion). And so I wondered whether Graves had mistaken 'Public Schools' for 'Public Works'? Or was it one of the malicious jokes for which Graves' book is famous? Did it amuse him to deliberately confuse an elite front line battalion with a pioneer battalion?[2]

.

Lionel Renton dismissed my theory.

> *To us the 18th Pioneers seemed like old men. They were not a fighting unit. No one, not even this Graves fellow, could mistake the Pioneers for the Public Schools Battalion. We knew them as the Navvies Battalion, being young and ignorant. In fact they were brave, hard working fellows and the 18th took very heavy casualties from shells and mortars.*

I asked whether it was possible that Graves could have muddled up the 16th Middlesex with the 20th Royal Fusiliers? Was one of the Fusilier Battalions formed as a Public School Battalion? Lionel Renton replied that it was possible but he had never heard of such a battalion. He told me that there were several similar battalions formed in 1914, but that they all were transformed into officer selection units. He repeated that there was only one active service battalion in France with the title 'Public Schools Battalion' and that was the 16th Middlesex.[3]

Graves' first libel concerns the night of 18th of July. His story is this:

> *The tall officer who came running towards us, his hands lifted in surrender, seemed surprised to find that we were not Germans. He claimed that he belonged to the Public Schools Battalion in our own Brigade. When I asked what the hell the game was he explained that he commanded a patrol... the patrol consisted of fifty men, wandering about aimlessly with their rifles slung, and, it seemed, without the faintest idea of where they were, or what information they were supposed to secure. The Public Schools Battalion was one of four or five similar ones formed in 1914 ...this alone was sent out, (to France) and proved a constant embarrassment to our brigade.[4]*

Captain Graves was seriously wounded early in the German counter-attack at High Wood (20th July). While Graves was in hospital a wounded brigade major told him a version of what had happened at High Wood.

> *When I asked whether they (2nd RWF) had held the wood, he told me, 'They hung on near the end. I believe what happened was that the Public Schools Battalion came away after dark; and so did most of the Scotsmen. Your chaps were left there more or less alone for some time.'*

Graves then quotes two letters, the first from Captain Cobart, 5th Scottish Rifles. 'At about 9.00am the troops on the left fell back before a counter-attack. They were all mixed up, Cameronians, Scottish Rifles, Public Schools Battalion. The debacle was stopped in mid-wood, and my company on the right re-took its objective.'

The second was written 30th July by the CO of the 2nd RWF, Colonel Crawshay in a letter to Graves.

> *We had a rotten time, and after succeeding in doing practically the impossible we collected that rotten crowd and put them in their places, but directly darkness came they legged it. It was too sad. We lost heavily. It is not fair putting brave men like ours alongside that crowd.*

At Lionel Renton's request I re-visited the IWM library and, once again, checked through the Regimental histories of all the battalions that were involved in the High Wood struggle. Having read them I was no nearer solving the mystery, but one interesting side light on regimental histories is their partiality. As literature these histories varied from those of high standard, such as Kipling's Irish Guards to the run-of-the-mill editions. The regimental history of the Royal Welch Fusiliers is edited by Dudley Ward and is a well-written and readable account, but he puts his own people in the best possible light. All the other histories that I read take the same approach.

The account of the part played by the 18th Middlesex pioneers takes up three pages in Everard Wyrall's history. It describes a scene of total confusion in the wood, of orders to dig trenches countermanded by orders to act as infantry, and then changing back again. This account, based on reports by Major Best and Captain Hill seems unusually frank and honest. Superficially the theory that '16PSB' was confused with '18PWB' is attractive but eventually I came round to Lionel Renton's belief that this was most unlikely. Both of us felt that Graves' allegations might be some twisted form of joke. This last theory is not as fanciful as it sounds. Paul Fussell writes in *The Great War and Modern Memory* that Graves had a very odd and mischievous sense of humour. *Goodbye to All That* was published in 1929. Fussell describes the book as 'theatrical', much of it written along the lines of a music hall farce. Fussell points out several leaps from fact into fiction, and many deliberate mistakes. An example is playing a tune on a machine gun, a piece of nonsense that Graves must have known that any ex-soldier would spot.

In the 1957 edition, that Graves re-wrote from his 1929 book, the author remarks that he began it as fiction. Later, in an essay PS to *Goodbye to All That* that was published in 1932, Graves states that he wrote the book to 'make a lump of money'. 'I have more or less deliberately mixed in all the ingredients that I know are mixed in to other popular books.' He lists them – food, ghosts, foreign travel, murders, kings, sports, suicides. 'But the best of all are battles, and I have been in two quite good ones.'...'So it was easy to write a book that would interest everybody.' [5]

Paul Fussell advises his readers not to fall into Graves' trap by taking him seriously, or taking anything in *Goodbye to All That* at its sight value. And yet many did take it seriously, and continue to do so. *The Times Literary Supplement*, reviewing the 1960 revised edition wrote:

'Apart from its exceptional value as a war document, this book has also the interest of being the most candid self portrait of a poet, warts and all, ever painted.'

Robert Graves is an extraordinary and fascinating literary character. Amongst many well known and well-read works he wrote what is probably the most entertaining and amusing book of the Great War. Contrary to the claim by the critic in the *TLS* it is not a 'war document', nor did Graves intend it to be. Building on the novel, that he rejected, Graves noted the success of the war memoir and set out to write a best seller in this genre. Fussell remarks that it is as much rooted in the London theatre and music hall conventions as in the war itself. Even Graves' prejudices have a theatrical ring to them. Though he was a wartime volunteer Graves imbibed all the snobberies and myths of an officer of the pre-war regular army. In the postscript added to his revised version he despises and patronises Egyptians, Greeks and other foreigners in Cairo in the nineteen-twenties (chapters 31 and 320). Periodically, through the book he professes to detest the

French. On the Northern French civilians '...their dirty little lives' (p140). He includes all British soldiers in his prejudice. 'The eighteenth century owed its unpopularity to its Frenchness. Anti-French feeling amongst most ex-soldiers amounted almost to an obsession.' 'Some undergraduates even insisted that we had been fighting on the wrong side: our natural enemies were the French' (p240). One can compare this with the pity shown towards the wretched conditions endured by the *poilu* at Montmorency barracks, and the sympathy for the plight of French civilians shown by Noel Peters and Alf Damon. Noel said, 'I liked the French. I learned a lot about cooking from those farmers and their wives.' Alf wrote, 'I often thought of the Fourcroy family. They were in my thoughts when the Boche broke through our lines in 1918.' As for Lionel Renton, he married a girl from Le Havre and lived in France between the wars, virtually becoming a Frenchman.

In his prologue to the version that he rewrote in Majorca in 1957, Graves ended, 'If any passage gives offence after all these years, I hope to be forgiven.'

Unfortunately the passages referring to the Public Schools Battalion did indeed give offence. Lionel Renton described Graves as 'highly mischievous'. To the Great War generation the word 'Mischievous' was far more damning than it is to ours today. Lionel Renton wrote, 'Since Graves cannot reply to explain to us (and it is doubtful if he would reply even if he was alive) we will never know the answer. But we can be certain of one thing. Whoever it was who was, or was not, running in and out of High Wood, it was not the Public Schools Battalion.'[6]

There is a sequel to this unhappy story. Fifteen years after Lionel Renton and I had this conversation about Robert Graves I picked up a copy of *The Bells of Hell go Ting-a-ling-aling*, by Eric Hiscock, who joined the Royal Fusiliers at the age of fifteen. My attention was drawn to a note in his book 'The University and Public Schools Brigade of the Royal Fusiliers was already becoming a misnomer by the summer of 1916'.

Searching through the Regimental History I discovered a story very similar, and running parallel, to that of the 16th Middlesex. Just as the 16th (Public Schools Battalion) was founded by a few wealthy citizens in August – September 1914 at Kempton Park, so 'The University and Public School Brigade', or UPS, was formed on the Epsom racecourse at the same time. And, just as the PSB was adopted by the Middlesex Regiment, so the UPS was taken under the wing of the Royal Fusiliers, becoming the 18th, 19th, 20th and 21st Royal Fusiliers. But though the 20th Royal Fusiliers had once been part of the UPS no one ever called it 'The Public Schools Battalion' and any connection with universities and public schools had long gone, as Eric Hiscock says, by the summer 1916.

There is one final theory, and this one is mine. Reading the biography of Henry Williamson, written by his daughter, Ann, I came on an attack on him by another ex-soldier of the Great War, none other than Robert Graves.[7] Graves appeared to dislike anyone who wrote about the Great War, or even those who had the potential to write. This made me think about his attack on the reputation of the Public Schools Battalion, and wonder again why Graves was so prejudiced against it. The answer may lie in Graves' childhood. Graves was born to a middle-class family in Wimbledon. His father was a Londoner of Scottish descent and his mother was German. Robert Graves attended several preparatory schools (all of which he loathed) and then went to a middle of the range Public School (Charterhouse – which he both disliked and despised). Graves, as Fussell remarks, posed as Irish, joined a Welsh regiment and made a cult of living what he saw as a Celtic life. So we can plainly see two phobias about his own background: London-English suburbia and the whole ethos of the Public School system. Both the PSB and the UPS Brigade aimed their recruiting campaigns, in August 1914, at young men with exactly the same background as Robert Graves: from comfortable haute bourgeois homes in the suburbs of London and sent, at an early age, away to a Public School. Thus a 'Public Schools Battalion' represented everything in his own past that Robert Graves was attempting to suppress and deny.

1. The location of 16PSB is shown in chapter 38, footnote 1.

2. The 18th (Public Works Battalion) were pioneers, attached to the Brigade for trench digging and other labouring work. Officers and men alike were too old for front line duty. But the nature of their work caused a steady trickle of dead and injured. Having worked continuously in the rain for almost twenty-four hours the 19th were ordered back for food and rest that they well deserved. Before they had time for either the Pioneers were ordered to march back to High Wood because the Germans had broken through and were pushing 10th Brigade out of the wood. The scene was one of total confusion, more like jungle fighting than anything seen in Europe. Scots, Royal Welch, Cameronians and Royal Fusiliers, all mixed up with the enemy infantry in the thick undergrowth, shell craters and fallen trees. The Pioneers fought bravely, despite their exhaustion and lack of food, until at last they were ordered to fall back.

3. The 16th Middlesex moved to the Somme in March 1916, joining 86 Brigade of the 29th Division. Graves, recently promoted to Captain joined the 2nd Royal Welch Fusiliers at Cuinchy, near Bethune. The 2nd RWF were part of 19 Brigade in 33rd Division. His Battalion moved to Fricourt to join the Somme battle, moving into line on July 14th 1916.

4. As well as the 2nd Royal Welch Fusiliers, 19 Brigade consisted of: 5th Scottish Rifles; 20th Royal Fusiliers and a company of Cameronians attached to the Brigade. Other units who were sent in to the messy battle in High Wood were the Divisional Pioneers, the 18th Middlesex, and possibly some reinforcements from the 20th RWF and the 2nd Gordon Highlanders, though the role of these last two units is not clear.

5. Robert Graves' *Goodbye to All That* was first published by Jonathan Cape in 1929. He re-wrote it and it was published by Penguin Books in 1960. Penguin re-printed the book 17 times, a tribute to its enduring popularity. The passages libelling the Public Schools Battalion run from pages 178 to 183.
Paul Fussell, *The Great War and Modern Memory*. Pub OUP 1977.
 See 'The caricature scenes of Robert Graves' in the chapter The Theater of War, pp 203-220.
'We are in no danger of being misled as long as we perceive that *Goodbye to All That* is no more 'a direct and factual autobiography' than Sassoon's memoirs. It is rather a satire, built out of anecdotes heavily influenced by stage comedy.'
'No one has ever denied the brilliance of *Goodbye to All That* and no one has ever been bored by it...'
'But to put it so solemnly is to risk falling into Graves' trap... Graves is a joker, a manic illusionist...' 'Being 'a Graves' is a way of being scandalously 'Celtish' (at school 'I always claimed to be Irish', he says in *Goodbye to All That*)'.

6. In fact, Lionel Renton and I were both wrong. At the time of our conversation Graves was still alive. Born in 1895 he lived until 1985.

7. Henry Williamson: *The Last Romantic* by Ann Williamson.
On the subject of the Great War see the central series of Williamson's series of novels *The Chronicle of Ancient Sunlight*, in particular *A Fox Under My Cloak*. *The Golden Virgin* and *A Test to Destruction*. *The Golden Virgin* includes a description of the first day of the Somme battles. Graves takes exception to this because he says that Williamson's battalion did not take part in it. This is an example of Graves' contrariness. Williamson took part in several major attacks, just as Graves did. Each writer had friends who survived July 1st. It did not take an enormous effort of imagination on Williamson's part to re-create July 1st in his novel without being physically present at that particular attack.

APPENDIX THREE

LANDSCAPE AND THE PHYSICAL EVIDENCE SIXTY YEARS LATER

My training was that of a sculptor, so it was the landscape and the materials that first attracted me to the old front line above the Somme. One has to walk the downs, and explore the steep, wooded dingles, to appreciate the skill with which the German planners and engineers made use of the high ground, and exploited and fortified the strongest features. Up until quite recently, the walker not only took in the broad strategy of the defence, but, on the immediate scale, observed and picked up many clues.[1]

To coincide with the 50th anniversary of the opening of the battle of the Somme the Imperial War Museum Photographic Library set up a 'Then and now' exhibition of the mine craters; photographs taken in 1917 and another set, each from the same spot, in 1966. My first trip, in the summer of 1968, was inspired by this exhibition. My objective was to draw all the mine craters along the Somme line. The Lochnagar Crater was easy to find because there was a signpost on the La Boiselle to Fricourt road, though the land around it was overgrown and the vast crater eroded and falling in.[2] The Hawthorn Redoubt Crater was much harder to find because the crater was totally overgrown and there was no clear path to reach it. It was through losing my way that I came on the two small British cemeteries that started this project. Here, at the crater lip and beside the Sunken Road lie the remains of those Middlesex men who died close to the German wire.

The landscape in the early seventies was quite different to the landscape today. Northern France has changed out of all recognition. Equally important, what is today a tourist site, was then a barren landscape that had only partially recovered from two wars. (Three if one counts the German invasion of 1870.) Apart from the growth of trees and shrubs, very little had changed since the villagers rebuilt their homes in a shattered and haunted landscape. The only tourists I saw were the rare coach-load of old soldiers, organised by the British Legion, and the occasional historian on a cycle. Recognising each other as English the historian and I slunk past without a word as though committing some act of indecency by visiting the place where our ancestors were slaughtered. No Frenchman dreamt that this wretched place would one day become a tourist centre. Taking their cue from the Communist Mayor of Albert, they discouraged interest in the period that they most wanted to forget. The Picards appeared to dislike, even detest their former allies.[3]

By 1976, farmers were beginning to fill in the larger shell and smaller mine craters. They also started to fell some of the woods and copses that had re-grown since the last desperate German offensive of Spring 1918. The only obvious reminder of the war was

Newfoundland Park that was established between the wars. Apart from the preserved (but not yet restored) furrows of the two front lines at the park, and the major mine craters, there appeared, superficially, little reminder of one of the most terrible and costly battles in Europe. And yet one only had to turn off the track into a bit of unploughed land, or into one of those tormented woods, to see material evidence all around. Lumps of displaced chalk, steel wire, cast iron shards, brass tubes and lead balls. There was too a mass of other assorted debris such as decayed petrol tins, perforated helmets, enamelled steel water-bottles, Toffee Apples, Lewis gun magazines and the broken barrels of trench mortars, but the former were the most common finds and those most indicative of the reasons for the disaster.

To take chalk first. Money was beginning to trickle into the area because the first road-widening schemes had started and a few entrepreneurs were enlarging, or building new houses. This brought in large earth-moving machines who began to cut into the chalk. The chalk exposed by JCBs and crushed by bulldozers was impressive stuff. Picking up a lump of it, one cannot crumble the surface, but one can carve it with a penknife.[4]

As if to emphasise my thoughts on the tough and homogenous quality of the Somme chalk builders were excavating a cliff to make way for the foundations of a house. They had opened up two tunnels for the twin tracks of a light railway. The tunnels were narrow but regular in section and skillfully cut into the chalk. German army engineers took full advantage of its excellent qualities as a tunnelling material and also its resistance to the shock of high explosive.

The British must have known this. Certainly the Royal Engineers knew it from their excavations to place high explosive for the mines. Guide-books to the region, such as Baedeker of 1913, note the number of refuges cut into the chalk, some like the Bergwerk at Beaumont Hamel, date back to the Middle Ages. It was the defender's ability to shelter safe underground through the bombardment, as well as the fatal delay between the explosion of the mine and the first wave of 86 Brigade climbing rising from their trenches, that allowed the defenders time to climb out of their deep shelters, take their positions and set up their machine guns.

The second material that could not be overlooked by anyone walking the fields, or peering into hedgerows, was the thickness and tenacity of the German barbed wire. This was specifically German because the British wire was thin, inferior and, by the mid-seventies, had rusted away. The stout and deadly German wire remained. Farmers made use of it for fencing. Neglected craters were filled with it, pushed there out of the farmer's way. Farmers also made use of the steel section that the Germans used to support the wire, to shore up trenches and to reinforce their dugouts. Much of this remains to this day and one can see an interesting variety of channel, I beam, angle and light railway section supporting fences or used in the rebuilding of pig-sties or cow-sheds.

The third family of materials is metal, starting with cast iron. This is still surfacing today and will do for decades. Some of it is lethal and claims victims every year. In 1976 the traveller could barely sit down to eat his sandwiches without encountering a rough edged shard of iron. (I do not exaggerate – very painful it was too.) Cycling up a rough farm track his wheel hits a bump in the hard-core surface. It is a live 18 pounder shell, nose cone and copper driving band intact.

He cycles on thinking that it might have been worse, it might have been one of the big ones. From time to time a farmer's plough hit one of the legendary Grands Obus and plough, tractor and farmer were vapourised. As well as the larger shells, lethal ordinance includes Mills grenades and Toffee Apples. In contrast the immense quantity of British 18 pounder shells were treated with a mixture of contempt and avarice. Unlike the 5.9s the 105s and the French 75 shells, that are still deadly, the 18 pounders were inert. Knowing this, the farmers harvested them, removed the nose cone and the driving band with a chisel and sold the brass and copper. The cast iron carcasses of the shells lay in a corner of the farmyard. Through the 'seventies and early 'eighties the scrapyards between Peronne and Amiens were piled high with them. Over the years the farmers and their children learnt to know those that can be exploited and those that must be handled with extreme care.

The final material evidence was the quantity of brass and lead. The brass cartridges and the lead shrapnel balls lay in the ploughed fields as testimony to the ferocity of the fighting. During the 'seventies one could still find these in any freshly ploughed field, as well as scraps of webbing and the brass buckles off equipment, despite the farm children, who earned pocket-money by picking up brass and lead to sell to scrap merchants. Machine gun cartridges were, of course, crucial. It was the ability of the defenders to bring their guns into action while the attackers were still struggling across the open fields, weighed down with kit, that cemented their victory. It was the shells loaded with shrapnel balls that killed so many of those pinned down in shell holes or wounded and lying in the open.

1. 'All the advantages of position and observation were in the enemy's hands, not in ours. They took up their lines where they were strong and we were weak, and in no place in the old Somme position is our line better sited than theirs, though in one or two places the sites are nearly equal. Almost in every part of this old front our men had to up hill to attack.'
John Masefield. *The Old Front Line.* p77 Spurbooks Ltd 1972. First pub Heineman 1917. See also Rudyard Kipling's masterly and poetic description of the German trench system and redoubts in *Irish Guards. The History in 2 volumes.* Vol 1 p225.

2. The two largest mine craters have survived nearly four decades after that exhibition, but most of the smaller ones have been filled in. The artist Richard Dunning bought the Lochnagar crater in order to preserve it as a memorial to the men who died there on July 1st.

3. Coincidentally, Richard Dunning, John Giles and Martin Middlebrook each visited the Somme about the same time. The latter wrote, 'There are few visitors to the Somme now. Although Albert is as near to London as is York, Liverpool or Exeter, it is not on the popular route to the south. The more isolated cemeteries sometimes do not see an English visitor in a whole year.' p295 *First Day on the Somme.* Martin Middlebrook wrote this in 1971 and it was a correct description of this quiet region of Picardy at the time. Ninety years on, the shopkeepers and hoteliers of Albert are making a lot of money out of the battle.

4. French soldiers in a similar trench landscape, that of Champagne, carved souvenirs and keep-sakes out of chalk. (The Dragon's Cave museum, Chemin des Dames.) There is also a display of Trench carvings in chalk, beneath the Hotel de Ville at Arras, and even a carved memorial in a cellar at Auchonvilliers. See *Trench Art.* Nicholas Saunders. Pub Leo Cooper 2001. pp107-08.

APPENDIX FOUR

CASUALTIES: 16TH MIDDLESEX
JULY 1ST 1916

IN ACTION. OFFICIAL VERSION
> 23 Officers 689 ORs
> Battalion Reserve (source Everard Wyrall)
> 9 Officers 79 ORs

Total 32 Officers and 768 ORs   Battalion strength 800

There is some confusion about whether the reserve went into the attack or not. Lionel Renton thought that the Battalion was too short-handed to have a reserve. Noel Peters said when he was sent by the RSM to bring them forward the reserve had already gone. Only a few cooks and the QM Sergeant remained at Auchonvillers. Noel ran back down the communication trenches to the front line where he found a scene of disorder with dead and wounded blocking the trenches.   Noel found it extremely difficult to talk about that day, but, when at last he did so, his memory was accurate and precise. He gave a picture of total confusion, shock and horror.   Each of the survivors that I interviewed bore out Noel's statement though not one had met the other since the First of July 1916.

CASUALTIES (OFFICIAL VERSION) COLONEL HALL

23 officers and 689 OR took part in the attack
Casualties
22 officers and 500 OR 'most of these within the first half hour of the attack'
Everard Wyrall '24 officers 500 OR'.
The Battalion Diary lists only 20 officers.
Everard Wyrall adds in 2 who died of wounds several days later. Everard Wyrall's list is based on the 86 Brigade casualty return. He checked this against the War office publication *Officers died in the Great War 1914-18*

Various unofficial accounts related that, by mid-day, there were only two officers left. The CO and a second lieutenant, both lightly wounded, and 189 ORs, either fit of only slightly wounded. (Noel Peters thought that the second lieutenant was named Forbes, but there is no Forbes on the list of officers who served with 16 MX)

For the full list of those killed on July 1st 1916 see the list at the back of Wallace Grain's history of 16PSB. There is also a useful list of the service record of all the officers who served with the 16th Middlesex.

GRAVES OF OFFICERS AND MEN OF THE 16TH (PUBLIC SCHOOLS) BATTALION. DCO, KILLED ON 1ST JULY 1916, OR DIED OF WOUNDS.

BEAUMONT HAMEL CEMETERY
TANQUERAY Lieut. Frederick Baron. 'B'Coy. Woburn, Beds. Age 24.
CROWDEN L/Cpl James. 42
LOCKE Pte Albert Mathama. 21.
MARTIN L/Cpl. Loughborough Junction. London.
MOODY Pte Walter Frederick. Mitcham. London. 18.
PUDDEPHAT Pte. R. Frederick Alfred William. Ealing. London. 19.
TAGG Pte. Frederic Alfred William. Ealing London. 19

HAWTHORN RIDGE CEMETERY
HESLOP Capt. George Henry. Mitcham Surrey. 21
HEATH Lieut. Henry James MC. Alton. Hants. 39
GODWIN Lieut. Harold Desborough.
HEATON Heaton. 2nd Lieut. Eric Rupert. Hove Sussex. 20 'Our youngest son.'
KING Sgt. Arthur Wilfred. 'C' Coy. Bedford Park. London. 30
CAIRNS Sgt. W H.
AUST Pte. A. 35
BAXTER Pte C R. 28
BONNICI Pte. C R. Malta. 33
CHAMBERS Pte. S. Biggleswade, Beds.
CRAIG L/Cpl. Bow London.
DAVEY Pte. Percy Frank. Holoway London. 18. 'In loving memory of our son who gave up all for King and Country.'
DAVIDSON Pte. L.
DeSILVA Pte. P R. Pandura. Ceylon.
DORAN Pte. Lucien Edward. 21. 'Born in London.'
DOUBLE Pte. H E. Kentish Town. London.
DURELL Pte. David. Carlyon. 36. 'Native of Fulbourn Cambridge.'
'ELDRIDGE' (See Iggulden)
ELEY Pte. A E. Camberwell London. 19. 'He was worthy of his mother's love.'
ELLIS Pte. S. Toronto Canada.
GOODERHAM L/Cpl. R C.
HARRIS Pte. J. Rainham Essex. 21
HEAPE L/Cpl. John Schofield. Bedford. 20
HOAD Pte. Walter. 'A'Coy. Warlingham. Surrey. 19
HOSKING Cpl. Herbert Noel. 'A' Coy. Finchley London.24. 'Student. University College School and The Royal School of Music.'
IGGULDEN Pte George. (Served as 'Eldridge') 'B' Coy. Fulham. 19
KEMBER Pte. Harold Dale. Twickenham. London. 30. 'Husband of Mary Kember.'

MARTIN Pte. Edward George. Brentford Middlesex. 24. 'Husband of Bessie Martin.'
MELLISH Pte A G. Wembley London.
MILNE-MILLS Pte. Kenneth. Wimbledon London. 26
MURPHY Pte Daniel. Kellystown. Co 'Wexford. 18
OSBORNE Pte. Philip John. Birmingham 21. 'BA of Birmingham University.'
PERRYMAN Pte. A. East Croyden
READ L/Cpl Walter. Rotherhythe. 20
ROBERTS L/Cpl. Ambrose. Gloucester Street London. 32
RUDD Pte. A G.
SAUNDERS Pte T H. Wood Green London.
STONE Pte Gordon. Dalston London. 21
STREETER Pte A. Edmonton London.
TAYLOR Pte John Frederick. Smethwick Staffs. 25
TAYLOR Pte L G H.
TRAMAGLIA Pte Speranza Archdale. Lombard Street London. 30

HAWTHORN NO 2 CEMETERY
MELHUISH Pte Warren LeSouef. Clevedon Bristol. 19

AUCHONVIILLERS CEMETERY
HERTSLETT 2nd Lieut Harold Cecil. Norton Heights Connecticut USA. 27 'Husband of Mrs Helen Hertslett'
ADDINGTON L/Cpl Cyril John Flinton. Merton Hall Road Wimbledon. 22
'Died of wounds.'
ASHBY pte Spencer W G.'Boy' Streatham London. 23
BOND L/Cpl Charles James. Brixton London
BOWSKILL Pte Edward. Clifton Bedford. 22
COLLETT Pte Frederick William. Beckenham Kent. 24
CROSS Pte Frederick William. Grays Inn Road London. 34
EDWARDS Pte George Charles. Willesdon London. 21
GARLAND Pte William Henry. Enfield London. 21
GRUTE L/Cpl. Hornsey. London. 24
HILDER L/Cpl. Died of wounds 4 July 1916
KNOTT Cpl Richard Stanley. Ryde IOW. 28
LATHAM Pte T
LEVESQUE Pte William Alexander. 'B'Coy. Wandsworth Bridge Road. Fulham London.
'Husband of Mrs Joanna Levesque.'
LOVETT Pte Richard Dale. 46. Son of Col Thomas A Lovett.
'He left his coffee estate in India to serve.'
ROBINSON Pte Walter Castle. Solicitor's clerk. Bishops Stortford Herts. 21
SHAMBROOK Pte Sydney Benjamin. South Hackney London. 31.
'Husband of Mrs Violet Louisa Shambrook.'

SHARP Pte Edward Horace. Harrow-on-the-Hill Middlesex. 19
SIMMONS Pte. Wendover Bucks. 24
TOLLMANN Pte Thomas James. Winchester Hants. 21
WILLIAMS Pte H S
There are many graves of men from other units killed in late June or early July 1916, Sappers (tunnellers) Gunners and Transport Drivers, and one grave from the arrival of 16PSB at Auchonvillers.
HEPBURN Pte F J. killed 26th April 1916

MAILLY WOOD CEMETERY
PEAKALL Sgt Harold Cardigan. West Ham London. 21

COURCELLES CEMETERY
Graves at Courcelles give a picture of casualties from counter-bombardment behind the line. Graves of the following units and Corps.
Royal Artillery Siege Batteries
Royal Field Artillery
Trench Mortar Battery
Ammunition Column of the Royal Garrison Artillery
Royal Engineers
Ordinance Corps
Army Service Corps

LOUVENCOURT CEMETERY
(Louvencourt was a field ambulance centre in July 1916)
SCOTT Pte F H W 18. Died of Wounds
KILLICK Pte Harold Bertie. Hornsey London. Died of Wounds 2nd July 1916
NICHOLS Pte W M. Cork Ireland 21. Died of Wounds 2nd July 1916

LEBUQUERE COMMUNAL CEMETERY EXTENSION. PAS DE CALAIS
MICHELMORE. Lieut. Robert Frank. D of Wounds 7th July 1916 aged 24.

FOOTNOTE.
I noted the names on grave-markers of all the 16th Middlesex men that I could find during the summer of 1978. There are other graves that I did not find, those who died of wounds, on the medical evacuation routes from the Somme to the channel ports. For the list of those who have no known graves on Lutyens huge memorial at Thiepval I must thank the staff at the Commonwealth War Graves Commission.

THE MEMORIAL TO THE MISSING OF THE SOMME AT THIEPVAL

The names of the missing of 16th Middlesex are to be found on Piers and Faces 12D and 13B.

ACKFORD, Private, WILLIAM T., G/2787, 16th Bn., Middlesex Regiment. 1 July 1916. Age 22. Son of the late Mr. R. H. and Mrs. E. M. Ackford. Pier and Face 12 D and 13 B.

ALLEN, Lance Serjeant, HARRY, G/252, 16th Bn., Middlesex Regiment. 1 July 1916. Age 37. Son of Samuel Allen; husband of Sarah Ann Allen, of 2, South Grove, St. Ann's Rd., Tottenham, London. Pier and Face 12 D and 13 B.

ALLEN, Private, RICHARD OSWALD, PS/1557, 16th Bn., Middlesex Regiment. 1 July 1916. Age 39. Son of Richard Charles and Lucile Allen, of 'Bradda', Letchworth Rd., Leicester; husband of Stella S. Allen, of 25, Fosse Rd. Central, Leicester. An Artist. Pier and Face 12 D and 13 B.

ARMITAGE, Private, HARRY, G/3003, 16th Bn., Middlesex Regiment. 15 July 1916. Pier and Face 12 D and 13 B.

ASSER, Second Lieutenant, HAROLD EDWARD, 16th Bn., Middlesex Regiment. 1 July 1916. Son of Edith Marian Asser, of 65, Windsor Rd., Ealing, London, and the late Arthur Edward Asser. Pier and Face 12 D and 13 B.

BAINBRIDGE, Private, ROLAND, G/1995, 16th Bn., Middlesex Regiment. 1 July 1916. Age 23. Son of the late William and Elizabeth Bainbridge; husband of the late Annie Bainbridge. Pier and Face 12 D and 13 B.

BALDWIN, Private, HENRY S., PS/2646, 'C' Coy. 16th Bn., Middlesex Regiment. 1 July 1916. Age 27. Son of Mr. and Mrs. William Baldwin, of 6, Fraser Rd., Lower Edmonton, London. Pier and Face 12 D and 13 B.

BARKER, Lieutenant, HAROLD WILLIAM, 16th Bn., Middlesex Regiment. 1 July 1916. Pier and Face 12 D and 13 B.

BENDER, Private, ERNEST G., PS/2367, 16th Bn., Middlesex Regiment. 1 July 1916. Age 24. Son of Heinrich and Ada Rose Bender; husband of May Helen Billers (formerly Bender), of 54, Oldfield Rd., Willesden, London. Pier and Face 12 D and 13 B.

BLUMER, Private, MURRAY P. H., PS/133, 16th Bn., Middlesex Regiment. 2 July 1916. Pier and Face 12 D and 13 B.

BOTTOM, Private, JAMES, G/12722, 16th Bn., Middlesex Regiment. 1 July 1916. Age 33. Son of the late Mr. and Mrs. Charles Bottom; husband of the late Alice Maud Bottom. Pier and Face 12 D and 13 B.

BROOKS, Private, SIDNEY J., PS/1966, 16th Bn., Middlesex Regiment. 1 July 1916. Age 20. Son of the late Mrs. Anna Brooks, of 7, Montefiore St., Battersea, London. Pier and Face 12 D and 13 B.

BROWN, Private, FRED, PS/2245, 16th Bn., Middlesex Regiment. 1 July 1916. Age 22. Husband of Grace Brown, of 42, Vanbrugh Park, Blackheath, London. Pier and Face 12 D and 13 B.

BRYANT, Private, CHARLES C., PS/1962, 16th Bn., Middlesex Regiment. 1 July 1916. Pier and Face 12 D and 13 B.

BURTENSHAW, Private, ALBERT W., PS/1737, 16th Bn., Middlesex Regiment. 1 July

1916. Pier and Face 12 D and 13 B.

BURTON, Private, JAMES, PS/1858, 'C' Coy. 16th Bn., Middlesex Regiment. 1 July 1916. Age 22. Son of Frances Campbell Burton, of 66, Leam Terrace, Leamington, Warwickshire, and the late George Burton. Pier and Face 12 D and 13 B.

BUTTON, Private, WILLIAM J., PS/1614, 16th Bn., Middlesex Regiment. 1 July 1916. Pier and Face 12 D and 13 B.

CAIGER, Private, SIDNEY, PS/1743, 16th Bn., Middlesex Regiment. 1 July 1916. Pier and Face 12 D and 13 B.

CASH, Lance Corporal, GEORGE SOUTHAM, PS/801, 16th Bn., Middlesex Regiment. 15 July 1916. Age 25. Son of John Oliver Cash and Ada Cash, of Wincanton, Somerset. Pier and Face 12 D and 13 B.

CHEESEMAN, Lance Corporal, GEORGE E., PS/1920, 16th Bn., Middlesex Regiment. 1 July 1916. Age 24. Son of George and Sarah Cheeseman, of 106, Godstone Rd., Whyteleafe, Surrey. Pier and Face 12 D and 13 B.

CHILTON, Lance Corporal, HERBERT R., PS/1924, 16th Bn., Middlesex Regiment. 1 July 1916. Pier and Face 12 D and 13 B.

CLARK, Private, ALFRED J., PS/1922, 16th Bn., Middlesex Regiment. 1 July 1916. Pier and Face 12 D and 13 B.

CLATWORTHY, Private, MAURICE WILLIAM, F/1639, 16th Bn., Middlesex Regiment. 1 July 1916. Age 24. Brother of Miss Violet Clatworthy, of High St., Dunster, Taunton, Somerset. Pier and Face 12 D and 13 B.

CLOSE, Private, RAYMOND, P/1434, 16th Bn., Middlesex Regiment. 1 July 1916. Pier and Face 12 D and 13 B.

COLE, Private, RAYMOND, 2421, 16th Bn., Middlesex Regiment. 1 July 1916. Age 19. Son of W. E. and Mary Cole, of 37, Westbourne Gardens, Hove, Sussex. Pier and Face 12 D and 13 B.

COOPER, Private, CHARLES E., PS/2397, 16th Bn., Middlesex Regiment. 1 July 1916. Pier and Face 12 D and 13 B.

COX, Private, HARRY, PS/57, 16th Bn., Middlesex Regiment. 1 July 1916. Age 21. Son of Harry Cox, of 26, Landguard Rd., Southampton. Pier and Face 12 D and 13 B.

CRAGGS, Private, COLIN C., G/1329, 16th Bn., Middlesex Regiment. 1 July 1916. Pier and Face 12 D and 13 B.

CRAWSHAW, Corporal, COLLIN A., G/2104, 16th Bn., Middlesex Regiment. 1 July 1916. Pier and Face 12 D and 13 B.

CURTIS, Private, THOMAS, PS/2227, 16th Bn., Middlesex Regiment. 1 July 1916. Pier and Face 12 D and 13 B.

DOSSETTER, Private, ALEXANDER, PS/2231, 16th Bn., Middlesex Regiment. 1 July 1916. Pier and Face 12 D and 13 B.

DOWNES, Serjeant, WILLIAM J., PS/2034, 16th Bn., Middlesex Regiment. 1 July 1916. Pier and Face 12 D and 13 B.

EVANS, Private, EDGAR W., PS/2459, 16th Bn., Middlesex Regiment. 1 July 1916. Pier and Face 12 D and 13 B.

EVANS, Lance Corporal, JOHN L., PS/2182, 16th Bn., Middlesex Regiment. 1 July 1916. Pier and Face 12 D and 13 B.

FENSOM, Private, SIDNEY, PS/2434, 16th Bn., Middlesex Regiment. 1 July 1916. Age 18. Son of Walter and Martha Louisa Fensom, of 3, Eastfield Rd., Hornsey, London. Pier and Face 12 D and 13 B.

FOOT, Lance Corporal, SAMUEL A., PS/1271, 16th Bn., Middlesex Regiment. 1 July 1916. Pier and Face 12 D and 13 B.

FREEMAN, Private, ARTHUR R., PS/12681, 16th Bn, Middlesex Regiment. 1 July 1916. Pier and Face 12 D and 13 B.

GAMMON, Private, HERBERT O. M., PS/956, 16th Bn., Middlesex Regiment. 1 July 1916. Pier and Face 12 D and 13 B.

GITTENS, Private, FRANCIS OWEN, PS/3155, 16th Bn., Middlesex Regiment. 1 July 1916. Age 19. Son of Joshua T. and Jane E. Gittens, of 10, St. Francois Valley Rd., Belmont, Trinidad, B.W.I. Pier and Face 12 D and 13 B.

GRAHAM, Serjeant, FRANCIS A., PS/1548, 16th Bn., Middlesex Regiment. 1 July 1916. Pier and Face 12 D and 13 B.

HAMER, Private, HENRY, G/1383, 16th Bn., Middlesex Regiment. 2 July 1916. Pier and Face 12 D and 13 B.

HAMKINS, Private, RUDOLPH B., PS/1539, 16th Bn., Middlesex Regiment. 1 July 1918. Pier and Face 12 D and 13 B.

HEFFILL, Lance Corporal, HAROLD FISHER, PS/1940, 16th Bn., Middlesex Regiment. 1 July 1916. Age 21. Son of Alfred and Eliza Heffill, of Ivy Cottage, Kensington Palace, London. Pier and Face 12 D and 13 B.

HERD, Private, CHARLES, PS/2823, 16th Bn., Middlesex Regiment. 1 July 1916. Pier and Face 12 D and 13 B.

HODGSON, Private, GEORGE, G/12735, 16th Bn., Middlesex Regiment. 1 July 1916. Pier and Face 12 D and 13 B.

HOWARTH, Lance Corporal, EDGAR, PS/1923, 16th Bn., Middlesex Regiment. 1 July 1916. Pier and Face 12 D and 13 B.

HUGHES, Private, VALENTINE C., PS/2457, 16th Bn., Middlesex Regiment. 1 July 1916. Pier and Face 12 D and 13 B.

HUNT, Private, JOSEPH EDMUND, PS/1810, 'D' Coy. 16th Bn., Middlesex Regiment. 1 July 1916. Age 21. Son of Mr. S. W. and Mrs. A. Hunt, of 'Olveston', Pizey Avenue, Clevedon, Somerset. Pier and Face 12 D and 13 B.

JACKSON, Private, ERIC, PS/1556, 16th Bn., Middlesex Regiment. 1 July 1916. Pier and Face 12 D and 13 B.

JENNER, Private, JAMES, PS/2623, 16th Bn., Middlesex Regiment. 1 July 1916. Age 25. Son of Edward Jenner, of 3, Marden Cottages, Woldingham, Surrey. Pier and Face 12 D and 13 B.

KEMPSTER, Private, ERIC G., PS/2329, 16th Bn., Middlesex Regiment. 1 July 1916. Pier and Face 12 D and 13 B.

KING, Private, ALBERT VICTOR, PS/2878, 16th Bn., Middlesex Regiment. 1 July 1916.

FOOTNOTE Pte Henry Hamer was killed on the 2nd of July 1916 and his body was not found. This is not surprising given the shelling of the 86 Brigade trenches and the chaotic conditions immediately after the attack. The death of L/Cpl George Cash is mysterious because he was killed on the 15th of July when the 16th Middlesex, with the rest of 86 Brigade, were withdrawn from the front-line to Mailly woods, though still within range of the German artillery. If Cash was killed by a shell behind the line what became of his body?

Age 19. Son of Henry R. King, of 58, Tovil Rd., Maidstone. Pier and Face 12 D and 13 B.

LARGE, Private, JAMES, PS/1738, 16th Bn., Middlesex Regiment. 1 July 1916. Age 23. Son of James and Grace Large, of 106, Sydney St., Brightlingsea, Essex. Pier and Face 12 D and 13 B.

LIVERMORE, Lance Corporal, PETER W., PS/1907, 16th Bn., Middlesex Regiment. 1 July 1916. Pier and Face 12 D and 13 B.

LONGWORTH, Private, CYRIL, PS/2169, 16th Bn., Middlesex Regiment. 1 July 1916. Age 25. Son of Henry and Ada Sabina Longworth, of 77, Whitton Rd., Hounslow, Middx. Pier and Face 12 D and 13 B.

MARTIN, Lance Corporal, FREDERICK, L/12769, 16th Bn., Middlesex Regiment. 1 July 1916. Age 27. Husband of Cissie Phillip (formerly Martin), of Victoria Villa, Victoria St., Hereford. Pier and Face 12 D and 13 B.

MILL, Private, ARTHUR GERALD, PS/2174, 16th Bn., Middlesex Regiment. 1 July 1916. Age 28. Son of John and Alice Rebecca Mill, of 28, Bushey Hill Rd., Camberwell, London. Pier and Face 12 D and 13 B.

MOORE, Private, FREDERICK, G/2975, 16th Bn., Middlesex Regiment. 1 July 1916. Pier and Face 12 D and 13 B.

MULLINS, Private, ALBERT, PS/2978, 16th Bn., Middlesex Regiment. 1 July 1916. Age 18. Son of Albert and Catherine Mullins, of 106, Grafton St., Bradford, Yorks. Pier and Face 12 D and 13 B.

MURRAY, Private, CHARLES E., PS/1893, 16th Bn., Middlesex Regiment. 1 July 1916. Age 22. Son of Mrs. C. Murray, of 81, Gwynne Rd., Battersea, London. Pier and Face 12 D and 13 B.

NELMES, Private, HERBERT, PS/2612, 16th Bn., Middlesex Regiment. 1 July 1916. Age 25. Son of Dan and Alice Nelmes, of 17, Goodyere St., Gloucester. Pier and Face 12 D and 13 B.

ORD, Private, JAMES W., G/2650, 16th Bn., Middlesex Regiment. 1 July 1916. Pier and Face 12 D and 13 B.

ORR, Second Lieutenant, JAMES KENNETH, 16th Bn., Middlesex Regiment. 1 July 1916. Age 21. Son of Dr. and Mrs. W. R. Orr, of Clydesdale, East Finchley, Middx. Pier and Face 12 D and 13 B.

OVERTON, Private, LESLIE, PS/2078, 16th Bn., Middlesex Regiment. 1 July 1916. Pier and Face 12 D and 13 B.

PAINTER, Company Serjeant Major, HERBERT G., G/564, 16th Bn., Middlesex Regiment. 1 July 1916. Pier and Face 12 D and 13 B.

PARRISH, Private, ALBERT E., PS/2564, 16th Bn., Middlesex Regiment. 1 July 1916. Pier and Face 12 D and 13 B.

PICKERING, Corporal, HERBERT, PS/2092, 16th Bn., Middlesex Regiment. 1 July 1916. Age 36. Son of the late John and Hannah Pickering husband of Rose Emily Pickering, of 117 George Lane, Woodford, Essex. Pier and Face 12 D and 13 B.

PIERCE, Private, ALFRED ERNEST, PS/2284, 'D' Coy. 16th Bn., Middlesex Regiment. 1 July 1916. Age 24. Son of Alfred and Rosetta Pierce, of 91, Sunnyhill Rd., Streatham,

London. Pier and Face 12 D and 13 B.

PURNELL, Captain, ARTHUR CHANNING, 16th Bn., Middlesex Regiment. 1 July 1916. Age 34. Son of the late J. A. Purnell and Emily Blandford Purnell. Pier and Face 12 D and 13 B.

RIEU, Private, ALFRED, PS/2260, 16th Bn., Middlesex Regiment. 1 July 1916. Age 37. Son of the late Dr. and Mrs. Charles Rieu, of 28, Woburn Square, Bloomsbury, London. Joined the Foreign Legion in France 1914, transferred to the British Army 1915. Pier and Face 12 D and 13 B.

ROSS, Private, EDWARD HOPE, PS/193, 16th Bn., Middlesex Regiment. 1 July 1916. Age 19. Son of Mr. and Mrs. D. Hope Ross, of Port of Spain, Trinidad, B.W.I. Pier and Face 12 D and 13 B.

ROSS, Private, STANLEY, PS/2304, 16th Bn., Middlesex Regiment. 1 July 1916. Age 21. Son of Richard Ross, of 3, Myrtle Rd., Sutton, Surrey. Pier and Face 12 D and 13 B.

SHIPP, Private, FREDERICK G., PS/2897, 16th Bn., Middlesex Regiment. 15 July 1916. Pier and Face 12 D and 13 B.

SHREWSBURY, Lance Corporal, ALEXANDER A., PS/1439, 16th Bn., Middlesex Regiment. 1 July 1916. Pier and Face 12 D and 13 B.

SPENCER, Private, FREDERICK PERCY, PS/519, 'C' Coy. 16th Bn., Middlesex Regiment. 1 July 1916. Age 26. Son of the late Edwin Spencer, of 92, Dennetts Rd., New Cross, London. Pier and Face 12 D and 13 B.

SPRENGER, Private, HERBERT, PS/1417, 16th Bn., Middlesex Regiment. 1 July 1916. Age 20. Son of Mr. A. E. A. and Mrs. K. C. Sprenger, of 1, Pynnont Rd., Ilford, Essex. Pier and Face 12 D and 13 B.

STROUD, Private, RAYMOND D., PS/1387, 16th Bn., Middlesex Regiment. 1 July 1916. Pier and Face 12 D and 13 B.

SUTEHALL, Private, JOHN, PS/1791, 16th Bn., Middlesex Regiment. 1 July 1916. Pier and Face 12 D and 13 B.

TAYLOR, Private, HENRY LEONARD, PS/2239, 16th Bn., Middlesex Regiment. 1 July 1916. Age 29. Son of Joseph Taylor, of 24, Ebsworth St., Forest Hill; husband of Ethel Ada Taylor, of 76, Caversham Rd., Kentish Town, London. Pier and Face 12 D and 13 B.

THOMPSON, Private, ERNEST, PS/3192, 16th Bn., Middlesex Regiment. 1 July 1916. Pier and Face 12 D and 13 B.

TUCK, Private, DAVID VICTOR THOMAS, PS/874, 16th Bn., Middlesex Regiment. 1 July 1916. Age 18. Son of Thomas John Tuck, of 5, Birkbeck Rd., Enfield, Middlesex, and the late Eliza Tuck. Pier and Face 12 D and 13 B.

WALKER, Private, ALFRED, PS/1609, 16th Bn., Middlesex Regiment. 1 July 1916. Pier and Face 12 D and 13 B.

WALTER, Private, ARTHUR E., PS/1819, 16th Bn, Middlesex Regiment. 1 July 1916. Age 18. Son of the late Herbert Allen and Alice Walter. Pier and Face 12 D and 13 B.

WARD, Private, FRANK, PS/1982, 16th Bn., Middlesex Regiment. 1 July 1916. Age 18. Son of Alfred Arthur and Caroline Ward, of 70, Hope St., Battersea, London. Pier and Face 12 D and 13 B.

WARNER, Private, FREDERICK V., PS/2053, 16th Bn., Middlesex Regiment. 1 July 1916. Age 37. Son of Matthew and Sarah Warner; husband of Elizabeth Warner, of 1, Cromwell House, Vauxhall Walk, Lambeth, London. Pier and Face 12 D and 13 B.

WATTS, Captain, TALBOT HAMILTON, 16th Bn., Middlesex Regiment. 1 July 1916. Age 27. Son of Dr. Fred Watts, of London. Pier and Face 12 D and 13 B.

WELLS, Private, MONTAGUE P., PS/1576, 16th Bn., Middlesex Regiment. 1 July 1916. Pier and Face 12 D and 13 B.

WEXHAM, Lance Corporal, ALBERT W., PS/1550, 16th Bn., Middlesex Regiment. 1 July 1916. Age 21. Son of George and Emma E. Wexham, of 45, Casino Avenue, Herne Hill, London. Pier and Face 12 D and 13 B.

WILKINSON, Serjeant, GEORGE JERRARD, PS/1236, 16th Bn., Middlesex Regiment. 1 July 1916. Age 29. Son of Amy Wilkinson, of 43, West Park, Eltham, London, and the late Rev. Willoughby Balfour Wilkinson. Educated at Uppingham and Caius College, Cambs. (two Musical Scholarships). B.A. Musician and Composer. Pier and Face 12 D and 13 B.

WINTERHALDER, Lance Corporal, EDWARD L., PS/1793, 'B' Coy. 16th Bn., Middlesex Regiment. 1 July 1916. Age 19. Son of Leo and Josephine A. Winterhalder, of 9, Station Rd. West, Canterbury, Kent. Pier and Face 12 D and 13 B.

WRIGHT, Lance Corporal, FRANK E., PS/2210, 16th Bn., Middlesex Regiment. 1 July 1916. Pier and Face 12 D and 13 B.

LIST OF THOSE KILLED DURING THE LATER SOMME BATTLES, WHO HAVE NO KNOWN GRAVE, WINTER 1916-1917

AMBROSE, Private, WILLIAM J., PS/1667, 16th Bn., Middlesex Regiment. 3 December 1916. Age 21. Son of William and Laura Clara Ambrose, of 85, Duncombe Rd., Upper Holloway, London. Pier and Face 12 D and 13 B.

BALDWIN, Second Lieutenant, HAROLD JOHN TAYLOR, 16th Bn., Middlesex Regiment. 23 October 1916. Pier and Face 12 D and 13 B.

BALDWIN, Private, THOMAS G., F/563, 16th Bn., Middlesex Regiment. 22 October 1916. Age 26. Son of William Baldwin, of 100, Shardeloes Rd., Brockley, London. Pier and Face 12 D and 13 B.

BATEMAN, Lance Corporal, FREDERICK, G/43321, 16th Bn., Middlesex Regiment. 23 October 1916. Age 27. Husband of Kate Sanderson (formerly Bateman), of 102, Elstow Rd., Bedford. Pier and Face 12 D and 13 B.

BRINTON, Corporal, CECIL IRWIN, G/1030, 16th Bn., Middlesex Regiment. 27 October 1916. Age 35. Son of Major and Mrs. G. Brinton, late of Southhampton.
Served in the South African War with Cape Mounted Rifles. Pier and Face 12 D and 13 B.

BRITTON, Lance Corporal, ARTHUR J., G/20200, 16th Bn., Middlesex Regiment. 28 February 1917. Pier and Face 12 D and 13 B.

BURVILL, Private, HARRY ROBERT, PS/1794, 16th Bn., Middlesex Regiment. attd. 22nd Bn., Manchester Regiment 2 September 1916. Age 24. Son of Harry and Eliza Burvill, of 15, Hubert Grove, Stockwell, London. Pier and Face 12 D and 13 B.

COLLETT, Private, ERNEST, G/2945, 16th Bn., Middlesex Regiment. 23 October 1916. Age 27. Son of the late Mrs. Emily Collett. Pier and Face 12 D and 13 B.

CORKER, Private, JAMES, G/1059, 16th Bn., Middlesex Regiment. 22 October 1916. Age 25. Son of William and Caroline Corker, of 48, Harvey Rd., Hornsey, London. Pier and Face 12 D and 13 B.

CUMMINS, Private, JOHN, PW/6298, 16th Bn., Middlesex Regiment. 28 February 1917. Age 33. Husband of E. Cummins, of 26, Steyne Rd., Acton, London. Pier and Face 12 D and 13 B.

DAVIS, Private, JOHN, G/25275, 16th Bn., Middlesex Regiment. 22 October 1916. Age 27. Son of John and Annie Davis, of 'Brookside,' Broad Lane, Bracknell, Berks. Pier and Face 12 D and 13 B.

FABIAN, Lance Corporal, PERCY L., G/201550, 16th Bn, Middlesex Regiment. 23 October 1916. Age 34. Son of Francis Harry and Annie Fabian, of 40, Galpins Rd., Thornton Heath, Surrey. Pier and Face 12 D and 13 B.

GRIERSON, Private, JOHN C., G/25287, 16th Bn., Middlesex Regiment. 23 October 1916. Pier and Face 12 D and 13 B.

HAYWARD, Private, FREDERICK, PS/2089, 16th Bn., Middlesex Regiment. 21 October 1916. Age 21. Son of William and Emma Hayward. Pier and Face 12 D and 13 B.

HEWITT, Private, WALTER F., F/2488, 16th Bn., Middlesex Regiment. 28 February 1917. Pier and Face 12 D and 13 B.

HULSE, Private, JOHN JAMES, G/23227, 16th Bn., Middlesex Regiment. 23 October 1916. Age 29. Son of Emma Smith (formerly Hulse) and John Smith (Stepfather), of Manor Cottage, Capel-le-Ferne, Folkestone. Pier and Face 12 D and 13 B.

HUNT, Private, WILFRED, 6684, 16th Bn., Middlesex Regiment. 28 February 1917. Age 25. Husband of Edith Hunt, of 2, Saxon Villas, Albion Rd., Great Yarmouth. Pier and Face 12 D and 13 B.

HURLEY, Serjeant, ARTHUR GEORGE, PS/2337, 16th Bn., Middlesex Regiment. 23 October 1916. Age 28. Son of the late William and Mary Ann Hurley, of Spaxton, Bridgwater, Somerset. Pier and Face 12 D and 13 B.

IVES, Private, GEORGE, G/40819, 16th Bn., Middlesex Regiment. 25 November 1916. Age 41. Son of Arthur and Eliza Ives, of 173, High St, Barnet; husband of Lily Ives, of 28, Wood St., Barnet, Herts. Pier and Face 12 D and 13 B.

KEAM, Private, CHARLES, G/40841, 16th Bn., Middlesex Regiment. 26 November 1916. Pier and Face 12 D and 13 B.

KENNETT, Private, ERNEST, PS/2062, 16th Bn., Middlesex Regiment. 25 November 1916. Pier and Face 12 D and 13 B.

LEADBEATER, Private, JOHN PHILIP, L/16363, 16th Bn., Middlesex Regiment. 22 October 1916. Age 19. Son of Mrs. Lilian S. Hannington, of 19IA, Stephendale Rd., Fulham, London. Pier and Face 12 D and 13 B.

(Noel Peter's friend 'Charlie' Leadbetter)

LEPPARD, Lance Serjeant, HAROLD J., PS/2290, 16th Bn., Middlesex Regiment. 25 February 1917. Pier and Face 12 D and 13 B.

PRATT, Private, BENJAMIN G., G/40349, 16th Bn., Middlesex Regiment. 23 October 1916. Age 29. Son of Benjamin and Emily Pratt, of 14, Woolett Rd., Maidstone; husband of Mrs. Attwood (formerly Pratt), of 3, Wargrove Cottages, Holborough Stream, Snodland, Kent. Pier and Face 12 D and 13 B.

ROGERS, Private, HERBERT E., G/23235, 16th Bn., Middlesex Regiment. 28 February 1917. Pier and Face 12 D and 13 B.

ROOT, Private, FREDERICK W., PS/1653, 16th Bn., Middlesex Regiment. 3 December 1916. Pier and Face 12 D and 13 B.

SHEARS, Private, ALFRED, G/43396, 16th Bn., Middlesex Regiment. 28 February 1917. Age 33. Son of Thomas and Annie Shears, of 148, Kyverdale Rd., Stoke Newington; husband of Elsie M. Shears, of 1, Springfield Rd., South Tottenham, London. Pier and

Face 12 D and 13 B.

SLOAN, Private, WILLIAM, PS/1149, 16th Bn., Middlesex Regiment. 25 October 1916. Age 25. Husband of Janet Neil McKerns Carr (formerly Sloan), of 21, Abercorn St., New City Rd., Glasgow. Pier and Face 12 D and 13 B.

VANE, Lance Corporal, ALMYR, G/43404, 16th Bn., Middlesex Regiment. 25 October 1916. Pier and Face 12 D and 13 B.

WHITE, Private, ALFRED, PS/2451, 16th Bn., Middlesex Regiment. 27 October 1916. Pier and Face 12 D and 13 B.

WOOD, Private, EDWIN J., G/40136, 16th Bn., Middlesex Regiment. 28 February 1917. Pier and Face 12 D and 13 B.

WREN, Private, BENJAMIN, G/40370, 16th Bn., Middlesex Regiment. 27 October 1916. Age 29. Son of Mary Elizabeth Wren, of 6, New Borough, Wimborne, Dorset, and the late John Wren; husband of Elizabeth Maria Wren, of 64, Woolley St., Bradford-on-Avon, Wilts. Pier and Face 12 D and 13 B.

THE DISBANDMENT OF THE 16TH MIDDLESEX

A list of officers who were original volunteers (The 'Originals') who were still serving with the Battalion in February 1918.
Maj. F.R.Hill. Capt. D.B.Tuck. Capt. H.M.James. Capt. Wegg. Lt.R.A.Pye QM.
During Operation 'Michael', the German onslaught a month later, the following former officers of the 16th were killed. Captain Launceton MC. Capt. Wegg. Capt. Tuck. Lt Stuart, and 2 Lt Bowden. Major Hill and Lt. Frayne were taken prisoner. Lt Frayne died of wounds while in the POW camp.

Neither Wallace Grain nor Everard Wyrall mention the fate of the 16th Middlesex Pipe Band in their histories. Noel Peters told me that the band went to the 2nd Battalion after disbandment. In the late 'seventies Noel gave me a photograph of the band taken at Woldingham. On the back Noel listed the members of the band and what happened to some of them. (I have listed them as he did. I am not sure whether they are in the same order as the photograph.)
'Piper MacFarlane not in photo won the MM after the 16 Batt was disbanded. Pipe Band went to the 2nd Batt MX in Feb 1918.
L.S.Pipe Major Charles Stewart 1152.
Piper John Grant 1144.
Piper William Sloane 2188. Wounded on the Somme, Oct 1916. Became Pipe-Major and founded the Scottish Pipe Band Association. Died June 22 1974.
Piper Fred Carruthers 1154
Ppr Norman MacDonald1148
Ppr Dougal McFarlane 1350
Ppr Henry Michelson 1154 (sic)
Ppr Thos Latham. Killed on the Somme 1-7-16
Ppr James Gilchrist 1930
Ppr John Kerr 1153
Cpl Thos Gibson on the right of photo.
Drummer William Sloane 2530. Killed on the Somme 1-7-1916

Noel told me that the Battalion transport had a good reputation and so were transferred, complete, to 29th Division. They were unlucky and once again the cause was Operation MICHAEL. In March 1918 the transport column was forming up, preparing to move, when a large shell landed in the middle of the horse-drawn vehicles, killing most of the Middlesex drivers.
I am twice indepted to the Commonwealth War Graves Commission: first in 1978 for their knowledge and help in locating the British cemeteries around Beaumont Hamel; and second in 2007 for extracting the names of those of the 16th Middlesex who have no known graves and who are commemorated on the Thiepval memorial.

ACKNOWLEDGEMENTS

Sitting in his dining room in Portsmouth, the table covered in papers and relics of his war, Noel Peters said to me, 'I have never told anyone this story before'.

'Why not?' I asked.

'Because no one was interested'. He said and then asked. 'Why are you interested?'

Explaining this interest was not easy. The need to know started with an accident. I got lost in the undergrowth looking for the Hawthorn mine crater. When I emerged I came on two small cemeteries, one on the upland, on the edge of a field of corn, and the other close to the road leading to Auchonvilliers, at the point that I learned later was the Sunken Road. There I came on the line of graves, each with it's familiar badge, that of the Middlesex Regiment. Here was a massacre of men from North London. I wanted to know how disaster happened. The start of the quest was as simple and naïve as that.

A second chance meeting happened at an Armistice Day dinner of the 7th Middlesex at Hornsey. I sat next to the curator of the Regimental Museum, Dick Smith. I told him about the shocking experience of blundering onto the graves of the 16th Middlesex. 'The Public Schools Battalion' He said. 'Come and see me at the Museum, I will see what I can sort out for you'.

The intense interest generated by the tragic events at Beaumont Hamel introduced me to a remarkable group of men, all of them born at the end of the nineteenth century. It was a great privilege to know them. As weeks passed into months, even into years, I got to know Noel Peters and Lionel Renton as friends as well as advisers and story-tellers. I never met Alf Damon, but I corresponded with him in Tasmania for a long time and through a large pile of letters. The other survivors of the Public Schools Battalion were all contacts of Dick Smith's who wrote to me through the late seventies. The Chelsea branch of the Red Cross introduced me to Sergeant Charles Quinnell MM who lived just down the road at the Royal Hospital.

The research period ran through the seventies while I was teaching at Chelsea School of Art. I had a job to do and a family to support so could not hurry the work. None of my advisers and friends lived to see the results published. Noel Peters died of cancer in 1979 and Lionel Renton not long afterwards. I lost touch with both Dick Smith and Alf Damon through a misunderstanding. In 1979 I moved to Northern Ireland to take up a teaching post at Ulster Polytechnic (today the University of Ulster). For a civilian living and working in the city of Belfast any suspicion of military activity could damage ones health. Alf told me that I and my family must move from a city in a state of virtual civil war and emigrate to Tasmania. Foolishly I wrote back joking that Belfast might be a turbulent city but compared to the Western Front it was a haven of peace. Alf did not reply, nor did I hear from him again. Despite many wounds he lived to the age of 85, dying in 1984.

I completed the first draft, then titled Some Desperate Glory, in 1981. It was far too long. The literary agent, Murray Pollinger was kind enough to read it and give me a criticism. 'You are attempting the re-write the history of the Great War.' He said. 'I have to tell you that it has been done. What you ought to do is re-write it concentrating on the story of the men who were there. But you will not do that.'

'I will.' I said. 'I've got to get it published – for them.'

Ten years after we returned from Ireland I rewrote the manuscript, cutting it by half and sticking to the story told me by the survivors. I re-titled it *Goodbye Picadilly*. Almost a decade later I went through the manuscript and virtually re-wrote it. The result is The Public Schools Battalion.

In the beginning of the search I relied on four museums and a library. The museums are listed, not in order of merit, because they are all important, but in the order in which I discovered them. My thanks to all the museum and library staff who were so helpful in assisting me in this research.

The Library of Printed Books, the Photographic Library, and the Archives at the Imperial War Museum

The Middlesex Regimental Museum at Bruce Castle in Tottenham.(Now closed)

Richard Dunning's museum in Mitcham. (now closed)

Major General A. MacLennan. The RAMC Library at Millbank (Closed)

Lieut' Colonel A.V.Tennuci.The RAMC Museum at Ash Vale, Aldershot.

The Middlesex Regimental Archives at Mill Hill. (Bombed by the IRA)

Some of the later, more general research took place in the museum to the 36th Ulster Division, then in the centre of Belfast.

My thanks to the BBC Archives, Caversham, for the permission to read the papers of 'Uncle Mac', and to the Commonwealth War Graves Commission for detailed reports on the British cemeteries around Beaumont Hamel and for the list of the men of the 16th Middlesex commemorated on the Memorial to the Missing at Thiepval.

I relied on two regimental histories through the search, Everard Wyrall and Wallace Grain, but more as frameworks than as accurate reports. Each used official reports rather than the evidence of survivors. For general reference I used Cruttwell's beautifully written account ot the Great War, which has the major advantage that the writer was there.

The story of Richard Dunning's struggle to preserve the Lochnagar crater as a memorial demands a book to itself. I met Richard in the early 'seventies because of the crater, but it was his museum in south-west London that influenced my work for decades, both in written form and in sculpture.   In particular the glass case one metre by two metres that appears at first glance to contain dried mud. This, in fact, is a section of soil that once covered the German Front Line exactly as it was excavated, containing both the war-like and the banal debris of life in a Front Line trench.

Dick Smith made contact with survivors of the 1st July 1916 who were kind enough to write to me:

John Wilson. Wirral. Merseyside

Albert Edwards. Cornwall

C.P.Lawson. London

Laurie Barrow. Croyden

Tony Chubb. Devon

George Jones-Walters. Surrey.

Three others who were not at Beaumont Hamel but were closely connected to the 16th Middlesex were:

Mrs Fanny O'Donnell. Guildford (Youngest sister of the Catchpole brothers, who enlisted under the name Tennant)

Colonel Benham Purnell RADC (nephew of Captain A.C.Purnell, Bombing Officer 86 Brigade)

Robert Taylor who allowed me to read the papers left by his father, Albert Taylor.

Military advisers who took part in the Battle of the Somme, serving with other units:

Sergeant Charles Quinnell. MM. Chelsea Royal Hospital.

Captain James. L. Crosbee formerly of the Royal Warwickshire Regiment, who I knew as a colleague at Birmingham School of Art.

The publisher David Unwin introduced me to Major Ynr Probert. RA whose guns preceded and supported the infantry on July 1st 1916.

Major Dick Smith MBE joined the Middlesex Regiment as a boy soldier in 1919. He knew many of the soldiers who survived the Somme battles, including Brigadier Hamilton Hall. Dick Smith rose to become an outstanding RSM in Libya and Tunisia in the Second World War. During the Cold War he was training adviser to the Malay Regiment. Dick Smith was more than curator of the museum at Bruce Castle, he was a walking encyclopaedia of information on the regiment.

My thanks to colleagues at Chelsea School of Art who gave me every encouragement in researching this project even though it was not strictly Fine Art. In particular I have to thank that fine sculptor and head of the Sculpture Department, George Fullard, who died at the age of fifty from wounds sustained as a young man at Monte Casino.

During the early stages of the book's genesis several literary experts helped and advised me on cutting and re-presenting this book: Frank Pike at Faber and Faber; Rayner Unwin at George Alan and Unwin; and the literary agent, Murray Pollinger. Not the least of my thanks go to my family and my colleagues in the 7th Battalion the Middlesex Regiment (DCO) TA, Colonel Gerry Gunnell (nephew of the Adjutant of 16 MX, Captain Cochram); Captain John Spencer-Richards and Captain Simon Enthoven, for their support and encouragement over the decades.

Finally, but most important, I want to note my gratitude to my dear wife Sylvie, and my daughters Sophie and Emma, who have had to endure my obsession with the massacre at Beaumont Hamel for thirty years. At every stage of the project Sylvie has encouraged, considered and aided the process that, in the end, led to this book.

Steve Hurst HANBOROUGH, WEST OXFODSHIRE. FEBRUARY 2007

BIBLIOGRAPHY

BAEDEKER. *Northern France: Handbook for Travellers 1909.* Leipzig. Baedeker Publications.

BARBUSSE. Henry. *Under Fire.* First published in Paris in 1917 when the author was in hospital recovering from wounds, *Le Feu* won the Prix Goncourt. The English translation was published in London in 1926 by Dents under the Everman label. Reprinted 1988.

BLUNDEN. *Undertones of War.* London. 1928.
Revised edition with preface by the author. Oxford. OUP. 1956.
BONE. Muirhead. *The Western Front: Drawings.* London. The War Office. 1917.

BRITTAIN. Vera. *Testament of Youth.* London. Victor Gollancz. 1966.

CLARK. Alan. *The Donkeys.* London. Hutchinson. 1966.

COOMBS. Rose. E. B. *Before Endeavours Fade: A guide to the Battlefields of the First World War.* London. Battle of Britain Prints International.

CORRELLI BARNETT. *The Swordbearers: Supreme Command in the First World War.* London. Eyre and Spottiswood. 1964.

CORRELLI BARNETT. *The Collapse of British Power.* Alan Sutton. Stroud, Glos. 1984.

CRUTTWELL. C.R.M.F. *The Great War; 1914-1918.* Oxford. OUP. 1934. Second edition reprinted 1969.

DIXON. Prof, Norman. *On the Psychology of Military Incompetence.* London. 1976. Jonathan Cape. 1994. Random House (paperback).

EVERARD-WYRALL. *The Diehards in the Great War.* London. Harrison and Sons. 1926.

FALLS. Cyril. *The History of the 36th (Ulster) Division.* M'Caw, Stevenson and Orr Ltd. Belfast. 1922.

FARRAR-HOCKLEY. A.H. *The Somme*. London. Batsford Books. 1964.

FUSSELL. Paul. *The Great War and Modern Memory*. Oxford. OUP. 1975.

GILES. John. *The Somme: Then and Now*. Plaistow Press. London. 1977.

GILLON, Capt Stair. *The Story of the 29th Division*. London. Thos Nelson and Sons 1925.

GRAIN. Wallace. *The History of the 16th (Public Schools) Battalion. The Middlesex Regiment (DCO)*. London. Private publication.

GRAVES. Robert. *Goodbye to All That*. London. Jonathan Cape. 1929. Revised edition with new prologue and many alterations by the author. London. Cassell. 1957. Republished by Penguin books in 1961 and 1979. (The difference between the first and later editions is important because Graves altered his story.)

HISCOCK. Eric. *The Bells of Hell go Ting-a-ling-a-ling*. (Royal Fusiliers.)

HOLT. Major Tonie and Valmai Holt. *In Search of the Better 'Ole: The life, the works and the collectables of Bruce Bairnsfather*. Portsmouth. Milestone Publications. 1985.

HOLT. Major Tonie and Valmai Holt. *The best of Fragments from France: Bruce Bairnsfather*. Phin Publishing. Glos. 1978.

HORNE. Alistair. *The Price of Glory: Verdun 1916*. London. 1962. Macmillan. 1993. Penguin (paperback)

JOAD. C.E.M. *The Diary of a Dead Officer: The Diary of Arthur Graeme West*. London. Alan Unwin. 1919.

JUNGER. Ernst. *Storm of Steel*. (In Stahlgewittern.) Germany 1920. First version in English. The *Storm of Steel*. London. Basil Creighton. 1929. New translation by Michael Hoffmann. London. Allan Lane. 2000

LEWIS. Cecil. *Sagittarius Rising*. London. 1966 (2nd Edition). Peter David Ltd.

LIDDELL HART. Captain Basil. *History of the First World War*. London. Cassell. 1930. Reprinted 1977.

MALELIEU. C.P. *Disenchantment.* Everyman Books. 1930?

MALINS. Lt Geoffrey. H. *How I Filmed the War.* London. Herbert Jenkins. 1920.

MANNING. *Her Privates We.* Privately printed 1929.
The Middle Parts of Fortune. (Bowdlerised version) London. Peter Davis. 1939. Unexpurgated version. London. Serpent's Tail Press. 1999.

MARWICK. Arthur. *Women at War 1914-1918.* Fontana. London. 1977.

MARWICK. Arthur. *The Deluge: British Society and the First World War.* Bodley Head. London. 1965

MASEFIELD. John. *The Old Front Line.* London. Heinemann Publishers. 1917. Re-published: Buckinghamshire UK. Spur Books. 1972.

MICHELIN. *Illustrated guide to the Battlefields.* Michelin. Paris. 1920.

MIDDLEBROOK. Martin. *The First Day on the Somme.* NY. W.W. Norton & Co Inc. 1972.

PARKER. Peter. *The Old Lie: The Great War and the Public School Ethos.* Constable. London. 1987.

PARSONS. I.M. *Men who March Away: Poems of the First World War.* Chatto and Windus. London. 1965.

PEARSON. C. A. Ltd. *The Western Front; Then and Now.* London 1928

PRIOR. Robin and WILSON Trevor. *Command on the Western Front: The Military Carreer of Sir Henry Rawlinson 1914-18.* Oxford. Blackwells. 1992.

REMARQUE. Erich Maria. *All Quiet on the Western Front.* London. Putnam and Co. 1929. Second impression 1967. Im Westen Nichts neues. Berlin 1929.

R.I.B.A. *Silent Cities; an exhibition of the Memorial and Cemetery Architecture of the Great War.* Royal Institute of British Architects. London. 1977.

SASSOON. Siegfried. *Memoirs of an Infantry Officer.* The George Sherston Trilogy. London. Faber and Faber. 1930.

SASSOON. Siegfried. *Collected Poems 1908-1956.* Faber and Faber. London. 1960.

SASSOON. Siegfried. *Siegfried's Journey.* Faber and Faber. London. 1930.

SAUNDERS. Dr Nicholas. *Trench Art.* Pen and Sword Books. Yorks. 2001.

TAYLOR. A.J.P. *War by Timetable: How the First World War Began.* Macdonald. London. 1980.

TERRAINE. John. *Douglas Haig; The Educated Soldier.* London. Hutchinson. 1963.

WALLIS-GRAIN. H.W. *The 16th (Public Schools) Battalion Middlesex Regiment and the Great War 1914-1918.* London. Privately printed. Edited by H.W. Wallis-Grain.

WEBSTER. Donovan. *Aftermath: the Remnants of War.* Constable. London. 1997.

WILLIAMSON. Ann. *Henry Williamson: The Last Romantic.*

WILLIAMSON. Henry. *The Golden Virgin.* London. 1960. Macdonald. 1964. Panther Books (Paperback). The sixth volume in a series of autobiographical novels, A Chronicle of Ancient Sunlight, *The Golden Virgin* describes the Somme battles, 1916-17.

INDEX

Acheux 122,135,145,200

Aire-sur-Lys 111

Albert 121,122,133,226,254

Allenby, General 137

Amiens 121, 122, 135, 147, 148, 155, 209, 222, 225

Ancre Valley 121,130,133,227

Anderson, Sgt 189,193

Annequin 70,78,93,101

Annezin 72,80

Arras 75

Auchonvillers122,127-130,132,133,139-141, 150, 153, 168,190, 192, 196,197, 203, 204, 208, 209, 211, 229, 255, 256

Aust, Pte 225

Authie 190,212,231

Bain-Kemp, Cpl 225

Barrow, Cpl Laurie 42,112-233,288

Beaucourt 227,228,130,136,170,172

Bethune 65,68-70, 75-77,85,88,110,117

Beaumont Hamel 122, 130, 142, 143, 148, 150,152,153,161,167,168,171,181,190, 191,194, 200-208, 254, 256, 262

Beauquesne 190

Beauval CCS 212

Beuvry 85,99

Biggs, Pvt Albert 88

Bird, Pvt Frederick Arthur 99

Blaxendale, Pvt George 105

Blunden, Lt Edmund 65,77

Bond, Pte 132

Boraston, Col 263,258

Boulogne 59-61

Bowman, 2/Lt 88,93

Bowskill, Pte 139

Brickstacks 80,87,101,127

Broodsiende 245

Brown, Pte George 97

Bruce, Pte Duncan 97

Burnett, Sgt 90

Bus-les-Artois 190

Cadmore.,Pte 88

Cairns, Sgt William 100,238,245

Cambrai 133

Cambrin 97

Cardiff Street Trench 171,172,185

Carey, Capt. (Adjutant at Kempton) 21,26

Caserne, see Montmorency

Catchpole (See Tennant)

Catchpole, Fanny (Mrs O'Donnel) 252, 253, 288

Catley, Pte. 220

Chubb, Pte. Tony 17,21,30,288

Cleghorn, Lt. 27,102-104,153-155,178

Clipstone, Notts. 50,51

Clutterbuck, Pte. 220

Cochram, Capt. F.S. (Adjutant Somme) 27,86, 112,183,187,188,200

Corbie CCS 122,225

Craxford, Pte. George 99

Cripps Cut Trench 171,172,185

Crosbee, Lt. James 160,256,288

Crowden, L/Cpl James 225

Crozier, Brig. F Percy 88

Cuinchy 73, 78, 87, 89,117

Damon, Cpl Alf 10 et seq

Dardanelles (29th Div) 138

Davey, Pvt. Frank 223

Dawson, Lt.

Deeves, 2/Lt MC 230-232

De Lisle, Gen. (GOC 29th Division) 138,157

Dixon, Prof. N F

Doullens 122-125,190,212,225

Doyle, Pvt. Bernard 105

Dunning, Richard 274,288

Edmunds, Capt. RAMC 90

Edwards, Pvt. Albert 42,217-219,288

Eldridge Pvt. 223

Eley, Pte 225

Ellis, Pte 225

INDEX OF MILITARY UNITS AND FORMATIONS